THE HONORARY COLONEL, NATAL CARBINEERS.

THE RIGHT HON.
LORD KITCHENER OF KHARTOUM, G.C.B., K.C.M.G.,
SIRDAR EGYPTIAN ARMY, 1899.

From the picture by A. S. Cope, R.A., in the possession of the Royal Engineers' Mess, Chatham.

BY PERMISSION OF THE AUTOTYPE FINE ART COMPANY, LIMITED, 74, NEW OXFORD STREET, LONDON, PUBLISHERS OF THE LARGE PLATE.

THE
NATAL CARBINEERS.

The History of the Regiment from its Foundation,
15th January, 1855, to 30th June, 1911.

Edited by the

Rev. JOHN STALKER, M.A.

The Naval & Military Press Ltd

Published by

The Naval & Military Press Ltd
Unit 10 Ridgewood Industrial Park,
Uckfield, East Sussex,
TN22 5QE England

Tel: +44 (0) 1825 749494
Fax: +44 (0) 1825 765701

www.naval-military-press.com
www.military-genealogy.com
www.militarymaproom.com

*In reprinting in facsimile from the original, any imperfections are inevitably reproduced
and the quality may fall short of modern type and cartographic standards.*

CONTENTS.

Introduction	Page	1
Chapter I.—Volunteering	,,	13
,, II.—Bushman Raids	,,	27
,, III.—Isidoi and Matyana	,,	34
,, IV.—A Zulu War-cloud	,,	41
,, V.—A Basuto Incursion	,,	51
,, VI.—Cetywayo's Coronation	,,	53
,, VII.—Langalibalele, 1873	,,	61
,, VIII.—The Zulu War, 1879	,,	80
,, IX.—The Boer War, 1899-1902	,,	122
,, X.—The Native Rebellion, 1906-7	,,	172

Annals:—1855—1911 ... ,, 214

Appendix 1.—Races	,,	300
,, 2.—Shooting Competitions	,,	307
,, 3.—Athletic Sports	,,	339
,, 4.—Cricket	,,	357
,, 5.—Regimental Lists:—		
(a)—Officers, 1855-1911	,,	360
(b)—Muster Roll of the Natal Carbineers, Boer War, 1899-1902	,,	377

ILLUSTRATIONS.

	PAGE.
Addison, C. B., Lt.-Col.	160
Barter, W. E., Lt.-Col.	280
Baker, W. G.	32
Bond, E., Trooper	96
Buntine, R. A., Major	216
Burkimsher, W., R.-S.-Major	224
Bowen, B., R.-S.-Major	224
Band, Regimental, 1908	288
Barker, W. W., Trooper	360
Clough, E. B., Trooper	32
Crompton, B., Lt.-Col.	160
Currie, O. J., Major	216
Currie, H. B., Lieut.	216
Chum-Chum	380
Erskine, R. H., Trooper	96
Farmer, F. C., Sergt.	272
Foxon, F. E., Lieut.-Col.	304
Green, Dean	48
Greene, E. M., Colonel	88
Gage, W. T., Major	304
Hyslop, J., Lt.-Col.	216
Helbert, G. H., Capt.	232
Hair, A., Lt.-Col.	312
Kitchener, Lord	*Frontispiece.*
Karkloof Troop	24
Knott, W., R.-S.-Major	224
Lyle, A., Captain	304
Langalibalele, Chief	380
Memorial, Isandhlwana	128
Memorial, Bushman's Pass	128
Memorial, Boer War	248
McKenzie, D., Colonel	136
Macfarlane, G. J., Lt.-Col.	152
Mackay, D. W., Lt.-Col.	208
Molyneux, W. H. A., R.-S.-Major	224

	PAGE.
Montgomery, J. W. V., Major	240
Miller, C. E. J. Trooper	272
Non-Commissioned Officers, 1865	16
,, 1879	56
,, 1882	72
,, 1887	80
,, 1907	296
Officers, Umlaas Camp, 1889	104
,, Reitspruit Camp, 1892	120
,, Balgowan Camp, 1899	176
,, Siege of Ladysmith, 1899	200
,, Taylor's Camp, 1905	256
,, Colenso Camp, 1909	320
,, ,, 1911	352
Owen, T. M., Major	344
Otto, Pete, Lieut.	376
Park Gray, W., Major	360
Royston, W., Colonel	64
Rodwell, C. N. H., Lieut.-Col.	240
St. George, Sir T., Lieut.-Col.	8
Shepstone, "Offy," Capt.	40
Sutherland, P. C., Doctor	48
Sergeants, 1892	112
,, 1894	144
Shooting Team, 1895	168
Sergeants, 1898	184
Shepstone, W. S., Lieut.-Col.	232
Shaw, D., Trooper	272
Stride, P. W., Captain	312
Sergeants, Colenso Camp, 1909	328
,, ,, 1911	368
Tatham, G. F., Major	160
Taunton, C. E. Major	264
Tent Pegging Team, 1909	336
Townsend, A. C., Major	344
Weighton, J., Colonel	192
Woods, J. P. S., Lieut.-Col	280
Watts, R., Trooper	360

Introduction.

On the 12th May, 1843, by a proclamation of Sir George Napier, Governor of the Cape of Good Hope, Natal became a British Colony, and its inhabitants, without distinction of colour, origin, language, or creed, were taken under the protection of the British Crown. The tardy annexation of this colony is an illustration of the long-recognised truth, impressed on many a page of history since the days of Queen Elizabeth, that Great Britain has had Imperial greatness thrust upon her. Sometimes she has had to make good by conquest the rights and privileges which had been peacefully transferred to her by purchase or treaty, and afterwards denied her; at other times her enterprising and adventurous sons, of a more daring spirit and proportionately greater in number than those of any other nation, boldly pushing forward till they become involved in difficulty and danger from which they cannot extricate themselves, have excited her maternal instinct to follow and protect them; and again she has had reluctantly to enclose within an extended frontier, and reduce to obedience and order, idle and thievish neighbours, who could not resist the temptation to prey on the fruits of her industry. But whichever of these or other reasons may have called for her armed intervention, the result has always been sooner or later the same,—an extension of her Imperial territory, with all its accompanying responsibilities, in spite of her disinclination for mere territorial aggrandisement.

1. DERELICT NATAL.—The first white man who voluntarily made a settlement at Port Natal was Lieutenant Farewell. Allured by the opportunities it seemed to offer to the hunter and trader, he landed there in 1824 with companions and hired servants for elephant and buffalo hunting and opening a trade by barter with the natives. He discovered that, only a few years before his arrival, the once teeming population had been slaughtered or dispersed by Chaka, the King of the Zulus, and the scourge of south-east Africa. A small remnant of the aborigines, lurking on the fringes and in the mountain caves and bushy kloofs of their native land, were maintaining a miserable existence; those in the mountains, when roots and small game failed them, resorting in their distress even to cannibalism, and those on the coast to fish-eating, which had been held till then in abomination by the

Bantu tribes. These poor wretches, gathered round the small band of English for the protection which white men could never refuse, acknowledged them as chiefs, and became their obedient vassals. This little State within the conquered territory of the Zulu King was tolerated by him, and even had a strip of land, twenty-five miles broad at its base on the Indian Ocean and extending inland of the same breadth for a hundred miles, ceded to it, on condition that it should not encourage or harbour refugees from Zululand. To the credit of their humanity, notwithstanding the risk to themselves of evading this condition, the English chiefs observed it only once; for learning that the first band of fugitives, on being sent back to Zululand, had been cruelly put to death, they took care to pass on to Pondoland all who afterwards fled to them for refuge. The grant of land awakened in Farewell's mind his old, but for some time dormant, design of founding a colony in Natal under the British Government. He wrote to Lord Somerset, Governor of the Cape, giving an account of his success and his hopes, and praying to be invested with magisterial authority over those whom he not unreasonably looked on as his subjects. But his scheme got no encouragement then, and up to the time of his murder, in 1828, it had not advanced a single step farther.

A petition was drawn up in 1834, to which the signatures of one hundred and ninety merchants and inhabitants of the Cape Colony were attached, and forwarded by the Governor, Sir Benjamin D'Urban, to the Secretary of State, praying that a State-protected settlement might be made at Port Natal. In support of the prayer of the petitioners a long array of arguments was adduced. Prominent among them was the statement, accompanied by a warning,—that the Bay there was naturally an exceedingly fine harbour, which could be vastly improved by art, and that there was a danger that if Great Britain neglected it much longer it would be seized by some other Power, with injurious consequences to British rule in South Africa, for already American vessels visiting Port Natal had opened a trade with the Zulus in muskets and gunpowder. The following year His Excellency acquainted the signatories that the Secretary of State had sent him a despatch stating that His Majesty's Ministers had fully considered their memorial, but, while duly appreciating their motives for sending it, the Government could not advise His Majesty to grant his sanction to their petition, as, in the state of the finances of the Cape at that time, any additional expense for the establishment of a new settlement would be highly inconvenient, and could not with propriety be incurred.

Among the Dutch farmers of the Cape Colony, especially those of its eastern province, the passive dislike of British rule, which they had felt from the first, had grown by what seemed to them a course of injustice and tyranny into positive hatred. That which put an end to their forbearance, as well as tried severely the loyalty of their British fellow-subjects, was the unjust dealing with the colonists after the Kafir war of 1835 by the infatuated Lord Glenelg, the Secretary of State for the Colonies. They who had suffered most were blamed and punished for the war; the Kafirs, who had been the aggressors, were pitied and rewarded. Thousands of Cape Boers made up their minds to forsake their native land, and a prospecting party, under Piet Retief, was sent forward to find a new home for them, where they might live the free life they had lost. Retief arrived at Port Natal when the English there, disappointed of recognition by the Home Government, were in the mood to welcome them, as friends certainly, and possibly as neighbours or partners. Pleased with all that he had seen and heard Retief led the way, followed by a thousand waggons, down the passes of the Drakensberg into the verdant desert of Natal. It was too fair a pasture for them to turn their backs on; but though they knew by hearsay and visible proof that the land was derelict, with the caution instilled into them by their long acquaintance with the character and claims of the natives, they resolved to bargain for a formal cession of it with its overlord Dingaan. They were to restore to him some hundreds of cattle that had been stolen from him by a neighbouring chief, and by way of salvage they should have the land they asked for. The recovered cattle were brought to him by Retief at the head of seventy Boers, the deed of cession was drawn and signed, and then the whole band of white men, thrown off their guard by the pretence of hospitality, were brutally butchered. Immediately Zulu bands were sent out to surprise the Boer camps that dotted the banks of the Tugela and Bushman rivers, and a ruthless massacre of men, women, and children was perpetrated. But the Dutch were not the men to flee, like craven Fingoes, before Dingaan's savage hordes. Re-inforced from over the Berg, and aided by the English and their native vassals from the Port, commando after commando went forth to avenge the slaughtered dead and punish the blood-thirsty Zulu. On each side there was shown a stubborn ferocity, upheld in the one by superiority of numbers, and in the other of weapons, such as had never been seen in the patched-up wars of the Cape frontier. But the end crowns the work, and Dingaan's Day, the 16th of December, is kept sacred by the Boers, as the Jews keep their Day of Atonement, to commemorate the last fight on the Blood River, which broke the tyrant's power, and established the white man's supremacy. If the bloodshed of their dearest and bravest gives a people a claim to land in South Africa, the Boers had earned Natal, for in less than one short year it had become the cemetery of hundreds of their dead.

After reverently burying the bodies of the seventy Boers treacherously slain by Dingaan's order, Pretorius and his commando returned from their decisive victory over the Zulus, bringing with them the deed of cession which they had found on the body of Retief. The Dutch, now fancying themselves independent of British sovereignty, and owners, both by treaty and conquest, of a rich and extensive country, at once proceeded, without any conscientious or political scruples, to divide the country among themselves, on a large and generous plan which in their eyes was both just and natural. Being a pastoral people, delighting in ample room and solitude, they apportioned out the land, so as to equal the number of their families, into farms of the extent of eight thousand acres each. For political and magisterial reasons they divided the whole country into twelve electoral districts, each of which was to return two members to the Volksraad. Meetings of the Raad were to be held quarterly at the newly-laid-out capital, Pietermaritzburg, named in honour of the two most respected Boer leaders, Pieter Retief and Gert Maritz. Any business that might arise between the stated meetings and require immediate despatch, was to be attended to by a Raad Committee, consisting of two or three members residing in or near Maritzburg. Thus it came to pass that the fair and fertile land, that once supported a dense population, as the still extant remains of stone kraals scattered over it testify, devastated by a cruel savage and for twenty years a waif, seemed likely again to be the home of a contented and prosperous people, under its new name of the Republic of Natalia.

2. BRITISH NATAL.—Before the emigrant Boers left the Cape Colony in 1836, they drew up a statement of their reasons for leaving their old home in search of a new, and added to it a renunciation on their part of subjection to the British Government. Allegiance is the tie that binds the subject for loyalty and service to the Crown in return for the protection

which it affords him, and cannot be so easily loosened as Retief and his followers imagined. It may be severed either by the Sovereign's abdication of his authority, as when the Romans re-called their legions from Britain in the beginning of the fifth century; or by the subjects' vindication of liberty against the abuse of the Sovereign power, as when the English, by the revolution of 1689, transferred their allegiance from James II. to William III., or the American colonists about a century later achieved their independence of the Mother Country. Since the British forcibly took possession of the Cape Colony and its dependencies in 1806,—a possession ratified by the Congress of Vienna in 1815—the Dutch at the Cape had been British subjects for thirty years. Great Britain was the paramount power in South Africa, and, though more tolerant than any other Sovereign ruler of free speech and action among her subjects, she was obliged, for the sake of her own colonists, to guard against the rise and approach of danger to them from over her borders. The existence of the Republic of Natalia would depend on whether it proved to be a safe and friendly neighbour to the Cape.

Not many years passed before Sir George Napier, Governor of the Cape Colony, was convinced that a permanent Republic of Natalia was an impossibility. By its high-handed dealing with the natives it was kindling a conflagration, which was likely to envelop the whole of South Africa, and it had within itself the fast ripening seeds of disintegration. On the overthrow of the Zulu King, Dingaan, the Boers proclaimed Panda his successor. But the change of king did not ameliorate the lot of the subjects. The oppression and savage cruelty that had been practised by Chaka and Dingaan were continued by Panda. Now, however, the settlement of the Dutch in their Republic of Natalia, and the fact of their having conquered Dingaan, induced many Zulus to seek an escape from the tyranny and cruelty of native despotism, by crossing the Tugela, and placing themselves under the protection of the conquerors. Thousands also of the aboriginals who had fled south and west in the time of Chaka's raids flocked back to the land they had been driven from twenty years before. At first both the refugees and the home-coming exiles were welcomed as useful herds and farm servants, but the inrush of them became so strong that the Boers, becoming alarmed for their own safety, resolved that it must be checked and regulated. A law was accordingly passed by the Volksraad limiting the number of Kafir immigrants to five grown men for each Boer family, and ordering the overplus to occupy the coast land between the rivers Umtamfuna and Umzimvubu, as long as they behaved well and were obedient to, and acknowledged the authority of, the Boer Republic. The territory thus arbitrarily assigned by the Boers to their redundant Kafirs was claimed by the Pondo Chief Faku.

Before the Boers had time to carry out their design of ridding themselves of their superfluous Kafirs by driving them over their borders, they made an attack on a Kafir tribe in Pondoland, which, though it may have been only of slight and passing importance to them, appeared to the Governor of the Cape Colony likely to imperil seriously the peace of his eastern frontier. Cattle and horses had been stolen from the farmers by the Bushmen, who lived near by in the Drakensberg. The Boers accused Ncapayi, one of Faku's tributary chieftains, of sharing in the raids and spoil of the Bushmen. They attacked him in Pondoland, killed and wounded a hundred and fifty of his people, and drove off three thousand head of cattle to recoup them for their losses and trouble.

While the Boers were thus recklessly making enemies of their Kafir neighbours beyond their borders, within, instead of consolidating their strength by conciliation and forbearance, they had suffered discord and lawlessness to grow almost unchecked till they threatened their community with speedy dissolution. They had already estranged the English at the Port, who (though having the prior claim to the ownership of the land) were from the first disposed to treat them as equals and friends, by interfering with the privileges of hunting and trading which they had enjoyed since 1824. Among themselves, the more unruly, setting the control of their leaders at defiance, were doing each as it seemed good in his own eyes. Many discontented Boers, who had stayed behind when the Voortrekkers left the Colony, had afterwards followed them with the intention of casting in their lot with them, but on making acquaintance with the unstable condition of the Republic of Natalia, they had gone back to their old life as the less of two evils. In the first year of the Republic, Captain Jervis, who had been sent from the Cape at the head of a force to occupy Port Natal temporarily as a military post of observation, had reported to Sir George Napier that he saw no probability of the emigrant Boers uniting under one head, for it was said that even of their Volksraad scarcely two of them agreed. In its last days Commissioner Cloete wrote of it that some of its most respectable and worthy burghers assured him that it was impossible for them any longer to live in such a state of anarchy as that into which the country was fast receding.

Sir George Napier and his advisers at the Cape were cognisant and observant of the position of peril to itself and others which the Republic had drifted into, and had forwarded their view of its situation to the Home Government. The Volksraad also had appealed Home, through the Governor of the Cape, for recognition as a free and independent State, and had proposed a treaty of alliance. The answer to these communications was an instruction to Sir George Napier to resume military occupation of Port Natal; and to the Boers, that the Queen could not acknowledge a portion of her own subjects as an independent Republic, but was willing to give them protection on their receiving a military force from the Cape. Accordingly Colonel Cloete was sent from the Cape with an armament sufficient to effect the Governor's purpose. He met with but a feeble and half-hearted resistance on the part of the disunited Boers, and that only at the harbour. As soon as the British effected a landing, the Boers retreated to Maritzburg. The soldiers' part of the business was happily ended: diplomacy would do the rest. Arms gave way to the toga.

Advocate Cloete, brother of the Colonel, was selected as Commissioner, and proceeded to Natal to state the terms on which Her Majesty's protection would be extended to her new colonists, and to examine and adjudicate on their claims to the farms which their Volksraad had already allotted. He was instructed to grant them titles to these farms on proof of bonafide occupation of them for twelve months previous to his arrival; and as a general rule in keeping with this liberal concession, and in consideration of their good qualities and the hardships they had undergone, he was enjoined, and as he was himself of Dutch nationality he was naturally inclined, to treat them generously. The Mother Country undertook to defray the cost of military protection. All sums accruing from the disposal of land, and from dues and customs collected on any part of the Natal coast, were to be applied exclusively to the maintenance of the civil government of the Colony. The Boers were to be indulged in their natural preference for their own customs and system of laws as far as was consistent with the following conditions,—that all the inhabitants of the new Colony were to be entitled, without distinction, to the impartial protection of the law, that no unauthorized aggression was to be made on the natives residing beyond the limits of the

Colony, and that slavery in any shape or under any modification should be absolutely unlawful. A proclamation drawn up in this gracious spirit was promulgated, which deprived the most hostile of their strongest argument for resistance, and commended itself to the more reasonable part of the emigrant farmers. Some of the irreconcilables, however, reckoning at a small value the possession of real property in a country where land was to be had for the taking, at once threw up their farms and trekked again over the Berg. Others of them, finding that the lines had fallen to them in pleasant places, stomached their disgust of British rule and stayed in Natal. Thus at last, after a long period of vacillation, of alternate advance and retreat, the Home Government had made its irrevocable decision, and from the 12th May, 1843, Natal became a British Colony.

3. OBSTRUCTION AND ENCOURAGEMENT.—The security which Natal offered to the lives and property of intending British colonists was extremely precarious. Thrust like a wedge into the side of savage Africa, with the thievish and restless tribes of Kafirland and Pondoland on its south-western border, the warlike Zulus on its north-east chafing under their defeat and humiliation by the white men, the hostile Boers over the Berg who sullenly resented and still hoped to recover the loss of what they considered their own blood-bought property, and a large portion of its population only half reconciled to British Sovereignty, its sole inlet for succour to its loyal inhabitants when in danger, or way of escape should they be overpowered, was by the sea at its only port. And to protect them against the rise of any or all of these unfriendly elements, there was only, besides their own right hands, a small body of troops, under the command of Major Smith, at Durban. As if in such circumstances the safety of the new possession was not sufficiently endangered, it was to be further jeopardised by opening its doors wide to the admission of all comers.

The evil which the Boers foresaw from the increase of Kafirs seeking their protection they would have found a remedy for, though at the cost of others. But now it was to be tolerated, if not encouraged, without limit. From the date of the annexation of the new Colony the principle that the British Empire shall be an asylum for the distressed, though condemned by the fears and prudence of the colonists, was acted on in Natal by the Government at Home. The rush of refugees in ever-increasing volume poured in and spread itself all over the land, hindering its industry and menacing its

Lieut.-Colonel Sir T. St. George, Bart.
First Commanding Officer, 1855-1856.

peace, till, when Governor West, in despair, hinted at the necessity of abandoning the Colony, a Commission was appointed to examine and report on the extent of the evil and to find a remedy. Better men to make the best of a bad business could not have been found than the five selected—Mr. Theophilus Shepstone, the Diplomatic Agent, Dr. Stanger, the Surveyor-General, two American missionaries, and a Lieutenant of the Royal Engineers. Their report, after stating the causes and extent of the large influx of the blacks and its danger to the whites, proposed that locations should be beaconed off for the Kafirs, that each location should be governed by a white magistrate and a competent staff of assistants, that it should be policed by a sufficient native force under European officers, that criminal offences and civil suits should be disposed of as much as possible according to the principles of British law, that there should be a complete registration of its inhabitants, with a census of their cattle, that the Native laws as to marriage and divorce should be remodelled, and that schools and missions should be established as a supplementary aid. Could these wise suggestions have been carried out, the character of the Kafir would have been transformed long ere this, and Natal would have had an abundant and steady supply of useful labour. But the whole expense of this generously devised scheme was to be borne by the white population, the Kafir Hut Tax being as yet no more than an idea to be afterwards timorously carried into practice, and the treasury of the infant Colony was unequal to the burden. The only part, therefore, that could be effected was to settle the Kafirs in the locations that had been marked off for them, and leave them there to live the idle and unprogressive life which their own laws and customs encourage and perpetuate.

If the Natal colonists found that the presence among them of a disproportionate and rapidly-increasing number of Kafirs proved to be more a curse than a blessing in time of peace, they still might indulge the expectation that it could be reckoned on as a substantial auxiliary of the colonial force in a time of war. The highest estimate of the number of blacks in the country when the Boers set up their Republic of Natalia was that given by Mr. D. C. Toohey before a Native Commission in 1852. He thought it could not exceed ten thousand: other witnesses put it at a much lower figure. By the middle of the century it had mounted at least twenty-fold to the alarming total of two hundred thousand. But as in peace the blacks are to the whites more a hindrance than a help, so they have been found in war. They are like the horde of camp-followers of a mediæval army—an encumbrance with a claim to protection. If the eyes of the Colony were blind for a time to the worse than worthlessness of its native population as an auxiliary in time of danger, they were opened by the breakdown of their trust in Kafir helpfulness under the test applied to it in 1851. The tale is told in "The Dorp and the Veld," by Mr. Charles Barter, in after years a captain in the Natal Carbineers Regiment. Mr. Barter was in Maritzburg when the news reached it of the outbreak of the Kafir War of 1850-53 on the eastern frontier of the Cape Colony, and he gives a vivid description of the excitement produced in the minds of all around him, some showing signs of dread, others of resentment and a desire of revenge. Many plans were proposed to secure Natal and even to send help to the Old Colony, the most notable of which was the one projected by Governor Pine and approved of by Sir Harry Smith, the soldier Governor of the Cape. It was to raise ten thousand of the Natal Kafirs and send them through Faku's country to attack the Cape's enemies in the rear. They were to be led by their own chiefs under the control of Mr. Theophilus Shepstone. The trysting day was fixed and the rendezvous was to be the Umzimkulu Drift. But the tryst was postponed again and again till it was named when it would no longer be heeded unless with derision. The scheme fell through, owing to the inertia or cowardice of the Kafirs, who were too evidently unwilling to risk anything for the country that gave them shelter. The plan was abortive, and the last that was heard of it was a notice in the "Natal Independent" of 10th April, 1851,— "Resident Agent Fynn, it is said, has collected an army of fifteen men." That may be called a newspaper skit, but it is enough to show that the grand Zulu expedition was a failure. The Kafir mountain was in labour, and there came forth a ridiculous mouse.

While the colonial Kafirs were showing themselves to be but a broken reed, there was pouring into Natal a class of immigrants of a totally different character, who were as welcome as ever were reinforcements to an outpost in war time disheartened and sore beset. Between the years 1848-51 over four thousand emigrants sailed from Home and were landed at Durban. They were brought out mostly under what was known as Byrne's Immigration Scheme. Mr. J. C. Byrne had arranged with the Government to bring out emigrants who were to pay £10 for their passage, and on reaching Natal were to receive grants of land varying, according to situation and quality, from twenty to fifty acres. To poor but energetic farmers and mechanics, who were bent on bettering their fortune and judged of land by its value in England, the free gift of fifty acres was an attraction that promised an easy competence. The unforeseen difficulties that confronted them, when they set themselves to the task of making a home in a new country so unlike the one they had left, were a severe trial to all, and appeared insurmountable to some. These within a year or two, despairing of success in Natal, made a second emigration,—to Australia most of them, captivated by the glowing accounts that reached them of fortunes made in a day at the gold fields there. But the residue were the right sort of pioneers for a new country, and if they did not prosper in farming they turned to other pursuits that promised better. As their condition in the Colony improved, they invited their friends and acquaintances at Home to join them here, and gave them advice derived from their own experience. In this way a tide of immigration set in for Natal which, if not very strong, was steady and wholesome. Vacant land was taken up, villages were settled here and there, and the towns enlarged, and within ten or twelve years of its foundation under the Queen the Colony could boast that it was at length a permanent portion of the British Empire.

Confidence and disappointment succeed each other rapidly in South Africa, and the year 1854, while it was taxing the strength of the Mother Country in the Crimea, saw an attempt made to bring the existence of Natal, the youngest of her colonial offspring, to a premature close. In that year, having her hands full in Europe and wearied with the succession of troubles in South Africa, Great Britain was easily persuaded that the Orange River Sovereignty was a worthless and expensive possession, and notwithstanding the entreaty of many of its inhabitants not to withdraw her protection, she hurriedly retired from it, just as two years before, by the Sand River Convention, she relinquished control over the emigrant farmers who had crossed the Vaal River. The Natal Boers, as a whole, only grudgingly tolerant of British rule, impatient of the lenient treatment of the Kafirs under it, and envious of what they deemed the happy release from it of their fellow-countrymen over the Berg, conceived the hope that, in Britain's embarrassment and peevish mood, they, too, might prevail on her to concede them their independence. They drew up a petition to the Home Government for the abandonment of Natal also, based on the following complaints, which, if not altogether groundless, were certainly exaggerated—that there was no redress of grievances, no protection for life and property, that the authorities here were interfering with, and trying to abolish, Roman Dutch law, that the Government was threatening to force through a County Council Ordinance, which would probably be followed by a burgher law, and that Natal had not yet representative institutions, but was still a Crown Colony. The petition had three hundred and thirty-nine signatures, and was duly forwarded by Governor Pine. Sir George Grey, Governor of the Cape Colony and Lord High Commissioner, wrote a forecast of its rejection in his despatch to Governor Pine, dated 30th December, 1854:—"I have to acknowledge your despatch, No. 59, of the 25th September last, transmitting a memorial, signed by 339 persons, praying that the District of Natal may be abandoned by Her Majesty's Government. I approve of your not having held out the expectation to the memorialists that such a course of policy would be adopted by Her Majesty's Government." The loyal Natalians, without condescending to mention it publicly, gave it a practical and conclusive answer by volunteering to defend the Colony under the flag which the others wished to be hauled down. Opportunely, to stimulate their loyalty, accounts of the endurance and courage of the British troops in the Crimea, and especially of the Charge of the Light Brigade at Balaklava, had just reached the Colony, and fired every British breast with pride and the spirit of emulation.

A naturally brave people never show their native character to better advantage than when they have to face difficulties and dangers by whose combined and overwhelming force, according to the calculations of prudence, their feebleness is far out-matched. The handful of British colonists in Natal at the end of 1854, if theirs had been only the courage of average humanity, should have counted the odds against them and surrendered at discretion. But as it always is with the men of their race, it was when their need was the sorest that their spirit rose highest. The psychological moment, as we are accustomed to call the favourable nick of time, had now arrived, and the man to call for a display of the old British spirit, as well as the men to make the response, were together on the spot.

CHAPTER I.

VOLUNTEERING.

His Excellency the Lieutenant-Governor of the Colony, judging correctly of the temper of the colonists, both the recent arrivals and the old settlers, and perceiving that the time was ripe for putting it to a successful proof, prepared an Ordinance which may be termed the Charter of the Natal Volunteer Forces. In submitting, for the consideration of the Legislative Council, a Draft Ordinance, under date 16th October, 1854, His Honour B. C. C. Pine, Esq., Lieutenant-Governor administering the Government of the District of Natal, states that:—
"It would be very desirable to encourage, by every means in our power, the formation of one or two small volunteer corps, which may, in some measure, supply the place of a mounted police. For this purpose, I would recommend that two mounted corps, each consisting of fifty men, should be formed, one in the neighbourhood of Durban, and one in this locality, the members of which should receive pay whenever called out for service, and also for a certain number of days' exercise in every year, upon the express condition that they are bound by bye-laws sanctioned and enforced by Legislative Enactment, to serve whenever called upon, at any distance not exceeding thirty miles from their general place of rendezvous. Such a force as this, if properly organised and trained, will not perhaps supersede the necessity of a mounted police force in the locality to which it belongs, but it will, I think, render a smaller police force sufficient; and considering the vast difference between the expense of the mounted police and that of the volunteer corps, the latter deserves every encouragement at the hands of the Government. A corps of this description has already, as you are aware, been formed in Durban, in a manner most creditable to the parties concerned. I think, in addition to small annual pay to the members of such corps, it might be advisable to make them grants of land, at the end of a given period, for efficient service."

The result of the foregoing suggestion was that the following Ordinance was enacted on the 15th of November, 1854:—

ORDINANCE,

Enacted by His Honour the Lieutenant-Governor of the District of Natal with the advice and consent of the Legislative Council thereof.

"To promote the Establishment of Volunteer Corps for the defence of the District."

Whereas it is expedient to promote the formation and establishment of Volunteer Corps for the protection and defence of the District, and for the maintenance of order.

Be it therefore enacted by the Lieutenant-Governor of Natal, with the advice and consent of the Legislative Council thereof, as follows:—

1. It shall be lawful for any number of persons residing in any parts of the District, with the sanction of the Lieutenant-Governor, to form themselves into Volunteer Corps, for military training and exercise.

2. It shall be lawful for every such Corps to make rules and bye-laws regulating the duties of its members, the enforcing of discipline, the nature of its arms and equipment, the number and rank of its officers and members, and its general place of rendezvous.

3. It shall be lawful for the Lieutenant-Governor, if he shall approve of such rules and bye-laws, to sanction the same by a Proclamation under his hand, and such rules and bye-laws shall thereupon have the force of law in the same manner as if the same were inserted in this Ordinance.

4. The members of every Corps shall have the power to elect their own officers, subject to the approval of the Lieutenant-Governor, who shall, if he see fit, issue Commissions under his hand to the persons so elected.

5. Every such Corps shall be entitled to the benefit of all fines and forfeitures levied under or by virtue of such rules and bye-laws as aforesaid.

6. No member of any such Corps shall be compelled to serve in any Militia, or other Military Force, which may be established in this District.

7. It shall be lawful for the Lieutenant-Governor, subject to the conditions hereinafter expressed, to cause pay to be issued to every man belonging to any such Corps, at a rate not exceeding six shillings per day, for every day on which he shall be called out for muster or actual service.

8. Provided that no such pay shall be issued to any man

for more than twenty days in each year, unless he shall be called out for actual service, and also unless such Corps and every member thereof shall be bound by its rules and bye-laws to serve in any part of the country, at least thirty miles from the general place of rendezvous, whenever called out by the Lieutenant-Governor, or by his order, to suppress insurrection, repel invasion, or to support the authority of the civil power whenever it appears likely in any case to be resisted; and every member failing so to do when duly required, shall be liable to a fine, not exceeding £10, to be recovered summarily in the Court of the Resident Magistrate.

9. Returns shall be transmitted to the Lieutenant-Governor, through the Colonial Secretary, half yearly, by the officer commanding every Volunteer Corps, or the Adjutant thereof, of the number of men and horses (if any) belonging to such Corps.

10. Whenever any Volunteer Corps shall be reduced below twenty men, rank and file, for a continuous period of six months, it shall become *ipso facto* disbanded.

11. This Ordinance shall commence and take effect from and after the publication thereof in the "Government Gazette."

GOD SAVE THE QUEEN!

Given at Pietermaritzburg, in the District of Natal, this 15th day of November, 1854.

By Command of the Lieutenant-Governor,

(Signed) WILLIAM C. SARGEAUNT,
Colonial Secretary.

By Order of the Legislative Council,

(Signed) EDMD. TATHAM,
Acting Clerk of the Council.

In terms of this Ordinance two volunteer regiments, the Natal Carbineers, in the Capital of the Colony, and the Royal Durban Rangers, at the port, were formed without waste of time. The 15th of January, 1855, the day when the promoters of the volunteer movement in Maritzburg held their first formal meeting, is the birthday of the former regiment. At that meeting the name selected for the newly-formed corps was "The Pietermaritzburg Irregular Horse." It was not till the 7th February following, that the original name was rejected for that which the regiment has ever since borne, "The Natal Carbineers."

The proceedings of the meeting of the 15th January, and of the adjourned meeting held a fortnight after, on the 29th, were reported in the local press of the day as follows:—

VOLUNTEER CORPS.

A meeting was held on 15th January inst., to discuss the establishment of a Volunteer Cavalry Corps.

Chairman: The Hon'ble W. C. Sargeaunt, Esq.

After a few brief introductory remarks from the chair, the proceedings of the meeting were opened by the following resolution by—

The Hon'ble Walter Harding, Esq., Seconded by Capt. Maxwell, R.N.

That a Mounted Volunteer Corps be established for the County of Pietermaritzburg.

Carried unanimously.

Proposed by Sir Theo. St. George, Bart., Seconded by C. Barter, Esq.

That the said Corps be called "The Pietermaritzburg Irregular Horse."

Carried unanimously.

Proposed by Sir Theo. St. George, Seconded by A. B. Allison, Esq.

That each member of the said Corps shall provide himself with a Horse and Gun (single or double barrelled) at his own Expense.

Carried unanimously.

Proposed by C. Barter, Esq., Seconded by Sir Theo. St. George.

That members of the said Corps shall wear no uniform.

Amendment proposed by Capt. Maxwell, R.N.

That the members of the said Corps wear a simple and inexpensive Uniform to be hereafter decided upon by a Committee appointed for that purpose.

Seconded by C. Baker.

Amendment carried.

Proposed by the Hon'ble W. Harding, Seconded by J. Bird, Esq.

That the services of this Corps shall be available in any part of the District.

Carried unanimously.

GROUP OF NATAL CARBINEERS, 1865.

Trooper J. McLean, Trooper J. Buchanan, Corpl. A. McLean, Sergeant T. Maxwell, Trooper W. Bell, Trooper J. Fannin, Trooper M. Stuart, Trooper Albert Allison, Jr.

Proposed by Capt. Maxwell, R.N., Seconded by Geo. Freshwater.

That each member of the said Corps shall provide at his own expense the necessary quantity of Ammunition required for practice upon Parade day, and that the quantity shall be determined by the Officer in command of the troop, due notice being given.

Carried unanimously.

Proposed by W. M. Collins, Esq., Seconded by Mr. Osborne.

That no troop of the said Corps shall consist of less than Thirty, or more than Fifty men;—and that each troop shall be officered by one Captain and one subaltern.

Carried unanimously.

Proposed by Mr. Raw, Seconded by A. Morrison, Esq.

That in addition to the troops Officers, there shall be a Colonel, Adjutant and Surgeon.

Carried unanimously.

Proposed by the Hon'ble W. C. Sargeaunt, Esq., Seconded by W. M. Collins, Esq.

That the Committee to determine upon the Uniform for adoption by the said Corps, shall consist of the following gentlemen:—viz.

        Sir Theo. St. George, Bart.
        Capt. Maxwell, R.N.
        A. B. Allison, Esq.

Carried.

Proposed by W. M. Collins, Esq., Seconded by C. Barter, Esq.

That at the next meeting of the members of this Corps, a Committee, composed of the undermentioned gentlemen, lay before such meeting draft bye-laws for the regulation and management of the said Corps, etc.,

        The Hon'ble W. Harding, Esq.
        The Hon'ble W. C. Sargeaunt, Esq.
        Mr. Raw.— Carried.

Proposed by Sir Theo. St. George, Bart., Seconded by W. M. Collins, Esq.

That A. B. Allison be appointed to act as Adjutant *pro tem.*, until a full meeting shall elect the Officers of the said Corps.—Carried.

Proposed by W. M. Collins, Esq., Seconded by Sir Theo. St. George, Bart.,

That the Acting Adjutant shall wait upon the members

of the said Corps (not present at this meeting), and submit to them a copy of the resolutions passed this day; for the purpose of obtaining their assent thereto.—Carried.

The meeting was then adjourned to Monday, the 29th inst.

Pietermaritzburg, Jan. 15, 1855.

At a meeting held on the 29th January, 1855, at the Court House, Pietermaritzburg, to discuss further preliminaries for the establishment of a Volunteer Cavalry Corps—

Chairman: The Hon'ble W. C. Sargeaunt, Esq.

The Chairman stated that he proposed to lay before the meeting a brief outline of what he considered should form the proceedings thereof, and to comment on the opposition which had arisen to the formation of a Corps on the principles contemplated. That there would be opponents to the measure was certain, and opposition in many cases did good, as it would cause those who did join the Corps in question to be united in stronger bonds, than if no opposition existed. However, there was one thing which he indeed regretted to see—namely, that those who did not wish to join, were not satisfied with condemning the measure and talking against it; but, in addition, distorted facts in such manner as to induce some who might be willing to join to stand aloof; and great use had been made for that purpose, of a resolution which had been adopted at the last meeting, viz., that the various members should find their own ammunition for practice;—it would have been as well had that resolution been accompanied with an explanation, that if the Corps came under the provision of the Ordinance for legalising the formation of the Volunteer Corps, each member would be entitled to a sum of 6s. per diem for 20 days' drill in each year. Thus each member would receive a sum of £6 per annum, from which amount the small cost for ammunition should be defrayed; that he considered it but common honesty, where opposition was raised to any measure, that the opponents should not only tell the truth, but the whole truth, otherwise false impressions on the measure must, as a matter of course, gain credence; that if the opposition proceeded, as it doubtless did in some instances from objection, or inability to comply with the regulations of the Corps, he would recommend the gentlemen so circumstanced to form a separate and distinct Corps for the protection of the City; such a Corps would undoubtedly be useful, and he (the Chairman) would be but too glad to co-operate.

The Chairman then stated that there were doubtless many present at the meeting who had no intention of joining the Corps, and that such gentlemen could not with any fairness expect to vote for the election of the officers of the Corps, or on the bye-laws; at the same time he wished to thank them for their countenance on the occasion. That the best mode of procedure, therefore, would be to agree to some general outline of the principle upon which the Corps is to be formed, and, having agreed, that those who are desirous of joining should sign a document containing these general resolutions, and the members thus signing to meet on some future day to decide upon the Uniform, Bye-laws, etc., etc.

The Chairman then read the Minutes of a former meeting held on the 15th instant. Tenders were submitted by the Clothing Committee to the members, setting forth the cost of Uniform, etc., etc.

The following report thereon from the Clothing Committee was then read by the Chairman:—

"The Committee appointed at the last meeting of the Members of the Pietermaritzburg Volunteer Cavalry Corps, beg to state that after having carefully considered the several tenders (now before the meeting) for the clothing of this Corps (which were called for by the members of the Committee, on the principle of fair dealing with the tradesmen of Pietermaritzburg and D'Urban), and having examined and compared the texture and quality of the samples forwarded therewith; they cannot, with a due regard to one of the resolutions passed at the last meeting, viz.:—

"That the members of this Corps wear a simple and inexpensive uniform, etc., etc."

recommend any of the tenders for acceptance, on the ground that such uniform is too expensive, and the material tendered of insufficient strength and durability.

"The lowest tender amounts to the sum of £4 19s.

"The Committee would suggest that a uniform, costing not much more than one-third of that amount, or certainly not exceeding £2, would be found to be better adapted to the purposes for which such a costume is generally intended, and, in reality, more serviceable than any other of a more costly description.

"The Committee, therefore, beg to lay before the meeting the estimated cost of such a Uniform; and respectfully suggest that the same be adopted by this Corps."

The Chairman then laid before the meeting the estimated

cost of the uniform proposed for adoption by the Clothing Committee, together with samples of material.

After some discussion, it was agreed that a general outline of the principles upon which the Corps should be formed, should be framed and adopted.

These being discussed, the following were adopted:—

TERMS ON WHICH IT IS PROPOSED TO FORM A VOLUNTEER CORPS IN PIETERMARITZBURG AND ITS NEIGHBOURHOOD.

1. The Corps shall consist of 100 Volunteers, including officers, and shall be called the "Pietermaritzburg Irregular Horse."

2. There shall be one Lieutenant-Colonel, one Captain, one Subaltern, and non-commissioned officers to each Troop.

3. They shall have a simple and inexpensive Uniform.

4. Their arms shall be a single or double-barrelled gun.

5. They shall be called out for exercise twenty days in the course of the year.

6. They shall be bound to proceed to the appointed place of meeting without delay (within two hours) after receiving notice, and to serve in any part of the district.

7. Non-Commissioned Officers to call out the Troop.

8. Any part of the Corps, provided not less than twenty men, with discretionary power in the Captain or Commanding Officer to increase the number, may be called out, within the period aforesaid, to support the authority of the Civil power, when it appears likely to be resisted.

9. It shall be in the power of the Commanding Officer in cases of great emergency, for the protection of the town, to call out the Corps, or part of the Corps, without waiting for orders from Government, and also when Governors, or other distinguished persons are arriving at, or leaving the Colony.

10. Rules shall be framed by the Corps, and sanctioned by Ordinance for enforcing discipline; offenders to be tried by Court Martial, chosen by the Corps. Punishment to be by fine. Amount of fines to go to the General Fund of the Corps.

(Signed by Eighteen Members.)

A resolution was then passed, to the effect—That the meeting should adjourn until Wednesday, the 7th proximo, to be held at the Court House, Pietermaritzburg, when further preliminaries for the regulation of the Corps, decision upon uniform, etc., etc., should be discussed; each subscribing member to the resolutions adopted at this meeting to be considered eligible to vote. Absentee subscribers to be permitted to vote by proxy.

Meeting adjourned accordingly.
Pietermaritzburg, 29th Jan., 1855.

It is unfortunate that the local newspaper of the approximate date does not give a detailed report of the meeting held on the 7th February, because, of the business done, some appears to have been accompanied with a show of excitement at the time, and a full report might be entertaining now. The bye-laws of the Regiment were passed; it was resolved, besides altering the Regiment's name, that the uniform should be blue with white facings; and, in addition to the headquarters troop at Maritzburg, a second troop was formed with Richmond as its centre, the inhabitants of that district having shown a warm interest in the volunteer movement. For the office of Lieutenant-Colonel there were two nominations, Sir Theophilus St. George and Mr. Walter Harding, and owing to the solid vote of the Richmond troop the baronet was elected. The complete list of officers selected was:—

Lieutenant-Colonel: Sir Theophilus St. George, Bart.
Captain: The Hon. W. C. Sargeaunt.
Lieutenant: Philip Allen, Esq.
Lieut. and Adjutant: A. B. Allison, Esq.
Surgeon: Dr. P. C. Sutherland.
Chaplain: Dean Green.

In the following correspondence between the Lieutenant-Colonel of the Carbineers and the Acting Lieutenant-Governor of the Colony, together with the proclamation by the Administrator in the "Government Gazette" of March 13th, 1855, it will be seen that an offer of the services of the regiment was formally made to the Government, and as formally accepted:—

"Pietermaritzburg, 15th February, 1855.

"Sir,—I beg to acquaint you for the information of His Honour, the Lieutenant-Governor, that after several meetings to consider the propriety of establishing a Volunteer Corps according to Ordinance No. 8, 1854, the enclosed rules and bye-laws have been accepted and signed by about forty Volunteers, who bind themselves to serve as set forth in the bye-laws themselves; and have further to request that you will obtain His

Honour's sanction to the formation of the corps as proposed, and further that you will obtain His Honour's sanction to the bye-laws under Section 3 of the Ordinance above stated.

I have, etc.,

THEO. ST. GEORGE, Lt.-Colonel.

The Honourable W. C. Sargeaunt, Colonial Secretary, Natal."

"Colonial Office, Natal, 2nd March, 1855.

"Sir,—In reply to your letter of 15th ultimo, I am directed by the Lieutenant-Governor to inform you that he has been pleased, under the provisions of Ordinance No. 8, 1854, to sanction the formation of a mounted corps, in the town of Pietermaritzburg, under the name of the Natal Carbineers. I am also to acquaint you that His Honour has given his approval to the bye-laws of the corps submitted by you, and that they will be duly proclaimed and published in the "Government Gazette" of 13th instant.

I have, etc.,

W. C. SARGEAUNT, Colonial Secretary.

Lt.-Colonel Sir Theo. St. George, Baronet, Pietermaritzburg."

PROCLAMATION.

By His Honor HENRY COOPER, Esquire, Acting Lieutenant-Governor, administering the Government of the District of Natal.

WHEREAS it is enacted by the Ordinance No. 8, 1854, entitled "an Ordinance to promote the Establishment of Volunteer Corps for the defence of the District," that it shall be lawful for every such Corps to make rules and bye-laws regulating the duties of its members, the enforcing of discipline, the nature of its arms and equipments, the number and rank of its officers and members, and its general place of rendezvous:—

And further that it shall be lawful for the Lieutenant-Governor if he shall approve of such rules and bye-laws to sanction the same by a Proclamation under his hand, and that such rules and bye-laws shall thereupon have the force of law in the same manner as if the same were inserted in the said Ordinance:—

And whereas a corps called the "Natal Carbineers" has been formed and established at Pietermaritzburg, in the County of Pietermaritzburg, and the said Corps having made the following rules and bye-laws for the regulation of the duties of its members, and the matters hereinbefore recited, which said rules and bye-laws have been duly submitted to me for sanction under the provisions of the Ordinance aforesaid:—

Now Therefore, I do hereby proclaim my sanction to the said Rules and bye-laws, and hereby direct their publication for general information.

GOD SAVE THE QUEEN!

Given under my hand at Pietermaritzburg in the District of Natal, this Sixth day of March, One Thousand Eight Hundred and Fifty-five.

(Signed) H. COOPER,
Lt. Coln. Commanding 45th Regiment,
Commandant.

By Command of His Honour the Acting Lieutenant-Governor,

(Signed) WILLIAM C. SARGEAUNT,
Colonial Secretary.

Rules for the formation of a Mounted Volunteer Corps for Pietermaritzburg and its neighbourhood.

1.—The Corps shall consist of two or more Troops, each Troop to consist of not more than fifty men, including Officers:—to be called the "Natal Carbineers."

2.—There shall be one Lieutenant-Colonel to be elected by the Corps; and one Captain, one Subaltern, and non-commissioned Officers to each Troop, to be elected by the Troop.

3.—They shall wear a simple and inexpensive Uniform.

4.—Their arms shall be a single or double barrelled Gun.

5.—They shall be called out for exercise twenty days in the course of the year.

6.—They shall be bound to proceed to the appointed place of meeting without delay (within two hours after receiving notice), and to serve in any part of the county of Pietermaritzburg or in any part of the District not being more than 30 miles from the general place of rendezvous.

7.—Non-commissioned Officers shall call out the Troop.

8.—Any part of the Corps, provided not less than twenty men (with discretionary power in the Commanding Officer to increase the number) may be called out within the limits aforesaid to support the authority of the civil power when it appears likely to be resisted.

9.—It shall be in the power of the Commanding Officer, in cases of great emergency, for the protection of the Town, to call out the Corps, or part of the Corps, without waiting for orders from Government, and also when Governors, or other distinguished persons are arriving at, or leaving the Colony.

10.—Rules shall be framed by the Corps, in accordance with the provisions of Ordinance No. 8, 1854, for enforcing discipline. Offenders shall be tried by Court Martial chosen by the Corps; punishment shall be by fine; the amount of fines to go to the general fund of the Corps.

11.—Sir Theophilus St. George, Bart, to be Lieutenant-Colonel of the Corps.

The hon'ble W. C. Sargeaunt, Esq., to be Captain of the Pietermaritzburg Troop.

Philip Allen, Esq., to be Lieutenant of the Pietermaritzburg Troop.

Mr. A. B. Allison, to be Lieutenant and Adjutant to the Corps.

P. C. Sutherland, Esq., to be Regimental Surgeon to the Corps.

Mr. G. K. Weston, to be Regimental Sergeant-Major to the Corps.

12.—The Uniform of the Corps shall be blue with white facings, consisting of a Shell Jacket, Overalls (strapped), Helmet (of Felt, Pith or Leather), with white cover, and Forage Cap.

13.—A Committee consisting of the Colonel and four members shall frame the bye-laws for the Corps.

BYE-LAWS.

1.—Applications for leave of absence shall be laid before, and decided upon by a Board, consisting of the Colonel and four non-official members.

2.—If any member be desirous of leaving the Corps he

KARKLOOF TROOP, NATAL CARBINEERS 1867.

Back Row—W. Jaffray, J. O. Jackson, J. J. Hodson, F. Buckml, F. E. Shaw, R. Otto, J. King, H. Kirby, W. Wray.
Second Row—Lieut. Parkinson, H. J. Stansfeld, M. Pannin, C. J. H. Turvin, F. Steer, Capt. C. Barter, W. C. Shaw, G. Ford, F. Methley, E. J. Tainton.
Front Row—J. Methley, W. Shaw, T. B. Vardy, Lieut. R. Lawton, P. Otto T. Priest.

may do so, by giving six months' notice thereof, to the Commanding Officer, or at any time by finding a substitute (to be approved of by the Committee named in the 1st Bye Law), or on payment of £5 to the funds of the Corps.

3.—The Commanding Officer shall have power at any time to call for Volunteers in case their services be required without the limits of the County.

4.—It shall be the duty of Officers commanding Troops, at the request in writing of any member thereof, on sufficient cause being shown by the applicant, to call a Court Martial, to investigate any cause complained of either against Officers or men.

5.—The Court Martial shall consist of a President and six members to be drawn by ballot from the whole Corps; the Commanding Officer to be President, and the Regimental Sergeant Major to be Acting Judge Advocate.

6.—Any member of the Corps absenting himself from drill, or service, unless absent on leave (except in cases of sickness or indisposition, when a certificate from the Regimental Surgeon or his Assistant must be produced) shall be fined in a sum not exceeding £10.

7.—Any member guilty of insubordination, disobedience of orders, or drunkenness when on duty, shall be liable to a fine not exceeding £2 for the first offence.

8.—It shall be lawful for the Commanding Officer, on any member appearing at muster in a slovenly state, either in person or accoutrements, to inflict a fine not exceeding 5s. on any offender who has been twice warned, and if the irregularities are further persisted in, after the infliction of such fine, to order a Court Martial on the party so transgressing.

9.—Any member not appearing at muster at the appointed time shall be liable to a fine not exceeding 6s., according to the order of the Commanding Officer.

The trumpet for saddling up shall sound half an hour before the time appointed for muster; and again five minutes before roll call.

10.—The first quarterly muster shall be on Monday, 2nd March next, and four following days.

The second quarterly muster shall be on the first Monday in June and four following days.

The third quarterly muster shall be on the first Monday in September and four following days.

The fourth quarterly muster shall be on the first Monday

in December and four following days:—The Corps to muster on the Market Square at 6 a.m., for three hours, and at 4 p.m., for two hours afternoon drill on each day.

11.—In the event of any officer dying or retiring from the Corps, his successor shall be elected by nomination and ballot.

12.—It shall be competent for the Commanding officer to call a general meeting of the Corps upon receiving a requisition signed by not less than ten members thereof, for the purpose of altering the Rules, or amending bye-laws.

13.—An Orderly Book shall be kept in which the Rules, bye-laws, etc., as sanctioned by Ordinance shall be entered, such Orderly Book to be open at all times for inspection by any member of the Corps; the expenses of printing, advertising, etc., to be paid out of the general fund of the Corps.

FOUNDATION MEMBERS.

Sir Theophilus St. George, Bart.
W. C. Sargeaunt.
A. C. Hawkins.
Philip Allen.
J. D. Nicholson.
O. Wirsing.
W. Wood.
P. C. Sutherland, M.D.
A. B. Allison.
S. Williams.
H. Pepworth.
J. Player.
G. Corlett.
E. B. Clough.
H. Coakes.
A. Mesham.
J. Jardine.
W. Griffiths.
M. Stuart.
G. Watson.
T. S. Colborne.
M. W. Goodwin.
T. Botterill.
J. McLachlan.
J. Radford.

T. W. Burchmore.
H. Fearne.
G. Macleroy.
J. Anderson.
L. F. McGill.
W. Hutchinson.
R. Spears.
T. Griffiths.
E. Pitcher.
G. R. Weston.
W. Hall.
Jno. Solomon.
W. G. Baker.
T. Fannin.
J. Wiggett.
Donald Moodie.
Dunbar Moodie.
W. Nicholson.
W. Pigg.
(?) Pigg.
J. T. Allison.
J. Millan.
Isaiah Solomon.
S. Grant.

CHAPTER II.

BUSHMAN RAIDS.

Among the many plagues that harassed the life of the stock farmer in South Africa, not the least irritating used to be the Bushmen, until they were mercilessly hunted down as vermin, or driven into the Kalihari Desert, where the remnants of them still find a miserable but free subsistence. As far as history is able to tell, they were the oldest occupants of Southern Africa, and had been driven South-westward by the Nomadic Hottentots into the Peninsula of the continent, and to some extent had commingled with them there. When the Dutch, in the middle of the seventeenth century, to break the long voyage to and from the East Indies, made Capetown their half-way port of call, they found the adjacent lands occupied by Bushmen and Hottentots. The Bushmen were in the lowest of the three stages of human advancement, that of hunters, and they have never risen above it into the pastoral, much less the agricultural stage. Their only domestic animal was the dog. Their food was game, when they could bring it down with their poisoned arrows; and failing that, roots, berries, wild plants, locusts, white ants, and reptiles. When they came in contact with the pastoral Hottentots, they allowed no chance to slip them of "lifting" their cattle and sheep. In consequence, they and the Hottentots were constantly at feud. The Dutch, as they spread out east and north from Capetown, and took to the business of stock-farming for the provisioning of the ships that touched at the port, became in their turn the prey of these pygmy marauders. At first the Dutch farmers tried hard, by presents and agreements, to induce their Bushmen neighbours to desist from their thievish practices. It was like trying to pull on a rope of sand. There was no chief who might bargain in the name of a tribe, for the Bushmen knew no higher form of government than the parental. In each case of theft, therefore, only the actual thief could be made accountable. They had no property, personal or real; and so, when they had devoured the cattle they had stolen, there was no indemnity to be got from them. But, "if they had no purse to tine, they had flesh to pine"; and it was on this principle that the Boers ultimately and of necessity dealt with and stamped out the Bushman plague.

Driven out of the Old Colony, and pursued far beyond its borders by the frontier farmers, some of the Bushmen who escaped made their home for years in the recesses of the Drakensberg; whence, impelled by hunger, and as opportunity offered, they descended into Natal, and harried the farms of the colonists. In the "Witness" newspaper of 30th July, 1847, there appears a long letter from Mr. Pretorius, who was then living on a farm, now called Edendale, only one hour's ride from Pietermaritzburg. For the most part, it is a complaint and denunciation of the imbecility of the Government; but the loss sustained by the writer might excuse his intemperate language. He says that forty oxen and sixteen horses were stolen from him by Bushmen, with the connivance of his Kafir neighbours. His nephew and four Cape Mounted Riflemen followed the spoor and recovered some of the stock, but all maimed or over-driven. Some had been wantonly killed, and their carcases left. The rest were never seen again. On another occasion of a similar raid, the Bushmen were pursued by a party of Kafir police, under a native sergeant. On being overtaken they expressed surprise at seeing Kafirs in pursuit of cattle stolen from Boers. They gave out that they were considerate and discriminating "caterans," for they were careful, though Kafirs and Englishmen paid them no blackmail, not to molest them, but they always drove their spoil from the pasture lands of the "Figs," as they called the Dutch farmers. From these and other notices of the like kind, that one comes across in the local newspapers of sixty and odd years ago, there can be no doubt that predatory incursions into Natal by Bushmen from the Drakensberg were very common, and too often successful in those days. From a concise and clear account of one of them given in the "Witness" of 10th December, 1847, we may learn the raiders' usual plan of operation and the small chance of ever recovering the booty:—"The four Cape Corps men, who left on the 26th ultimo, accompanied by Mr. G. Rudolph, returned to town after an absence of a week. This party proceeded to Mr. Oosthuise's farm on the Bushman's River, whence sixty-three horses had been stolen. The men arrived at the farm on the day following their departure hence, being six days after the theft had been committed. Mr. Oosthuise pointed out the spoor, and the next morning the party started in pursuit of the marauders. Having followed the track through the open country up to the Drakensberg for about nine hours, they found that the Bushmen, instead of crossing, had wheeled round and taken a course along the valleys on the sides of the mountain. They then passed through the Umkomaas, and on the road between that river and the Umzimkulu, there were found, at different intervals, the remains of six horses that had been killed by the Bushmen. These generally lay at the top of steep ascents, where they had probably dropped from the fatigue of over-driving. The spoor, followed for several days, was at last obliterated by the heavy rains that fell during the pursuit."

The Regiment was little more than a year old when the services of a portion of it were offered and accepted to pursue an audacious gang of thieves and recover their booty if possible. Early in 1856, a report was brought to Maritzburg that Bushmen had driven off four hundred and sixty head of cattle belonging to Mr. G. Naude, a Boer, then farming in the Upper Umgeni district. The news produced an emotion in the City similar to the feelings of affront and injury in the household of the Baron of Bradwardine when Davie Gellatley sang out "Our gear's a' gane," after Donald Bean Lean's "creagh" on the lands of Tully-Veolan. The Carbineers, prompted partly by a sense of duty, and partly by the impulse of curiosity and adventure that urged Edward Waverley to penetrate the Highlands and make himself acquainted with the freebooter and his lair, eagerly volunteered to ride out to the rescue. On the 5th of March a party, consisting of Lieutenants Wirsing and Allison, Sergeant Player, Corporal Wiggett, Troopers Walton, Greaves, Maxwell, Moodie and Parish, under the command of their Colonel, Sir Theophilus St. George, started from Maritzburg for that purpose. The "Natal Guardian" contains the following account of the expedition:—

"The first patrol, consisting of ten of the Carbineers, started about 7 a.m. on Thursday, 5th March. It was a fine morning, and men and horses were in capital spirits. After some trouble with one waggon on the Town Hill, we arrived at Reit Spruit, where we had breakfast, and reached Mr. Prellar's farm before dark. The working party of the 45th, with their waggon, had joined us on the road up the hill. Near the river, where the road crosses Mr. Prellar's farm, we outspanned for the night, and leaving the corporal and two men in charge of the waggon, the Lt.-Colonel with the remainder of the men rode over to pay Mr. Prellar a visit and buy some sheep. We were all highly pleased with the kind way in which that gentleman received us. He did all he could to oblige us After a good night's rest in the tents, which were pitched in the evening and struck again in the morning under the able direction of our corporal, we started early and outspanned at a beautiful spot on Mr. Collison's farm, Maritzdaal, where a very pretty mountain stream, overshadowed by gigantic yellow-wood trees and smaller bushes, supplied us with delicious water for our breakfast, and afforded a most refreshing bath. An orderly, sent by the Lt.-Colonel who had preceded us to Mr. Fannin's farm, brought us the order to march at once to that place, where we met with a hearty welcome from a very amiable family, and after having partaken of some refreshments, we started again on our journey. Mr. G. Fannin, who very kindly accompanied us and remained with us until we returned, gained the good opinion of everyone of us. The waggon road to the old military post being farther round, we left our waggon with a guard, and took a footpath which saved us three or four miles, and here began our troubles. We ought to have reached our camp the same night, but owing to the waggon being upset, and afterwards sticking fast, we had to pass the night in the veld without food or other covering than our blankets. Our active adjutant, Lieutenant A. B. Allison, volunteered, though the night was very dark, to ride over to the waggon, a distance of seven or eight miles, to bring the tent and other necessaries, which he succeeded in doing by two o'clock in the morning. On the Saturday, about 11, we reached the site of the old military post, where we pitched our camp and decided on making the best of the time left to us. Accordingly, on Sunday, we started immediately after service, about a quarter to eight, guided by Mr. Botha, who brought us on the spoor of the marauders, till we reached a prominent hill, close to Spijoen Kop, where he pointed out the line of road we had to take. About 3 p.m. we rounded the first spur of the Drakensberg, and, after an hour's hard riding, reached the summit, and continued for about two hours till within five miles of the main range. Having so far succeeded as to have followed the path of the robbers through a most difficult pass, want of time prevented us from prosecuting our researches farther, as we had to be in Maritzburg by Tuesday evening. Therefore passing a second night—and a very cold one—in this elevated spot, after eight hours in the saddle, we, the next morning, turned our horses' heads homeward, and reached the camp about noon. On the road, we found in different spots, fifty-five head of cattle which had been, in the usual wanton and disgusting manner, butchered by the Bushmen."

A second patrol was despatched on the 13th March, and their doings are thus recounted by one of the party:—

"The second patrol party of the Carbineers, consisting of Quartermaster Wood, Sergeant Anderson, Corporal Williams, Troopers McElroy, Grant, Pepworth, Ablett, Mesham, and Corlett, under the command of Captain Allen, started from the city at 6.30 a.m. on Monday, 13th March, and reached the tents, pitched by the former party, on the site of the old Native Police post, and long since abandoned, that evening. We started from thence in a Scotch mist, and soon got wet through. After climbing the hills at this place we, in a few miles, fell in with the spoor, which we followed for ten or twelve miles, till we reached a place we called Tiger Kloof, in consequence of having surprised a splendid tiger there, and the adjutant, who was left behind by the first party, to be our guide, being under some misapprehension that we would not fall in again with bush for some miles, the order was given to off-saddle and pitch the tents, which we were not sorry to hear, for we were all thoroughly wet, and the wood was wetter still, which very nearly resisted the united attempts of all present to be of any use to us; but at last patience and perseverance conquered the difficulty, and all got a pannikin of coffee and a biscuit, after which we turned in in wet blankets and on wetter grass. The following morning we started again, the weather still being very bad, and after a march of some miles, we first saw towering above us to all appearance an inaccessible precipice, but which, we were soon shown, was not so bad, for the Bushmen had succeeded in driving the cattle up the steep side of it. By the time we reached the top we were all tolerably well blown. This ridge and the flat table land had been explored by the first party, so we pushed forward on the spoor, passing a great number of dead cattle which the Bushmen, according to custom, stab as they get tired, being driven very fast, and leave slowly to die. In this place we found it no easy matter to keep the spoor, the mist being so exceedingly thick, so after roaming about for some time, we pitched our tent again for another night on the edge of a steep precipice, where we had ten times the trouble of kindling a fire that we had before, but after two hours' patient blowing we were rewarded by seeing a cheerful blaze, and our usual spirits returned with hot coffee.

"On Sunday morning we had church parade, which was one of the most solemn sights a man could see, being very many miles away from any human being. From this point we started in quest of the spoor, which we soon found and followed on towards the Drakensberg, which at this point appears to be close at hand, but it took us some hours' hard riding before we could aver that we were under the point known as Giant's Castle. We rounded this point of the range on a mere apology for a path with, we may safely say, a fearful decline on our left of 1,000 or 2,000 feet below. If any man had been unfortunate enough to miss his footing or make a false step, down to the bottom he must inevitably have gone. Most of us were obliged to hold on to the grass to prevent ourselves from falling, but after two or three narrow scrapes with the horses we got down all right. The Captain's horse fell from a height of fifteen or twenty feet into a spruit, and the Quartermaster's horses were both slightly injured. We reached the bush where the last lot of cattle were recaptured (which is situated over the middle source of the Umkomanzi), or rather what remained of them, for we had passed sixty-six dead ones on the road. We off-saddled here, and took our Sunday dinner of coffee and biscuit with a piece of bacon cooked on a ramrod; but here we found to our sorrow that the horses would not eat the grass, which is of a very rank and wiry nature. Our party were soon engaged in cooking, bathing, exploring, etc., and many geological specimens were brought away. We were all agreed that this locality is, without exception, the most inhospitable we had ever been in.

"After resting here for about two hours, we started on our return, and after climbing the almost inaccessible sides of the mountain for about two hours, we once more beheld the source of the Impafane on our left, and the other source of the Umkomanzi on our right, but only for a short time, as the mist soon came down. After wandering about for a long time, we again got on the spoor, and trekked away until we were within a mile or two of Corlett's Kloof, where we off-saddled for the night and got a good fire, for the Captain had taken the precaution of ordering every man to carry a small quantity of dry firewood. Many of us had travelled all over the Colony and neighbouring countries, but we had never seen anything so miserably dreary and desolate as the country is in this part of the Berg. But all parties will profit by the trip, from the Government downwards, so far as experience is concerned, which will, if we should again be visited by Bushmen, prove of infinite value to the country. We know the directions they take, and can easily intercept them by

Mr. E. B. Clough.
One of the only two surviving Foundation Members.

Trooper E. B. Clough.
Foundation Member of the Regiment, 1855.

Mr. W. G. Baker.
One of the only two surviving Foundation Members.

sending one party, a strong one, by the Illovo, and a party of fifteen or so to follow up the spoor, who will be required to watch every movement in their rear, and the larger party will get round by the Umzimkulu, when, hemmed in on both sides, they must inevitably fall; at least this seems to be the prevailing opinion of all connected with the two parties which have just returned, and we could now in two hours, night or day, be in readiness to start, which we could not have done with any degree of success before we were acquainted with the road and direction. We breakfasted after some hard riding at Grobbes' Drift, and reached the tents just before sundown, where we had a magnificent bed of dry grass, which was the only dry bed we had while we were away. The weather was still wet, and continued so until we reached the Dargle, the residence of Mr. T. Fannin, one of the most generous and open-hearted gentlemen we ever met with. He treated us as friends; in fact, we were unanimous in believing him to be, with his family, a thorough specimen of the true old English gentleman. We gave him three cheers—and they were real cheers. From here we took our homeward road, and reached Reit Spruit before sundown from where, after a short stay, we reached the top of the Town Hill just in time to catch the rain, which gave us a good drenching for the last time, while we groped our way on foot and led our horses from the top of the hill to the bridge. When we were dismissed, we had a much higher opinion of one another, and we one and all hold the highest praise of Captain Allen as a leader, and there is not one man but would volunteer to go with him again to-morrow."

CHAPTER III.

ISIDOI AND MATYANA.

In April, 1857, the Carbineers eagerly expected, and indeed were under orders, to take part in punishing a rebellious tribe under the chief Isidoi, on the southern border of the Colony. To their great disappointment, however, the Governor, on further information and advice, deemed it unnecessary to employ their services.

Isidoi was a young and hot-headed Kafir who, on his coming of age in 1850, had been deputed by Government to rule his deceased father's tribe, located in the basin of the Umkomanzi River. He was warned that neither the tribe nor the land was his, and that his tenure of the chieftainship was conditional on his obedience and good service to the Government. This warning had to be repeated on his afterwards showing signs of insubordination, and a magistrate, Mr. Hawkins, was placed over him. At the marriage of one of Isidoi's Kafirs and a girl of a neighbouring tribe under Umshukangubo, a quarrel arose, assegais were used, and one man was killed and two wounded. On hearing of this, Isidoi led five hundred of his men against the other tribe, killed their chief and twenty of his followers, plundered their huts, and brought his temerity to a climax by mutilating the body of Umshukangubo. When summoned twice, first by the magistrate and then by the Governor, to appear and account for his deeds, he each time defiantly disobeyed. To the natives in Natal, Isidoi's case was of far greater interest than an ordinary faction fight. They estimated its importance, not by the loss of life, but by the claim to independence which Isidoi practically asserted, not only by levying war in his own name, but more emphatically by mutilating the dead body of his enemy. If the Governor took a lenient view of his conduct, and did not at once and adequately punish him, it would mean, as they would interpret it, that the smaller tribes in the Colony might be absorbed or exterminated by the fiat of the larger. It was well for Natal that it had in Mr. Theophilus Shepstone one who, from his intimate knowledge of Kafir customs and feelings, could appraise this business at its proper value, and had the courage and tact to deal with it promptly and effectively. He organised and commanded an expedition against Isidoi, consisting of two native levies of four hundred each, one under his brother, Mr. John Shepstone, the other under Mr. Moodie, and supported by detachments of the 45th regiment and the Cape Mounted Rifles. The orders he gave were that Isidoi was to be seized, and the cattle, horses, and guns belonging to his tribe; that no huts were to be burnt, nor women and children harmed; and that no assegai was to be used except to overcome offered resistance, as the Government's object was to punish one of its own subjects and not to shed blood. These firm and humane instructions were carried out precisely, for the rebel tribe, confronted by an overwhelming force, wisely surrendered and submitted to a fine, part of which was in charity remitted afterwards, of ninety per cent. of their cattle. Isidoi, who had fled across the Drakensberg, was deposed, and none of his family were to be allowed to succeed him. Zatshuke, a Government induna, was appointed and submissively accepted in his place. The conduct of this expedition against Isidoi is a pleasing contrast to that of the one subsequently sent against Langalibalele. The friends of the late Sir Theophilus Shepstone may point to them both and say proudly:—

"Look here, upon this picture, and on this."

Matyana was the chief, not hereditary, but appointed by the Government, of a tribe of between three and four thousand settled in Klip River County, near the Zululand border. One of the men of the tribe being sick, two witch-doctors were called in to "smell out" the person who caused his illness. They charged a certain Sigatiya with being the culprit. Matyana, accepting the charge against him as indisputable proof of his guilt, condemned him without further ado to banishment. Those sent to carry out the sentence seized the unfortunate man, beat him with sticks, bent back his arms till his shoulder-blades were dislocated, and so maltreated him that he died on the road. His widow at once went in to Ladysmith and reported the murder to the magistrate there. A message was sent to Matyana to appear in person about the matter. Instead of going himself he sent three of the men who had caused Sigatiya's death. Summoned again, he sent his indunas to explain the facts of the case to the magistrate. Ordered a third time to come himself to Ladysmith, he still refused. When a report was made to Government of his repeated evasion, and at length defiance, of the magistrate's orders, it was resolved to send a force of volunteers, burghers, and natives sufficient to arrest him. The Governor, in his order calling out the Carbineers, indicates that he expected the success of the expedition to depend on its celerity.

"Colonial Office, Natal, January 9th, 1858.

"Sir,—I am directed by the Lieutenant-Governor to instruct you to collect, without delay, a force of about fifty men, to proceed on active service to the County of Klip River, to join the force to be assembled there, and to proceed against the native chief Matyana, the force, when complete, to be under your command. His Excellency, having taken into consideration the delay that would ensue if commissariat was to be provided for said force, has been pleased to authorize you to offer each man, proceeding on this expedition, pay at the rate of 12s. per diem without any rations.

"I have the honour to be, Sir, your obedient servant,

"ACTING COLONIAL SECRETARY.

"To Major Philip Allen, Natal Carbineers."

In compliance with this order, the regiment assembled on the 11th January, and the following members turned out:—

MARITZBURG TROOP.

Major Allen.
Captain Allison.
Lieut. and Adjutant Wirsing
Lieutenant Wood.
Surgeon Sutherland.
Quartermaster Player.
Sergeant Wiggett.
Corporal Pitcher.
Trumpeter Hall.
Trooper Coakes.
Trooper Dobson.
Trooper Greaves.
Trooper Griffiths.
Trooper Grant.
Trooper Hall.
Trooper Hutchinson.
Trooper Jardine.

Trooper Lloyd.
Trooper Maxwell, J.
Trooper Maxwell, W.
Trooper Mesham.
Trooper Millan.
Trooper McCabe, Senr.
Trooper McCabe, Junr.
Trooper Moodie, Dunbar.
Trooper Moodie, Donald.
Trooper Moreland, J. H. B.
Trooper McGill.
Trooper Parish.
Trooper Pittam.
Trooper Regan.
Trooper Richards.
Trooper Wilson.

RICHMOND TROOP.

Captain Hawkins.	Trooper Hambridge.
Sergeant Dacomb.	Trooper Leadley.
Trooper Arbuthnot.	Trooper McLeod.
Trooper Baseley.	Trooper Mills.
Trooper Cook.	Trooper Nicholson.
Trooper Crouch.	Trooper Schmidt.
Trooper Godden, J.	Trooper Shires.
Trooper Godden, W.	Trooper Strapp.

It may here be mentioned that the Natal Rifles, another volunteer corps which had been formed in Maritzburg, had also been called upon to turn out; but, at a meeting held by them to consider the call, it was resolved respectfully to decline it, unless reasonable commissariat accompanied the expedition and an assurance was given that their services would be actually required. The Government replied that circumstances did not permit of compliance with the conditions under which they were inclined to volunteer for the service proposed to them in conjunction with the Natal Carbineers.

One who went on the expedition gives this interesting account of it:—

"On the morning of the 11th January, the city was in a great bustle. Those who were staying, and those who were going, were all on the qui vive, as if it had been fair-day instead of one of a military nature. The day was intensely hot, and the horses of those who had come in from the country had already done some duty. About 11 o'clock the regiment, mounted and armed, fell in and marched down Commercial Road. When a couple of miles out of town, His Excellency overtook the troop, and after a hearty cheer, pushed on to the scene of dispute. At Britton's, there was an off-saddle for an hour; the troop then rode on to Pole's, at Lidgetton, about twenty miles, where, after the fatigues of a scorching day, they looked for slumber within the house, in empty waggons, or under the cool canopy of the heavens. Lieutenant Wood, having the day before taken the route the regiment was to follow, had advised Mr. Pole to anticipate no small demand on his larder, for which ample provision had been made. On Tuesday, the 12th, daybreak found them in the saddle. The weather continued intensely hot. After an off-saddle, the next stage, Mooi River, was reached at noon. Here Mr. D. Gray, who had been put on his guard by Lieutenant Wood, provided a breakfast of abundant and good fare, and it is said to be an undisputed fact that the warriors' attack on very large loaves had the effect of making them look "small by degrees, and beautifully less." For the sake of man and beast, a rest of two hours was allowed, after which they pressed on to Nickson's, at Bushman's River. Here, as at other stages, the exhausted energies of the cavalcade were replenished as thoroughly as if Mr. Nickson had had a month to prepare. Wednesday's sunrise saluted the troop marching for Blaauw Krantz, where the horses had a run for a while, and the men rested. Refreshed with a few minutes' lounge, they pressed on and made for Mr. Schultz's at Colenso. Hence the party proceeded to Ladysmith, which was reached, after an off-saddle, about sunset, all the inhabitants turning out to receive them.

"The heavy fall of rain on Tuesday, Friday, and Saturday, favoured the horses by cooling the ardour of the men and staying the orders of the officers for the onward march. The public offices were converted into barracks. On Saturday the Carbineers were joined by the Natal Frontier Guard, and were reviewed by His Excellency the Governor. At daybreak on Sunday the march re-commenced. As half-way houses were now not to be met with, three waggons with provisions were added to the cavalcade. After a trek of about fifteen miles, a halt was made for breakfast. A few kraals were seen here and there, but no signs of alarm, fear, or resistance were discovered. Another off-saddle took place at Sunday's River, and thence, after a long and tedious ride, the natives of the kraal appointed for the halt gave up some of their huts for the accommodation of the wearied horsemen for the night, a proper guard being mounted. Here the force was joined by a party of Boers, who mustered thirty strong, under Commandant Maritz. At this kraal a small troop of thirty head of cattle arrived as a peace-offering from Matyana. with a further offer to pay any fine that might be demanded as an atonement for his offence. On the Monday morning the route lay through a pleasant country, studded with trees in park-like beauty. About midday the first of Matyana's kraals was reached, which was entirely deserted. In all the listlessness produced by midday heat, a moving mass was seen on the top of the hill on the other side of the valley, where the horses were grazing. In a few minutes the horses were caught, saddled, and mounted. The approach of the natives, who had preceded the main body on horseback, and had been taken for spies, dissipated the alarm, and brought the explanation that the party consisted of friendly natives. From this spot, not hitherto marked on the map, the roadless track to Matyana's chief kraal lay through a broken, stony country, and after travelling for about forty miles the kraal in question was reached. These headquarters were deserted, and herds of cattle in the valleys abandoned to their fate were collected and given in charge of native attendants. Here Langalibalele's warriors, consisting of five regiments of one hundred men each, were assembled, and appeared to have attended to co-operate against Matyana in case of resistance. For two days and nights the encampment remained at this place, without any signs of the enemy.

"On the Friday, half a day's march brought them to a stony country, beyond which it was impossible to proceed except by scrambling through ravines. A guard was told off, of those whose horses were least able to travel, to remain with the waggons, whilst the main body proceeded in quest of Matyana. As they were not able to return to the waggons for the night, half-a-dozen natives were sent to them with three days' provisions. On Saturday evening the whole troop assembled at the waggons, and a start was made to return to the open country. On Sunday morning church parade was held, the service being read by Captain Hawkins, and the remainder of the day was a halt. On Monday, at daybreak, the cavalcade turned their faces homewards. They had not proceeded far when a native presented himself, showing a wound in his head, which he stated had been inflicted by Matyana's people; he also said that the waggons, which were about ten miles in rear, had been attacked. This led to a right-about march, which ended in the discovery of the waggons in a state of safety, the alarm given by the native not being correct. The troops then returned to Ladysmith, from whence they proceeded to Pietermaritzburg, which was reached on Saturday, after a long journey and an absence of twenty days. Before leaving Ladysmith, the following order by the Lieutenant-Governor was published:—'Ladysmith, 27th January, 1858. The volunteer force being about to return to their homes, the Lieutenant-Governor desires to congratulate them on the satisfactory manner in which they have carried out the recent operations against the insubordinate Chief Matyana, and which have achieved a success which has reached His Excellency's just expectations. The Lieutenant-Governor offers his sincerest thanks to these corps for the loyalty manifested by them, in so readily coming forward to aid him in the due administration of the law, although such service necessarily involved on their part a loss of valuable time and no slight personal hardships. His Excellency has learned with much satisfaction from the officer in command, that the corps have performed their duties with alacrity and in an orderly manner. By His Excellency's command,

          P. ALLEN, Acting Colonial Secretary.'"

Though the force sent out neither captured, nor came into conflict with, Matyana, for the chief escaped to Zululand and his tribe offered no resistance, nevertheless the results of the expedition were most salutary. Matyana was outlawed, and his tribe fined seven thousand head of cattle, for serious offences which he and they insolently thought they might make light of. The other chiefs and tribes in the Colony learned that, feeble as the magistracies scattered all over the land seemed to be, there was behind them an irresistible power that would promptly and with severity vindicate their lawful authority whenever anyone dared to set it at naught. And the Boers, who went out against the rebellious chief, returned with a new feeling of respect for the firmness and fairness of the Government.

Captain "Offy" Shepstone, C.M.G.,
Commanded Regiment 1872 to 1880.

CHAPTER IV.

A ZULU WAR-CLOUD.

In 1856, Cetywayo's jealousy of his brother Umbulazi, whose pretensions to the Zulu throne were, as he feared, favoured by their father Panda, led to a civil war, which began and ended with a sanguinary battle, or rather a massacre, on the Zululand bank of the river Tugela. Umbulazi's forces, far outnumbered by the other side, were hopelessly defeated. Of his party, himself, five of his brothers, and three thousand men were slain; the rest narrowly escaped into Natal. It was said then:—"All parties acquainted with the Zulu country represent Cetywayo, the victorious son of Panda, and now probably actual sovereign, as a second Chaka in character; restless, reckless, and bloodthirsty, and cherishing withal no friendly feeling toward the white man. He now commands all the hot young blood of the country, who have been kept from troubling their neighbours only by the order and more prudent counsellors of Panda, whose experience extends back to the horrors of a former period, but who now are hors-de-combat before the rampant spirit of young Zululand." One of Panda's wives, fearing Cetywayo for her two young sons, fled with them into Natal for the protection which she knew the Colonial Government would not deny her, and settled with them at Bishopstowe.

Early in 1861, Mr. Theophilus Shepstone, ever ready to act the part of pacificator regardless of the trouble and risk to himself, made a journey into Zululand with the design of trying to obviate the intrigues and bloodshed which, as his knowledge of the unsettled mind of the Zulus regarding the succession warned him, would take place on the death of Panda. He succeeded in persuading the King and his indunas to come to a decision on the question. They named Cetywayo as successor to his father.

In the middle of the same year, Cetywayo gathered a large armed force on the bank of the Tugela. He would have it believed afterwards that he had only assembled a hunting party; but the Natal Government and colonists suspected that the game was on their side of the river, and was nothing else than the two refugee sons of Panda. This suspicion was confirmed to almost a certainty when messengers came to the Natal Government from Panda and Cetywayo, after the storm had blown over, with a request, which was refused, for the surrender of the refugees. If the suspicion was well founded, the danger of the purposed raid was averted by the prompt action of the Natal Government. The force sent to the border showed Natal's determination to resist the threatened inroad, and Cetywayo, "letting 'I dare not' wait upon 'I would,'" withdrew his warriors.

It was felt, however, that for the security of the Colony more was required than a call to arms whenever its safety was endangered, and that the Zulus should be taught that to mass armed men on the border, though it might be a pastime to them, was the cause to their neighbours of serious and intolerable damage. And this feeling was clearly expressed at the time. "The first thing apparently necessary is the adjusting of a proper understanding with the ruling powers in Panda's country. If Cetywayo already represents the government, then he should be taught to know that pranks such as he has been playing are not to be repeated, and that some arrangement must be made to guarantee the non-recurrence of acts, which it is perhaps difficult to construe into a casus belli, but the repetition of which is particularly undesirable." But though the Government were justified in calling out all their forces to defend the Colony from invasion, and were confident that the call would be readily obeyed, they could not take the responsibility for the blood that would inevitably be spilt, on the one side as well as on the other, before the Zulus could be taught the lesson they much needed of respect for their neighbours' rights. That was a work which had to be done some day, but it was too formidable to be ventured on by Natal alone and so early in her lifetime.

The troops, both regulars and volunteers, were called out by a proclamation, published by the Governor in the Gazette of the 17th July:—"Whereas information has reached me showing the disturbed state of the Zulu people, and deeming it necessary that measures should be taken to watch the frontier of the Colony, I therefore proclaim and make known that I have directed an advance of Her Majesty's troops and the volunteers to be made towards that border. Should events threaten any danger, early notice will be given thereof. The present movement is simply precautionary, and intended to prevent any undue alarm on the part of the inhabitants."

On the 16th July, the Carbineers assembled on the Maritzburg Market Square, which has always been their rendezvous, and marched for their destination on the border. The following members turned out for this expedition:—

MARITZBURG TROOP.

Lt.-Colonel Allen.
Captain Allison.
Lt. and Adjutant Wirsing
Lieutenant Wood.
Quartermaster Player.
Sergeant Williams.
Sergeant Pepworth.
Corporal Corlett.
Corporal Maxwell, J.
Trooper Ashton.
Trooper Adendorff.
Trooper Allison.
Trooper Button, E.
Trooper Button, E. T.
Trooper Bressler.
Trooper Crowe.
Trooper Colborne.
Trooper Greaves.
Trooper Griffiths.
Trooper Holliday.
Trooper Henderson.
Trooper Hurchisson.
Trooper Lamond.
Trooper Lidmonsky.
Trooper Maxwell, T.
Trooper Midgeley.
Trooper Moreland.
Trooper McLeod.
Trooper Perl.
Trooper Shires, J.
Trooper Shires, T.
Trooper Stuart.
Trooper Smith.
Trooper Shaw.
Trooper Solomon, Isaiah.
Trooper Taylor.
Trooper Walker.

KARKLOOF TROOP.

Captain Proudfoot.
Lieutenant Parkinson.
Surgeon Armstrong.
Sergeant Varty.
Trooper Archbell, F.
Trooper Archbell, W.
Trooper Archbell, J.
Trooper Barter.
Trooper Buchanan.
Trooper Dicks, H.
Trooper Dicks, G.
Trooper Fannin.
Trooper Hare.
Trooper Hall.
Trooper Jackson, E.
Trooper Jackson, J.
Trooper Kirby.
Trooper Methley.
Trooper Moorby.
Trooper Norton.
Trooper Prirsh.
Trooper Pratt.
Trooper Spiers, W.
Trooper Spiers, C.
Trooper Shaw, S. W.
Trooper Shaw, W.
Trooper Shaw, F.
Trooper Stevenson.
Trooper Trotter.
Trooper Varty, G.
Trooper Westbrook.
Trooper Wray, J.
Trooper Wray, Jos.

The following account of the expedition was given by a correspondent to the "Natal Witness":—"The regiment left Pietermaritzburg on Thursday, 16th July. After stopping for a few minutes at Brewer's for refreshments, an off-saddle was made at Liversage's, where a good supply of oranges was obtained. One man who was thrown lost his horse, and that of another man was missing until late, when it was eventually found. The march was continued, it being expected that the waggons, which were ahead, would outspan at York, but we found that they had moved on to Rooi Spruit, which was reached at dark. The military had just arrived. On the way, we tried first one place then another, but the inhabitants had flown; a few fowls and a solitary pig being all that was left. Pursuing the march, the baggage waggons were overtaken, one of which would evidently be compelled to get additional motive power before it could proceed. On arrival in camp, the horses were off-saddled and tents pitched, and a ration of oats was issued. The next day, 17th July, after a hurried breakfast, tents were struck and loaded on the waggons with all the heavy equipment, and the march was resumed, the military having preceded the regiment by an hour. Lt.-Colonel Allen had arrived the preceding evening. His horse must have been a capital walker, or easy jog-trotter, for the regiment was kept on the jog till Greytown was reached without further adventure. Here it was found that several waggons, containing the families of adjacent farmers who had deserted their homes, were coming in for the protection of the laager. The Karkloof Troop here joined the column. Orders were received that evening to march at 8 the next morning. Consequently a sharp look-out was kept for forage, the three or four pannikins of oats which were issued being quite insufficient. Eventually supplies of capital oat hay were obtained. No one knew where it came from, but the horses had a good feed.

"On Thursday, 18th July, punctually to the time ordered, Greytown was left. As the column wended its way coastwards, spirits were enlivened by the voices of the songsters of the troop assisted by a flute. Thus the day was passed until the house of the guide was arrived at, a plentiful supply of forage doing the needful for the horses. Here the regiment was joined by the Cape Corps. The march was then resumed, a halt being made for a short time at the top of rather a steep hill for the purpose of assisting the waggons, if necessary; however, they got up without assistance. The march was then resumed until the stream which waters the Hermansberg district was reached, and a halt was made for the night. By this time the men had settled down into working order; the occupants of each tent formed gangs and worked accordingly. Thus whilst a portion belonging to each tent was pitching the tents, others obtained supplies from the commissariat. The guard was mounted after supper, and a quiet night was spent. Friday, 19th July, saw the column, after an early breakfast, resuming the march, several families being met on their way to the Greytown laager. Shortly afterwards a pig was encountered, which soon became a prize pig, and was placed on the waggon. A little way farther on the Cape Corps turned off to their destination, viz., Van Staden's. Continuing on the track, a large force of armed natives was seen. Ten men were immediately told off to pay them a visit and see who they were, and it was found that they were our own people. A rest was now called and the horses off-saddled, and after an hour's graze the march was continued till 4 p.m., when it was decided to outspan for the night in beautiful undulating country. Here the only item of interest was the arrival of two citizens, one of whom had the unusual appendage of a white hat, in consequence of which he was taken for the Lieutenant-Governor and accorded three hearty cheers; when it turned out that the gentleman instead of being His Excellency was merely a surveyor! Attention was, however, soon drawn to another object of interest. Far away on the hills of the Zulu country, stretching away for miles, were to be seen fires, and it was thought that they might be the watch-fires of the Zulu army. In consequence, the guard was increased, and most judiciously posted. Saturday, 20th July, the men were aroused early, and the tents having been struck, sunrise saw them on the march, the country now becoming more hilly and, in consequence, difficult for waggons. A halt was made about 1 o'clock in a very agreeable place, with good water and grazing. After a stay of about two hours, which were well utilized in bathing and washing, the march was resumed, but progress was slightly delayed by a rather comical looking piece of ground. However, as the road lay that way, down that track must they go; so a portion of the troop, giving their horses to the others to hold, at it they went, and by dint of reims, etc., some pulling their hardest to keep the waggon from going head foremost on to the oxen, whilst others doing their utmost on one side to keep it out of a deep valley, all got safely to the bottom, and were rewarded with a sack of lemons from a neighbouring missionary. Ascending to the opposite side, a halt was called for the night, and tents were pitched as before, there being plenty of firewood at hand. Here it was found on enquiry that the Zulus had not crossed the border. An order was now issued for a patrol, to open communication with the coast column, to start early the next morning, the men comprising it getting extra rations for themselves and horses.

"The doings of the main body must now be left, to narrate the proceedings of the patrol. After an early breakfast, and having obtained extra ammunition, a start was made by 7.30, and proceeded in the direction of the Mapumulo Mission Station. Here the party reined up, and having dismounted with military precision, a welcome present was made in the shape of a well-laden basket of oranges and naartjes. Getting directions for the road, the party proceeded, and a most disagreeable hilly country was encountered, until the neighbourhood of Piet Hogg's was reached, when the country became most delightful. After going a short distance out of the way, this gentleman's house was reached by about 12.30. It was found that the rumours of war had made no impression on him or his family; but seeing our party, he really thought that something must be up, so thought he would remove his family to a more secure position. The party were glad to find that he did not carry out his idea until he had given them some dinner—and a first-rate dinner it was—also a good feed of mealies was provided for the horses by generous Mr. Hogg. Remounting, under the guidance of a native tracks were made for the lower drift of the Tugela. After taking an occasional shoot into a wrong track, it was ascertained that the troops under Major Williamson, instead of being at the Tugela, were at the Nonoti; so, getting another guide, we arrived there about 9 p.m., the camp consisting of about fifty of the Durban Rangers, forty of the 85th, and ten of the Cape Mounted Rifles. Having off-saddled and fed the horses, the party was heartily welcomed by those with whom they were already acquainted. On Monday, 22nd, orders were received to return, and having had breakfast, a start was made. Mr. Bennett, who resided on the spot, treated the party with great hospitality, and kindly sent his son to guide them on their way. Travelling by a different route to that on which they had come, Mr. Colenbrander's station was passed, he kindly supplying coffee and cigars. Piet Hogg's was arrived at by sunset, and the party were again treated in first-class style, he not only supplying them with what was good to eat and drink, and plenty of it, but also providing a good night's rest. After an excellent night's rest and another substantial meal, the party mounted, and at 9 o'clock proceeded on their way. To commemorate the great kindness of their host, a rhyme was composed in his honour, which runs as follows:—

1. ' 'Twas Saturday night, when we camped in sight
　　Of the Mapumulo missionary post,
　That an order came out that a patrol was to scout
　　Next morning on the road to the coast.

　Chorus—Come, Carbineers, around without delay,
　　　　　We'll travel o'er hillocks high and low.
　　　Come, saddle up, saddle up, come boys haste-
　　　　away,
　　　And to jolly Piet Hogg's we'll go.

2. Now Piet has a wife, children, pigs, and cattle too
　　And a house in a very pleasant spot,
　So to Piet's we shaped a course, to get a feed for man and
　　　horse,
　　For the weather was tarnation hot.

3. Off-saddled at his place, Piet showed a smiling face,
　　Bade us welcome, and invited us to dinner;
　So with fowls and ham, and with potatoes, bread and rice,
　　By jingo! our stomachs got no thinner.

4. Then success to Mr. Hogg, may they never stop his grog,
　　Nor his family hard-up be,
　But enjoy good health and abundance of wealth,
　　For a stirring good fellow is he.'

"Just as they were starting, Major Williamson and a party of horse hove in sight. His arrival was awaited and despatches were conveyed from him. Being now better acquainted with the road, the journey became considerably shortened, and the mission house was reached without adventure, the missionary in charge again supplying an abundance of fruit. In the meantime the main body had moved to Monkey Hill, about three miles from where the patrol had left it, and on reaching the camp the party was received with hearty cheers from their comrades. The main body, after taking up this position, had had to strengthen it by the erection of a stone wall in one part, and a wattle fence on the other, so that, in conjunction with the natural defensive properties of the site, it was almost impregnable. The Lt.-Governor had visited the camp and, after expressing himself as highly pleased with what had been done, had returned to the city. On one night great inconvenience was sustained by a very heavy windstorm, which blew down two of the tents; but as the shelter of the fluttering canvas was better than total exposure, the occupants remained underneath. On Wednesday, 24th July, a letter from Cetywayo, of a very amicable nature, was received, and in consequence a few of the men who had special business to attend to were allowed to return to their homes. The few of the Durban Rangers who were with the regiment marched to join their troop on the coast, and the Colonel, accompanied by an escort of three men, paid a visit to headquarters about twenty miles distant. The men, especially the Karkloof troop, stuck well to the erection of the defences; the neighbouring natives supplied the men with tywala, maas, fowls, etc. An amusing incident is reported as having happened here. It would appear that one man was very keen that his charger should receive his full share of oats, and for fear that any animal, either two or four legged, should be inclined to share them, he comfortably took his seat near his horse until it had finished the feed, when he found to his disgust that he had been feeding some one else's horse all the time. When this became known, the unfortunate individual had to stand the chaff of the whole camp. On Thursday, 25th July, the defensive works were proceeding rapidly when the Lt.-Colonel returned at midday with the intelligence that, so far as the volunteers were concerned, our labours would cease in a few days. On receipt of this intelligence, leave was granted to more men who were anxious to return to their homes, being followed by the main body in the course of a few days, and the city was reached without further adventure. The success of the expedition was conduced to by the quiet unassuming bearing of all the officers towards the men, and, combined with the general unity and good temper of all ranks, rendered the trip one of many pleasant recollections."

At the next sitting of the Legislative Council, in August of this year, a resolution was passed thanking the forces:—

"Legislative Council Chambers,
"Natal, 14th August, 1861.

"Sir,—I am commanded by the Legislative Council of Natal to transmit to you the enclosed resolution expressive of

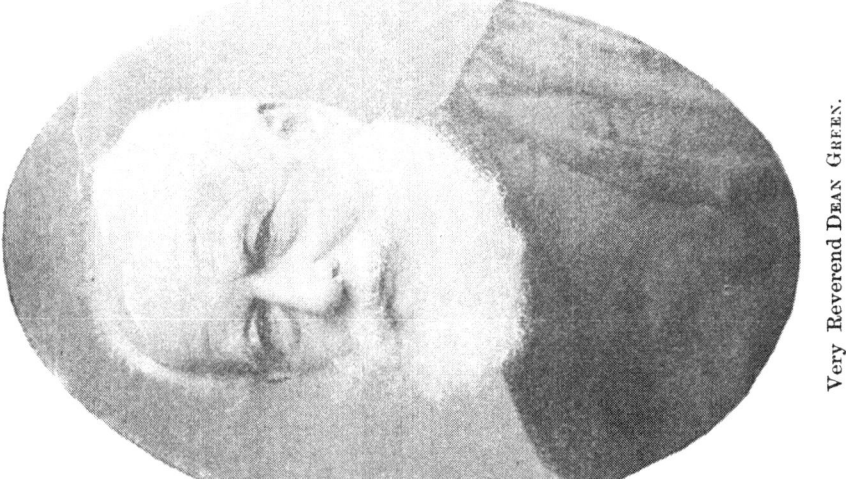

Very Reverend Dean Green.
First Chaplain of the Regiment, 1862.

P. C. Sutherland, M.D.,
First Surgeon of the Regiment, 1855 to 1877.

their appreciation of the services rendered to this Colony on a late occasion by the volunteers under your command, and I am further to request that you will communicate the same to those officers and men whose services were called into requisition.

"I have, etc.,

"W. MACFARLANE, Speaker."

"Resolution passed by Legislative Council, 13th August, 1861:—

"That this House has pleasure in placing on record its high sense of the services rendered by those bodies of Her Majesty's troops and volunteers, under the command of Colonel Grey, who with so much energy and enthusiasm advanced on an important and dangerous duty, to the northern borders of the Colony."

Letter of thanks from His Excellency, the Lieutenant-Governor:—

"Colonial Office, Natal, 7th August, 1861.

"Lt.-Colonel Allen, Natal Carbineers.

"Sir,—I am directed by His Excellency, the Lieutenant-Governor, to convey to yourself and the officers and men of the volunteer force, employed recently under your command in watching the Zulu border of the Colony, His Excellency's thanks for the promptitude and efficiency with which this important service has been performed.

"I have, etc.,

"D. ERSKINE, Colonial Secretary."

Letter from Commandant of Her Majesty's forces:—

"Commandant's Office, Natal, 17th August, 1861.

"Sir,—I have it in command to transmit, for your information, a copy of a district order of this date, embodying a resolution of the Legislative Council of Natal, and to request that you will communicate the same to the corps under your command:—

'The Commandant takes this opportunity of signifying his approbation of the mode in which the various and arduous services required of them in the late operations in the field were performed by the officers, non-commissioned officers and men of the Natal Carbineers under your immediate command upon the occasion referred to.'

"I have, etc., W. H. DRAGE,

"Captain, 85th Regiment,

"Acting District Adjutant, Natal.

"Lt.-Colonel Allen, Natal Carbineers."

CHAPTER V.

A BASUTO INCURSION.

In 1865, while war was going on between the Dutch of the Free State and the Basutos, under the chief Moshesh, some of the men of the Boer commandoes, who owned land on both sides of the Drakensberg, sent their cattle down to their Natal farms, partly for winter pasture and partly for safe-keeping. Regardless of its neutrality in the war, a band of Molappo's Basutos invaded Natal and, scrupulously limiting their depredations to the refugee stock, drove off a large number of cattle and sheep. In an unsuccessful attempt to recover the booty on its way to Basutoland, four Dutchmen were killed in Van Reenen's Pass. Sir Percy Douglas, the Commandant and Acting Governor of the Colony at the time, promptly called out a force, consisting of regulars, volunteers, and natives, to proceed to Basutoland and exact redress. The Carbineers, who mustered on the Market Square on the 3rd July and, under a volley of hurrahs from a large crowd of spectators, left Maritzburg on this service, were:—

Lt.-Colonel Erskine.	Trooper Linton.
Captain Williams.	Trooper Maclean, W. A.
Lieutenant Pepworth.	Trooper Maclean, Jno.
Sergeant Corlett.	Trooper Martin.
Corporal Maxwell.	Trooper Stuart.
Corporal Clough.	Trooper Sherrie.
Trumpeter Ford.	Trooper Smith.
Trooper Allison.	Trooper Taylor.
Trooper Buchanan.	Trooper Wallis.
Trooper Burchmore.	Trooper Wood, Thos.
Trooper Dick.	Trooper Wolhuter, F.
Trooper Doig.	Trooper Wolhuter, T. C.
Trooper Ensor.	Trooper Wood, D.
Trooper Erskine.	Trooper Zeederberg, B. J.
Trooper Fannin.	Trooper Zeederberg, J. J.
Trooper Greaves.	Trooper Parry.
Trooper Hansmeyer.	Trooper Moodie.

The march of the punitive force was stopped at the border of the Colony by the order of Sir Philip Wodehouse, Governor of the Cape Colony and Lord High Commissioner. Intent only on preserving British neutrality, and regarding its maintenance as of first importance, he deemed a fine of ten thousand head of cattle on the Basutos a sufficient atonement for their trespass on Natal. The volunteers were at once sent home; the rest of the force was kept for months on the border to receive the fine at Moshesh's convenience, and to guard against another invasion. The High Commissioner's peace with dishonour policy was approved by the Home Government, Mr. Gladstone being at the time Chancellor of the Exchequer and Leader of the House of Commons. Natalians judged quite differently of his conduct in this affair. By a resolution of the Legislative Council a complaint was sent Home of his indifference to the honour and safety of a British Colony; in Durban his effigy was burnt; and the Carbineers sent him a crinoline and other articles of female attire.

CHAPTER VI.

CETYWAYO'S CORONATION.

There were some who, either in the spirit of the busybody that never misses a chance for petty criticism, or from political animus against Mr. Shepstone and inability to judge aright of his character, pronounced his expedition to crown Cetywayo as a tinsel and tawdry effort to exert a presumed but vain influence, which would fail of a good and lasting impression on the King and of benefit to his subjects and Natal. They purposely misrepresented the expedition, or were blind to its real design. It was a humane and patriotic idea, conceived in the mind, and realised by the hopeful and unselfish will, of the Secretary for Native Affairs. In his address to his escort, on dismissing them to their homes when they returned to Natal, he disclosed to them that the sole purpose of his journey to Zululand was to be the means, if possible, of saving human life there and of confirming and augmenting Natal's prestige. If any justification were required of Mr. Shepstone's motives and his plan for giving effect to them, it can be found in the cordial support which he received from two men who have endeared themselves to Natalians for their services and personal worth, Harry Escombe and Charles Barter.

Mr. Shepstone's proposal, though it met with the approval, did not receive the official authorization of the Government. The volunteers, therefore, who composed his escort, were not called out, but offered to serve for the occasion. Those who left Maritzburg on the expedition were:—

Quartermaster Niekerk, Isaac.
Sergeant-Major Taylor, John.
Corpl. Fletcher, Charles Edw.
Corpl. Moodie, **Alfred**.
Corpl. Shepstone, Geo.
Corporal Clough, E. B.
Tpr. Bourke, Geo.
Tpr. Boshoff, S.
Tpr. Chatterton, J.
Tpr. Jones, E. T.
Tpr. London, W.
Tpr. McDonald, John M. G.
Tpr. Potterill, F.
Tpr. Pannewitz, J. A.
Tpr. Raw, Crick.
Tpr. Zeederberg, Louis.

They left at 2 p.m. on the 28th July, meeting the detachment of the Karkloof Carbineers at Baynes's Drift, the whole of the mounted men being then under the command of Captain Barter, of the Karkloof Carbineers. A correspondent of the "Witness" sent to his paper at intervals a lengthy and particular report of the trip to Zululand and back.

"1st August, 1873.

"The different contingents mustered at Baynes's Drift, and were joined the same evening by the Secretary for Native Affairs. The march yesterday was intentionally a short one to guard against any contingency which might arise from the unaccustomed moving of such a large number of men and material. Most perfect good humour and discipline prevail, and the conduct has been all that could be desired. The band of the Maritzburg Rifles performed each night to an appreciative audience. Along the road we have met with great hospitality and civility.

"5th August, 1873. We had hard work to get up the hill near Mr. Hulley's farm, having to double span the waggons. A halt was made on the top of the Noodsberg. Camped near Mr. Dykes' farm. The Umhloti drift was very bad, and Mr. Shepstone's waggon nearly capsized, all the waggons getting stuck. Mr. Mills kindly sent a liberal supply of bananas and pineapples. Sergeant-major Taylor here found it necessary to return on urgent private affairs, he having gained the good-will of all by his strict attention to duty and general conduct. Leaving the Umhloti early, we breakfasted near a coffee plantation, a stream near by being resorted to by every one to remove traces of the dusty ride. Encamped at Rev. Grout's mission station, having so far experienced good weather.

"Tugela, 6th August, 1873. Reached here at 4 p.m., being met by the coast volunteers (Alexandra and Victoria Mounted Rifles and Durban Volunteer Artillery), the volunteers now numbering 123. Great difficulty experienced in crossing the Sinquasi drift. The column leaves here to-morrow and crosses into Zululand.

"Tugela, Zulu side, 8th August, 1873. Crossed the Tugela to-day and encamped a mile from the drift. The men were now informed that they were under the Mutiny Act. Spare time is occupied in cooking, looking after horses, and playing cricket and quoits.

"9th August. On the banks of the Tugela, from which

it will take us eight days to reach the Royal Kraal. Zulus proved very friendly, bringing eggs, etc., to sell. Health of all excellent.

"Amatikulu, 10th August. Reached here yesterday after a long trek of 16½ miles. The principal waggon stuck in the drift till 9 p.m., 36 oxen being inspanned to pull it out. Advantage was taken of the proximity of the river for the purpose of washing clothes. A present of fat oxen was received from Cetywayo. The camp was pitched with military precision.

"Amatikulu, 10th August. Church parade was held this morning, the men being formed into square, and a short service was read by Major Giles (who is in command of the whole of the volunteers). The band played after the service. The kraals are all vacated except by the izisalakazi (old women), men, boys, and girls having preceded us to the Coronation. Horses all well. We turn them out at night, there being splendid grass for them.

"St. Paul's, 12th August. Our start was delayed this morning by horses straying, four or five still being missing. A further instalment of fat oxen in good condition was received from Cetywayo. Natives prove very friendly, women, girls, and children collecting to see the column go past.

"Magwasa. Two men started back to look for the missing horses, catching up the column the next morning with all the runaways. The band played, to the delight of the crowds of our dusky visitors. Four koodoo were seen, also tracks of buffalo.

"White Umfolosi, 17th August. The column encamped here on the edge of the bush country and fifteen miles from Nodwengu, the Royal Kraal. Owing to the death of Masipula, the Zulu Prime Minister, it was necessary to stay here for four days. The country round is very broken and stony. Athletic sports, etc., were held, also a cricket match between the coast and up-country volunteers, which resulted in a win for the latter, the following members of the regiment helping their side to victory, viz., G. Shepstone, A. Moodie, Bourke, Nourse, and Raw.

"25th August. The camp was moved back to-day about 400 yards for sanitary reasons. A party was formed to inspect the scene of the murder of Piet Retief and his followers. Traces of many huts were found, the judgment-seat was seen, beads, etc., being taken as relics. On returning to camp the welcome order was given to push on to Nodwengu to-morrow.

"Umfolosi. The final halting place was reached this morning, and the camp was pitched close to a Norwegian mission station in sight of three of the Royal Kraals. John Dunn here met the column. On the line of march the troops were disposed as follows:—An advance guard of twenty men followed by a troop, then Mr. Shepstone's waggon, followed by another troop, succeeded by the two guns of the Durban Artillery. At the mission station the Norwegian flag was saluted. The camping ground was a bleak open spot,—nothing but stones. The band played in the evening, exciting great curiosity.

"At Umfolosi the expedition was met by Mr. John Dunn with directions as to the spot to be occupied near Cetywayo. But as on enquiry it appeared that all the water had been contaminated by the long encampment of large bodies of men in the neighbourhood, it was resolved not to shift the camp, which had been pitched on the banks of a small stream, from which, it was afterwards ascertained, the water used by Cetywayo was daily carried. After the camp had been formed, several of the leading men of the country came to offer their hearty welcome. The band, which was hidden from view by a small bush, struck up during the interview. They had never heard or seen such a thing before and, until brought nearer at their request, it was amusing to watch the struggle between their dignity and their curiosity, and to note that, what seldom occurs with a Zulu, the latter triumphed.

"On the 28th August, Cetywayo paid his long put-off visit to Mr. Shepstone. He approached the camp at 3 p.m., accompanied by about fifteen hundred followers. Major Giles had prepared the escort to receive him, the mounted volunteers with the artillery being drawn up on the right. The shaking of hands by Mr. Shepstone was the signal for the firing of a salute by the Durban Artillery. Cetywayo expressed his pleasure and thankfulness at the coming of the expedition, walked towards the camp, listened to the band, and watched the movements of the mounted volunteers, which were most creditably performed, considering the nature of the ground.

"On Monday, 1st September, preparations were early commenced to carry out the Coronation. A large marquee, brought for the purpose, was erected in the central space of the military kraal, being decorated inside with shawls, blankets, and other showy articles which had been brought as presents. At noon the whole of the party proceeded to the Umbambongwenga kraal, where the ceremony was to be per-

1879.
Trooper Miller, Trooper B. C. Clarence, Trooper A. Muirhead, Trooper W. W. Barker, Trooper C. Tatham, Corpl. H. Stirton, Trooper W. Grainger.

formed, leaving the camp in sole charge of five or six natives. Major Giles organised the procession, which entered at the lower gate, the band playing. The brilliant uniforms of the officers formed a contrast with the costumes of the clergy and the miscellaneous dresses of the party. The Mounted Volunteers, Artillery, and band of the Maritzburg Rifles formed up on the right of the marquee; Cetywayo and his councillors, with Mr. Shepstone and his party, being on the left. When order had been established, Cetywayo expressed a wish to examine the guns. The peculiarity of the breech loading was explained to him, at which he was much surprised, but seemed disappointed that the guns were not larger.

"After speeches had been made by Mr. Shepstone and the Zulu councillors, Cetywayo was conducted to the marquee by Mr. Shepstone and his own party. When all had entered, the doors were closed, being guarded by two sentries of the Durban Artillery. A scarlet robe and a crown were then placed on Cetywayo's head, and he was then led to his seat outside, and after a few moments Mr. Shepstone rose and proclaimed him to the assembled multitude as their king. The proclamation occupied about a quarter of an hour, after which the Artillery fired, with great regularity and effect, a salute of seventeen guns, the Mounted Volunteers also saluting, and the band playing. Heralds were then sent out to make known the new laws. This operation took fully half an hour.

"The volunteers had dismounted and linked their horses in line in sections of fours, one man to a section. The proclamation being ended, all the thousands of Zulus present lifted their shields, and struck them sharply with sticks, in token of applause. The sound is strange and startling to anyone hearing it for the first time, and it terrified the horses. They wheeled suddenly to the left, and seemed charging down on where the Royal party was sitting. This belonged to a class of accidents that sometimes produce disasters, and for the moment one seemed likely to happen. The horses were, however, soon under control again. Cetywayo at once saw what had taken place, and exclaimed, "They have left their horses, and these are startled at the noise of the shields." The quickness with which the accident was remedied soon changed the aspect of affairs, and turned adverse criticism into admiration at the smartness with which the mischief had been stopped.

"On 3rd September, the camp was broken up, and the homeward journey commenced with a moonlight march, the column bivouacking out that night in the open. Leaving

Hlabatini, Entonjaneni was passed, and the Makwobanene having been crossed, the camping ground, which had been used on the march up, was reached. Here it was notified that those who wished might leave and return direct to their homes. The Karkloof Carbineers branched off and took a more direct route back. Previous to their departure, the following communication was read, on parade, to the volunteers, from Mr. Shepstone:—

'Camp, Entonjaneni, 4th September, 1873.

Sir,—The Karkloof Carbineers are to break off to-day from the main escort, and I cannot allow the occasion to pass without asking you to convey to them, as well as to the whole escort, my sincere thanks for their services, and for the confidence they have shown towards me, in volunteering as they did to follow me on an expedition, the end of which could not always clearly be foreseen. I regret the necessity which compels us to separate so early on our way home, but I feel that it is my duty to release those members of the escort whose personal affairs demand their presence at their homes, and I may add that the conduct of all has been such as to make me feel an earnest desire to meet their private wishes as far as I can. I shall take a later opportunity of saying what I feel on this subject.

I have, etc.,

T. SHEPSTONE,
Secretary for Native Affairs,
Commissioner, Zululand.

Major Giles, Commandant of Volunteers.'

"The main escort reached Verulam on the 15th September, and broke up, the different regiments proceeding to their respective headquarters. Before dispersing, the following address was presented to Major Giles by Mr. Shepstone:—

'I take the opportunity, afforded by the arrival at their homes of our Verulam companions, to say a few parting words to you all, and indeed to all who have at any time formed part of the expedition. We have returned from carrying out most successfully a service of the most novel and interesting character,—one not undertaken for mere fanciful, or indeed sentimental, objects, nor because we wish to interfere in, or busy ourselves about, the installation of a neighbouring ruler. The truth is, we found ourselves, as a Colony, accidentally placed in a position which called upon us to do a signal service to humanity, and at the same time to advance the interests of our Colony, or to abandon that position for ever. You must not, therefore, measure the results of your long march by the gratification or disappointment which the spectacle, you took part in and witnessed, caused to each of you, for after all that could be but a secondary consideration. You are entitled to congratulate yourselves on higher achievements, upon having been the means of saving much human life, besides securing to your adopted country a position which it must be careful never to lose. This is not the time or place for discussing political questions, but I may assert my belief that the results of the expedition will make full amends for all our toil and trouble, and more than justify all the expense the Colony has been put to. We have re-entered Natal wiser, and I am sure, better men than when we left it. Our journey has been marred by no accident, or want of harmony, or sickness, and we have all had much to learn in discharging the different duties that devolved upon us. In so far as the interests of the volunteer principle are concerned, the expedition has undoubtedly been invaluable as a lesson taught by actual experience. You who have served upon it are certainly foremost in practical knowledge of all Natal volunteers, because it has shown you your weak points as well as your strong ones. It is not improbable, from my position, that I may be associated with you upon occasions on which real hard work may be required of you. I naturally, therefore, take a deep interest in your efficiency, and feel entitled to so far act the true friend to you as to remind you that the experience of this expedition has still left you a good deal to learn. I have been much pleased at your conduct towards the natives, a point of extreme importance towards the success of the expedition; at your ready submission to the discipline considered necessary to accomplish that success; and at the cheerfulness with which you have at all times performed the duties required of you. It will be my pleasant duty to make known these sentiments to His Excellency, the Lieutenant-Governor. I tender my thanks to your commandant, Major Giles, for the ready way in which he, on all occasions, met my views, and for the zeal with which he carried out what was necessary to the success of the expedition. I also wish to express my appreciation of the self-sacrificing spirit, and the prompt and zealous manner in which your officers acted under his directions. I sincerely thank you all for your confidence in me, which you showed by volunteering to accompany me on an expedition, the end of which could not always clearly be seen, and the success and safety of which depended so much on its leader. I take this as a great compliment, and value it accordingly, and think we may fairly share with each other the success which we have achieved. This is the first occasion on which the volunteers of Natal have crossed the boundary of Natal in an organised body. The whole has been an experiment of the most searching kind, from which valuable lessons may, and will, I am sure, be gathered. Let us all diligently learn these lessons, and let the remembrance of thus acting together, and of the good-fellowship which has prevailed along the whole of the expedition, always remain to be a bond of brotherhood amongst its members; and may I be allowed to so far identify myself with the expedition and with you, my companions, as to be looked upon by you as the senior member of the brotherhood. I request Major Giles to communicate what I have said to those officers and men of the expedition who may not now be present. In all probability we shall separate in a few days, and as this is the last opportunity I shall have of addressing you, I congratulate you on the happy termination of our expedition, and I bid you farewell with my most sincere thanks and warmest wishes for the prosperity and happiness of every man who has honoured me by escorting me to Zululand.

T. SHEPSTONE.

Verulam, 15th September, 1873.'"

The business which took Mr. Shepstone to Zululand, and if unaccomplished would have made of his journey a useless trouble, and the Coronation itself but a paltry pageant, was to gain the new King's, and through him the nation's assent to a series of laws which would make Zululand a safer abode for its inhabitants and a better neighbour to Natal. These laws, drawn up by Mr. Shepstone, sworn to by Cetywayo, and accepted by the crowd of assembled Zulus, before the Coronation, were:—1st. That every person publicly accused shall have a fair trial and, on condemnation, a right of appeal to the King. 2nd. That the death penalty shall in no case be inflicted without the King's sanction. 3rd. That minor offences shall be punished by fine instead of death. Besides assenting to these laws, that to us are only reasonable but were revolutionary in Zululand, Cetywayo agreed to give Amatonga labourers a safe and assisted passage through his country to Natal, and to protect them on their return journey.

CHAPTER VII.

LANGALIBALELE.

There are two motives powerful enough to overcome the natural indolence of the Kafir and induce him to work steadily for a time,—his desire for cattle and for wives. When the Diamond Fields were discovered, a third motive temporarily prevailed on the Kafir to take his labour there,—his desire to become the possessor of a gun. In Natal no Kafir is allowed to have a gun unless the Magistrate of his district has registered it and given him a licence to own it; and great care is exercised in granting natives permits to keep firearms. In Griqualand West, where the Diamond Fields are, there was no such stringent law, and the facility for getting guns there was as great an attraction of Kafir labour as the high rate of pay. The young men of the Amahlubi tribe, living under their chief Langalibalele, at the foot of the Drakensberg, that part of Natal nearest to the Diamond Fields, were specially tempted to go and work for guns, because it was easy for them to smuggle them into their location without having to submit them for registration, and perhaps confiscation, by their Magistrate. The account which one of these young Kafirs gave of his trip to the Fields, and the way in which he disposed of his earnings, may be taken as a sample of what was done by many others of his tribe. Umlanduli had paid eight head of cattle for a daughter of one of his chief's indunas, and he went to the Diamond Fields to earn, in the first place, the £5 required for a licence under the new marriage regulation. After five months' work, at twenty-five shillings a week, he had earned enough for his immediate wants. He bought one gun for £10, another for £6 10s., and with more than enough in his purse to pay for his marriage licence, he started for home.

Mr. John Macfarlane, Magistrate at Estcourt, got to know that there were unregistered guns in the Amahlubi location, and ordered the chief to send them in to the Magistracy. Langalibalele's reply was, "You must give me the names of the people; I cannot do anything unless you give me the names." The Kafir is a shifty fellow, and Langalibalele was a Kafir of the Kafirs; but in his Magistrate, Mr. Macfarlane, and

Mr. Shepstone, the Secretary for Native Affairs, he had to do with men who knew his character thoroughly, and were as resolute as he was wily. When Langalibalele, driven from his many subterfuges, at last bluntly refused to send in the guns, saying that they had been earned at the Diamond Fields and he should retain them, the Magistrate sent him notice that, "as the vessel in which he kept his offences was full to overflowing," he had reported him to the Secretary for Native Affairs.

With the Secretary for Native Affairs, Langalibalele resorted again to the shifts which his Magistrate had forced him to abandon. In April, when summoned to Maritzburg by Mr. Shepstone, he sent his induna, Mabudhle, "with a lie in his mouth," to say that he had actually set out to obey the Secretary's order, but had been obliged to go back owing to an attack of sciatica. The excuse was at the time admitted, but Mabudhle was directed to inform his chief that he was wanted on urgent business, and must manage, by waggon or some other way, to come down to Maritzburg. After some delay a third message was sent to him, to which he replied that he was too ill to obey the summons, and would not come down to Maritzburg.

In July, from 7th-16th, the Colonial Volunteers assembled at the "Great Northern Camp," near Estcourt, for drill and military manoeuvres. If Estcourt was chosen for the place of meeting in the expectation that Langalibalele and his tribe would be overawed by a display of military force in their neighbourhood, that object was entirely missed. The comment on the doings at the camp, by some of Langalibalele's warriors who had gone to criticise them, was "If that was the way they managed their shooting, and those were the plans upon which they shot, Langalibalele's people could easily manage them."

During the Secretary's six weeks' absence from the Colony for Cetywayo's Coronation, the business concerning Langalibalele lay dormant, at least on the Government's side. The chief, however, was not idle, for a letter, dated 5th August, was sent to Mr. Shepstone from the Secretary for Native Affairs of the Cape Colony, beginning, "I have the honour to transmit herewith copy of a letter from the Governor's Agent at Basutoland, having reference to a rumour current among the Basutos, to the effect that a Zulu chief intended to resist an order from the Natal Government to deliver up a number of guns, and that he had asked two Basuto chiefs to allow him to send his cattle into their country for safety." In another letter, dated 3rd September, he says the name of the Zulu chief is Langalibalele.

On the 4th October, Mr. Shepstone, being by that time back at his post, again sent an order to Langalibalele to come down to him, and for impression's sake, selected as his principal messenger on this occasion, Mahoiza, the induna to the Magistrate in Maritzburg. Not till the 28th of the month was the messenger allowed to see the chief, and only then after having been stripped of his clothes on the suspicion, as it was said, that he was carrying firearms concealed. There is no doubt that Mahoiza, in his report of his reception by the chief and his people, gave an exaggerated account of their incivility; but if the treatment he got from them was not meant as a studied insult to the Government in the person of their messenger, it was at least discourteous and offensive.

It was time to make an end of the Government's controversy with Langalibalele. Eight months had already been spent in the vain endeavour to persuade the chief to come either to Estcourt or Maritzburg to answer for the unregistered guns held by his people. However desirous the Government were that their difficlulty with the Amahlubi tride and its chief should be kept secret, it was impossible that of the many messages, carried by different messengers, that had passed between the parties, some should not leak out, or that a degree of credit should not be given to the vapouring of Langalibalele's Kafirs, especially of those who, having guns of their own, would be sure to indulge in unlimited boasting. The whole Colony, natives and Europeans, was already in a state of excitement. Natal colonists, though they "dwell in the midst of alarms," are very far from being prone to panic fear. But towards the end of the year, so near and serious seemed the crisis of the long-drawn dispute, that the farmers in the neighbourhood of the Amahlubi location sent their families into laager, and made up their minds for a fight. An attempt was afterwards made to turn this fact, which was really the effect of Langalibalele's threatening attitude, into the cause of his flight and all its disastrous consequences. The apologists of the chief tried to prove that he was perfectly innocent of rebellion, and that from the beginning to the end of his trouble with the Government he was only actuated by fear. They would have it believed that both whites and blacks alike, by some mysterious centrifugal force, were repelled against their will from the limits of the Amahlubi location.

The order was issued to raise a force of Europeans and natives to capture the chief, and strong enough to make resistance, if his followers should be so foolish as to offer it, utterly hopeless. But even when the troops had reached Estcourt, so eager were the Government that the difficulty should be got over peacefully, that Mr. Shepstone said, "If he (Langalibalele) would only meet His Excellency and explain his conduct, no harm whatever would happen,"—the last clause evidently being equivalent to an assurance of a safe-conduct. But it was then too late. Langalibalele was already aware that preparations were being made to surround him, and that his neighbour chiefs and their followers, from whom he expected sympathy if not assistance, were on their way to intercept his retreat. His first concern then was for his own safety, next for his cattle and his armed clansmen; the old men, women, and children might shift for themselves. His sciatica, which prevented him from taking a comparatively easy journey to Maritzburg, did not hinder his flight across an almost impassable mountain. And he had a full day's start.

Major Durnford, in command of the Carbineers and mounted Basutos, set out to seize the Bushman's Pass, the Amahlubi tribe's only exit from the Colony. He was foolishly given the order, "not to fire first," by Sir Benjamin Pine, and he foolishly accepted it, and still more foolishly obeyed it to the letter,—an order which Mr. Shepstone disapproved of as soon as he heard of it; too late, however, for his disapproval, if it had been heeded, to prevent mishap.

Hardly had the men, who volunteered to assist in escorting Mr. Shepstone into Zululand for the installation of the King, settled down again in their homes, than they were required to do duty of a totally different character. The chief Langalibalele having set the Government at defiance, it was decided to despatch a force to capture him. For this, the services of the Regiment, in addition to the Karkloof Carbineers and the Weenen Yeomanry Cavalry, were demanded. At the assembly in Maritzburg, on 30th October, 1873, every man answered the roll-call, and as Captain Shepstone was at the time absent from the Colony, the command devolved on Lieutenant Woodroffe. A photograph of the force was taken before they set out. A large number of the citizens witnessed their departure and bade them God speed. The following composed the contingent from Maritzburg:—

Colonel W. Royston
Commanded Regiment 1881 to 1888

Lieutenant Woodroffe.
Quartermaster Niekerk, I.
Sergeant-major Taylor, J.
Sergeant James, G.
Sergeant Button, J. T.
Sergeant Whitelaw, W.
Corporal Moodie, A.
Corporal Shepstone, G.
Corporal Fletcher, C.
Trumpeter Holliday, H.
Trooper Boshoff, J. C.
Trooper Boshoff, D. J.
Trooper Berning, W.
Trooper Bourke, E.
Trooper Bower, T.
Trooper Bond, E. (killed).
Trooper Church, A.
Trooper Chatterton, W.
Trooper Davis, A.
Trooper Doig, D.
Trooper Egner, Jas.
Trooper Erskine, R. H. (killed)
Trooper Ford, T.
Trooper Freeman, J.
Trooper Gilligan.
Trooper Goodburn (substitute for Doig, W.)
Trooper Jones, G.
Trooper Kahts, F.
Trooper Keytel, P.
Trooper London, W.
Trooper Macdonald, A.
Trooper Murphy, P. R.
Trooper Pannewitz, J.
Trooper Pepworth, H.
Trooper Potterill, C. D. (killed)
Trooper Player, J.
Trooper Pistorius, C.
Trooper Royston, W.
Trooper Raw, Crick.
Trooper Shepstone, A. J.
Trooper Spettigue, T.
Trooper Vanderplank.
Trooper Wheelwright, W.
Trooper Zeederberg, L.

The rendezvous at Fort Nottingham was reached on Saturday, 1st November. The next day orders were issued that the Carbineers, Natal and Karkloof, leaving Fort Nottingham that (Sunday) evening, were to proceed to the positions mentioned in the official plan. It will be interesting to compare the official plan for settling off-hand the business of Langalibalele and his tribe, with Captain Barter's description of the attempt to work it out; if only that we may see how the best laid schemes, as they seem to be while as yet they are only on paper, may fall to pieces when the time comes to carry them out,—so wide sometimes is the divergence of practice from theory. The light-hearted confidence in which the orders, signed by the Commandant and the Governor, set the task of guarding and keeping up communications, extending over many miles of some of the most rugged country in the world, shows that difficult and tedious operations were begun without adequate preparation for them, and in profound ignorance, as Captain Barter's story will prove, of the extent and character of the ground over which they had to be conducted.

OFFICIAL PLAN.

On Monday next, 3rd November, the troops and details of armed police and natives, as per margin, will be posted as shown in the accompanying sketch, the troops (regulars and volunteers) being in support of the natives, acting under the orders of the Resident Magistrates.

The whole to be in position by 8 a.m., with the undermentioned exceptions, viz.:—Mr. Allison, with 500 armed natives, to seize the Champagne Castle Pass *before* 5 a.m., and to hold it at the summit, communicating with the detachment at Bushman's Pass on his right, and Captain Lucas's party on the left.

He will watch any possible (and at present unknown) approach up the mountain between these two points (Champagne Castle and Bushman's Pass). Captain Barter, with one troop of Karkloof and half a troop of Maritzburg Carbineers, will advance up the Giant's Castle Pass, to which there are two approaches, one easy, the other difficult, leaving the half troop of Maritzburg Carbineers at its head so posted as to guard both approaches, and will proceed along the Plateau on the mountain top to the head of the Bushman's Pass by 5 a.m., which he will occupy and hold with the Karkloof Troop.

He must be in position at the Bushman's Pass by 6 a.m., and will communicate with Mr. Allison's party on the hill top, to his own left.

Captain Barter will carry with him provisions for twenty-four hours, and three feeds for his horses.

Captain Lucas, R.M., with 500 armed natives, supported by the Frontier Guards, who will be posted at David Gray's, the left of the position, will be in position by 8 a.m., his right at the foot of the Champagne Castle Pass, his left resting on the little Tugela River, feeling the right of Captain Macfarlane's party.

Captain Macfarlane, R.M., with 500 natives, supported by the Weenen Yeomanry and Burgers, will be posted with his right feeling the left of Captain Lucas's force, and his left resting on the left bank of Bushman's River, about ten miles from Estcourt, in the direction of the Table Mountain. He will be posted by 8 a.m., and will communicate with the Maritzburg natives on his left.

The Maritzburg natives will be posted with their right on the right bank of Bushman's River, in communication with Captain Macfarlane's left, their own left resting on the Giant's Castle Pass.

To be in position at 8 a.m.

Captain Hawkins, R.M., at Richmond, with 500 natives of his district, supported by the Richmond Mounted Rifles, will occupy the country between the Umkomaas and Umzimkulu Rivers, as per sketch, preventing any escape in that direction, the Richmond Rifles acting in support, under his directions.

The whole to be in position by 8 a.m. on the named day.

Her Majesty's Troops, with the head quarters and half a troop Maritzburg Carbineers, will be in position at Meshlin at the hour named, in readiness to support Captain Barter at either the Giant's Castle or Bushman's Passes, as may be required.

Communications will be kept up with the Giant's Castle Pass by the Maritzburg natives, Umbundo's Tribe being employed on the mountain top between Giant's Castle and Bushman's Passes.

The head-quarters detachment will march from Maritzburg on Thursday next, at 1 p.m., after the men have dined, and camp for the night at Riet Spruit, nine miles out, where they will be joined by the Maritzburg Carbineers on the same day. On Friday, they will march at least half way to Fort Nottingham (twelve miles), and on Saturday to Fort Nottingham, where they will encamp, being joined there by Captain Barter's Troop of Carbineers by 3 p.m. on that day.

The volunteers will provide camp equipment, commissariat, and transport of every description, including that required for the reserve ammunition, according to the Volunteer law.

There will be with each troop of volunteers 100 rounds of ball cartridge for every man in it: and when in position on Monday morning, the 3rd November, they will be provided with three days' provisions, and will have made the necessary arrangement for future supplies.

Submitted to H. E. the Lieutenant-Governor for his approval.

(Signed)   T. MILLES, Lieut.-Colonel,

Commandant.

I concur in these proposed arrangements,

(Signed)   BENJAMIN C. C. PINE.

CAPTAIN BARTER'S ACCOUNT.

Camp at Meshlynn,

Thursday.

I have no time and little strength to write you a detailed account of the sad events which have marked the commencement of the expedition which was, I hear, called a Government picnic. But the public will want to know the facts, and I will do my best to satisfy them.

You know that we all met at the rendezvous on Saturday afternoon; after twenty-four hours of great discomfort, owing to a continuance of misty rain, the Natal Carbineers and the Karkloof Carbineers were ordered out for active service.

Intelligence had been received that Langalibalele had retired into the throat of the Bushman's Pass with the intention of escaping southward to his brother who, I believe, lives on the St. John's River. The task imposed upon the Volunteers selected, aided by about a score of Basutos from the tribe Umbunda, but now Hlubi, was to occupy the head of the Pass and prevent the escape of the rebel chief. We were to start at 8.30 p.m., and be in position at the same hour the next morning. Preparations having been previously made, one hour was allowed for final arrangements, and by that time we were in the saddle carrying forty rounds each; provisions at the rate of three days per man and spare ammunition being carried on pack horses. The expedition was under the command of Major Durnford, R.E. At 1 a.m. we crossed the Mooi River for the second time within a mile from Meshlynn, when it was discovered that two of the pack horses were missing, and that these two not only carried a portion of our ammunition, but the whole of our store of provisions. Our Basuto scouts not being able to find them, we up-saddled at 3 a.m., and proceeded up what is called the Game Pass, which ascends the lower range of the Kahlamba, under Giant's Castle, but a little to the south of it. I must premise that the data, on which the orders were based, were a sketch which shows a plateau or flat top between the summit of this Pass and the head of the Bushman's River Pass. We shall see how this was verified. Travelling through the night we emerged upon the said plateau and for some time rode over a fine grass country. Suddenly, however, turning to our right we found ourselves facing a stupendous mountain, the sides scarred and scoured with water furrows, and discovered that this obstacle lay between us and our destination. All this time our Commanding Officer pressed on, eager to fulfil his instructions, the men occasionally munching dry biscuit washed down by a drop of rum. After one or two minor inequalities of ground we came to the edge of an abrupt descent of grass, very slippery and long, so trying to the necessarily dismounted men that a considerable number were knocked up by the time they had got to the bottom; crossing the Loteni River close to its source we commenced the ascent of a precipitous hill which in any other place would be called a mountain. How horses and men struggled up by a succession of springs and rushes was a miracle, but the ascent was not accomplished without accident. Major Durnford, pulled back by his horse, rolled many feet down a precipice, dislocating his shoulder and otherwise injuring himself in the head and body. Full of energy, however, he struggled on to the top, which the greater part of us reached minus our remaining pack horses, one of which was supposed to be seriously hurt, if not killed. A mile of easier travel along a ledge we off-saddled where there was good water and grass, a little after noon. Here we left Lieut. Parkinson and Sergt.-Major Otto to bring up stragglers and collect pack horses, and with a force reduced to thirty-two rank and file we proceeded onward at about 2 p.m.

A short ride brought us to the Umkomaas with no very abrupt descent. The scene before us was savage in the extreme. Down the sides of the mountain hung ribands of water showing the spot to be the very birthplace and nursery of rivers. Above, huge krantzes frowned, whilst the masses of unburnt grass, hanging like a vast curtain, gave a sombre and malignant aspect to the scene. How we slipped and struggled, fell to get up and struggle again, or lay panting on the ground, despairing of accomplishing the task, would be tedious to tell. Trooper Fannin was the first man out about sunset, myself the last about 8 p.m. I should say that this pass is the one mentioned in the "Witness" as little known except to Bushmen, etc., and certainly little known to the Government who represented the country as a plateau. Had Mr. Popham been at home he could have corrected this mistake, as it was here that his cattle were slaughtered by Bushmen some years ago. The last part of the ascent is terrific, among boulders of immense size on sloping ground, offering no hold to anything except naked foot. When some hundred yards from the top Major Durnford fainted and lay where he fell, through the night being sedulously attended by Trooper Erskine, of the Carbineers, who twice descended with brandy and other comforts, stayed with him through the night, and with the assistance of two Basutos, brought him out of the Pass between 1 and 2 a.m. We had linked horses and camped out at a height, by aneroid, of 9,100 feet above level, and after a few hours of such sleep as the intense cold would permit, were again in the saddle a little after 2 a.m. Proceeding over a rough and stony surface we began to near our destination, and at about 6.30 on Tuesday morning (*instead of* 8.30 *on Monday morning*) occupied the Pass, wearied and jaded, but in thoroughly good spirits.

I have hitherto omitted the important fact that it had been announced to us that Mr. Allison, the late Border Agent, was to be on the spot at the original hour appointed, with a large force of natives to support us. Why he failed us will be a matter for enquiry. Our Commanding Officer formed us in single line across the Pass, and we proceeded to make a careful inspection of its depth. All seemed quiet at first, and we congratulated ourselves on our success. We had seen some natives above, but as they showed no hostility we took little notice of them. A large herd of cattle was feeding above, and, as hunger has no law, Major Durnford gave orders for the Basutos to stab one, as of course it would not do to fire a shot. This was not effected till four or five had been wounded, as there was no means at hand of securing them. One was at last slaughtered, and such was the raving hunger of the men that some of them ate pieces of raw meat.

By this time a large party of natives had gathered in our rear and might be seen approaching in a body. We at first supposed them to be part of Allison's contingent, but we were soon undeceived. Major Durnford, after some conversation with Elijah Kambule, whose behaviour throughout was excellent, rode off to parley with them, refusing my offer to accompany him. I afterwards rode up with a trooper, seeing their excited gestures and knowing that trouble was brewing. It appears that the elders and headmen had no wish to commence hostilities, but were unable to control the younger. This was shortly afterwards seen, for when a number of them came up the rocks on either side, and, taking position, deliberately covered our little troop, they were deaf to every order and remonstrance of their elders, though in one case enforced by a blow.

We had set outlooks along the ledge of rocks on both sides,

and were soon apprised that the men from above were calling those from below to come up. This we had orders to resist, but not to fire the first shot, the consequence of which was that the men forced through us and soon both sides of the opening were lined with enemies. Some were mocking and jeering at us, some sharpening their assegais on the rocks and calling out to us to bring the real army.

The plot thickened for a long time; the men had stood quietly seeing themselves caught in a trap, commanded by the pointed guns of their foes, and compelled to remain inactive. At length several of the oldest and steadiest men of the Karkloof Carbineers came to me and said that it was very plain we were surrounded and caught in a trap, that there was neither support nor open country behind them, and that as they could not accomplish the work they were set to do, they ought to retire before the numbers increased or the excitement reached a climax. These feelings were not calmed by Sergt. Clark, who loudly shouted that we were going to be murdered, etc., and whose experience in Kaffir warfare gave his words authority.

I decidedly thought, and think still, that to match thirty-two men, jaded and sick with hunger, even with the very efficient aid of the Basutos, would have been madness. In defence of home and country men will face fearful odds, but I hold that the arrest of the rebels would not have compensated for the loss we have already sustained. Had we arrived before any portion of the tribe, there is no doubt we could have held the Pass as long as our ammunition lasted, though the injunction to await their fire involved the certain sacrifice of one life. But our ammunition gone, and night upon us, what must have occurred? In our actual position I am perfectly certain that had we not retired, few, if any, would have lived to tell the tale. The first volley would have struck many down, and though the men would have fought well, with the ball once opened, they would have served principally for targets, the enemy having the advantage of position, knowledge of the ground, and the feeling that they were fighting for their chief and their home. They were surprised at first and a bold dash might have struck a panic, but as they drew together and saw their strength and our weakness their insolence increased, while the confidence of our men diminished. Our Commanding Officer, as gallant and determined a man as ever breathed, would have cheerfully sacrificed not only us, but himself, in the execution of his orders. He is doubtless right from his point of view, and had he insisted, I am sure the men would have obeyed his orders. He yielded very reluctantly to my remonstrance, though not before making an effort to provoke hostilities. We were now allowed to commence by forcing the natives who were above the Pass, back into it. This necessitated a diversion of the little force. The natives, moreover, determined to run no unnecessary risk, simply gave way slowly, while on the other side they were gathering. This was the side that commanded our retreat, which they meant to intercept. My own impression was that, if they gained their object of keeping the Pass open, they would not care to molest us. The result showed that I was mistaken.

When the word was given to retire, the men formed fours and retired at a walk as steadily as on parade. The front was then reduced to half sections, and as they were forming files, from either side the fire began; as we turned and entered the gorge, with a stony hill close, the bullets fell like hail. I drew a pistol and looked at the hill, but could see nothing but little jets of smoke and, feeling sure that it was all over with us, cantered on. Just as we rounded the corner nearest the hill poor Erskine was struck, and I am certain that he was dead before reaching the ground. He had supported the Major in his wish to occupy the Pass, and had behaved with that gallantry which distinguishes all his family. Sergt. Varty's horse falling dead, he seized the grey which had carried poor Erskine, to be again unhorsed by a chance shot. This time he must have been lost but for the assistance of Troopers Fannin and Spiers, one of whom caught the led horse and the other helped to shift the saddle from the dead steed to the living one. This was all I saw of the fearful ride. Elijah Kambule fell whilst riding beside Major Durnford. The Major, leaping a gully, was beset by two Kaffirs, one of whom seized his bridle. The ready pistol disposed of one, and a parting shot rolled over the other. In the throat of the Pass we met our comrades whom we had left behind. Trooper Taynton had a narrow escape here. He had stayed behind to look for a missing haversack, when three of our Basutos warned him that two of the enemy were coming down. They took shelter behind a rock, and after exchanging a few shots one of the enemy fell and the other ran up the Pass.

Arrived at the bottom we took a path suggested by Trooper Fannin, and plunging into the recesses of the Umkomanzi, and following the valley for miles, reached the camp

1882.
Sergt. H. Brewer, Corpl. T. Edwards, Trpr. C. Tatham, Sergt. W. Edwards, Corpl. D. McKenzie, Regl.-Sergt.-Major E. M. Greene, Sergt. Geo. Ross, Sergt. A. Hair, Q.-M.-Sergt. H. Stirton. Sergt. W. Barker.

without further molestation, having been out fifty-two and a half hours, of which forty and a half were spent in the saddle and climbing hills, having crossed a country such as no cavalry corps has, probably, ever before attempted, and doing even this on dry biscuit sparingly administered.

I make no comments, leaving facts to speak for themselves.

It will be noticed that Captain Barter, like a good soldier, says not a word in disparagement, hardly even of criticism, of his commanding officer at the unfortunate affair of the Bushman's Pass. In his "Stray Memories," published more than twenty years after, he writes:—

"Durnford was there, the Engineer;
A man to those he trusted dear:
As eagle bold, with haughty crest,
Yet with deep feeling, though represt;
Cool and contemptuous in tone,
No counsel pleased him but his own:
Proud of his flag, a soldier born,
He held the Volunteers in scorn."

The critical moment—when the Carbineers, formed in single line, were extended across the Pass,—either for them then to retire as being too weak to hold the position, or forcibly to resist the further advance of the Kafirs, was lost by their commander. No one has ever questioned that Major Durnford was a brave soldier, but not many will deny that at Bushman's Pass he wanted the combination of moral courage and common sense to act on his own judgement in an emergency which his superior officer, when giving him his orders, could not foresee. When Nelson, fighting in the van at the battle of Copenhagen, was told that Admiral Parker was flying the signal for his recall, he declared that he couldn't see it: he put the telescope to his blind eye.

After reading this narrative of the event, written by an honourable gentleman, and bearing unmistakably the internal evidence of truthfulness, one cannot but conclude that, drawn up across the Bushman's Pass that fatal morning, the handful of men and their commander, jaded and faint, disappointed of the supports they were encouraged to rely on, and fettered by an absurd order, were the victims of the bungling and ignorance of the authors of the "official plan"; and one wonders, too, not that five fell, but that any got away. For long after, reproaches were freely cast from side to side, on the one hand by Major Durnford and his small party of staunch friends, and on the other by the Carbineers and the vast majority of their fellow-colonists. But they were silenced for ever when it became known that, little more than five years afterwards, and by a strange freak of Fortune, the same commander, and two-and-twenty of the same Regiment, who had carried bitter thoughts of one another in their retreat from the Bushman's Pass, had fallen together, fighting side by side to the last, on the field of Isandhlwana.

In his official report Major Durnford speaks gratefully of the kind and assiduous care which poor Erskine took of him after he was injured in the ascent of the Pass. He also refers to the "solicitude shown for my safety by many of the force during the retreat," and adds, "I should never have returned but for the assistance I received."

The tribe of the rebel chief having succeeded in keeping the Bushman's Pass open, some escaped by it over the borders of the Colony; others took refuge in the caves of the Drakensberg.

On November 8th, Meshlynn Camp was abandoned for the Headquarter's Camp. From here patrols were despatched to scour the rough country along the base of the Drakensberg where small parties of the rebels were hiding. These "ratting expeditions," as they were called, were disagreeable work. A force, consisting of fifty Carbineers and the Artillery, was sent to shell a large bush which concealed some of the enemy, and a few of the rebels were killed.

On November 12th the camp was again shifted, and on the 16th the town troop returned to Maritzburg. Trooper A. J. Shepstone remained behind on special duty in charge of native levies on the Drakensberg, and Trooper Wheelwright was appointed interpreter to Sir Benjamin Pine, the Lieutenant-Governor.

Two flying columns were now organized to follow in pursuit of the rebels. One, consisting of about fifty men of the Natal Frontier Guard and Weenen Yeomanry, with fifteen hundred natives, the whole under the command of Captain Allison (late of the Natal Carbineers), was to follow on the spoor through the Bushman's Pass. The other, of about fifty men of the Carbineers and Richmond Mounted Rifles, with fifteen hundred natives, under the command of Captain Hawkins (also late of the Carbineers), was to march along the foot of the Drakensberg towards Nomansland, now known as Griqualand East. The object of this column was to intercept

Langalibalele should he attempt, as was thought probable, to make for that country.

The latter column assembled near the Impendhle mountain, and pushed on as rapidly as swollen rivers and the absence of roads would permit. Near the source of the St. John's River the column was met by Adam Kok, the Griqua chief, and some of his men. From information obtained here it was plain that the rebels were not moving in this direction, and the column retraced its steps until the Manzimyama River, now called Mkomazaan, was reached. As native guides reported the existence of a pass across the Drakensberg in this neighbourhood passable for horses, it was decided to cross the mountains in the hope of striking the spoor of the rebels or of falling in with Allison's column. The solitary surviving waggon was left behind, the remaining scraps of biscuit and coffee were placed upon pack-horses and oxen, and the long climb up the mountain began.

After several days' march, mostly on foot, the rebel spoor was struck, and signs were found of Allison's column being ahead. Shortly afterwards, Captain Allison's column was found on the banks of the Orange River, which was much swollen by recent rains. A punt was improvised, by sewing raw bullock hides together, and the rapid river crossed with a few mishaps. The united columns then pushed on, and from the abandoned cattle, and other indications, it was soon seen that the rebels were not far ahead and moving rapidly. After a march, mostly on foot, of some ten days, through a wild uninhabited country, the western crest of the Maluti mountains was reached, from which the more open and inhabited portion of Basutoland was visible and the column's whereabout ascertained, which until then had been somewhat uncertain.

That night parties of rebels were met with, and the next day it was ascertained that the column had driven the main body of them into the arms of the Cape Frontier Armed and Mounted Police sent up into Basutoland to intercept them. After a slight skirmish, the rebel chief and his headmen surrendered to the Cape forces. Meanwhile the Natal column, unaware of this, pushing on rapidly down the spurs of the Maluti, came upon a large body of rebels occupying Basuto kraals. These were promptly stormed, and the flying rebels pursued for some miles. The deserted huts were then occupied, and the tired men and horses revelled in their first square meal (of green mealies) since leaving Natal. A few days later, the rebel chief and his headmen were handed over to the Natal column, together with between 6,000 and 7,000 head of cattle and some hundreds of horses. The return march was made through the Free State, the column reaching Natal on Christmas Day, 1873.

Traversing rapidly the wildest and most rugged country in South Africa, following a trail leading no one knew whither, with scarcely any supplies beyond live beef, and during the storms of a very wet season, the march of this flying column was a most creditable achievement. The results were, however, well worth the hardships and risks, as the best possible effect was produced on the native population by the sight of the rebel chief and his headmen, who had defied the Government, brought back in chains, and their cattle confiscated.

At the opening of the next session of the Legislative Council, His Excellency in his speech said:—

"In the course of the military operations against this Chief, lives were lost, which, unfortunately, were all those of Her Majesty's subjects. I regret even the deaths of the misguided men who had lifted their arms against the Government which had so long protected them. I still more regret the loss of those loyal men, native as well as European, who gallantly fell in defence of their country; and particularly do I deplore the loss of those brave men who fell at the Bushman's River Pass.

"I observe with pleasure that a monument is being erected to their memory by private subscription; but I would ask your Honourable House whether you should not contribute some small sum for this object, so as to identify the Colony, through its representatives, with this memorial.

"I cannot too much praise the conduct of the Military, the Volunteers, and the Native Forces, who were engaged during the recent operations, and special praise is due to that gallant column which, amid dangers and difficulties of a no ordinary kind, followed the fugitive Tribe over the Drakensberg, and assisted in their capture."

On the work and conduct of the column sent in pursuit of Langalibalele, Captain Allison reported:—"I have also much pleasure in testifying to the excellent and steady conduct of the Volunteers throughout the whole of this tedious and difficult march. I have had no occasion to reprimand a single man. The force appeared to be held together and animated by but one feeling, and as the end drew near, weariness and privations were forgotten, and they pressed on to the work cheerfully and well."

In a Government notice, His Excellency expressed his thanks to the force in these words:—"His Excellency desires to convey to the whole of the Volunteer Force, engaged in the late operations against Langalibalele, his most sincere thanks for the gallantry, patience, and endurance which they exhibited throughout the campaign."

By a resolution of the Maritzburg Municipal Council a copy of the following letter was sent to the parents of Troopers Erskine, Bond, and Potterill:—

"Sir,—We, the Mayor and Town Councillors of the Borough of Pietermaritzburg, would express our deep and unfeigned regret for the loss which you have sustained in the expedition against the chief Langalibalele, and most sincerely offer you our condolence and heart-felt sympathy which, we are sure, is universally felt and expressed by the community at large. Though we do not consider it belongs to us to enquire whether your brave and gallant son was unnecessarily exposed to danger, or not sufficiently supported, this we leave to be explained hereafter; we are, however, satisfied that your courageous son has fallen in the discharge of an honourable duty which his love of home and country had voluntarily imposed upon him.

I have, etc.,

P. DAVIS, SENR., Mayor."

The Regiment, at a meeting held on the 9th December, resolved that it should go into mourning for six months. It was also decided to devote £60 for a corps memorial, and letters, couched in the following terms, were sent to the parents of those who were killed at the Pass:—

"Dear Sir,—We, the undersigned, as comrades of those members of the Natal Carbineers who lost their lives whilst engaged in the recent expedition against the rebel chief Langalibalele, desire to express to you the esteem in which your late son was held by us for his admirable qualities as a volunteer, not only as willing and active for any duty he was called upon to perform as a trooper, but constantly ready to render personal assistance to those of us who were suffering from fatigue and illness. We feel that we cannot speak too highly of our appreciation of his good qualities, nor the loss which the corps generally, and each of us individually, have sustained. We trust that this expression of the feeling with which your son was regarded by his comrades may be of some consolation to you in your great affliction."

On the 4th November, 1874, the first anniversary of the fatal affair at the Bushman's Pass, a monument, erected to the memory of those who fell, was unveiled by Mrs. Pepworth, the wife of the then Mayor of Pietermaritzburg. In addition to the Regiment, representatives of every volunteer corps in the Colony were present. The monument bears the following inscription:—

"Robert Henry Erskine,

Edwin Bond,

Charles Davie Potterill,

of the

Natal Carbineers.

In a good cause they perished,
wept for, honoured, known.

———

One country;

One interest; one object;

The same effort; and the same death.

———

This monument is erected by the Colonists of Natal and the Natal Carbineers in memory of those who fell in the discharge of their duty at the Bushman's River Pass, 4th November, 1873.

———

The Natal Carbineers
mourn the loss of their comrades who fell, while taking part in suppressing the rebellion of the Hlubi tribe under Langalibalele, at Bushman's Pass, November 4th, 1873.
'Gently they laid them underneath the sod,
And left them with their fame, their country, and their God.'"

On the 16th January, 1874, Langalibalele was brought to trial before a court consisting of the Lieutenant-Governor, Sir Benjamin Pine, president as Supreme Chief of the Native Population, Mr. Theophilus Shepstone, Secretary for Native Affairs, several Resident Magistrates, Native Chiefs, and Indunas. He pleaded guilty to the charge of rebellion in the indictment, and the inquiry of the court into the circumstances was to ascertain the measure of his guilt. The trial of his sons followed, when further evidence implicating the chief was given. The tribe was next tried, and sentences were awarded of from two to three years' imprisonment with hard labour; but in the majority of these cases the prisoners were located on farms, with their female relatives and connections, and worked out their terms of imprisonment there. One of the chief's sons, who had fired on the troops, was sentenced to imprisonment for five years; the others, for various terms. The rebel chief himself was condemned to banishment for life, and an arrangement was come to with the Government of the Cape Colony for detaining him on Robben Island, whither he was sent. In 1886 he was allowed to return to Natal, and after spending three years in peace and obscurity at the kraal of Tetelegu, a Kafir chief residing in the Zwaartkop location, he died there in 1889.

CHAPTER VIII.

THE ZULU WAR.

For two generations Zululand was turned into a military camp, and in the opinion of its people war was the only business worthy of its manhood. By a law, instituted by Chaka and enforced by his successors, all the able-bodied men were classified in regiments according to their years, and they were not allowed to marry till they had "washed their spears" in the blood of an enemy. Only once, and that about the middle of their career as a nation of warriors, had they been checked by a serious defeat. It was when the Boers discomfited them at the Blood River in 1838. But time had healed their wounded pride of invincibility, and under Cetywayo, both as heir and successor to his father Panda, their old confidence in their prowess was restored, and the younger generation were as keen for war as ever their fathers had been. Their national independence, too, was not only a proud honour to themselves, but it was to the other native tribes, especially those who had wholly or partially been subjected by the white man, their last, but, as they believed, their surest hope that the black man would yet regain all that he had lost and once more be the master in South Africa. The future of the South African natives depended on Zulu prestige.

The river Tugela, generally fordable for eleven months in the year, separated the war-camp of Zululand from the Colony of Natal. On the one side was an army of savages, whose thirst for blood was stronger even than their love of plunder; and on the other, a handful of intruders, visibly growing rich by the peaceful industry to which, as their Zulu neighbours observed with surprise and contempt, they were persistently addicted. Civilization and barbarism, thus placed in immediate proximity the one to the other, could hardly avoid a clash. The temptation from the one side of the river gave rise to alarm from the other; and the time of suspense, until the Zulus should throw off restraint and the fears of the colonists be realised, was too painful to be of long duration.

In 1876, for a breach of the Zulu marriage law, a massacre, uncommon even in Zululand for cruelty and the large

CAMP, MARITZBURG, 1887.

Tpt.-Major A. J. Molyneux, Sergt. Tilney, Sergt. Muir, R.-S.-Major Molyneux, Sergt. Brewer, Sergt. Worman.
Sergt. Cooke, Sergt. Whittaker, Sergt. Foxon, Sergt. Hair, Sergt. Hutton, Sergt. Comrie.
Sergt. Powell.

number of victims, was perpetrated, and the news of it carried to Sir Henry Bulwer, Lieutenant-Governor of Natal. He at once sent messengers to Cetywayo to remonstrate with him and remind him of his coronation promises. The reply, amazing and monitory to His Excellency, was insolent and defiant. It ran, "I do kill, but do not consider that I have done anything yet in the way of killing. Why do the white people start at nothing? I have not yet begun; I have yet to kill; it is the custom of our nation, and I shall not depart from it. The Governor of Natal and I are equal; he is Governor of Natal and I am Governor here."

Several events that followed close on one another after 1876 combined to irritate Cetywayo by exciting within him, as they could not fail to do, feelings of envy, chagrin, and impatience. He had the mortification to see that the role of champion of the South African natives was being played by second-rate chiefs in default of the Zulu King, who should have been the leading actor; that what he looked on as a field of conquest, open to him whenever he chose to enter it, was suddenly closed against him; and that he who had vaunted of his independence and power was hampered, even in what he claimed as his proper sphere of liberty, as though he were a ward in pupilage. For Secocoeni, a chief living in the north of the Transvaal, had won for himself from all the South African blacks the renown, which Cetywayo burned to eclipse and surpass, of having successfully resisted the Boers; the annexation of the Transvaal in April, 1877, brought the Dutch, whom Cetywayo regarded as his natural and hereditary enemies, under the protection of the British crown; and a long-standing dispute, between himself and the Transvaal Boers, about a strip of land between the Buffalo and Pongola rivers, was terminated, not by a war of conquest as he desired, but by the award of arbitrators appointed by Sir Henry Bulwer. The jealousy and sense of humiliation and restraint produced by these occurrences, made the cloak of subordination, which he had worn since he was crowned, unbearable now, and would render any opportunity to insult and provoke Natal not unwelcome.

In July, 1878, one of the wives of Sirayo, a Zulu chief of some importance, fled into Natal for protection. She was followed two days after by two sons of Sirayo at the head of seventy or eighty men, seized in a police hut twelve miles on the Natal side of the border, carried back into Zulu territory and there killed. Shortly after, a similar offence was committed by the sons and followers of the same chief. When a demand for the surrender of Sirayo's guilty sons was made on Cetywayo, he spoke of the outrages as "boyish freaks," and suggested that they would be sufficiently condoned by a fine of £50. In September, Umbeline, another chief, made a raid with the connivance if not by the orders of Cetywayo into the Transvaal territory, and killed men, women, and children in a kraal of friendly natives. About the same time two English surveyors, while employed professionally in British territory near the border, were interfered with and molested by Zulus. These acts, which none but a savage bent on war would do or allow to be done, to a peaceful neighbour, though perhaps not specially heinous in themselves, were sure indications of a hostile feeling and purpose in the minds of Cetywayo and his people, and natural emanations of the aggressive spirit which the Zulu military system fostered. They were like puffs of smoke through the rifts of a volcanic mountain, that tell of the fires beneath and warn the surrounding country of danger.

In September, 1878, Sir Bartle Frere, Governor of the Cape and Lord High Commissioner, arrived in Natal, with full power to settle any trouble that Cetywayo might be brewing. He had spent the previous nine months in King William's Town while the Gaika and Galeka risings were being suppressed, and while studying the temper and motives of the Cape frontier Kafirs, had found evidence that their discontent and resistance had been fomented from Zululand. He had already been a year and a half in South Africa, and during that time, owing to prolonged and wide-spread trouble by the natives, his attention had been given to investigate the causes of their restlessness, and to arrive at a clear understanding of their aims. The conviction had been forced upon him that the desire among them was universal to rid themselves of the white man, and that the belief was rooted in them that all that was wanted to gain the end desired was the combination of their powers simultaneously and for the one object. It was no novice, therefore, to the character and aspirations of the South African natives, who came to Natal as High Commissioner when the relations between the Colonial Government and Cetywayo were on the point of rupture. Sir Bartle Frere's mind was made up that the time had come to deal firmly with the Zulus even at the risk of war. But he did not take the final step without the concurrence and support of the most reliable authorities. In 1876, Sir Henry Bulwer wrote to Lord Carnarvon, Secretary for the Colonies, "It is evident that he

(Cetywayo) has not only been preparing for war, but that he has been sounding the way with a view to a combination of the native races against the white man." Later on he wrote, "There can be no question as to the right of interference to such extent as is necessary to secure the objects in view, namely, the better government of the Zulu people, and the security of British territory from constant danger." And when the crisis came in 1878, as Governor of Natal he signed Sir Bartle Frere's ultimatum to Cetywayo. Nearly a year before Sir Bartle Frere came to Natal, Sir Theophilus Shepstone wrote to him, "One thing is quite certain, that if we are forced into hostilities we cannot stop short of breaking down the Zulu power, which, after all, is the root and real strength of all native difficulties in South Africa." It is perhaps not too much to say that, out of every ten of the British colonists of South Africa, nine approved of all that Sir Bartle did as High Commissioner, and that of the dissentient one-tenth many have since come round to the opinion steadfastly held by the nine.

Resolved to do the duty which his office and circumstances required of him, and backed by the best-informed advice, Sir Bartle Frere sent his ultimatum to Cetywayo on the 11th December, 1878, and allowed him thirty days for his answer. It demanded: 1. The surrender of the sons and brother of Sirayo for trial by a Natal court, and the payment of five hundred head of cattle for non-compliance with the two former demands. 2. The surrender of Umbeline. 3. A fine of one hundred cattle for the offence of surrounding and obstructing two Englishmen while surveying British territory. 4. The existing military system to be reformed, and all men allowed to marry as they came to man's estate. 5. The appointment of a British Resident in Zululand or on its immediate border. 6. The missionaries who had settled in the country were to be left unmolested, as in Panda's time.

No. 708.

Commandant, Volunteer Office,
November 23rd, 1878.

Sir,—I am directed by the Lieut.-Governor in Council to acquaint you that His Excellency has determined to call out the Volunteer Corps under your command for service.

I am therefore to direct you to make all necessary preparations, and to march not later than the 30th instant, via Greytown, to Helpmakaar.

The transport necessary for your Corps will be provided by the Military authorities, to whom you will send in a requisition specifying amount of transport required, and the day on which it will be wanted.

You will make your own arrangements for provisions for your men and forage for your horses, while on the road, but, after arrival at Helpmakaar, rations and forage will be issued by the Military Department on daily requisitions certified by yourself.

You will send to this Department a return of the actual marching out strength of men and horses, as also to the Deputy-Adjutant-General.

On arrival at Helpmakaar you will report yourself to the Senior Officer at that post, under whose command you and your Corps will remain until further orders.

Your Corps will commence pay on the day on which you march, at the rate established by law.

You will send in at once requisitions to complete your ammunition to (70) seventy rounds per man, which will be carried on the line of march. If necessary, directions with reference to reserve ammunition will be forwarded hereafter.

I have the honour to be,

Sir,

Your Obedient Servant,

C. B. H. MITCHELL, Major, R.M.,
For Commandant, Volunteers.

GOVERNMENT NOTICE No. 365, 1878.

Colonial Secretary's Office,
Pietermaritzburg,
November 25th, 1878.

His Excellency the Lieutenant-Governor in Council has been pleased to direct that the following Mounted Corps of the Colony be called out for actual military service, and stationed until further orders, under the command of His Excellency the Lieut.-General Commanding the Forces in South Africa, at the places expressed against their names:—

Natal Carbineers—Helpmakaar, Umsinga.
Buffalo Border Guard—Helpmakaar, Umsinga.

Newcastle Mounted Rifles—Helpmakaar, Umsinga.
Natal Hussars—Pot Spruit, Umvoti.
Durban Mounted Rifles—Pot Spruit, Umvoti.
Isipingo Mounted Rifles—Pot Spruit, Umvoti.
Stanger Mounted Rifles—Thring's Farm, Lower Tugela.
Victoria Mounted Rifles—Thring's Farm, Lower Tugela.

The Acting Commandant of Volunteers will take steps for carrying out this direction.

By His Excellency's Command,

C. B. H. MITCHELL,
Colonial Secretary.

When the thirty days had elapsed without the slightest notice of the ultimatum having been taken by Cetywayo, the High Commissioner committed to the Commander-in-Chief the task of enforcing his demands. As Lord Chelmsford declared that he could only protect Natal by acting on the offensive, the forces were ordered to cross into Zululand at three widely separated points of the border and converge in their march on Ulundi, Cetywayo's chief kraal, where it was expected the first and only battle of the war would be fought.

"REGIMENTAL ORDER, 26th NOVEMBER, 1878.

The Corps being ordered out by His Excellency the Lieut.-Governor, members will parade in heavy marching order on the Market Square at 9 a.m., on Friday, 29th instant.

THEO. SHEPSTONE, JUNR.,
Captain Commanding N.C."

In consequence the Regiment mustered at the time specified, the following men answering to their names:—

Captain T. Shepstone.
Lieut. and Adjt. W. Royston.
Lieut. F. J. D. Scott (K.)
Qr.-Master W. London (K.).
Sergt.-Major Dan Scott.
Q.-M.-Sergt. W. Bullock (K.).
Far.-Sergt. J. Hall (left 16th January, 1879).
Sergt. Mackenzie.
Sergt. F. Methley.
Corpl. J. Symons.
Corpl. W. Mileman.
Corpl. A. Matterson (invalided home early in campaign).
Corpl. Merryweather.
Trumpeter C. Scott.
Tpr. C. Bissett.
Tpr. J. A. Blaikie (K.).

Tpr. H. Brewer.
Tpr. W. Barker (E.)
Tpr. G. Ball.
Tpr. W. Borain (K.).
Tpr. Byrne.
Tpr. C. G. S. Christian.
Tpr. P. Comrie.
Tpr. B. C. Clarence.
Tpr. H. W. Davis (K.).
Tpr. Deane (K.).
Tpr. Dickinson (K.).
Tpr. W. Edwards (E.).
Tpr. C. Fletcher (E.).
Tpr. E. M. Greene.
Tpr. W. Granger (E.).
Tpr. A. Hair.
Tpr. Hawkins (K.).
Tpr. Hayhow (K.).
Tpr. J. Hutton.
Tpr. J. Hay (D.).
Tpr. Haldane (K.).
Tpr. R. Jackson (K.).
Tpr. F. Jackson (K.).

Tpr. D. Little.
Tpr. H. Lloyd (joined Feb., 1879).
Tpr. W. Lumley (K.).
Tpr. A. Muirhead (E.).
Tpr. G. J. Macfarlane.
Tpr. Moodie (K.).
Tpr. G. T. Macleroy (K.).
Tpr. Mendenhall (K.).
Tpr. H. P. Pennefather.
Tpr. J. Ross (K.).
Tpr. G. Ross.
Tpr. Rock.
Tpr. W. Shepstone.
Tpr. Symons.
Tpr. C. Slatter.
Tpr. H. Stirton.
Tpr. W. Sibthorpe.
Tpr. Swift (K.).
Tpr. W. Tarboton (E.).
Tpr. E. Tarboton (K.).
Tpr. Whitelaw (K.).
Tpr. Woodhouse.

[K., killed; E., escaped; D., died. Those not marked were out on patrol.]

The following men joined after Isandhlwana:—

Tpr. Wales.
Tpr. W. Cook.
Tpr. Cranford.
Tpr. C. Lavender.
Tpr. D. Hollington.
Tpr. Collins.

Tpr. A. Pearse.
Tpr. C. Tatham.
Tpr. H. Gibson.
Tpr. W. Craik.
Tpr. Miller.

After parading, the men were marched to the Drill Shed, where new belts were issued, each of which carried 120 rounds. They were then dismissed, to parade again at 2. Four wagons had previously been sent forward.

> "Farewells were said with hearts so light,
> To loved ones near and dear;
> Each man was burning for the fight,
> And ne'er a one showed fear."

The Regiment mustered again in front of the Market House, where a large number of spectators was gathered to bid them good-bye, a special platform having been erected for the ladies. When they were drawn up in column, Lord Chelmsford arrived, and after inspection addressed them. He had not previously had an opportunity of inspecting the Regiment, but from what he had heard he was perfectly confident that, should it ever come into action, it would behave in a manner worthy of the reputation it had attained and of the City to which it belonged. He was pleased with their equipment and general appearance, and after again expressing his confidence in them, he wished them good luck on their expedition. Their Excellencies, the High Commissioner and the Lieutenant-Governor, also came to say good-bye, and rode down the line. The order was then given to form fours, and about three o'clock, amidst hearty cheering and with the good wishes, sympathy, and confidence of everyone in the City, they marched away to the strains of the 24th band, playing "Let Me Kiss Him for His Mother," and "The Girl I Left Behind Me."

The first off-saddle was just beyond Cremorne, where two horses were lost, the unfortunate owners having to follow the Regiment on foot. Next morning tents were struck at six o'clock, and a start was made. The waggons sticking on the Red Hill, the Regiment halted some time on the top, and progress was but slow. After an off-saddle at Comins', the night was spent with the 24th Regiment at the Umgeni. The following day Carbutt's Hill was reached after two off-saddles and a tremendous thunderstorm, which lasted two and a half hours. Next day Purcell's was passed, and a halt made at the Umvoti Drift, but as the waggons had not come up with the tents, everyone slept in the open. On Tuesday (2nd December) the Regiment was played into Greytown by the band of the 24th, and camped on the Market Square.

On Friday, the 5th, they left Greytown, being played out of town by the 24th band. At Burrup's they halted, and passed the night in delightful weather. After an early start next morning a halt was made in the Thorns. The road was both stony and dusty, and, owing to the scarcity of grass, forage had to be issued for the horses. After crossing the Mooi River, the Regiment halted for the night at Horsley's. The Tugela was crossed next day, and Sandspruit the day after that.

On the 9th December Helpmakaar, the destination of the Carbineers, was reached, all being well. Here the Newcastle

Mounted Rifles and Buffalo Border Guard were found already encamped. On the road up the Regiment had been most hospitably treated. Men and horses soon settled down to work, and all were well and fit for duty. Up till the 8th January the men were kept hard at work in Helpmakaar, there being two mounted and one foot parade daily, so that not much time was left for recreation. The health of all was extremely good, the only drawback being the scarcity of water for the horses, three of which died.

Colonel Russell, 12th Lancers, was appointed to the command of all the mounted forces, much to the discontent of the Volunteers and Police, who protested. They considered that the Government, who had promised that they should be under the command of Major Dartnell, had broken faith with them. Protesting, however, was of no avail, and being told that they had either to submit or return to Maritzburg, they reluctantly fell in with the arrangement. It is hardly necessary to say that the objection to this appointment was not owing to any personal feeling towards Colonel Russell, who throughout the campaign was most popular with the Colonial Forces under his command.

On the 8th January the Regiment, together with the other mounted men, moved to Vermaak's farm as an advance guard, where they remained for two days. Here all excess baggage had to be left. After Isandhlwana the owner of the farm fled into laager, and the baggage was looted.

Though it is unnecessary to detail the plan of operations, it may be stated that the Regiment was attached to what was known as the Centre Column, under the command of Colonel Glyn, C.B.

On the 10th January the column encamped on the right bank of the Buffalo River at Rorke's Drift. On the evening of that day orders were issued that the troops should cross the following morning.

At daybreak on the 11th January the mounted men and natives crossed the drift, the arms, blankets, etc., being ferried across in a small punt, the men and horses swimming. All the Regiment passed over without mishap, a fact no doubt due to their being colonial and accustomed to fording and swimming swollen rivers from early boyhood. The operation was covered by Harness's battery, which occupied a knoll overlooking the points of passage, but no opposition was attempted, and by 6.30 a.m. the whole of the troops were on the left bank. After getting their arms, etc., the mounted men were

Colonel E. M. Greene C.M.G. V.D.,
Commanded Regiment 1891 to 1902.

sent out on a patrol. Ten men of the Regiment were told off to capture some cattle, and, although Zulus were to be seen armed with assegais and guns in the krantzes, they drove the cattle from the kraals, even entering the huts and loosening the calves, and disarmed several natives. They were not fired on, though the Zulus could be seen on the cliffs all round. Some cattle had to be left, but most of them were captured. On reaching the top of the hill they found that the remainder of the Regiment, together with the other mounted men, had moved on some distance, and the few in charge of the captured cattle found it a difficult job to drive them from their feeding ground. They only succeeded in this by fixing bowie knives as goads and by touching up some of the most troublesome behind. On the return of this small party to the Buffalo they found that their comrades had also captured a lot more cattle, some eight hundred oxen and two hundred sheep in all being brought in.

At 5 a.m. on the 12th January, a force under the command of Colonel Glyn, the Carbineers forming the advance guard, left camp to reconnoitre the country to the eastward, where the kraal of the chief Sirayo was known to be situated. Lord Chelmsford and his staff accompanied this force, which, after a march of about five miles, arrived at a ravine in the valley of the Bashee River, and captured a number of cattle. A small body of Zulus was seen on the hills above, and all the mounted men were sent against them, Lieut. Royston and four Carbineers being in advance to draw their fire. One who was present thus describes what happened:—"We all marched towards the hill in column of fours, and when about 150 yards from the Zulus we were fired on. If the Zulus had had any knowledge of firing they might have done great execution here, for, as might have been expected with troops under fire for the first time, there was a little confusion, as the leading horses all shied at the firing, and we were rather huddled together, but the Zulu bullets went far over our heads. As no word of command was given to dismount or commence firing, we, on our own account, dismounted and opened fire, the Zulus immediately retiring. Major Dartnell then rode up to us and spoke some cheering words to us to advance, and we were then taken up the hill at a killing pace, for when we arrived at the top we were all dead beat, and had there been an army waiting for us I fear none of us would have had legs or breath to retire. However, there were but few Zulus, I should say about a hundred, on this hill, although a short distance off in a gully, where it was impossible for mounted men to venture, numbers were in hiding, and these were left for the native contingent. Some thirty Zulus were killed, eight or nine of them by the Carbineers themselves." For their steadiness and general behaviour on this occasion the Regiment gained the praise of Colonel Russell.

From the 14th to the 19th January the column remained in the same position, and during this time waggons and stores continued to be brought up from Helpmakaar and ferried across the Buffalo, and bad places in the road were rendered passable by strong working parties.

After the affair at Sirayo's kraal, more cattle were brought back to camp, and were sold to the contracting butcher for a mere song. The members of the Regiment, having a day off, assisted him in crossing his cattle over into Natal, and the day being blazing hot they spent it mostly in the flooded river. It was on this day that Tpr. Dixon, of the Newcastle Mounted Rifles, was drowned, an event which cast a gloom over the whole camp. From this time to the 20th January the Regiment was employed in long and hot patrols, but never came across more of the enemy or their cattle. On 14th January a patrol was sent, under Lieut. Royston, as far as Manzinyama Spruit. They found the kraals deserted. On the 15th a reconnaisance was made as far as the Isipezi. Only a few mounted Zulus were seen. Kraals were deserted and cattle removed. One prisoner was taken. On the 18th a patrol was sent in the direction of the Ityotyosi, the Regiment acting as the advance guard. Neither men nor cattle were seen.

On the 20th January the Regiment moved to camp at the ill-fated Isandhlwana Hill. The new camp was distant about eight miles from the Bashee Valley, on the left hand side of the road which was being pursued to reach Ulundi. There were considerable misgivings on the part of officers of experience, including Major Dartnell, in regard to the selection of this site, owing principally to the broken and wooded country in its immediate rear, which offered ample cover for a large force of the enemy to concentrate unseen and attack suddenly.

The camp was pitched during the afternoon in the following order:—Beginning on the extreme left were the 2-3rd N.N.C., 1-3rd N.N.C., R.A., 2-24th, Volunteers and Mounted Infantry, the N.M. Police, and the 1-24th on the right. The waggons were all parked between the camp and the hill at the back, and behind them, immediately against the base, the headquarters tents were pitched with their waggons beside them, the hospital being close by on the Nek. Late the same evening, after the camp was pitched, an order was sent round for the 3rd Regiment N.N.C., together with the Mounted Police and Volunteers, to prepare themselves for a start at daybreak next morning, and take with them one day's rations, for the purpose of beating up the country opposite to us, viz., the Malakata Hills, close beyond the kraal of an old chief, Ugamadane, who had previously surrendered. The Police and Volunteers, 120 in all, were under the command of Major Dartnell, and they left the camp at 5.30 a.m. on the 21st January. After a march of about three hours, the Indawene stream was reached, and a halt made for lunch. Here the party separated, the Carbineers, under Capt. Shepstone, ascending the Ndlazagazi heights to co-operate with the native contingent. Major Dartnell with his party, having found the enemy in considerable strength, pursued his reconnaisance no further, and rejoined the Carbineers, who by this time had joined forces with the N.N.C. It was then decided to send the Carbineers to reconnoitre and ascertain the exact strength and position of the enemy. Under Lieut. Royston, they galloped up to within 600 yards of the enemy, who immediately extended in skirmishing order and tried to surround them. Though they did not fire a shot, our men, acting up to their instructions and having seen enough, wheeled round and rejoined their main body. The Zulus did not follow far. As it was now late, nearly six o'clock, and the officers in charge of the native contingent reported their men as tired and hungry, Major Dartnell deemed it advisable not to attack.

Orders were given to bivouac for the night at the head of the Mangeni Valley, both to prevent the enemy from entering the broken country towards the Tugela, which appeared to be his intention, and also to be in a position to attack early the next morning. Our natives, however, were evidently faint-hearted about fighting, and in order to give them confidence by increasing the backbone of European troops, Major Dartnell during the night sent a note to the General describing the situation, and asking that two companies of infantry might be sent out to support him. In his opinion this extra "stiffening" would be all that he required. Blankets and provisions were sent out from camp on pack horses, and arrived at the bivouac just before dark. A dreadful night was spent in the bivouac, which was formed in a hollow square, three sides of which were made up of the 3rd N.N.C., the fourth by the Mounted Police and the Carbineers, the horses being ringed in the centre. About midnight—fires having been seen on the opposite hill where the Zulus were—a few shots were fired by the outlying picket, and (for what reason will never be known) one of the corners, No. 1 Company 1-3rd N.N.C., gave way and fled across the centre of the square, causing a general stampede of the horses, until, upon being met by the men of the other battalion who stood firm, the torrent was stemmed and the alarm found to be false. At the first alarm the Mounted Police and Carbineers lay down in line with bowie knives fixed and cartridges inserted, after having told off a guard for the horses in a quiet and soldierlike manner, their officers walking about cheering the men and keeping them acquainted with what was going on. The Carbineers were then divided and were posted, one here and another there, among the natives to give them confidence in case of a further alarm, false or real. No greater compliment than this could have been paid to the steadiness and splendid behaviour of the Carbineers, albeit the duty was far from pleasant. A trying three hours brought daylight, during which time there was another false alarm which, however, was not taken much notice of.

Before daylight the force was under arms and moving towards where the enemy had been last seen. On arriving at a point from which the camp was in sight a large force was seen leaving it, much to the surprise and discontent of the colonial forces, who hoped they were going to have the fighting to themselves and under their own officers. This force proved to be four companies of the 2-24th and four guns R.A., under command of the General. The Carbineers and Mounted Police, under Major Dartnell, were ordered off to get round on the right flank, between the position of the enemy and Matyana's stronghold. After skirmishing over the hills they found a body of the enemy on a hill to the right among whom were some mounted men. Major Dartnell gave orders for the Carbineers and Police to ride after them. At 800 yards they opened fire, greatly to the astonishment of the Zulus who stood jeering at them, and even at this distance brought down a number. Seeing this the enemy fled up the hill as hard as they could; but, as it turned out, not fast enough to escape the men of the Carbineers, who, putting their horses to full speed, gained on them and shot many running. Indeed, dead shots were made in this manner at 600 yards. Three horses were captured, and the stern chase continued until the men of the N.N.C. were met, when the Carbineers returned and left their sable allies to finish the business. Over sixty of the enemy were killed. Matyana himself, chased for miles and nearly overtaken by Captain Shepstone, only saved himself by jumping off his horse and dropping over a steep krantz. His horse was brought into camp. A halt was then made for tea and biscuits and to await the General's arrival. The General's stay was short, and his instructions on leaving were that the force under Major Dartnell was to return two miles back to the head of the Mangeni gorge and wait there, his intention being that the whole camp at Isandhlwana should be struck that afternoon, and the entire force moved forward to the spot selected as Dartnell's halting ground. This intention, it is needless to add, could unhappily never be carried into effect. But the orders were at once acted on, and on our arrival the staff was found already there looking through field glasses at some large bodies of Zulus, who were about ten miles away, massed in close proximity to the camp. This was about half an hour after noon, and it was then that the first uneasy suspicion was aroused with regard to the welfare of the camp.

Reports now came to the General that heavy firing was being heard in the direction of Isandhlwana, and Lord Chelmsford galloped up to the top of a neighbouring hill, and every field glass was levelled at the camp. The sun was shining brightly on the white tents, which were plainly visible, but all seemed quiet. In the meantime a message had been received by Lt.-Col. Harness from camp by a messenger, supposed to be Tpr. Hayhow, N.C., saying, "For God's sake come with all your men; the camp is surrounded, and will be taken unless helped." In consequence of this message Lt.-Col. Harness immediately moved off towards Isandhlwana, and sent the messenger to inform Lord Chelmsford of his intention. The General ordered the messenger to go back, and shortly after, with the Carbineers and mounted men as escort, started to return to camp and ascertain the position of affairs and what had occurred there. About three miles of the return journey had been traversed when a mounted man was seen approaching and speedily recognised as Commandant Lonsdale, who proved to be the bearer of most dreadful news. Those who were present when he told his tidings to the General will never forget the scene. It appeared that, feeling unwell, he had ridden quietly back to the camp at Isandhlwana. Riding on unsuspectingly he had got within ten yards of the tents when he was fired at, and then recognised that all the men he saw about him in red tunics were Zulus, and that the camp was entirely in the enemy's hands. Turning his pony away with some difficulty, he fortunately escaped, and was thus able to bring the news to Lord Chelmsford.

As soon as his sad tale was told, orders were sent back for the rest of the column to return at once, and meantime the Carbineers and the others who had joined them were halted. In order, if possible, to obtain further information, mounted patrols were detached to the crest of the adjoining ridge to watch the progress of events. They ascertained that the enemy seemed to have beaten the troops, to be firing the tents, and taking away large quantities of stores. A scouting party of Carbineers, under Lieut. Royston, was sent forward to approach as near the camp as possible, and they reported that nearly all firing had ceased and that everything was in possession of the enemy. Orders were now given for the remainder of the column to march for Isandhlwana forthwith. It was quite four o'clock when they reached the party, including the Carbineers, who had been first ordered to return to camp, and the order for the march was established, the N.M. Police and the Carbineers being on the left flank. Before a start was made the General addressed the men, stating that the camp had apparently been taken by the enemy during their absence, and that he relied on them to retake it. On arriving within two miles from camp the column was halted behind a ridge, and advanced scouts sent out to reconnoitre, but no signs of the enemy were visible, and the march was resumed, all precautions being taken. By the time the vicinity of the ill-fated camp was reached it was completely dark. A halt was made, and the guns fired four rounds into the camp. After a short advance, another halt was made and the shrapnell fire repeated. Meanwhile Major Black and three companies of the 2-24th were sent to take possession of a koppie which commanded the camp: they announced their success by three hearty cheers. The remainder of the column then moved on to the site of the camp, where they bivouacked for the night. Such precautions as were possible were taken to guard against surprise, as it was known that large bodies of the enemy were in the vicinity.

It is almost impossible to realise the horrors of the night, spent as it was on the battlefield among the bodies of both friend and foe. By the dim and misty light were to be seen, mixed up with the bodies of horses, oxen, and mules, the mutilated corpses of friends, ay, even of brothers, men who had fallen where they stood, regulars, police, volunteers, loyal natives, showing true loyalty and devotion in the one cause of their

Queen and country. Well does the inscription on the tablet, erected in St. Peter's Cathedral to the memory of the Natal Carbineers and other Volunteers who fell on that fatal day, express what might even have been, of some, their dying thought:—"Stranger, tell England we died doing our duty." During the night the glare of burning kraals for miles within the Natal border raised anxious thoughts for the safety of the Colony, and there were several alarms in which shots were fired—the Carbineers proving their steadiness by not firing a single shot.

As daylight began to appear, the order was given for the march to be resumed, and the column, the Carbineers forming the advance guard, tired out, and ill at ease with regard to the safety of their comrades and friends (for no opportunity was given of looking for anyone), proceeded rapidly on their return route. They had not gone far when a large impi of the enemy was met with, and it was concluded that it was the victorious army which had set out from Isandhlwana, attacked the post at Rorke's Drift, and were now returning to Ulundi. Preparations were made to resist this force, but they, having been so thoroughly defeated at Rorke's Drift, were disinclined to take the offensive, and both forces proceeded on their way. On Rorke's Drift being reached, all were delighted to find that the brave little garrison had succeeded in repelling the attacks of the enemy. The sight of so many dead Zulus around the heroically defended post served to cheer the spirits of our men. The Regiment bivouacked for the night in a cattle kraal adjoining the laager, but owing to the number of false alarms not ing the laager, but owing to the number of false alarms not much sleep could be had.

The following paper, "Before and After Isandhlwana: a Reminiscence," though it first appeared in the "Greytown Gazette" of 20th December, 1903, was written expressly for a place here, with the purpose of conveying some idea of the consternation spread throughout Natal by the news of the disaster:—

"On the night of the 30th November, 1878, I was present as a guest at a banquet, given to celebrate St. Andrew's Day, in the Maritzburg Victoria Club. I have since attended St. Andrew's banquets that were more enjoyable, but it stands out in my memory distinct from all the others because of a speech at it by the Rev. Mr. Ritchie, at the time military chaplain for Natal. He told us that just as he was leaving home for the Club that afternoon his wife said to him, 'Now, don't forget the poor boys who marched off to the front yesterday,' meaning the Natal Carbineers, who had gone out in high spirits to the Zulu war. Mr. Ritchie, as brave a man as ever breathed, seemed to me to be needlessly solemn, and my neighbours must have felt so too, if one might judge by their looks. I have often thought since that to him, as to a Highland seer, coming events were casting their shadows before. But he failed at the moment to transmit his own foreboding to his audience. We hilariously drank the toast, 'Success to the Carbineers,' and sat down as if satisfied that the prayer was already answered, for we feared no evil to them.

"In the following January I agreed with a Maritzburg friend who, like myself, had just got a fortnight's holiday, to ride up after the troops for the sake of spending a day with our two or three Carbineer acquaintances. As we had plenty of time for the trip we were content to get over short stages in a leisurely way, and so, reaching Greytown at the close of our first day out, we put up for the night at Wood's Hotel. In the afternoon of the following day, January 23rd, as we were thinking of saddling up for the next stage, a trooper of the Natal Mounted Police came spurring in on a hard-ridden horse, and spread dismay around him before he had time to say a word. He was carrying sealed despatches from Lord Chelmsford to Sir Bartle Frere, but he had seen the field of Isandhlwana with its heaps of dead, and he electrified us all with his hurried account of the sight that had, as was still evident, unnerved him. He did not attempt to enter into particulars, and even if he had tried he would certainly have failed, for the horror of the whole disaster had prevented his mind from noting its details. A council of two was then held, and after a short debate on the question, 'Shall we turn back, stay for a while where we are, or go forward?' we decided, partly under the influence of shame to abandon an expedition deliberately begun, and partly drawn on by the fascination of the frightful, to go forward. At Burrup's we saw the first sign of panic. The landlord was alone in his hotel, he had already sent his family into Greytown, and he was hastily making things as secure as he could before following them. We got a scanty meal from him, but the best he had to offer us, and pushed on to Mooi River. A company of the Engineers, that had halted here the day before on their way up to the front, had hurriedly thrown up a sod fence so as by it and the river to enclose and, in case of a Zulu attack, to give a slight protection to, the hotel and its outbuildings within about an acre of ground. We found two companies of the 4th Regiment bivouacked

Trooper Edwin Bond,
Killed at Bushman's Pass, November, 1873.

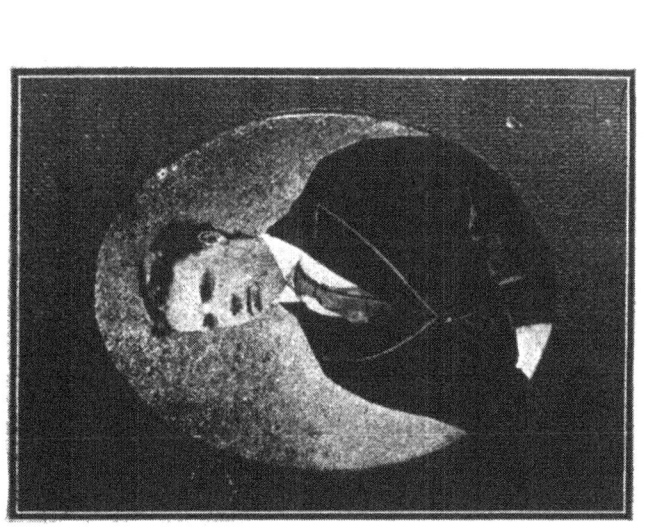

Trooper R. H. Erskine,
Killed at Bushman's Pass, November, 1873.

within the enclosure, and with them we passed a quiet but miserable and rainy night.

"Starting early next morning we had the way all to ourselves till we reached the steep and rocky road leading down to the Tugela. Then we began to meet, and with rapidly increasing frequency, small and straggling bands of Kafirs returning from the front. But how different from the regiments of native levies we had seen some weeks before marching down Church Street, Maritzburg, at a proud, swinging pace to the accompaniment of their war chants that sounded like a strong wind blowing through a forest! Now there was no singing, and not even the loud and merry talk of Kafirs on the road, but either suppressed conversation or an absolute silence, and looks that plainly showed anxiety and depression. And the change was quite intelligible. They had lost confidence in the Umlungu with his loss of the Isandhlwana camp, they had been disbanded as an encumbrance, and they knew what they had to expect if Cetywayo's impis should sweep over Natal. The Tugela was alive with Kafirs fording it, some singly, most of them in parties hand in hand, and all using their ox-hide shields as buoys when they had to swim. Having crossed by the punt we were told at the hotel by the landlord and the punt-keeper, its only occupants then, that we should have to go back almost immediately, for all the white people between the Tugela and the Zulu border who had not already fled had been ordered into laager at Helpmakaar. Accordingly, after resting and baiting our horses, and indulging in a long and serious talk and a short and slender snack, we turned back on our morning's ride and reached Mooi River again about sundown.

"After a late dinner, as the five guests staying in the hotel that night—one of them, Mr. Smith, being a surveyor for whose hustling by Zulus reparation was demanded in the High Commissioner's ultimatum—were seated round the dining room table, smoking, chatting, and leisurely drawing on a "nightcap," in came the landlord, Mr. Horsley, and dramatically placing before them a rifle and two fowling pieces, said, 'I have been warned that a Zulu impi is coming down to-night to destroy the punts here and at the Tugela. I am an old soldier and a Government servant in charge of this punt. From here I shall not budge till further orders.' On being questioned he told us that his own Kafirs had got notice of the purposed attack, had given him a well-meant warning, and then taken themselves off, as they said to stay meant to be assegaied.

How the others passed the night I cannot tell; but, for myself, I did not sleep a wink. I did not undress, but lay down on the bed, with a loaded revolver in my grip, to watch and wait for what was to be the signal to begin making such use of my weapon as might be permitted me before the end came. Everything was painfully still within the house, but from outside I heard the river ceaselessly and the wind by fits. The flow of the one would sound at times to my terrified mind like the rushing of hundreds of naked feet, and in every gust of the other I read 'U-su-tu! U-su-tu!' the war cry of Cetywayo's impi. Our small party in the dining-room had broken up late, and in January the Natal sun rises early; but no sleepless night of mid-winter at Home ever seemed half so long to me as that night of agony at Mooi River. Before daylight my friend and I were up and attending to our horses. Half an hour or so later we were cantering homeward, with revolvers handy, and, as the Spaniard says, 'the beard on the shoulder.'

"On the top of the hill just above Greytown we were stopped by a patrol party of five Dutchmen, each well mounted and with rifle butt on his thigh. They questioned us closely about all that we had seen and heard since we left the Tugela, and seemed much interested in the story told by Horsley's Kafirs. At Greytown we learned that many women and children from the farms round about had come into the laager, that parties like the one we had met were out on all the roads leading to the Zulu border, and that, Sunday as it was, preparations were being energetically made to give the Zulus a hot reception. After a two hours' rest we were again on the road. At York we were once more put under strict examination. We noticed that there was much more excitement there than we had found at Greytown. Some of the York residents had already gone, and others were just going, to Maritzburg. The throng of fugitives in every kind of conveyance increased as we proceeded, and between Albert Bridge and the City it vividly reminded us of Lord Macaulay's description, in his 'Lay of Horatius,' of the flight of the country folk to Rome. As we had observed in the course of our long ride that day that the fear of the Zulu increased in the proportion of the distance from him, so at Maritzburg we found it at the climax. Loop-holed walls of sandbags had been built up from the extreme sides of Longmarket and Church Streets, right across and in front of the Post Office, so as to make a fortress of the centre of the town; wells had been dug and provisions stored within that area; and those residing outside had orders to hurry to the quarters already allotted to them within it at the signal of three guns fired from Fort Napier. Happily these wise precautions were never needed, and the scare gradually faded away, leaving only a memory of an anxious time, for the Zulu Dabulamanzi proved to have no better right to be classed among first-rate Generals than the English Lord Chelmsford."

JOHN STALKER.

We must now return to the doings of those ill-fated men who were left at Isandhlwana on the 21st January. The following most interesting and graphic account by Tpr. W. W. Barker, N.C., who was fortunate enough to escape, needs neither introduction nor comment.

"On 21st January all the available mounted men went on a patrol, only those remaining in camp who were on duty, or whose horses had sore backs or otherwise were not fit for riding. I was on vidette duty next day with every available man under Lieut. Scott. We left camp at about 4 a.m., and the Carbineers were posted to the direct front and left of the camp, from three to five miles away. Hawkins, my bosom friend, and myself were posted on a hill to the extreme front, quite six miles from camp, and arrived on the hill about sunrise. After being posted for about a quarter of an hour we noticed a lot of mounted men in the distance, and on their coming nearer we saw that they were trying to surround us. We gave the usual signal, but had to retire off the hill post haste, as we discovered they were Zulus. We retired to Lieut. Scott, about two miles nearer camp, and informed him of what we had seen, and he decided to come back with us, but before we had gone far we saw Zulus on the hill we had just left, and others advancing from the left flank where two other videttes, Whitelaw and another, had been obliged to retire from. Whitelaw reported a large army advancing, 'thousands' I remember him distinctly stating, and he was immediately sent back to camp with the report. This would be about eight a.m. He returned with a message to Lieut. Scott that we were to watch the enemy carefully and send back reports of their movements. Shortly afterwards, numbers of Zulus being seen on all the hills to the left and front, Trooper Swift and another were sent back to report. The Zulus then remained on the hills, and about two hundred of them advanced to within three hundred yards of us, but on our advancing they retired out of sight, and a few of us went up to this hill where the Zulus had disappeared, and on a farther hill, at about six hundred yards' distance, we saw a large army sitting down. We returned to Lieut. Scott, who was then about three miles from camp, and reported what we had seen. Hawkins and I were then sent back to camp to report a large army to the left front of the camp. On our way back we noticed the Zulus advancing slowly, and when about a mile and a half from the camp we met the rocket battery, who enquired the enemy's whereabouts. We advised the officer to proceed to where Lieut. Scott was stationed, but he asked if he could get up a hill to his left. We informed him that the Zulus were advancing towards that hill, and most probably would be seen on it within half an hour. The officer decided to proceed up this hill, and the battery was, half an hour afterwards, cut up to a man, just as they arrived, I believe, on the top of the hill in question. (We, the videttes, were at the time in a donga firing at the Zulus, and witnessed the cutting up of this battery without their having time to fire a single shot.)

"Hawkins and I reported to an officer, staff, I believe, about the advance of the Zulus, and as we left camp to return to Lieut. Scott, another Carbineer, I am not sure of his name (Hayhow), galloped in and reported Zulus in every direction advancing. He was then sent on to the General with some report, and was never seen again alive by any in camp, although he is reported to have given a dispatch to the General, who sent him back to camp, at which the poor fellow never arrived. As Hawkins and I were returning to the vidette outpost we noticed the mounted Basutos to the extreme left of the camp in skirmishing order, and masses of the Zulus on all the hills. Firing was then heard for the first time, as although we had been within two hundred yards of the Zulus, we had strict orders not to fire the first shot, and no shot, up to then, had been fired on either side. We reported ourselves to our officer, who immediately advanced us (the videttes having all retired to where Lieut. Scott was stationed) against some Zulus who were coming on slowly. Heavy firing was then heard on our left, and being fired on we returned the fire, posting ourselves in a donga. (It was from this donga we saw the rocket battery cut up.) We were obliged to retire, but at every cover we dismounted and fired. We would then be about two miles and a half from camp. We retired slowly, never allowing the Zulus to come closer than two or three hundred yards of us. As some of us had nearly expended our ammunition we retired to camp for more, and saw, as we retired, soldiers being despatched in skirmishing order, to the extreme left, some companies being nearly two miles from camp. Arriving at camp we found our quartermaster and his sergeant busy opening ammunition boxes and serving it out to all who asked for it. Poor London, the quartermaster, had been struck by a stray bullet, but not badly wounded.

"As we left the camp Col. Durnford rode up to us, followed by some mounted natives, and shouted to us, 'Carbineers, hurry up and follow me.' We followed him to a donga about a mile from camp, where we dismounted, Hawkins, myself and others giving our horses to one of Durnford's natives to hold, promising to tip him when the fight was over. However, he left our horses after a time and rejoined his troop. Colonel Durnford collected all the mounted men, police and volunteers, some eighty in all, and here for about half an hour we kept the Zulus in check, the donga being in direct front to the camp. Although there must have been fully five thousand Zulus they never advanced nearer than two hundred yards of us, and eventually retired. A lot of the men having expended their ammunition, we were ordered back to the camp. This would be about 10.30 or 11 a.m. As I had procured ammunition on the former occasion when I had returned to camp I did not require more, but tied up my horse to the horse lines, next to another horse I had in camp, intending to change saddles later on, as the horse I had been riding had had a hard time of it, and I wished for a fresh horse, as I then thought that when the Zulus broke we should pursue them. Few at that time had any idea that the camp was practically surrounded and that there was any chance of defeat. I then went down the hill to our immediate front, about a hundred yards from our lines, and joined some Carbineers, Hawkins, Swift, two Tarbotons, and Edwards, and commenced firing. The Zulus were then advancing from the donga we had just left. After firing about a dozen shots I noticed, or rather heard, a rush from behind, and on looking round I saw the soldiers who were left in camp literally surrounded by Zulus, who had evidently come in from the rear, and as soldiers and natives repassed us in confusion we retired back to our Carbineer lines. The artillery now retreated in the direction of the Nek to the right of the Camp.

"As the Carbineers were now all separated, some loosening their horses from the lines thinking, at least I did, we were retreating to rally on some point, on coming to the horse lines I found one of my horses shot in the side and kicking on the ground. Luckily it was the one not saddled. I mounted my horse, the Zulus being busy now all over the camp stabbing the soldiers, and made in the direction of the Nek in rear of the camp. I was joined by W. Tarboton here, but being met by the Zulus we were obliged to retire back towards the camp, which was now a mass of Zulus. We then went in the direction we had seen an artillery carriage go, to the direct right of our lines, and saw the gun upset, it being immediately surrounded by the Zulus. This point, from what I heard afterwards, was the only point that the Zulus had not surrounded, and we two got through here. After riding for about half a miles or less, Tarboton asked me to return with him to look for his brother whom he had missed, and as I had lost my comrade Hawkins at the same time I willingly returned, but just as we got in sight of the camp, from a hill we both for the first time realised what had happened; the camp was completely surrounded and the people were being massacred by the Zulus. We were then obliged to fly as Zulus were following fugitives up.

"Up to this time I had never thought of disaster, but only that we were retiring on a point to rally; but the defeat was only too palpable, and we had to spur and hurry on our jaded horses over the most awful country I had ever ridden. Riderless and wounded horses were galloping past and tumbling down precipices and gullies. Here I heard for the first and only time the awful scream of a terrified or mad horse. He was a black horse with the saddle turned round, and as he passed us and went crash against a mounted man in front of us, rolling over the krantz, this awful scream was heard. Zulus seemed to be behind, before, and on each side of us, and as we hurried on we had to leave poor fugitives crying and begging us not to leave them. Many were shot as we rode past them, but we met no Carbineers or volunteers whom we knew until we neared Fugitives' Drift, when we caught up C. Raw, and well it was for us two, as his men, mounted Basutos, were already on the Natal side of the river, and had it not been for these Basutos I doubt if a single white man would have escaped by Fugitives' Drift, as they kept the Zulus in check while the few escaped. As we ascended the hill on the Natal side the firing of the Zulus was very good, and I saw a contingent native drop just in front of us, and shortly after we passed another who had been shot. The Zulus would then be about nine hundred yards off.

"As soon as we got out of fire Tarboton and I waited to see if we could find any of our fellows, and as I fancied I saw a man who I thought was Hawkins some way down the hill, I rode back, but it turned out to be Lieut. Higginson, so he informed me, of the native contingent, and had got hurt in the river where his horse was washed away. As my horse was too tired to carry two, I assisted him to mount, and he rode away leaving me to follow on foot. Tarboton, Henderson, and Raw, recognising him on my horse, took the horse from him and came to meet me with it, of which I was right glad, as I had run for about three miles. Higginson told them he could not have walked any further, and he knew I was fresh, and that he was sending the horse back for me. Raw obtained a horse for him by dismounting one of his Basutos. We gave our horses a rest here for about an hour, and I can tell you they needed it, as we (the Carbineers) had been in the saddle since 4 a.m., and had had a lot of galloping about. My poor horse had come down twice with me along the Fugitives' Track. I should say it was now about 4 p.m. Higginson was the last man to have seen Melville and Coghill, whom he had left at the drift, and it will be remembered that it was from information received from him that their bodies were discovered and the colours of the 24th found.

"On our arrival at Helpmakaar, about sundown, Capt. Essex ordered us to assist in making a laager. We worked for about an hour, but being refused any food, and several horses having been jumped by flying natives, we decided to leave our horses with Raw's Basutos, and went to a store where we were kindly given some beer, sardines, and biscuits by the man in charge, the first food we had tasted since the day before, it being then about eight p.m. Messages having been sent for us either to come into laager or remain outside, several of us decided to do the latter, as our horses were not allowed in the laager and we were afraid of them being jumped. I forgot to mention that at Helpmakaar five other Carbineers had arrived, three having escaped by Fugitives' Drift, but we did not meet them as we were escaping, viz., Edwards, Sibthorpe, and Muirhead, the latter having seen the last of poor Macleroy, who had been wounded in the thigh early in the day. As the Basutos saddled up and moved away, I know not where, we, about a dozen mounted men, made tracks, as all kinds of rumours were brought in by natives, and arrived at a place, about 2 a.m., which I afterwards found was Dundee, although I had not the slightest idea of the direction in which we were travelling. We let our horses out to graze, and got about two hours' sleep, and about five o'clock had a meeting, there being about eighteen men who had escaped and arrived during the night. Most were in favour of proceeding to Ladysmith, but poor Tarboton (who had hopes of finding his brother as he had mounted his horse before W. Tarboton had at Isandhlwana), and I, with one or two of the police, returned to Helpmakaar, where we were welcomed by Sibthorpe and Granger (Carbineers), who had lost their horses, and we were given a good breakfast. About an hour after this we, the mounted men, were ordered to saddle up and take despatches and post to Rorke's Drift, no news having been heard from there. The despatches were entrusted to Tarboton and myself. About five miles from Helpmakaar we met the General and staff, when we heard for the first time of the safe arrival of the General's column at Rorke's Drift and of the gallant defence of that post. We were gladly welcomed by Major Dartnell and the late Captain Davey, but the General was very gruff and short with us as we did not get out the post and letters quick enough for him, Major Dartnell himself assisting us. We were then sent on with the post to Rorke's Drift, and rejoined our regiment just as it was starting from there."

After the foregoing circumstantial account of the doings at the Isandhlwana camp it is hardly necessary to add more; but the following references to the gallantry of those members of the Regiment who remained in camp, taken from the account given by Mehlakazulu, the captured son of Sirayo, will be found of interest. After relating the Zulu proceedings up to the actual commencement of the fight, he says:—"The mounted men (Carbineers) retired very slowly on seeing the Zulu army. On seeing the English troops retiring, the Mkandapemvu regiment advanced. The mounted men retired and advanced four times. We just went on and they retired before us, our Zulu army appearing to become more numerous every moment. There is a little red hill which overlooks Isandhlwana within sight of the camp, and there the Ngobamakosi, to which regiment I belong, came into contact with two troops of mounted men. Some of these men had white stripes up their trousers (Carbineers), and there were also men dressed in black (probably N.M.P.), but none of the native contingent on the brow of this hill. The Ngobamakosi and Uve regiments attacked on this side. The English force kept turning and firing, but we kept on; they could not stop us. But on the side of this little hill there is a donga into which the mounted men got and stopped our onward move there; we could not advance against their fire any longer. They had drawn their horses

OFFICERS, UMLAAS CAMP, 1889.

Top Row—Vet.-Surgeon Wiltshire, Lt. Whittaker, Lt. Sinclair, Capt. McKenzie, Capt. Weighton, Lt. G. F. Tatham, Qr.-Mr. Hicks, Capt. Shepstone, Capt. Ross, Lt. Willson, Lt. Tilney.
Second Row—Lt. Hair, Capt. Von Bulow, Major Menne, Lt.-Col. Royston, O.C., Capt. Macfarlane, Capt. Addison.
Front Row—Lt. Ehlers, Lt. Cooke, Surgeon-Capt. Hyslop, Lt. C. Tatham.

into this donga, and all we could see were their helmets. They fired so heavily we had to retire. We kept lying down and rising again. At this time the wings of the Zulu army were running on both sides above Isandhlwana and below to Rorke's Drift. The men in this donga were firing on the chest of the army. Then when the firing became very heavy, too hot, we retired towards the left wing, towards Rorke's Drift, and they withdrew. On seeing us retire towards the Buffalo they retired on the camp, fearing lest we should enter the camp before they could get to it, and that the camp would not be protected. The Carbineers on entering the camp made a strong stand there, and their firing was very heavy. It was a long time before they were overcome, before we finished them. When we did get to them they died in one place all together. They threw down their guns when their ammunition was done, and then commenced with their pistols, which they used as long as their ammunition lasted. And then they formed a line, shoulder to shoulder, and back to back, and fought with their knives. The Carbineers were on the right front of the camp. When they were rising out of the donga, and retreating on the camp, we shot two Carbineers. When they reached camp the Carbineers jumped off their horses and never succeeded in remounting them. They made a stand and prevented our entering the camp, but things were then getting very mixed and confused, what with the smoke, dust, and intermingling of mounted men, footmen, Zulus, and natives, it was difficult to tell who was mounted and who was not."

The following extract from the official narrative of the Zulu war is also of interest:—"Colonel Durnford, on his return to the neighbourhood of the camp, appears to have remained near the mounted men who, by holding the watercourse on the extreme right, were keeping the Zulus at bay. These, however, finding a direct advance impossible, extended to their left, and crossing the watercourse still lower down, out-flanked the mounted men and threatened to cut off the retreat. On this, it would seem that Colonel Durnford determined that the forces under his command should adopt a more compact formation, and that, with this object, he ordered the 'Retire' to be sounded. This was done, and the time of its occurrence appears to have been just previous to the rush of the Zulus which penetrated the defensive line. The troopers, whose horses had been under cover in the watercourse, rode back some fifteen hundred yards, and took up a fresh position on the eastern slope of the Nek, over which a stream of fugitives must now have been hastening. But the stony koppie to the south was already in the hands of the enemy, and from the west their right horn was rapidly closing in, so that on this spot the final stand was made. Here Colonel Durnford, with a party of mounted volunteers and others, who had rallied round their commanding officer, held their ground gallantly; but attacked from all sides by overwhelming numbers, when the last cartridge had been fired, the end could not long be delayed."

Of this last stand by Colonel Durnford and the handful of Carbineers, Mr. C. Barter writes in his "Stray Memories":—

"And yet, on Isandhlwana's plain,
Between the slayers and the slain,
At head of a Colonial band
He made a last and desp'rate stand.
They fought and died, and, sooth to tell,
With those he scorned the hero fell.
They rest alike in honour's grave:
None can be braver than the brave!"

So ended the fatal day. It is not within the province of these pages to enter into the controversy, which raged long and fiercely, as to who was responsible for the overwhelming defeat. It is sufficient for us to record that the men of the Natal volunteers—for we must not forget that the Newcastle Mounted Rifles, Buffalo Border Guard, and Natal Police were also represented in the gallant band—when called upon to show their devotion to their Queen, their country, and their duty were not found wanting.

It is needless to say that the sad news was received in Pietermaritzburg, and indeed throughout the Colony, with the greatest consternation and anxiety, or that sympathy with the relatives of the killed was felt and expressed on all sides.

"Corporation Notice.—The Mayor and Town Council of Pietermaritzburg feel that they cannot but express how deeply they sympathize with the relatives and friends of those who have so recently fallen in the service of their country, and desire therefore to convey to each and all their heartfelt condolence. By order of the Council,

W. Francis, Mayor."

A letter, in the following terms, was received by Captain Shepstone from the Maritzburg Rifles:—"Sir,—I have in command to express to you on behalf of the officers, non-commissioned officers, and men of the Maritzburg Rifles, the profound sympathy they entertain towards yourself and the officers and men under your command at the present period of reverse and disaster, when so many of your brave corps have been numbered with the slain on the field of battle. The officers, N.C.O., and men of the Maritzburg Rifles fully share in the universal public ascription of praise accorded to your corps for its distinguished gallantry and efficiency under arms, and deeply regret to have learned the very severe and unprecedented loss the corps has suffered in the discharge of its duties.—I have, etc., T. J. E. Scoones, Lieut. and Adjt., Maritzburg Rifles."

The whole of the Regiment having lost every article of their kit, which was left behind on 21st January, fresh supplies were sent up, the late Mr. J. D. Holliday being indefatigable in his exertions to forward the necessary goods, but owing to the dearth of transport it was some time before they were received.

On the 24th January the Regiment left Rorke's Drift for Helpmakaar, being joined on the road there by those men who had been so fortunate as to escape from Isandhlwana. On arrival at Helpmakaar the waggons were laagered and all the men inside, as described by one present, "in a beastly mess." The waggons were gradually drawn away and a sod wall substituted for them. The inside of this wall was re-veted with bags of flour and mealie meal, but as no arrangements had been made for drainage the natural consequence, after a few days' rain, can better be imagined than described. The inside of the laager was like a pond, the stench was overpowering, and the men all huddled inside at night with but one blanket apiece. It is needless to say that before long the fever fiend began his deadly work, and several members of the Regiment were soon down with it. The hospitals were in such a disgraceful state that dying men preferred to keep out of them.

After a time all the members of the Regiment who were down with fever, but well enough to be removed, were taken to Ladysmith, where a hospital was established. Here, thanks to the kindness of the inhabitants of that town, particularly Mr. George Tatham and Mrs. Knight, who rendered every assistance in their power, and to whom many of the men owe their lives for the care and attention bestowed on them, all recovered. Troopers Edwards and Hay were too ill to be moved. Edwards recovered, but Hay, to the regret of all, died on 4th March, and was buried in the cemetery of Helpmakaar. In consequence of the effect it might have on the sick, no military honour was paid to the dead at this time.

About this date Captain Shepstone left the **Regiment** temporarily to take charge of a force of mounted Basutos, and the command devolved on the only other officer present, namely, Lieut. Royston, who was well qualified for the position. Writing of this gallant and popular officer, an ex-member of the Regiment says:—"Had it not been for Lieut. Royston, who stuck to the corps through thick and thin, I fear we should have been left to the tender mercies of the military who, over and over again, did their best to make us do the dirty work. But Royston was one in a thousand, and would not allow us to be sat upon, and I must say the Regiment should always be proud of having had such an officer as Lieut. Royston (now Lieutenant-Colonel), and I am sure his severance from the Regiment will always be missed, especially by those who had the pleasure of serving under him during the trying time of the Zulu war."

On the 15th February the Regiment left Helpmakaar for Dundee, the strength then being but one officer, three non-commissioned officers, and twenty men. Here they stayed with the mounted infantry, under Colonel Russell, 12th Lancers, until 1st March. During the whole of this time patrols were sent out daily, scouring the whole country. Though there were night alarms occasionally, no forces of the enemy were seen.

On March 1st the Regiment returned to Helpmakaar, and on the 5th it was joined by a few recruits from Maritzburg. During this month a reconnaissance was made into Zululand, and a few kraals burnt, with the object of drawing off attention from the force entrenched at Eshowe.

Shortly afterwards the Regiment was despatched to Newcastle to form the escort of His Excellency the High Commissioner, Sir Bartle Frere, on his visit to the Transvaal, and accompanied him as far as the border. From this point His Excellency considered it advisable, for political reasons, to proceed without an escort, and the Regiment remained in Natal. In a parting order, His Excellency expressed his thanks for the satisfactory manner in which the duty had been performed and the good conduct of the men. The Regiment returned to Helpmakaar, but in a few days was ordered to proceed to Dundee with the N.M. Police, to join the camp there with the reinforcements of Imperial regiments arriving from England.

On 1st May the advance towards Zululand was begun, and a large camp was formed on the right bank of the Buffalo river at Landtman's Drift. The Regiment accompanied the column, and had to undertake very heavy duties in connection with scouting and patrolling, long patrols being undertaken daily into Zululand in addition to constant vidette duty on the heights surrounding the camp. The work was especially hard on the horses, whose daily ration consisted of five pounds of grain and whatever scanty herbage could be picked up in the veld. The cheerful manner in which the hard work was undertaken, and the valuable assistance rendered at this time by the Regiment, was specially noticed by General Newdigate, commanding the column. During the reconnaissances made into Zululand by the cavalry brigade, 1st Dragoon Guards and 17th Lancers, detachments of the Regiment invariably accompanied as guides.

In May a column, of which the Regiment was a part, under the command of General Newdigate, was sent to revisit Isandhlwana and bring away the abandoned waggons still lying there. No signs of the enemy were observed until the last valley before Isandhlwana was reached, when signal fires were seen. Half of the Regiment, with other mounted men, under the command of Colonel Drury Lowe, formed the advance guard, and by 9.30 the ridge by the camp was reached. It was found that the grass, intermingled with a luxuriant crop of mealies and forage, had grown up over the whole site of the camp. In the grass lay bodies in all directions. Everything was hidden at first sight, and required searching for. Whilst preparations were being made to harness the horses to the empty waggons, all, except those on vidette duty, were allowed to wander over the scene of the disaster. Naturally the members of the Regiment made at once for the spot their lines had occupied, and endeavoured to find relics of their dead comrades. On searching over the ground the bodies of Colonel Durnford, Lieut. Scott, and others were found. Lieut. Scott lay partially under a broken piece of a waggon, and had not been mutilated or touched after death. Both the bodies of Colonel Durnford and Lieut. Scott lay right in the midst of the young colonists who had fallen in defence of their country, and judging from the position in which they all were, they must have made one last gallant stand and died together. Time did not admit of any attempt at burial, but, as far as possible, the bodies found were covered over. Many interesting relics were brought away. A start back was made at 12.30, Rorke's Drift was reached at 3.30, and the Regiment returned to Landtman's Drift.

On 1st June, General Newdigate's division crossed the Blood River. Up to this time there was every chance of the Regiment, or what now remained of it, being allowed to go with the column. It was, however, Lord Chelmsford's policy not to permit any of the troops who were with him in his former disastrous advance into Zululand to accompany his new force. The only corps granted this honour was the No. 5 Battery, Royal Artillery, for, having only one other battery, he was obliged to make this exception. General Newdigate applied to Lord Chelmsford for leave to take the Regiment in with his division as his personal escort and as guides, but at the last minute this was refused. Colonel Drury Lowe also applied for the services of an officer and several men as guides to his cavalry brigade, but this also was refused. The members of the Regiment then petitioned the Lieutenant-Governor in the following terms to be allowed to re-cross the border:—"To His Excellency Sir Henry Bulwer. The petition of the undersigned members of the Natal Carbineers humbly sheweth: That your petitioners have been for the last six months in the field on active service, and in the disaster of Isandhlwana lost twenty-two of their comrades. Your petitioners, in consequence, are anxious to re-cross the border with General Newdigate's column, and to see the campaign brought to a successful termination, the General having expressed a wish to secure their services as his personal escort. Your petitioners therefore pray that Your Excellency would be pleased to take into consideration the request set forth in this petition, and your petitioners, as in duty bound, will ever pray. (Signed by twenty-six members of the Regiment)."

The Regiment was now placed under the orders of Colonel Degacher, 2-24th Regiment, and by him they were detailed for vidette duty and to patrol the borders, and also to supply orderlies for mounted duty in carrying despatches to Dundee, the nearest telegraph station.

During the time the late Prince Imperial was at the front the Regiment frequently formed his escort, but although they had volunteered for the duty on the day on which he met his death they were not allowed that honour. On 3rd June they proceeded to Koppie-Alleyn to escort the body from that place to Dundee.

On 25th June a detachment of the Regiment accompanied a force which was sent to Isandhlwana for the purpose of burying those who had fallen on 22nd January. Waggons, picks, and shovels were taken. The battlefield was reached by 9 a.m., and the bodies of the following were buried where they were found, viz.:—Lieut. Scott, Troopers Davis, Borain, Lumley, Hawkins, Dickinson, Tarboton, and Blaikie. They were lying together, between the road and the 24th camp. About four hundred yards higher up the bodies of Moodie and Jackson were found close together. Swift was lying on the Nek under the koppie. Dead bodies were found very thick near the spot where Lieut. Scott and the others were. Search was made for the other bodies, but without success. Enquiries were made from the party of the 24th, who were also engaged in the task of burying their comrades, but they had come upon no Carbineers. Search was made all round where the waggons had stood and where London and Bullock were last seen, but without success. After burying all that were found, the men were extended in skirmishing order, and the country along the line of retreat was thoroughly searched. Poor Macleroy's remains were found about a mile from the Nek, in which place his grave was dug. Time did not permit of further search being made, and the force reached Rorke's Drift at sunset. On the 26th June another force, sent to complete the task, found the remains of Q.M. London, the only means of identifying him being his uniform. The bodies of Bullock, Ross, and Deane were also found, besides four others unrecognisable. By this time it was extremely difficult to identify anyone, a few bones and rags being all that was left. Only two bodies were never discovered. The bodies of Q.M. London, Ross, and Deane were in the 1-24th camp, not far from Lieut. Scott and the others; and of Bullock, in the 2-24th camp. Of those that could not be recognised, three lay a short distance from the Nek, to the right of the path which the bulk of the fugitives had taken; one on the right of the Nek, up under Isandhlwana hill, close to where the 24th found a company of their men who had fought it out in a position they had evidently taken among the rocks. The grass was very long, and it was not till it was trodden down by the working parties that the bodies could be discovered. In recognition of the services of the burial parties, Mr. J. D. Holliday, already mentioned as the Regiment's agent in Maritzburg, sent the following telegram to Lieut. Royston:—"Please accept yourself, and convey to your men, the heartfelt thanks of the community for the sacred duty you have so generously and feelingly performed."

On the 26th July orders were received for the Regiment to return to Maritzburg, their services being no longer required. During the whole of the last two months their duties had been very heavy. Standing to arms at 4 a.m. on cold winter mornings was far from agreeable. Six videttes had to saddle up at this hour and occupy three different posts about two miles from camp, and there they had to remain till 7 p.m. At 9 a.m. patrols for the day were sent out and did not return till dark. Orderlies, sometimes two and three a day, were required to ride to Newcastle, Utrecht, Ladysmith, Conference Hill, etc., and men and horses frequently knocked up.

On the 28th July the Regiment left Landtman's Drift for Maritzburg at 9.30 a.m., after a very flattering address from Colonel Degacher, commanding the post. A highly complimentary order on their leaving him was also issued by the same officer.

The Regiment reached Maritzburg on the 1st August The following account of their arrival is taken from the "Natal Witness" of the 2nd:—"Yesterday, long and anxiously waited for, our Volunteers returned once more amongst us. It had been anticipated that the Natal Carbineers would not arrive until to-day, and arrangements were made to do honour to the occasion by parading the Rifles with their band, and the general turning-out of the public. 'Our Boys,' though, when once within hail of home, lost no time in pushing on, and yesterday afternoon, between 3 and 4 o'clock, the news travelled rapidly through the community that they had gained the outskirts of the city. Shortly before, four mounted men, with Captain Shepstone and Lieut. Royston at their head, were descried making their way down Church Street, and numbers went to meet them. Near the Post Office quite a large crowd had gathered round to cheer them. As the travel-stained men drew up there was much enthusiastic hand-shaking between long-parted friends; Captain Shepstone and Lieut. Royston being the recipients of the most hearty greetings. When something like order had been obtained, the Mayor (Wesley Francis, Esq.), taking off his hat, called for three cheers for the Carbineers, which were given with great lustiness again and again, amidst cries of 'One for Royston.' His Worship the Mayor then mounted a carriage in front, and said:—'Captain Shepstone, officers, non-commissioned officers and men of the Natal Carbineers, we did not expect you this afternoon, or we would have been better prepared to receive you. (Hear, hear.) We thought you were not coming till to-morrow, when the Rifles and their band were going to turn out in your honour. I will read you the address which has been prepared on behalf of the burgesses.

CAMP, 1892.

Back Row—Q.-M.-Sergt. Munro, Sergt. Dick, Sergt. Bennett, Capt. Chules (Ordnance), Sergt. Lyle, Sergt. Buchanan, Sergt. Methley, Sergt. Hyslop, Sergt. Cockburn, Sergt. Mason, Sergt. Walters.
Second Row—Sergt. Meyer, Sergt. Owen, Sergt. Comrie, R.-S.-Major Molyneux, Sergt. Holmes, Sergt. Tranmer.
Front Row—Sergt. Colville, Sergt. Bell, Sergt. Knott, Sergt. Dodd, Sergt. Rodwell, Sergt. Townsend, Sergt. Hayes.

"To the Officers, Non-commissioned Officers, and Troopers of the Natal Carbineers.

"We, the burgesses and inhabitants of the City and Borough of Pietermaritzburg, take the earliest possible opportunity of expressing to you, as we hereby do, through our representative His Worship the Mayor, the great pleasure we have in hailing your return to the City, after enduring the protracted hardships and dangers of active warfare in connection with the Zulu Campaign, in which we are proud to know you have so eminently distinguished yourselves.

"Under ordinary circumstances the return to their families and accustomed vocations of a Body of Volunteers could not fail to furnish an occasion of unalloyed gladness and rejoicing. In regard to yourselves, such sentiments will be entertained this day in their fullest force by every inhabitant. But when we, remembering the gay departure of the Natal Carbineers from the Market Square on the 29th November last, now witness how thinned have become their ranks and numbers through the cruel hand of War, the tear of sorrow involuntarily starts from the eye and bedews the cheek from the recollection of the fallen comrades left behind and the knowledge of the grief which, as a consequence, has invaded the bereaved homes, and indeed has been shared in by all.

"Yet while thus paying the loyal tribute of regret to the esteemed and brave departed, be assured, none the less, of our gratification that so many of you have returned in safety to reap the Laurels of your Patriotism and high Devotion to Duty and to enjoy the congratulations awaiting you on every side.

"In common with other sections of the Volunteer Forces of Natal which have been engaged in the Field, in combating for the interests of the British Empire and yielding hearty and efficient service to Her Majesty not only within but likewise in Territory outside the confines of Our Own Colony, it has already been your good fortune to have obtained the highest praise from Officers in Chief Command of the British Forces who have marked and recorded with commendation your Gallantry and Efficiency at all times. Permit us to say it is our earnest hope, as also our confident expectation, that the services rendered in the Zulu Campaign by the Volunteers of Natal; services which without doubt have contributed, in no insignificant degree, to the success of the Queen's Arms, may yet be awarded by our Gracious Sovereign the meed of still further and substantial recognition. Meanwhile we shall beg your acceptance personally from us of a memento of the Estimation in which these services are held by the inhabitants of the City.

"Conscious of our inability materially to add to the value of the just encomiums already conferred on the Volunteers by Officers so competent to judge as those alluded to, it now only remains for us, on this auspicious occasion of re-union, most cordially to welcome you back to resume amongst us your usual pursuits as our highly valued Citizens and Fellow Colonists. We wish you health and happiness; and cherish an ardent desire for the conclusion of so thorough and satisfactory a Peace as shall foster the best interests of the Colony, conserve those of the British Empire at large, and avert from one and all the calamities of renewed war.

"On behalf of the Burgesses and Inhabitants of Pietermaritzburg.

"W. FRANCIS,
"Mayor.
"Pietermaritzburg, August, 1879."

"At the conclusion of the reading of the address, the crowd cheered again and again. The Mayor, still addressing the men, said:—'On behalf of the burgesses I have to invite you to honour them with your company, to a public luncheon in the Park on Thursday next, when they will be better prepared to extend to you, that welcome which is your due, than they are to-day. On behalf of the citizens and myself, I wish you a hearty welcome back to your hearths and homes.' (Renewed cheering.)

"Captain Shepstone, in reply, said:—'Mr. Mayor, this address has taken us by surprise. We were not aware until we came to the bottom of Chapel Street that you were going to present us with an address this afternoon, and consequently we are not prepared with a written reply. As for myself, I think I can say the same for Lieut. Royston, I should like to make a written reply to the address, and as we have a parade to-morrow I would ask you to postpone receiving a reply till that time.' The men then broke off and returned to their homes amidst hearty cheering."

On the following day the Regiment paraded to return Government equipment and to read a reply to the address from the Corporation. The reply ran as follows:—"To His Worship the Mayor, burgesses and inhabitants of the City. Mr. Mayor, on behalf of Lieut. Royston, non-commissioned officers and men of the Natal Carbineers, I have to thank you, and through you, the inhabitants and burgesses of the City for the very enthusiastic reception you have given the corps on its return from active service, and the very kind expressions which your address contained. We cannot but feel very deeply the sad loss the corps has sustained, which we realise most keenly on an occasion, like the present, when we are receiving the affectionate welcome of our relations, friends, and fellow-citizens. The happiness of our return to our homes, and our pleasure in being so cordially received is tempered by the recollection of those whom we have lost; their memory we cannot too highly honour, and it is the wish of the whole corps that some suitable and lasting memorial should be made to them. It is very gratifying to the corps to feel that you appreciate its late services, and I feel sure that you will all be pleased to know that the officer commanding the district in which they served has spoken in high terms of praise of the conduct of Lieut. Royston and the men, and of the manner in which they have performed their very monotonous and trying duties. Again thanking you for your hearty welcome. —I am, etc., on behalf of the Natal Carbineers,

T. SHEPSTONE, JUNR.,
Captain, N.C."

Captain Shepstone said he wished to supplement what he had just read by a few words. He thought the man who ought to be in the position he (Capt. Shepstone) was in was Lieut. Royston. (Cheers.) To him was principally due the credit the Regiment had obtained by its onerous duties. There could be no better officer than Lieut. Royston, and he had proved it on many an occasion. The success of the Regiment had been chiefly due to the exertions he had made and the soldierlike qualities he had exhibited. He asked them to give three cheers in his honour—a call most heartily responded to. Lieut. Royston returned thanks for the reception accorded to him, and said he was not aware he had done anything to merit such praise. The Regiment then marched off amid hearty cheering.

The following telegram was received by Captain Shepstone from His Excellency Sir Bartle Frere:—"His Excellency desires to send to you and the Natal Carbineers his hearty congratulations on your return home after what is, His Excellency trusts, the conclusion of the operations to make their homes secure." To which Captain Shepstone replied:—"On behalf of the Natal Carbineers I thank His Excellency for kind congratulations."

In a despatch to Lord Chelmsford, the Secretary of State for War says:—"I note with great satisfaction the part taken by the colonial troops in recent operations, though I deeply regret the losses they have sustained."

The following General Order No. 18, issued by the General Commanding in South Africa, expressive of his appreciation of the services rendered by the Volunteer Corps and other Colonial Forces of Natal during the late Zulu War, was published for general information in the "Government Gazette" of 23rd December, 1879.

GENERAL ORDER, No. 18.

Pietermaritzburg, August 2nd, 1879.

By order of the General Commanding, the Mounted Volunteer Corps in Natal are released from further services, and will proceed at once to the Headquarters of the respective Corps, when the men will be dismissed to their homes.

The General Commanding desires to convey to the Volunteers his appreciation of the services rendered, and of the ready obedience to orders and soldierly qualities they have displayed during the eight months they have been in the field.

The General Commanding wishes also to take this opportunity of thanking all the Colonial Forces—Mounted Police, Volunteers, Local Forces, and Native Levies—all of whom have performed good and loyal service; and although all have not had an opportunity of meeting the enemy, they have probably, by their services along the border, prevented an invasion of the Colony, and thus assisted in bringing the war to a conclusion.

By order,

G. POMEROY COLLEY, Brig.-Gen.,
Chief of the Staff.

In the official Precis of information on Zululand, 1879, Major Newdigate in expressing his opinion on the Colonial Corps, says:—

"The Natal Carbineers were excellent men, well acquainted with the Country and well mounted."

On the 8th October, a dinner was given by the Maritzburg Rifles in honour of the Natal Carbineers. Captain George Matterson proposed the toast of the evening in a most eloquent speech. Captain Shepstone replied, and after thanking them for their kindness, mentioned the dissatisfaction that had arisen through the regiment not being allowed to recross the border, and concluded by proposing the health of the popular Commandant, Major Dartnell.

On the 8th October, the remains of the late Lieutenant Scott, having been exhumed from the battle-field, were re-interred in the Pietermaritzburg cemetery. Lieutenant Royston was in charge of the firing party, who turned out in their frayed and tattered uniforms. The band of the 99th Regiment was present and played the funeral march. General Clifford and many others attended.

The Regiment also attended the re-interment of the remains of the late Lieutenant-Colonel Durnford.

In November, at the opening of the Legislative Council, the Regiment once more formed the escort to His Excellency, the Lieutenant-Governor. In the course of his opening speech, His Excellency, in referring to the recent war, said:—"The honour and reputation of the Colony were well upheld by the little band of Natal Volunteers and N.M. Police, who took part in the fatal engagement of Isandhlwana, and who fell, nearly all together, where they fought, showing the example of a noble courage that ought never to be forgotten in Natal, and a devotion to their duty which was faithful unto death. The sacrifices entailed upon many of the volunteers, whom services in the field compelled to leave their ordinary occupations, professions, and pursuits, for a period of many months, the public spirit, the soldierly qualities, and the excellent conduct exhibited by all ranks of the colonial forces, and the good service rendered by them, are such as to call for my special notice and gratitude."

In the Legislative Council the following resolution, a copy of which was sent to every man concerned, was unanimously passed:—"That this Council thanks the Colonial Forces, N.M. Police and Volunteers, for the alacrity and bravery with which they went to the front when called upon by the Imperial Authorities, showing by their whole conduct during the war, and by the glorious death of many of their number, that the colonists are willing, at any sacrifice, to take their part in the defence of their country and homes." Mr. John Robinson, in speaking to the resolution, referred in glowing terms to the volunteers, expressing the hope that the name of the Natal Carbineers would never die out—a name which had now a halo of glory round it of which any colony might be proud.

In December a special burial service was held on the battle-field of Isandhlwana, Bishop Macrorie officiating.

The report in the "Natal Witness," of August 9th, 1879, which takes up four columns of that issue of the paper, describing the Public Luncheon in the Park to the Natal Carbineers, is here condensed.

Thursday was set apart as a holiday in Maritzburg, and the elite, not of the City only, but of the Colony, gathered in the Park to do honour to the remnant of the Natal Carbineers on their return from the Zulu War. His Worship the Mayor, W. Francis Esq., presided, supported on his right by His Excellency, Sir Henry Bulwer, and on his left by Captain Shepstone. After a substantial repast had been partaken of, and the usual complimentary toasts duly honoured, Sir Henry Bulwer, in reply to the toast of "His Excellency, the Lieutenant-Governor," said:—"We rejoice to know that when the danger of that fierce death came suddenly upon them, our men faced it bravely, and that they gave up their young lives gallantly and nobly, and that their death was a soldier's death, a death honourable to all men, and we know that Natal honours the memory of these dead, because their memories honour Natal. We can claim for the Carbineers, and all Natal forces, engaged in this war, that they have done their duty right-well, and that they have worthily upheld the reputation of this Colony. They have been kept out during many long trying months, under exceptional circumstances, and at no small sacrifice to many amongst them, and throughout all this, in the field and in the camp, and the day of battle, and in the long night of routine work, whatever they were called upon to do, whatever duty was placed upon them, amidst disaster, and sickness, and discomfort, they have done that duty bravely and well." The Mayor, in proposing the toast of "The Carbineers," made two promises; first, of a medal to the survivors, if not offered by the Mother Country then by the Colony, and second, of a public monument to the memory of the fallen. In reply, Captain Shepstone, for himself and his comrades standing up around him, assured their entertainers that they would sooner have gone into action again and again than be overwhelmed by the kindness that awaited them at home. The Chief Justice, Sir Henry Connor, proposed the toast, drunk in solemn silence, of "The Memory of the Fallen," and insisted that to fall in battle, as they knew from the days of their Latin Grammar, was an honourable and a beautiful thing, and to call his task a melancholy one was the last thing in the world that he could think of. He knew some of those who had fallen, and when he remembered them now, he remembered them with this recollection, "They have fallen at Isandhlwana," and that brought them back before him with a halo round them which they would never have had had they not fallen so. If they were dead their memory bloomed over their graves. He remembered very well at the Crimean war there was a song going about connected with the Alma, the refrain of which was:—

> "What will they say in England?
> What will they say in England?
> They will say, 'It is nobly done'."

And that was what had been said in England regarding the Carbineers, 'It was nobly done.'

Captain Shepstone then made two presentations from the Carbineers; the one to Lieutenant Royston, of a gold watch and an address, the other, of a handsome time-piece and an address, to "Old Holliday."

Other speakers were, Mr. J. W. Akerman, M.L.C., Major-General Clifford, Colonel Mitchell, Lieutenant Royston, and Mr. J. D. Holliday.

In a despatch to the Lieutenant-Governor, the Secretary of State for the Colonies writes:—"Her Majesty has desired the Secretary of State for the Colonies to express to the Government of Natal, her indebtedness to the local volunteers for the services rendered by them in the recent operations in Zululand, and at the same time to make known her sense of their admirable behaviour on all occasions when employed before the enemy."

More than three years after the Carbineers had left Maritzburg for the front, on the 17th December, 1881, at the distribution of medals on the market square to those who had been in the Zulu campaign, Sir Evelyn Wood, who presided, said:— "We have learnt much from the war, but in my opinion nothing so remarkable as the devotion to duty shown by the Natal Carbineers and Newcastle Mounted Rifles. When these corps left Isandhlwana on 21st January, 1879, for Matyana's district, there remained in the camp 25 men (?Carbineers 28), who were mostly employed on outpost duty. Seven of these, separated from their troops next day, managed to escape, and, with one exception, reached Helpmakaar together and unshaken. I have only now heard of a gallant act performed by the straggler whose late arrival is well explained by his having, during the retreat, given up his horse to an officer who was exhausted. Into this matter it will be my pleasing duty to enquire further. These Carbineers, hearing at Helpmakaar, that their commanding officer, Mr. Offy Shepstone (whom I am glad to see here to-day), had got to Rorke's Drift, immediately rejoined him. Those who remember the state of feeling induced by events of that time will justly appreciate this soldier-like action. I have been three times to the spot where the remainder laid down their lives, and was on the first occasion accompanied by men who had fought with us and a Zulu induna who fought against us. He took part in the annihilation of your comrades who disdained to fly, and what I learned from him, and from others on each succeeding visit, has increased my admiration for those Natal Carbineers and Newcastle Mounted Rifles who stood and fell round Colonel Durnford. No greater proof of devotion was ever given by a body of soldiers. Let us recall the scene. These men were sent forward to check the advance of the Zulu army on the camp. Pushed back by ever increasing and overwhelming numbers, they formed up at last on that gentle slope where the monument to an officer who fell with them has now been erected by his widow. In front of them and to their right crept on a restless surging wave of black bodies which, though constantly smitten with leaden hail, broke but to sweep on again with renewed force. Half a mile in their left rear stood the Nodwengu regiment, as yet motionless, but ready to complete the death closing circle. Past this devoted band there rushed a terrified crowd of non-combatants, hurrying from the already burning camp, through the rapidly narrowing outlet, over the fatal Nek. But all this confusion, and the certainty of a cruel death, served but to deepen the resolution to cover the retreat. There they stood; there they fought; and there they died. The record of what colonist soldiers did is there in silence and in death, but none the less a living record now, aye, and for ever."

A tablet erected in St. Peter's Cathedral is inscribed:—
"In memory of the Natal Carbineers, and other Colonial Volunteer Corps, who fell with Colonel Durnford, R.E., on the fatal day of Isandhlwana, January 22nd, 1879.
'Stranger, tell England we died doing our duty.'
(Here follow the names of those killed).
This tablet is erected by their admiring fellow-colonists and comrades."

CAMP, REITSPRUIT, 1892.

Top Row—Qr.-Master Lyle, Capt. W. S. Shepstone, Capt. C. E. Taunton, Capt. D. McKenzie, Lieut. C. G. Willson, Lieut. W. G. M. Sinclair, Lieut. J. McKenzie, Lieut. W. A. Vanderplank.
Second Row—Lieut. A. Hair, Capt. and Adjutant J. Weighton, Major G. J. Macfarlane, Lt.-Col. E. M. Greene, O.C., Capt. C. B. Addison, Capt. G. Ross, Surgeon Captain J. Hyslop, Surgeon Lieut. G. C. Henderson, Lieut. G. F. Tatham.
Lying Down—Lieut. W. A. Tilney, Lieut. F. E. Foxon, Lieut. C. A. Martin.

True to his promise made at the distribution of the Zulu war medals, Sir Evelyn Wood brought the conduct of Trooper W. W. Barker to the notice of the Horse Guards, unfortunately, however, without the result desired, as will be seen from the despatch in reply to his application.

"Horse Guards, War Office,
10th March, 1882.

"Major-General Sir Evelyn Wood, V.C., etc., etc. Sir,— I am directed by the Field Marshal Commanding in Chief to acknowledge your letter of 6th instant, and to acquaint you in reply, that the statements re Trooper Barker, Natal Carbineers, at the battle of Isandhlwana, on 22nd January, 1879, having been carefully considered, His Royal Highness desires me to state that, while Trooper Barker's conduct on the occasion referred to is deserving of every commendation, there does not appear to be sufficient ground, according to the terms of the statute, for recommending him for the distinction of the Victoria Cross."

The crushing defeat at Ulundi, on the 4th July, 1879, broke the military power of the Zulus. A few weeks after, Cetywayo was captured and banished. The British Government having thus restored its honour, impaired at Isandhlwana, seemed in haste to wash its hands of Zululand. To escape the trouble and responsibility of governing, it partitioned the whole land among John Dunn, a Zuluised white man, and twelve native kinglets. This arrangement, though it multiplied the chances of internal strife, minimised the risk of a combined attack by the Zulus on the colonists of Natal and the Transvaal. The only semblance of authority which Britain retained in Zululand was the appointment of Sir Melmoth Osborn as Resident. But, like a watchdog with teeth drawn and claws pared, and good only for barking, the Resident had no power to interfere effectively between the jealous and rival kinglets, and only served to send timely warning when they were likely to break bounds and disturb the tranquillity of their white neighbours. It is to the honour of Sir Melmoth that, though his life was threatened again and again, he held tenaciously to his difficult and thankless post till, after the Boers under Lucas Meyer had "come cranking in and cut from the best of all the land a huge half-moon, a monstrous cantle out," what was left of Zululand was annexed by the British Government in 1887 and incorporated with their Colony of Natal.

CHAPTER IX.

THE BOER WAR, 1899-1902.

After the British defeat at Amajuba, and the subsequent retrocession of the Transvaal to the victorious Boers, the ardent loyalty of the colonists of Natal seemed all of a sudden to sink almost to extinction. But it was alive nevertheless, and as warm as ever. Its apparent diminution was the result partly of their vexation that, while they saw clearly what political wisdom required to be done for progress and freedom in their corner of the Empire, the leaders of the English Parliament appeared to be blind to it; partly of anger that they and the other loyalists of South Africa had been so lightly and heartlessly sacrificed to the Boers. For years, and with growing impatience, they watched the increasing arrogance and tyranny of the Transvaal oligarchy, in the expectation, rising at length to certainty, that the time was coming when the cup of Boer iniquity would be full and the Home Government be forced to reverse the Gladstonian policy. The accession of Mr. Chamberlain to the Colonial Office, with his firm and well-known conviction of the importance of Britain beyond the Seas, and his sympathy with the feelings of colonists, was the first sign to Natalians that a new order of things would soon begin in South Africa. Then followed in close succession, and in the same hopeful direction, the appointment of Sir Alfred Milner, as High Commissioner; his quick perception of the real object of the Boers of Graaf-Reinet:—"Loyal! it would be monstrous if you were not"; and his conference with Paul Kruger at Bloemfontein as the forlorn hope of peace.

The discovery of the rich gold fields of the Witwatersrand not only saved the Dutch Government of the Transvaal from fast approaching bankruptcy, but poured into their hands, as they thought, the means of realising an idea which had taken possession of their minds since Amajuba, viz., of ousting British rule from South Africa and erecting a Dutch Republic which should extend from Cape Town to the Zambezi. With this object in view they spent, but secretly under the name of public works, a large part of their annual revenue, which in ten years had increased twentyfold, in the purchase of guns, rifles, and ammunition, and the hire of trained artillerymen, from

France and Germany. They also built forts, in Johannesburg to overawe and quell the Uitlanders, and around Pretoria as bulwarks of that city's protection. The Uitlanders were forbidden to own firearms of any kind, and though they outnumbered the Burghers, and contributed at least nine-tenths of the revenue that flowed into the public treasury, they were denied civil rights and the smallest voice in the control and distribution of the finances. When they clamoured for the franchise, it was promised them on their fulfilment of certain conditions that at first seemed fair and realisable. But as the time drew near when the conditions would soon be complied with, new laws were again and again passed which raised the qualifications required for enfranchisement, till it became clear that there was no intention to admit the Uitlanders to burgher rights. The promised franchise was like the mirage of the desert; it vanished as it was approached. Paul Kruger and his clique, like the witches in Macbeth, paltered with the Uitlanders in a double sense, they kept the word of promise to the ear but broke it to the hope. Their determination to keep political power exclusively to themselves was revealed by the President himself, in an unwary moment, when he replied to an advocate of the Uitlanders, "You see that flag? If I grant the franchise, I may as well pull it down." In reality it was not a republic that the Transvaal was zealous to maintain, but an oligarchy by the Boer minority of its inhabitants. In the Cape Colony and Natal, Dutch and British colonists were politically on an equality; but in the Transvaal Republic, British subjects were the helots of the Dutch. The injustice of the Boer Government towards the British advanced so near to the end of human endurance that in March, 1899, a petition, signed by 21,000 of them, was sent Home containing a statement of their grievances and a prayer that Her Majesty, as Suzerain of the Transvaal, would protect her subjects there, secure a reform of the abuses they complained of, and a recognition of their rights. Sir Alfred Milner, in a despatch to Mr. Chamberlain, informed him that the position of the Uitlanders was intolerable and that the case for intervention was overwhelming. On the 30th May, at Bloemfontein, the High Commissioner met the Presidents of the two Dutch Republics in conference. He insisted on the redress of the Uitlanders' grievances, but as President Kruger's concessions were unsatisfactory, the conference came to nothing.

The propaganda of Dutch republicanism, which had its

headquarters in Pretoria, was a specially bitter grievance to loyal Natalians, because it was inciting within their borders to a civil war for which neither they nor their Government had given the slightest provocation. For more than half a century Britons and Boers had lived in Natal side by side in amity. In markets and agricultural shows, sports, and rifle associations, they had bargained and vied with one another to their mutual advantage and enjoyment. The Government of Natal had treated both races alike, or, if it had made any difference between them, the balance of favour had been on the side of the Boers. The town constituencies, which were almost exclusively British, returned fewer members of Parliament, in proportion to the number of voters, than those of the country; and consequently, at the outbreak of the Boer war, Natal had what was with good reason called a farmers' Parliament. The system of farmhouse schools carried education, in Dutch as well as in English, to isolated and outlying families all over the Colony. And it was the Dutch farmers of Umvoti, Klip River, and Weenen Counties who primarily enjoyed that security of life and property which the Imperial Government had won for South Africa when it broke the power of the Zulus in 1879. In short, Natal had enabled Briton and Boer to live together in peace and comfort in the only way possible, by treating both alike on a footing of equality. And what return were the Natal British to get from their Boer fellow-colonists for having dealt with them as brothers? As time passed on after the declaration of war, colonial towns, occupied almost entirely by British tradesmen and artisans, were seized and plundered; the homesteads of British farmers, as far south as Mooi River, were singled out by former neighbours for wanton destruction; and if the Boers had taken Maritzburg, as they were confident they would, their intention was, and they did not blush to avow it, to hold the women and children as hostages for the surrender of Natal. Within a few weeks from the outbreak of the war there seemed to be nothing, except the dilatoriness of the Boers themselves, to prevent the greeting, telegraphed to the Transvaal President by General Louis Botha when he began his march to invade Natal, from being temporarily fulfilled, "May the Vierkleur soon wave over a free harbour." And all this misery and humiliation was intended, and in part accomplished, for the realisation of a vain dream of an Africander Republic from the Zambezi to Cape Town—a dream that the leaders of the Africander Bond had beguiled the ignorant and bigoted Boers with for twenty preceding years.

To appreciate the feelings and aims of the South African Dutch it is necessary to recall to mind how they fretted under the stringent rule of the British, their grievances which they attributed to it, and the sacrifices which they made to escape from it throughout the whole course of the century which closed with their effort to expel it from South Africa. The Voortrekkers of 1837 left their homes in the Cape Colony, thereby renouncing for ever, as they believed, the control of the British over them, with the purpose, publicly declared by them at their exodus, to seek peacefully and honestly for a home for themselves in the wilderness. The fair and fertile land of Natal, swept almost clean of human beings by Chaka, the Attila of South-East Africa, invited them to end their wanderings in it, and they claimed to have won a freehold title to it by their victory over Dingaan at the Blood River. After a fruitless struggle to retain it, and smarting with the sense that they had been wrongfully dispossessed, they relin-- quished the prize to which Great Britain asserted and enforced her prior claim. Resuming their trek, they found across the Vaal River a settlement ample enough to gratify to the full their love of isolation and individualism, and there for a whole generation they lived their own manner of life, almost free from authority of any kind and entirely liberated from alien interference. The Transvaal Boers of 1899, were the sons and grandsons of the Voortrekkers and the heirs of their spirit and traditions. At the close of the year 1880, they began what everybody outside their borders scoffed at as a hopeless war to undo the British annexation of their country in 1877, and in three months' time they ended it with a world's wonder—their acquisition of self-government under the suzerainty of Great Britain. Elated by the result of their successful skirmish at Amajuba, magnified by them into a Marathonian triumph, and enriched with the gold which they drew without toil and in ever increasing volume from the mines of Johannesburg, they would have been more than human if they had not grown to count their prowess as invincible and their resources as unfailing, and to arrogate to themselves, a numerically insignificant band of simple farmers, the right to keep in perpetual subordination the growing multitude of immigrant Uitlanders from Britain, America, Germany, and France, the strongest and most enlightened countries of the world. Their courage might win applause from brave men, but their infatuation could only be deplored by their best friends. They had to learn with pain and disappointment the lesson which reason and history should have taught them, that their endeavours to arrest the onward march of civilization and enterprize in South Africa would be as futile as Mrs. Partington's to sweep back the tide of the Atlantic with her mop.

On the 22nd September, Mr. Chamberlain broke off the unavailing attempts,—which he had continued, with unexpected patience, much longer than was consistent with prudent consideration for British supremacy in South Africa,—to persuade the Transvaal Government to deal justly and fairly with the Uitlanders. In a despatch of that date he informed President Kruger that it was useless to continue the discussion which had lasted for months, and that the British Government would consider the matter afresh and make their own proposals for the settlement of the question. To that despatch President Kruger replied on the 9th October, with the concurrence of President Steyn of the Free State, with an ultimatum which was to be accepted by the British Government, or war would be declared by the two Dutch Republics, within forty-eight hours. The ultimatum demanded:—(1) That all British troops near the border should be instantly withdrawn. (2) That all recently arrived reinforcements should be removed from South Africa. (3) That the troops then on the sea should not be landed. Of course the answer to this "audacious defiance," as Lord Salisbury termed it, could be no other than instant rejection.

The official reply from London, dated 10th October and despatched through Sir Alfred Milner, was in these words:— "Her Majesty's Government have received with great regret the peremptory demands of the Government of the South African Republic, conveyed in your telegram of the 9th October. You will inform the Government of the South African Republic in reply that the conditions demanded by the Government of the South African Republic are such as her Majesty's Government deem it impossible to discuss."

Mr. Conyngham Greene, Her Majesty's representative in the Transvaal, at once quitted Pretoria, and the Boers hurried on their preparations for the invasion of Natal.

Natalians, thoroughly convinced that under Mr. Chamberlain and Sir Alfred Milner there would be no repetition of the Amajuba surrender, and knowing besides that it was not the Transvaal only that was at stake now, as in the Boer War of 1881, but the whole of British South Africa, at once took up arms and entered with grim determination on the long-foreseen conflict. The whole Empire knows, and has handsomely acknowledged, the loyal service rendered by Natal in the three years' war that began in 1899.

In anticipation of an inevitable war between the South African Republic and the British Empire, the officer commanding the Natal Carbineers had taken steps to prepare his regiment to mobilize at the shortest notice. Mobilization orders, with the date left blank, had been issued to all squadron officers, and it only required a telegram of one word to each squadron leader to set the whole regimental machinery in motion. At last the day arrived when Briton was ordered out to face Boer, for on the morning of the 29th September, 1899, the day after President Kruger commandeered his burghers, orders were received for the Regiment to mobilize for active service. The "one word" was duly wired to each squadron leader, and the Carbineers were once again buckling on their armour.

At this time the Natal Carbineers Regiment was officered as follows:—

STAFF:

Lieut-Colonel E. M. Greene, Commanding.
Major C. E. Taunton. Major D. McKenzie.
Major G. J. Macfarlane. Major C. B. Addison.
Captain J. Weighton, Adjutant.
Captain A. Lyle, Quartermaster.

SQUADRON OFFICERS:

No. 1 Squadron (Head Quarters).
Lieut. C. N. H. Rodwell; Lieut. A. C. Townsend; Lieut. W. E. C. Tanner.

No. 2 Squadron (Head Quarters).
Capt. W. S. Shepstone; Lieut. W. J. Gallwey; Lieut. G. W. Nourse.

No. 3 Squadron (Nottingham Road and Camperdown).
Capt. A. Hair; Lieut. B. Crompton; Lieut. W. Bartholomew.

No. 4 Squadron (Richmond and Richmond Road).
Capt. F. E. Foxon; Lieut. E. Lucas; Lieut. W. Comrie.

No. 5 Squadron (Estcourt and Weenen).
Lieut. D. W. Mackay.

No. 6 Squadron (Ladysmith).
Lieut. G. F. Tatham; Lieut. D. Sparks.
No. 7 Squadron (Dundee and Newcastle).
Capt. C. G. Willson; Lieut. W. A. Vanderplank; Lieut. W. T. Gage.

During the campaign there were promoted to commissioned rank:—as Lieutenants, A. W. Smallie, T. M. Owen, R. Ashburnham, J. P. S. Woods, T. Duff, R. A. Cockburn, and A. Wylde-Browne; and promotions amongst the officers were:— Capt. Weighton to be Major; Lieutenants Rodwell, Nourse, Crompton and Lucas to be Captains.

Lieut. T. M. Owen was appointed Paymaster to the Volunteer Brigade and remained in Maritzburg where he did excellent service during the campaign.

Captain Crompton, upon promotion, was given command of No. 3 Squadron, Captain Hair taking over the command of No. 5 Squadron.

Captain G. F. Tatham was, early in the siege of Ladysmith, placed on the Volunteer Brigade Staff, and continued in that position till the relief.

Lieut. Ashburnham obtained leave to proceed to England in March, 1900, and did not return.

The following officers of the Natal Medical Corps were attached to the Regiment from time to time, and their services were very highly appreciated:—Captains O. J. Currie and R. A. Buntine, and Lieutenants H. B. Currie and J. E. Briscoe (attached to No. 5 Squadron on the Relief Column). There were also attached from time to time the following Veterinary Surgeons:—Lieutenants J. P. Byrne, F. Verney (No. 5 Squadron, Relief Column), and S. T. Amos.

At the outbreak of the war, and during the siege of Ladysmith, the Regimental Sergt.-Major was that smart little soldier "Benny" Bowen, late 3rd Dragoon Guards. When the Regiment reached Highlands after the siege he fell ill of enteric fever and succumbed to the disease. He was an excellent warrant officer, and all the time he was with the Carbineers he was most popular. As his successor the Regiment was fortunate in securing Staff Sergt. W. Burkimsher of the 9th Lancers, a man who in every way has proved himself worthy of the responsible position which he still holds.

By the evening of the 1st October, Nos. 1, 2, 3, 4, and 6 squadrons were in Ladysmith. Two or three days later they were joined there by the Newcastle troop, and on the 26th October by that of Dundee, owing to the evacuation of the towns from

Memorial erected by the Regiment at Isandhlwana to the Memory of the Members who fell on January 22nd, 1879.

Memorial to the Natal Carbineers who fell at Bushman's Pass, 1873.

which these troops respectively took their names. The Ladysmith squadron, being composed of local men, was detailed to furnish guides for practically every unit in the garrison as well as for units on outpost duty, and the services rendered by them in that capacity were highly appreciated. The remaining squadron, No. 5 of Estcourt and Weenen, kept to their own recruiting ground. Under the command of the gallant and capable Major Duncan McKenzie, who had hurried back from England to take his place in the Regiment, the men of that squadron, by their thorough knowledge of the ground, which for months to come was to be the scene of the fiercest fighting in the whole course of the war, and their acquaintance with the ways and wiles of the enemy, could not fail to be of value in the field out of all proportion to their weakness in number.

Short of abandoning the cause of the Uitlanders altogether the British Government did everything in their power to avoid war in South Africa. They indicated their readiness to accept the least concessions from the Transvaal that would deliver their clients from degrading subservience; and even when their relations with the Republics were strained to the breaking point, they purposely refrained from taking the legitimate and prudential steps necessary for the defence of their South African colonies, lest such action on their side should be taken on the other as a challenge. In the middle of August, the total strength of the Imperial force for the defence of the frontier, marching for hundreds of miles with the Dutch Republics, was little over 6,000 men, consisting of two regiments of cavalry, three batteries of field artillery, and six and a half battalions of infantry. At such a crisis so ill met it is not surprising that Lord Wolseley, the responsible administrator of the war department, losing patience with the diplomatists still eagerly straining after a hopeless peace, wrote to the Secretary of State on the 3rd September:—"We have committed one of the greatest blunders in war, namely, we have given the enemy the initiative. He is in a position to take the offensive and, by striking the first blow, to ensure the great advantage of winning the first round."

The Home Government's blunder, a failing which leaned to virtue's side, was foreseen by South African loyalists long before it was pointed out by the Commander-in-Chief, and as early as July, the attention of the Colonial Office was indirectly and ineffectually called to it by the Government of Natal in a comparative statement of the weakness of their colony, and the strength of the Transvaal. On the 6th of September they sent a second and more pressing appeal for help, which was so far successful that before the end of the month the Imperial forces in the two South African colonies were raised to 22,000 men by reinforcements from India and the Mediterranean. Thankful for this small relief, and yet aware of its inadequacy, the Natal Government unfortunately impaired its insufficiency still further by a blunder of their own. Sir George White, who had just then come to take supreme command of the troops in Natal, would have drawn and kept together the army of 12,000 men allotted to him, but advised by the Civil Government of the importance of the coal fields, and assured by General Penn Symons that the force of 4,000 under him at Dundee was sufficient for their protection, he courteously allowed his better judgement to be overruled for a time. The mistake was proved and paid for a short while after.

It was on the 20th October that the first battle of the war was fought. Early in the morning of that day, the troops, under General Penn Symons, suddenly discovered that Talana Hill, which overlooked their camp and the town of Dundee, was occupied by the enemy in force. At once the cavalry were sent round the left flank of the Boers to intercept their retreat, the guns moved forward, unlimbered and came into action in front at a range of 2,300 yards, and the infantry were ordered to the enemy's right to storm the hill on that side. The three lines of the Dublin Fusiliers, the Rifles, and the Irish Fusiliers passed the first 1,000 yards of the advance with few casualties and reached the plantation which stretched half-way up the hill. Between it and a rough stone wall which ran below the summit, there lay an open space, several hundreds of yards across. It was a fire zone such as the Gordons rushed through at Dargai. Starting from the wood their losses were heavy, among them the brave but over sanguine Penn Symons, before they reached the shelter of the wall. Under its cover, they sorted themselves, and took breath to face the 200 yards of boulder-strewn steep that rose above them. Gallantly led by their officers, and pelted by the Boer riflemen in front and shrapnell from their own artillery behind them, they scrambled their way up, and the hill was won and cleared. The British loss was 41 killed and 180 wounded in the engagement, and 200 cavalry—18th Hussars and mounted infantry of the Dublin Fusiliers and the Rifles—surrounded and taken prisoners by the Boers in their retreat. And what was gained by the victory of Talana? It had a two-fold moral gain: the Empire was reassured that as in the past there was scarcely a task in war too arduous for the

British soldier, and the Boers were undeceived of their delusion that the conquest of Natal was to be made with but little trouble.

The day after the battle the Boers mounted guns, superior in weight and range to those of their enemy, on Impati, a hill farther than Talana from Dundee, and began, in security to themselves, to shell the town and the British position. Shifting his camp out of range, Colonel Yule, who succeeded General Penn Symons, hoped that with reinforcements from Ladysmith he might still be able to guard the collieries, and he telegraphed his plan to General White. The answer was:—"I cannot reinforce you without sacrificing Ladysmith and the Colony behind. You must try to fall back on Ladysmith. I will do what I may to help you when nearer." So there was nothing for it but to evacuate Dundee. On the 22nd the retreat began, under the expert guidance of Colonel Dartnell of the Natal Mounted Police, and by a circuitous route well to the eastward of the railway, for it was known that the line had been cut by the Boers.

On the 21st October, the day after Talana, Sir George White sent out General French with a sufficient force to restore railway communication with his detachment at Dundee. As soon as the British topped the rise above Elandslaagte the Boers hurriedly left the station there, and, on the hills behind it, took up a strong position fortified by the two Maxim-Nordenfelds taken nearly four years ago from the Jameson raiders. The Boer stronghold had to be approached over a series of heights and hollows that alternately exposed and hid General French's advancing lines. The enemy resisted stoutly to the very end, but the four attacking battalions, in spite of their serious losses, pressed forward unflinchingly, each straining emulously of the others, to reach the same end—the Devons, the Manchesters, the Gordons determined to erase the blot of Amajuba from their regimental records, and the Imperial Light Horse, composed of refugees from the Rand, burning to requite their tormentors for the insults they had had to bear from the failure of Jameson's raid till their ignominious expulsion from Johannesburg. At the point of the bayonet, and shouting "Majuba, Majuba!" they carried the summit and drove off or captured the last of its defenders. The flight of the Boers was turned into a rout when the Lancers and Dragoons, who had stolen round the hill-foot to the rear, charged through the scattered fugitives once and again before the darkness fell. The line of rail between Ladysmith and Dundee was again clear of obstruction, but except for the capture of the Boer guns, stores, and prisoners, Elandslaagte, like Talana, was a victory of the Pyrrhic kind. The day following, owing to the swarming of the Free State Boers as for the assault of Ladysmith, General White ordered French's force to return with their utmost speed.

Mindful of his promise to General Yule, Sir George White on the 24th marched from Ladysmith, with as large a force as could safely be spared from the garrison there, and drew up his lines at Rietfontein, about seven miles to the north-east. As usual the Boers were in a strong posture of defence. They occupied the hill of Tinta Inyoni on which they had contrived to drag up some of their guns of heavy calibre. General White on his part had no mind to dislodge the enemy, while the Boers, conceiving that to be his aim, kept on the defensive most of the day. His object was to hold them where they were, and so prevent them from intercepting the Dundee column, now little more than a day's march from Ladysmith. The affair of Rietfontein should have been only an artillery duel; but the Gloucesters, by some mischance whose explanation was lost by the death of the Colonel, advancing as if to the assault, exposed themselves needlessly to the fire of the enemy's riflemen. Their losses were, their commanding officer and five men killed, and forty wounded. The Natal Carbineers, too, ordered from the right flank, to counter an outflanking manoeuvre of the enemy on the British left, came under a destructive fire. They lost, in killed, Sergt. A. E. Colville and Trooper W. Cleaver, and in wounded, Troopers E. Taylor, E. Russel, W. J. Freeman, R. A. Richmond, P. Ballantyne, G. W. Teasdale, R. J. Raw, R. J. Mason, and E. E. Smith. At the close of a day designedly consumed in Fabian tactics, Sir George White led his men back to Ladysmith. Early in the morning of the 26th, the column from Dundee, smeared with mud, hungry, dazed from want of sleep, but not dispirited, was received with cheers of admiration and welcome by the garrison in Ladysmith. The Boers had been staved off, the retreat of the 4,000 skilfully and successfully conducted, and the blunder of the Natal Government rectified at last; but the achievement of it all had cost a high price in lives and suffering.

It would have been too much to expect of brave men that they should submit to a blockade without a struggle. Besides, they foresaw that in the case of a siege, Long Hill and Pepworth Hill, each about four miles distant, would be invaluable either as bulwarks for the defence, or stations for the bombardment of the town. For these reasons it was decided to offer battle on

Monday the 30th. A bold plan of operations for that day was carefully prepared, but in its execution it went sadly awry, partly by misfortune and partly owing to an underestimate of the enemy's strength in position and numbers. On the eve of the battle a force of 1,100 men, with a battery of mountain guns on pack mules, set out under the command of Colonel Carleton to occupy Nicholson's Nek and protect the left flank of the fighting line. About the same time the Natal Carbineers were sent out to the far right, with orders to hold the Nek between Lombard's Kop and Bulwana at all costs, so that they might keep, for General French's cavalry in their rear, a safe passage when the right time came for the intended charge on the Boer left. With two squadrons Colonel Greene held Bulwana, and Major Macfarlane with one squadron held Lombard's Kop. At midnight the infantry and artillery commanded by Colonel Grimwood moved out to take post for the attack of Long Hill, and a body of reserves under Colonel Ian Hamilton followed them a few hours later.

On the way to Nicholson's Nek, Carleton's mules unaccountably took fright and stampeded, carrying with them the mountain guns and all the ammunition except what had been served out to the men. Fearing to press on to the Nek, Carleton climbed the nearest koppie, and there, surrounded and more than decimated by riflemen under cover, after fighting till their ammunition was spent, 37 officers and 917 men, the survivors of the party that should have covered General White's left flank, surrendered to the Boers.

As the battle developed in the morning General French, on the right wing, was surprised to find that the enemy's line extended far beyond what was presupposed to be its limit on the south-east, and it needed all his vigilance and skill to save himself from being surrounded and cut off. The head of Colonel Grimwood's column marched straight to the post assigned to it, but in the dark the guns in the middle and the infantry following them turned off to the left. When daylight came Colonel Grimwood, without guns and with only half his infantry, found his task too much for him, and from that time onward, while the battle lasted, he had again and again to send for reinforcements, both from the stray part of his own column and from the reserves, to enable him to hold his own. Before midday, Sir George White was aware that his plan had miscarried, but what at last settled his wavering decision was a message from Colonel Knox, in charge of the small garrison left in Ladysmith, that the Free State Boers were threatening the town from the south-west. The retreat was ordered, and the retiring infantry was successfully protected by the energy and self-sacrificing heroism of the gunners. If the British had an unpleasant surprise at the extent of the enemy's line, they got another of quite a different sort when a shell flew over their heads and exploded far beyond any that had been shot from their batteries that day. Captain Lambton came on the field, just in time to cheer the one side and depress the other, with a naval gun that was a match for the Boer "Long Tom." In Ladysmith the civilians—most of them refugees from Dundee and elsewhere in northern Natal, and even from the Transvaal—were panic-stricken ever since the first shell from Long Tom on Pepworth Hill burst over them in the morning; and when they saw the troops returning, wearied and in disarray, they read in the sight the signs, not merely of an unsuccessful battle, but of a lost cause. The sinister name of "Mournful Monday," given to the day of the unlucky engagement, indicated the popular view of the situation.

In three days more, the investment of Ladysmith was complete. During these days of grace stores were hurried in, and many useless mouths got rid of by rail. Amongst the last who left before the town was hemmed in was General French; but he to give, on other scenes of the theatre of war, a splendid display of the knowledge of the Boers and their method of fighting which he had gained by a few days of acting in Natal.

The week that followed the closing of the line of railway running south, the last door of exit from Ladysmith, was spent by the antagonists within and around the town in making preparations to accomplish the tasks which they had severally and deliberately undertaken—by the besiegers, to harass and subdue, and by the besieged, to endure and repel.

On the 9th November, a section of the enemy, more venturesome and impatient than the rest, exchanged the security of their entrenchments for the risk of an open attack; but their onset, feebly supported and due to impulse more than sound judgement was easily met and driven back. As this abortive essay happened on the birthday of the Prince of Wales, the garrison showed their loyalty by firing a salute of 21 shotted guns into the enemy's lines. On both sides there ensued weeks of lull—the situation relative to each other in which they found themselves being considered. The Boers contented themselves with keeping a firm grip on what they complacently regarded as their prize, while they detached spare commandos to raid Natal to the south and east; and Sir George White was satisfied to detain the bulk of their forces around him in the expectation of relief before long.

The monotony of the exchange of shells day after day between the British and the Boers was broken on the morning of the 8th December. Of all the Boer gunners, those on Gun Hill seemed to enjoy more than their fair share of the pastime of shelling Ladysmith, and it was resolved that they should be deprived for a time of the means of keeping up that sport. For this purpose Sir Archibald Hunter led out 500 Natal Volunteers and 100 Imperial Light Horse to surprise Gun Hill; but up to the moment of setting out he kept not only the men but even the officers in ignorance of the business in hand, for it was suspected that sometimes military information, which should have been confined to the garrison, had somehow been conveyed to the enemy. Leaving Ladysmith before midnight, and guided by Major Henderson of the Argyll and Sutherland Highlanders, they reached the foot of Gun Hill at 2 a.m. There General Hunter left Major Rethman with 100 of the Border Mounted Rifles to protect his left flank, and Colonel Royston with 300 men of the Natal Carbineers, Border Mounted Rifles, and Natal Mounted Rifles, to guard his right. The rest of his party, 100 of the Imperial Light Horse under Colonel Edwards and Major Karri Davies, and 100 Natal Carbineers officered by Major Addison, Captain and Adjutant Weighton, Captain Foxon, and Lieutenants Bartholomew and Vanderplank, began to scale the almost perpendicular rock that rose above them. Using the utmost caution, even slipping off their boots, to creep up in silence, they had climbed to within a few yards of the summit unnoticed, when there was a faint challenge, "Wie daar?" followed in an agonized shriek by "Schiet, Stephanus, hier kom de verdomde rooineks, schiet, schiet!" and then one wild volley was fired on them by the alarmed and excited guard. "Come on, boys. Fix bayonets," shouted Captain Foxon. The word "bayonets" alone, for the things it stands for were not there, had a magical effect; it was the "Hey, presto" at which the Boer piquet vanished on the instant, leaving everything, even their private documents and letters, behind them. The Imperial Light Horse rushed on "Long Tom," the Carbineers found the howitzer; then a charge of gun cotton wrapped round the breech and muzzle of them and exploded by Captain Fowke and Lieutenant Turner of the Royal Engineers, and these two guns could harm Ladysmith no more. Their task accomplished, they left Gun Hill. At daylight they marched into town in triumph, carrying with them the breech-blocks of the two big guns, and dragging two maxims which they had captured on their way back, as the trophies of their night's work. In the course of the day, Sir George White paraded the whole Volunteer Brigade, and after thanking those of them who had taken part in the previous night's expedition, he complimented them all on their conduct generally, which, he said, was "a credit to the Empire." In addition to this public recognition by the General, the Carbineers were gladdened with a congratulatory letter from the Gordon Highlanders with whom they were on excellent terms.

Official reports of the exploit of the Volunteers, from two sources the most interested in it, Ladysmith and Pretoria, were published in Maritzburg simultaneously a few days after the event.

From Sir George White:—"9th December. Last night I sent out General Hunter with 500 Volunteers under Royston, and 100 Imperial Light Horse under Edwards, to surprise Gun Hill. The surprise was admirably carried out and was entirely successful, the Hill being captured, and a 6 inch gun and a 4.7 inch howitzer destroyed with gun cotton by Captain Fowke and Lieutenant Turner, R.E., and a maxim was captured and brought to Ladysmith. Our loss: One man killed; Major Henderson, Argyll and Sutherland Highlanders, wounded; two men slightly wounded."

"Pretoria, 9th December:—The British at Ladysmith scored a success between one and two in the morning. A body of men crawled up the ravine and carried one of the Kopjes constituting the Lombard's Kop Boer position on which one big creusot and one howitzer were put out of action with dynamite, after which the force retired. Major Erasmus and Lieutenant Malan will be court-martialed in connection with the loss of the cannon. Besides the big guns the Boers also lost two maxims."

Those who were in Maritzburg at the time will not readily forget with what pride these paragraphs were read and re-read by old and young. They struck an exultant chord in the hearts of Natalians everywhere, for they told of a glorious feat by "Our Boys."

In emulation of the success of the Volunteers at Gun Hill, four companies of the 2nd Rifle Brigade set out on the night of the 11th to destroy a 4.7 inch howitzer on Surprise Hill. But it was hardly to be hoped that the enemy would be taken at unawares again in a similar fashion, and after so short an interval. The Rifles drove off the guard from the hill and

Colonel Sir DUNCAN MCKENZIE K.C.M.G., C.B., V.D.,
Commanded Regiment 1903 to 1906

destroyed the gun, but were waylaid as they were returning and suffered the loss of 11 killed, 43 wounded, and 6 missing.

As the new year opened there was evidence of a change of temper in the two belligerents. "Black week," the 10th to the 17th December, in which three British defeats were chronicled, fixed immovably in the defeated, both the Mother Country and her Colonies, the determination to fight to a finish this time; and elated the victors with the expectation that Magersfontein, Stormberg, and Colenso would be followed, as Lang's Nek, Ingogo, and Amajuba had been, with an offer of surrender from the British Government. But when the news spread among them that Lord Roberts was on the way out to take command of the British forces in South Africa, with Lord Kitchener as the chief of his staff, and that Sir Redvers Buller was recovering strength to force the passage of the Tugela, the Boers could not but conclude that the end was not yet and that, if it was necessary for them to repeat, with emphasis, the staggering blows of Magersfontein and Colenso, their commandos detained around Ladysmith must be set free without delay. The arguments of the younger and more enterprising section, urged by General Botha and Commandant De Wet, prevailed over the caution of General Joubert and the elders, and at a krijgsraad held on the 5th January, it was decided by a majority 'to finish the business of Ladysmith by assault off-hand instead of the tedious process of starvation.

The Platrand was the name given by the Boers to a plateau about two miles south of Ladysmith, 600 feet above the level of the Klip River, stretching more than two miles from east to west, and divided by two neks into three unequal lengths—Caesar's Camp, Waggon Hill, and Waggon Point. It was the key to Sir George White's circle of defence and was chosen by the Boers for the delivery of their attack next day (6th January), with a force of 4,000 men—2,000 from each of the Republics. At about three in the morning the sentry of the Imperial Light Horse on the Nek between Waggon Hill and Waggon Point, hearing some noise from the donga above which he was posted, challenged and fired. A volley and a rush of Boers followed. It happened that an extraordinary party of over 100 men, Sappers, Bluejackets, and Gordon Highlanders, were at work all that night preparing to mount a 4.7 inch naval gun on Waggon Point. On the outburst of firing these men left their work and hurried forward to the help of the handful of Imperial Light Horse. About an hour after the attack on Waggon Hill the other end of the Rand was assailed by the Transvaal storming party. They had slipped between the Manchester piquet at the east corner of Caesar's Camp and the patrols of Royston's Volunteer Brigade, and were making their way by the left flank to the rear of the Manchester position, when they were faced by a company of the Gordons, under Captain Carnegie, and gradually pushed back and round to the south front of the Platrand. From the beginning of the attack till daybreak, close and confused fighting was kept up all along the south face of the plateau, but fiercest at its extremities around the naval gun on Waggon Point and Manchester Fort on Caesar's Camp, each side where it was pressed attracting help from its supports. When the sun rose it showed that the assailants had effected a lodgment on the far edge of the summit from which, covered as they were by the outcrop of rock there, it would be hard to dislodge them. Soon, however, it was made manifest that their losses could not be repaired, and far less their original strength increased, by reinforcements from Bester's Valley behind them. Two batteries of artillery in rear of the Rand, the 53rd under Major Abdy at the east end, and the 21st under Major Blewitt at the west, firing over the heads of their infantry, poured such a storm of shrapnel on the reverse slope of the Platrand as made it impassable and kept the Boer reserves all day on the safe side of Fourie Spruit. By midday, though neither side could yet claim the victory, the Boers were morally defeated. The firing had almost ceased, and it was believed by the defenders that their enemy were just waiting for sundown to make a safe retreat. Suddenly, at one p.m., as if the preceding ten hours had never been, a rush was made as fresh as at first for the 4.7 inch naval gun at Waggon Point. It was bravely led by Commandant de Villiers and Field-Cornet de Jagers, but could only result in a grand spectacle of Homeric fighting and the sacrifice of brave lives on both sides. General Ian Hamilton, who had charge of the Platrand section of the Ladysmith defences, would have been content to hold the enemy where they were till nightfall, as much perhaps to spare the brave though foiled foe as his own exhausted men; but Sir George White, fearing that the assault might be prolonged to a two days' battle, gave orders to drive them from his precincts that day. From the opposite side of the town three companies of the Devons were summoned to make the final charge. Their line never wavered, though it showed many gaps before it covered the 130 yards of open ground, and at the point of the bayonet they cleared the Platrand of those who had clung to it so tenaciously for sixteen hours. The Boers fled before the bayonets, but not all of them to safety. A terrific thunderstorm in the afternoon had made a foaming torrent of the usually insignificant Fourie Spruit, and by its swollen waters many of the fugitives, too eagerly seeking escape from British bullets, were swept away. Ladysmith was saved by a part of its thin-drawn line of defenders, but at the cost of 424 in killed and wounded.

A result of the failure of the Boer attack on the 6th of January was to satisfy the garrison that their fortifications, manned by resolute defenders, were impregnable to Boer assaults. Its disheartening effect on the Boers was attested by the sudden access of "leave-plague" which raged without intermission, in spite of all the efforts of the commandants to suppress it, so long as they continued to laager around Ladysmith, and culminated, when at last the siege was raised, in the general cry of "Huis toe!"

The following paper, entitled "Within Beleaguered Ladysmith," was written primarily for the "Ladysmith Gazette," and appeared as its leading article, 3rd November, 1906, but with the ulterior object of its re-publication in these pages:—

"It is now seven years since the mind and heart of the whole British Empire began to be drawn irresistibly for a time to Ladysmith. For there the Dutch and British contestants for the prize of South African supremacy had at last come to grips, and it was felt, both by the two combatants and the world of onlookers that, whether Boer or Briton should ultimately win, the palm depended on the issue of that encounter. British sympathy with their beleaguered countrymen was of course but temporary, and the lapse of seven years, it may be hoped, has carried away with it the last remnants of suffering inflicted in the four months' siege; but each recurring anniversary revives the memory of both, and will recall it as long as our pride of race endures. As the siege went on the feelings of the British people in the Mother Country and the Sister Colonies—wrath at the sudden blockade, pity for the sufferers by it, irritated impatience of its long continuance, and delirious joy at its relief—were fully and freely made known. Not so, however, the innermost sentiments of those who struggled through and survived the four months' agony. The noble reticence of the brave man, arising from shame at his own momentary weakness and the desire to cheer the hearts of his less courageous fellow-sufferers, has buried in oblivion whatever of bitterness, complaint, and despair may have been thought or said when temper and patience were sorest tried. What we are permitted to know of the story of the siege of Ladysmith from within is not a full, true, and particular account of what must have been but a sad time throughout. It can hardly be doubted, that for pity's sake, a veil of forgetfulness is cast over many an instance of pardonable human frailty, and that much of the dark and gloomy tints required for a faithful picture has been purposely left out and the most has been made of the bright and cheerful.

"Just before the little town was invested train loads of faint hearts and useless mouths were sent down to Maritzburg. Even then there had to be a second sifting of the feeble from the strong, and a crowd of undesirables was relegated by Sir George White, with the consent of General Joubert, to the safety—within the lines of investment, but beyond the danger zone—of a neutral location which the garrison christened Fort Funk. After this process of exhaustion, which recalls that pursued by Gideon when he picked his small band of heroes, freed of "whatsoever was fearful and trembling," to fight the hosts of Midian, General White and a company of men, women, and children, all alike stout of heart though not equally strong of arm, were left within the narrow circle which was for four long months to be the unpitied target of the Boer artillery. They say that eels in time get used to skinning, and it was not long before the shrieking of the shells, at first a general horror, came by familiarity to be almost unheeded even by timid women and children. When a bombshell burst there would immediately follow a scramble by relic hunters for its fragments. Cave dwellings were hollowed out in the high banks of the Klip River, and when, on Big Ben, Long Tom, Black Jack, Silent Susan, Slim Piet, The Coughing Machine, Weary Willie, and others of the enemy's well-known guns becoming unusually troublesome, the townspeople left the streets temporarily for the river, they would facetiously intimate that they were gone for a change of scene and air to the Back Beach. Church services were kept up regularly all through the siege, for the townsfolk, morning and evening, in the wonted places of worship, and for the military in their lines. The defenders would have belied their national character and traditions if they had not beguiled dull care with amusements both out-of-door and indoor. King Henry V.'s soldiers, to while away their idle time at the siege of Rouen, made themselves a bowling green of which the traces still remain. Sir Francis Drake, while waiting for the Spanish Armada, amused himself with a game of bowls, and insisted on finishing his play before he would attend to business. Their descendants and successors at Ladysmith, in the intervals of serious duty, sought health and cheerfulness in cricket, polo, athletic sports, concerts, dances; and on quarter rations and Adam's ale they had the audacity to celebrate St. Andrew's Day, Christmas, and the New Year, if not duly, at least in a fashion that was both hearty and exceptional. Among many other signs of the garrison's determination to keep up their spirits, in spite of their many discouragements, was the publication of newspapers at short intervals during the four months. How these tried to sugar over whatever was essentially bitter may be gathered from the following extract from the "Ladysmith Bombshell" of 9th December, 1899.

> " 'For we're waiting, rather weary. Is there such a man as Clery?
> Are there any reinforcements? Is there any army corps?
> Shall we see our wives and mothers, or our sisters and our brothers?
> Shall we ever see those others who went southwards long before?
> Shall we ever taste fresh butter? Tell us, tell us, we implore.
> Shall be answered—"Nevermore."''

"It is sometimes said that most of Charles Dickens's characters are mere caricatures of real life; that Mark Tapley, for example, whose extraordinary craze to find himself in circumstances so miserable as to bring him credit for feeling jolly in them, had his prototype only in the writer's brain. But, as we grow in years and experience, to our astonishment we every now and again come across one of his children of real flesh and blood instead of, as he was to us before, paper and ink only. Whoever hears or reads the story of the siege, as told by any of the besieged, will say that not one but many a Mark Tapley must have been shut up in Ladysmith for four months seven years ago."

JOHN STALKER.

When it was known in Ladysmith, immediately before the battle of Colenso, that Sir Redvers Buller's preparations to force his way through the enemy's lines were nearly complete, Sir George White organized a Flying Column of four regiments of cavalry, four batteries of Royal Field Artillery, four battalions of infantry, fifteen mixed companies of infantry, and two detachments of colonial forces. This mobile column was exercised nightly and held in readiness to break out as soon as the opportune time should come to join hands with the column of relief. But in the course of the month of inaction that followed "Black Week," though the will of the garrison to strike a blow for their own deliverance continued as firm as ever, hunger and sickness, affecting horse as well as man, had so reduced the strength and mobility of his flying column that Sir George White was constrained to disband it, at least for a time. When General Buller was about ready for his second attempt to relieve Ladysmith another flying column was constituted, and it was signalled to him that the besieged would do their best to make a sally whenever he gave them the word, but that he must not trust too much in their power to co-operate effectively.

After his unsuccessful battle of Ladysmith, 30th October, 1899, Sir George White was obliged to admit that he could not keep the field, and that the best service he could render was to hold a large part of the Republics' forces around him and thus limit the extent of the invasion of Natal. Before the siege was ended he had to make the more painful confession that he could do nothing towards his extrication. But he would listen to no suggestion of surrender, and when one was signalled to him by General Buller, despondent after his repulse at Colenso, he professed to believe that the message had been intercepted by the Boers and tampered with in its transmission. All through the long siege he and every man under him, by watchfulness, industry, and ingenuity, did everything that could be done to hold the Boers at arm's length and keep the flag flying.

On 2nd November the effective garrison of Ladysmith was 13,496 men and 51 guns. With the civilian population of 5,400, and about 2,400 kafirs and Indians, the number to be provided for reached a total of over 21,000. According to an inventory made by Colonel E. W. D. Ward, Director of Supplies, there was in store at that date bread stuff for 65 days, meat 50 days, groceries 46 days, and forage 32 days. But for the careful husbanding of these stores and their distribution in half and even quarter rations, the siege must have ended to the heart's content of the enemy early in the new year. Moreover, as the garrison's hope of breaking through the cordon of investment was gradually relinquished, the necessity of maintaining their animal means of transport and mobility proportionally diminished. By the end of the year the transport oxen within the lines had been converted into biltong. Then came the turn of the horses. It was hard for the mounted men to see their equine friends and dependents driven to slaughter, but sentiment had to give way to stern necessity. The poor horses that could no longer be fed had to be turned into food for the men. In the preparation of horse flesh for consumption by the sick and the sound, Colonel Stoneman, Army Service Corps, and his assistants showed ingenuity and versatility that would have done credit to a Parisian chef. From their laboratory they issued chevril soup for the troops, condensed chevril soup for the sick in hospital, chevril jelly for the sick and wounded, and chevril paste as a substitute for potted meat. The water of the Klip River, to the amount of 12,000 gallons a day, was filtered in improvised condensers as a preventive against enteric fever; and the Indian Coolies turned their skill as market-gardeners to the benefit of the besieged in general and their own profit in particular. By these and similar devices Sir George White felt justified in sending Lord Roberts this assuring message on the 28th January:—"By sacrificing the rest of my horses I can hold out for six weeks, keeping my guns efficiently horsed and 1,000 men mounted on moderately efficient horses."

"Hope deferred maketh the heart sick," and it was a heart-sick garrison that wore through the long days of February, 1900. Again and again the attention of the besieged was strained to the signs of battle beyond the high hills south of Ladysmith. They could hear the roar of General Buller's artillery, and sometimes see the bursting of his shells on the hill tops, but always their hopes sank as the firing died down, and were extinguished for the time by the signalled intimation of the General's failure and change of plan. Their rescuers, notwithstanding their strenuous efforts to bring succour, seemed only to tantalize. But on the 14th of the month welcome news, inspiring sure confidence, came to Sir George White from Lord Roberts:—"I have entered the Orange Free State with a large force especially strong in cavalry, artillery, and mounted infantry. Inform your troops of this, and tell them from me I hope the result of the next few days may lead to the pressure on Ladysmith being materially lessened." On the 27th, Amajuba Day, General Buller signalled Lord Roberts's capture of General Cronje and his whole army of over 4,000 men; and next day he heliographed:—"I have thoroughly beaten enemy.

Believe them to be in full retreat. Have sent cavalry to ascertain what way they have gone." Late in the afternoon of that day, the 28th, mounted men in khaki were seen riding rapidly across Bester's Valley towards the town. They were the vanguard of Lord Dundonald's mounted brigade—Major McKenzie's Estcourt Squadron of the Natal Carbineers, Imperial Light Horse under Major Bottomley, and Border Mounted Rifles commanded by Captain Gough of the 16th Lancers.

It was intolerable to the Ladysmith garrison to see the enemy, that had kept them in durance for 118 days, trekking away to the north and west, with all their guns and baggage, on the morning of the 1st March. With the design of intercepting them a small flying column moved out consisting of portions of the Liverpool, Devon, and Gordon infantry, two guns of the 10th Mountain Battery, part of the 53rd and 60th batteries R.F.A., two squadrons of the 5th Dragoon Guards, and as many of the Natal Carbineers as were thought to be efficient. At Pepworth Hill they were slightly engaged with the enemy's rearguard, but it was evident that men who had only with difficulty accomplished a march of four miles were physically unable to do more than ply the enemy with their artillery. The spirit was willing but the flesh was weak. Next day Sir Redvers Buller humanely ordered their return to Ladysmith.

For two reasons Sir Redvers Buller could not pursue the Boers retreating from Ladysmith. After three months of arduous campaigning he was in need of horses, clothing, and drafts from Home to make up the wastage of battle and disease; and on the 3rd March, the day on which with his victorious army he made his triumphal entry into Ladysmith, Lord Roberts, making for Bloemfontein, telegraphed to him:— "The Natal Field Force is to act strictly on the defensive until such time as the operations of this column have caused the enemy to withdraw altogether from, or considerably reduce their numbers in the Drakensberg Passes." His first business was to disperse the enfeebled defenders of Ladysmith to recuperate in clean and healthy camps, and send the sick, numbering upwards of 2,000, down to the Maritzburg hospitals as fast as his means of conveyance allowed. Then he began to give his whole attention to the reorganisation of his army, preparatory to his final advance against the enemy still clinging to northern Natal. At the same time the Boers, finding that they were not pursued, set to work to entrench themselves on the Biggarsberg

CAMP, STEEK SPRUIT, 1894.

Top Row—Sergt.-Major Mason, Sergt. Grafton, Sergt. Townsend, Sergt. Lyle, Sergt. Baxter, Q.-M.-Sergt. Munro, Sergt. Mitchell, Sergt. Colville, Sergt. Cockburn, Sergt. Meyer.
Second Row—O.-R.-Sergt. Dick, Sergt. Budd, Sergt. Comrie, R.-S.-Major Molyneux, Sergt. Buchann, Sergt. Hayes, Sergt. Denne, Bandmaster Dunn, 3rd D.G.'s
Front Row—Sergt. Runciman, Sergt. Rodwell, Sergt. Owen, Sergt. Guttridge, Sergt. Methley, Sergt. Mapstone, Band Sergt. Kielly.

to bar his way to the north. For more than a month it was as if the generals on both sides had agreed to an armistice.

North of Ladysmith Natal is roughly in the shape of an isosceles triangle, of which the base is the Biggarsberg stretching from the boundary of the Free State to Helpmakaar close to Zululand, its apex is Lang's Nek leading into the Transvaal, its western side is the Drakensberg range, and its eastern the Buffalo River separating it from Zululand. On the 10th May, General Buller set his army in motion to drive the invaders out of this triangle. His intention was to force the enemy to the north of Newcastle before attempting the passage of the Drakensberg. Screened by Lord Dundonald's mounted men he led a strong force of infantry and artillery towards Helpmakaar with the object of turning the enemy's left flank and rolling up their whole line of defence on the Biggarsberg. On the morning of the 13th, Uithoek, which had been neglected by the Boers though it dominated the extremity of their line resting on Helpmakaar, was scaled by the mounted men and soon after occupied in force by Hamilton's brigade of infantry. The mounted brigade then swiftly skirted the semicircle of the hill of Helpmakaar from Uithoek to the first line of the enemy's trenches on the Biggarsberg and, joined by Bethune's force, charged straight for the first entrenchment and drove its occupants to their second line on the farther side of Helpmakaar Nek. The Boers were taken by surprise. Hitherto they had been accustomed to select and prepare their battle-ground, and it was not on Helpmakaar they had fixed for a fusilade of their adversaries. Stormed at from Uithoek on their front and Helpmakaar Nek on their left they held their ground till dark. In the night, knowing that their line of defence on the Biggarsberg was now untenable, they retreated with their usual rapidity northwards to Beith.

Lord Dundonald's mounted brigade, with the Natal Carbineers scouting in front, took up the pursuit on the morning of the 14th. Two or three times that day, in his march of 25 miles, he came into action with the enemy's rearguard but without bringing them to a resolute stand. During the night he learned from his patrols that Dundee was deserted, and at 9 a.m. next day he recovered that town over which the Vierkleur had been flying for seven months. Here the whole army stayed a day for a much-needed rest. Resuming the pursuit on the 17th the mounted brigade entered Newcastle at 10 p.m., only twelve hours after the Boers passed through it on their way to occupy and entrench Lang's Nek and make their last stand on that spot in Natal which recalled to them the happiest memories of victory.

By a reconnaissance well to the north of Newcastle Lord Dundonald discovered that the Boers were already ranged in large numbers, and with heavy guns posted, on the heights of Amajuba and Pougwana and on the sides of Lang's Nek. Doubtless they were looking forward confidently to a day of what they called "splendid shooting" when, themselves safe by their invisibility, as they had been at Magersfontein and Colenso, they would mow down our men exposed in the open, as they would be, in delivering the wonted frontal attack. Sir Redvers Buller adroitly encouraged them in this hope by ordering Sir F. Clery to make a feint of preparations for storming their strongholds, while he himself led, behind the cover of his cavalry, a strong force of artillery and infantry to Botha's Pass, about ten miles south-west of Lang's Nek, by which he meant to turn the enemy's right flank.

Owing to their eagerness to concentrate their numbers on and about Lang's Nek the Boers had not spared men enough to protect their right wing. General Buller's first care, as soon as he reached the scene of his outflanking operations, was to secure the heights from which it could be dominated. From the summit of Inkwelo, a lofty and isolated hill situated about six miles north of the Pass, the whole field of the coming battle could be overlooked, and guns posted on its slopes could shell Lang's Nek on the one side and the crest of the Drakensberg on the other. This commanding height was seized by the Natal Volunteers without any opposition, for happily the enemy lacked either the men or the will to occupy it, and heavy guns were quickly dragged into position on its sides. From Van Wyk hill, facing the mouth of the Pass and commanding the whole of its southern jaw, the Boer piquets were driven off by the South African Light Horse. Between these two hills the Boers were occupying two inferior and less important heights, Spitz Kop and Inkweloane. The South African Light Horse captured Spitz Kop without having to fight for it, and it was at once occupied by three battalions of infantry and a battery of artillery. Of the four hills which stood in a line of seven or eight miles in front of the Drakensberg, Inkweloane alone was left for a short time in possession of the Boers. By these preliminary successes and arrangements General Buller made it impossible for the enemy, with any regard for their own safety, to contest his advance through the Pass.

At 10 a.m. of 8th June the infantry began their ascent of Botha's Pass and after a stiff climb of four hours they reached the top. The Drakensberg presents a lofty and precipitous mountain side only towards Natal. From the summit there begins, not a reverse and correspondingly steep slope as one would expect but, a tableland stretching far into Basutoland and the Free State. On the plateau above Botha's Pass the Boers in a long line of trenches were awaiting the coming of their enemy. But just as our infantry appeared on the ridge the men of the 3rd mounted brigade rushed up the steep slopes of Inkweloane, dragging up with them two guns of the R.H.A. battery and, before their infantry supports were alongside of them, they had begun enfilading the left of the Boer lines. The 11th brigade of infantry on the crest swung round on the enemy's right, and the 2nd brigade charged in upon his front. Two hours before dark the Boers were in flight, heavily shelled by our artillery, and setting the grass on fire to hide their retreat. By his brilliant strategy Sir Redvers Buller had gained a firm footing in the Free State, and turned the flank of the Boer army in Natal, at a cost of only fifteen casualties, two killed and thirteen wounded. One can hardly bear to think what his losses would have been had he tried to dislodge the enemy from Lang's Nek in the way they expected.

After an entire day spent in the laborious task of dragging his guns and supplies up Botha's Pass General Buller, on 10th June, was only two days' march from Volksrust, the first Transvaal town beyond the northern border of Natal. General Clery's column was still facing Lang's Nek from the south, and between his and General Buller's force, when it should reach Volksrust, it seemed possible to entrap the whole of the Boers still in Natal. Only at Alleman's Nek, which cleft Verzamel Berg, could the Boers hope to check the British advance on Volksrust. An encounter here might be avoided by a detour round the northern end of Verzamel Berg, but time was precious and it was resolved to force the Nek. Two thousand Boers with a long range field gun and two Vickers-Maxims were holding the Nek and, though for want of time they were not entrenched, they found good cover behind boulders and bush. The action began at 1.30 in the afternoon with an artillery duel and, the enemy's fire having been subdued in an hour's time, the Dublin Fusiliers, the Dorset, the 2nd Queen's, and the 2nd Surrey regiments led the attack, supported by the Middlesex and 2nd West Yorkshire regiments. By a succession of short charges by the infantry and by the well-timed and accurate firing of the artillery the defenders were steadily pushed along the Nek from end to end. In the night the

Boers retreated, but they had gained their object. They had fought what was in reality a rearguard action to give their army on Lang's Nek time to escape with their guns and waggons. When General Buller marched into Volksrust next day, the rear ranks of the Boer invaders of Natal were miles ahead of him on the road to Standerton.

The following order was issued on 16th June:—"The General places on record his high appreciation of the services rendered by Brigadier-General Dartnell and the Natal Volunteers in the arduous operations which have resulted in the expulsion of the enemy from Natal territory. They have borne their full share, and their efforts throughout the last eight months have largely contributed to the successful issue. The General fully realises the sacrifices cheerfully made to remain in the field, and feels the time has come when he ought to release as many as possible from duty so patriotically undertaken. He therefore asks General Dartnell to undertake the defence of Dundee and a section of the eastern frontier, and allow the volunteers not required to return. They have earned the respect and confidence of every one and, when now leaving, carry the best wishes of their late comrades."

In obedience to this order the Regiment left Charlestown for Dundee on the 15th, and arrived there on the 18th, having bivouacked at Ingogo, Newcastle, and Dannhauser on their way down. Here a tiresome time of more than three months of mounting guard, patrolling, and scouting dragged slowly to an end, and seemingly with but little to show for it all, relieved only by an interesting and rather exciting advance on Vryheid, and it was with more than satisfaction that orders were received on 8th October to return to their homes. On the following day the Regiment returned to Maritzburg after an absence on active service of a year and eight days.

It was generally believed that the Boers would sue for peace after the loss of their capitals, Bloemfontein and Pretoria, and Johannesburg, the source of their wealth and arrogance; but the belief was erroneous, because it was arrived at without the consideration that they were not an urban but a rural population. The Free Staters were willing to let their capital go on circuit with the restless and peripatetic President Steyn, and to the Transvaalers the saloon carriage which accommodated President Kruger was a good enough substitute for Pretoria. As for the gold-field, before it was discovered they had lived and enjoyed the simple life on their isolated farms, and a return to it now would be no great hardship. To them, therefore, the loss of these three cities did not involve the end of the war, as it should have done if they had known when they were beaten, but it changed the character of their warfare from regular and formal to guerrilla. The effect of this obstinate determination to prolong a hopeless struggle was to keep South Africa in turmoil for a year and a half after it should have entered into the enjoyment of rest and peace, till at last the opposition of the Boers was worn down by Lord Kitchener's "drives" and blockhouses.

The Regiment was again called upon to take the field in consequence of a threatened inroad of the Boers from the Zululand border. Orders were received on the 18th September, 1901, and by the 22nd the whole Regiment, despite the very bad weather prevailing at the time, had assembled at Maritzburg. The Ladysmith troop were sent back to their own district on the 22nd, and were employed in watching the western border. The remainder of the Regiment formed part of a mobile column under Colonel Mills, and left Maritzburg on the 29th of September for Greytown, one squadron having gone on by rail. Greytown was reached the following day, and it was found that the advance squadron had been sent on to Untunjambili.. On the 1st October the column moved on the Magistracy at Krantzkop, where it remained until the 13th. During this time the only real work to be done was frequent patrolling, and outposts were stationed at Solitude, Sir Garnet's Road, and Untunjambili. The Regiment, recalled to Greytown on the 13th October, after waiting there one day, returned to Maritzburg. Before being dismissed the whole of the Volunteer Brigade were thanked by His Excellency the Governor.

On the 11th March, 1902, the services of the Ladysmith troop were called upon in consequence of an inroad of the Boers in the Upper Tugela district, and the troop proceeded in that direction, but fortunately their services were only required for a few days.

Before the Natal Carbineers were relieved from their long and faithful service in the field the two Boer Republics had ceased to exist. On the 28th May, 1900, Lord Roberts, by proclamation at Bloemfontein, had annexed the Free State and given it the name of the Orange River Colony; and on the 1st September he had in a similar way added the Transvaal Republic to the British Empire under the name of the Transvaal Colony. Yet, although their capitals had been captured and their armies broken up into fragments, the stubborn Boers kept up a sullen resistance. But their warfare was now of the guerrilla character and carried on by marauding bands acting independently of each other. Patience and hard work, and the extension by Lord Kitchener of lines of blockhouses that secured district after district as each was cleared by his "drives," slowly but surely wore down the remnants of Boer opposition, till the last of them, exhausted and heartless, with their leaders, Generals Botha, Delarey, and De Wet, driven at length to surrender, accepted the British terms of peace at Vereeniging on the 31st May, 1902.

In no war that history tells of has such humanity been shown by the stronger to the weaker side as in that waged in South Africa from October, 1899, to May, 1902. While the war went on, surrendered Boers and their families, and even the wives and children of enemies still in arms, to the number of 110,000 in August 1901, were supported at the expense of the British Government in concentration camps established in the pacified parts of the Transvaal and Orange River Colonies, and in Natal and the Cape. Short of the restoration of independence, the terms offered to the Boers at Vereeniging were more than merciful, they were magnanimous. The crimes of treason and rebellion by British subjects in Natal and Cape Colony were punished with a leniency hitherto unheard of anywhere. And to crown its generosity the British Government made the late Republics a free gift of £3,000,000, and granted advances in the shape of loans amounting to £5,000,000, free of interest for two years and afterwards repayable over a period of three years with three per cent. interest, to repatriate the banished prisoners and assist them and the impoverished enemies fresh from the field of war to restock their farms and make a new start in life. By these means, and as her chief intention in adopting them, Great Britain paved the way for the speedy and lasting reconciliation of British and Boers in South Africa estranged the one from the other by the long and devastating war. It remains for the two races to forget the bitter feelings of the past, and to strive to make their quarter of the British Empire over the Seas as prosperous and progressive as are the other three—Canada, Australia, and New Zealand.

N.C. DIARY OF THE BOER WAR.

1899.

29th September.—The Regiment was ordered out for active service on the 29th September, 1899, Nos. 1, 2, 3, 4, and 6 Squadrons assembling at Ladysmith on the evening of the 1st October, 1899. The Newcastle troop, a portion of No. 7 Squadron, assembled at Newcastle but, owing to the evacuation of that town, proceeded to Ladysmith two or three days later. The Dundee troop assembled at their headquarters, and were utilized by General Penn Symons until the troops retired from Dundee. No. 5 Squadron, Estcourt and Weenen, served on the Relief Column under General Buller.

2nd October.—Nos. 1, 3, and 4 Squadrons received orders to patrol the O.F.S. border, No. 1, under Major Taunton, watching the country between Olivier's Hoek and Tintwa passes, No. 4, under Major Macfarlane, working from Blaauwbank, and No. 3, under Major Addison from Bester's Station. A guide for each squadron was provided from No. 6 (Ladysmith). Before leaving, the squadrons were addressed by Col. Knox, C.B., R.A.

12th October.—On the 12th October, the Boers crossed the border at Tintwa Pass. This was reported by Major Taunton. In consequence, a reconnaissance in force, under Colonel Knox, C.B., R.A., was sent from Ladysmith in the direction of Tintwa Pass, but only came as far as Dewdrop. The remainder of the Regiment, who had been left in Ladysmith, accompanied this force. The Military Intelligence Department, disbelieving the information sent in by Major Taunton that the enemy had crossed, the force returned to Ladysmith. Major Taunton then (at great personal risk), with but a few men, made a further reconnaissance of the enemy's camp and reported to Ladysmith accordingly, but apparently no notice was taken of this important information. Those Volunteers who formed part of the force will never forget the muster at "Tin Town" to join the

Regulars. The night was pitch dark, the mud knee deep, and confusion reigned. After a good deal of delay the force was put into some sort of order and, all things considered, matters might have been worse.

16th October.—On the 16th October, No. 1 Squadron was relieved by the Border Mounted Rifles, and proceeded to the vicinity of Walker's Hoek, midway between No. 3 Squadron at Bester's and No. 4 at Blaauwbank. The remainder of the Regiment (No. 2 Squadron and Newcastle troop), under Lieutenant-Colonel Greene, left Ladysmith and took up a post at Klip Kraal, on the left of No. 3 Squadron, to watch the passes in the Berg in that direction.

18th October.—The enemy made no forward move until the 18th October. On the morning of that day Colonel Greene reconnoitred to the foot of the Berg, in the direction of De Beers and Van Reenen's Passes, and, observing a large force of the enemy, retired parallel with them (but unobserved by them), at the same time reporting to Ladysmith. He joined hands with Major Addison, near Bester's Station, and attacked the enemy. In the meantime the enemy's main body was observed by Nos. 1 and 4 Squadrons proceeding along the Van Reenen's Road towards Ladysmith in very strong force. Reports were sent to Ladysmith accordingly. This Boer column, hearing firing in the direction of Bester's Station where Colonel Greene was engaged, at once sent large reinforcements there. On observing the rapidly increasing numbers of the enemy, and having in the meantime received instructions from the General Officer Commanding to retire upon Ladysmith, Colonel Greene withdrew his force to Nicholson's Nek. In this engagement Trooper Spencer was wounded in the arm, and Lieutenant Gallwey was taken prisoner. The Boer casualties were one killed and five wounded. It was unknown at the time what had happened to Lieut. Gallwey. Colonel Greene waited a while to see if any signs of him were forthcoming, and a party went out for the purpose of seeing what had happened to him, but the enemy's fire was too hot, and they had to return unsuccessful. Nos. 1 and 4 Squadrons had

Lt.-Col. G. J. MACFARLANE, C.M.G.

also come into contact with the enemy, and shots were exchanged. Fortunately they had no casualties. All the squadrons returned to Ladysmith during the night of the 18th, and the following day pitched their camp outside the Ladysmith Showyard.

20th October.—On the 20th October the Regiment formed part of a column which made a reconnaissance in the direction of Elandslaagte, where the enemy were known to be, during which No. 3 Squadron captured four Boer scouts. On this reconnaissance the good news was heard of the victory at Talana Hill, marred at the same time by the loss of General Penn Symons. The latter news was keenly felt by the Regiment, the gallant officer having always shown a warm interest in, and appreciation of, the Volunteer Forces in Natal. It is understood that General French, in command of this reconnaissance, intended to engage the enemy this day, but from information received he postponed the action till the day following, when he fought the brilliant engagement known as Elandslaagte.

21st October.—The Regiment stood to arms the whole afternoon of the Battle of Elandslaagte, but unfortunately, with the exception of the Ladysmith troop, took no active part in it. That night two squadrons, for some unknown reason, were sent to occupy the vicinity of the Railway Station, whilst the remainder vacated camp and bivouacked on the other side of the Klip River.

22nd October.—On Sunday, the 22nd, the discouraging news was heard of the evacuation of Dundee. The Dundee troop came into Ladysmith, but returned almost immediately to assist in guiding General Yule's retreating column.

24th October.—On Tuesday, 24th October, the Regiment formed part of a column which went out to the north of Ladysmith to prevent those forces of the enemy to the west of Ladysmith from intercepting the retreating column from Dundee. The engagement known as Rietfontein or Tinta Inyoni ensued. The Regiment, in conjunction with the other volunteer mounted regiments, were successful in obtaining a position from which they could pour in a flank fire on the enemy's main position. To obtain this point of vantage a most exposed piece of ground had to be crossed under a very heavy fire, and there were several casualties:—Sergt. Colville killed, Trooper Cleaver mortally wounded, and wounded, Corporal Richmond, Troopers Taylor, Russell, Freeman, Ballantyne, Teasdale, Raw, Mason and Smith. This was the first occasion on which the Regiment came under shell fire. Fortunately before doing any harm the Boer guns were silenced by our artillery. The flank fire soon drove the enemy from their position, and orders were given to retire.

25th October.—This day the Volunteer Brigade went out to assist in bringing in the Dundee column, and met it in the Sunday's River Valley. Colonel Royston had imperative orders to bring in the column to Ladysmith that night, and so, although they were already outspanned and laagered, he insisted on their marching on at once as far as Modder Spruit, where they would be met by another force from Ladysmith. Throughout a terribly wet and dark night, the Volunteers held the stony kopjes on the Helpmakaar Road known as Vlak Plaats, a most important position to cover the retreat. It is only fair to state that the greatest credit is due to Colonel Royston, Commandant of Volunteers, and to the Volunteer Brigade generally, for the safe conduct of the Dundee column to Ladysmith; any delay taking place would have led to dire disaster. The Regiment formed the rear-guard into Ladysmith.

27th October.—The Regiment patrolled east of Ladysmith, one squadron joining a column which proceeded to Modder Spruit, but returned the following morning.

28th October.—Easterly patrols were made, resulting in the discovery of the enemy entrenching themselves and mounting guns north of Ladysmith.

29th October.—Forty men of No. 4 Squadron, under Major Macfarlane, were sent to occupy Lombard's Kop, and

Nos. 3 and 7, under Lieut.-Colonel Greene, to occupy Bulwana. Their horses were sent back to Ladysmith, the instructions being that these positions had to be held at all cost.

30th October.—The remainder of the Regiment left Ladysmith at 1 a.m., and proceeded to hold the Nek between Lombard's Kop and Bulwana. "Mournful Monday" was the significant name given to the day of the battle known as Farquhar's Farm or Lombard's Kop. None of the Carbineer squadrons was heavily engaged, and there were no casualties among them. During the day the Boers shelled the Carbineer Camp at the Showyard, and some narrow escapes were recorded. A general retirement to Ladysmith was made about 1 p.m.

31st October.—No. 5 Squadron (Estcourt and Weenen), with the Durban Light Infantry, were reinforced by the 2nd Dublin Fusiliers and Natal Field Artillery. During October the Squadron, under Lieut. Mackay, did a lot of patrolling and scouting towards the Upper Tugela. Major McKenzie arrived from England on 2nd November, and took command of the Squadron.

2nd November.—The Regiment formed part of a column sent out to attack a Boer laager to the west of Ladysmith. The column moved out at 2 a.m. The Boer laager, lying under Table Hill, was shelled by our guns, and the enemy cleared out. Our force retired to Ladysmith under a very heavy shell fire from the Boer guns on Table Hill and Telegraph Ridge. No casualties. It was on this day that communication with the outer world was cut off, and it was recognised that Ladysmith was closely besieged. No one, however, imagined that the siege was to last for four long weary months; confidence was strong that it would be for but a few days.

2nd November.—The Colenso mounted men had a sharp skirmish with the enemy on the Colenso-Ladysmith Road, one of the Dublin Fusilier mounted men being killed, and several of the enemy killed and wounded. The Boers shelled the Camp from Grobler's Kloof.

3rd November.—Colenso evacuated, the garrison retiring on Estcourt.

3rd November.—On 3rd November a force under General Brocklehurst went out to attack a Boer convoy north of Ladysmith, but, a part of his men becoming hemmed in by the enemy, he found it necessary to call for reinforcements, and the Artillery and Mounted Volunteers were sent to him. From the moment of their setting out, this force was subjected to a heavy fire. The Volunteer Brigade was ordered to take and hold Middle and End Hills. End Hill was found to be occupied by the enemy, and our men came under a heavy cross fire upon gaining the summit. The enemy was driven off the hill, which was held by the Volunteer Brigade. Major Taunton, who was with No. 1 Squadron, was killed. He was setting a most soldierly example of coolness and pluck, and his great loss was keenly felt by every member of the Regiment. He was buried in the Ladysmith Cemetery the following day. A cairn, raised by the members of No. 1 Squadron, with whom he had been so long associated, marks the spot where he fell. Trooper Webber was severely wounded, and, while gallantly rescuing him from his dangerous position, Troopers Miller and Watts were themselves wounded, and Trooper D. A. Shaw, who also assisted, had a bullet through his tunic. For their gallantry on this occasion, Troopers Miller, Watts and Shaw were afterwards awarded the D.C.M. The Carbineer casualties in this engagement were:— Killed, Major Taunton; mortally wounded, Sergeant F. G. Mapstone; and wounded, Corporal W. McCullough, Troopers W. Anderson, C. E. J. Miller, A. Paine, R. Watts, S. E. Waugh, and C. W. Webber. From this time a most monotonous period ensued. The Volunteer Brigade furnished daily a piquet for the defence of the eastern side of Ladysmith between Caesar's Camp and Helpmakaar Ridge. A night piquet was also established on the river banks in the town and, owing to the unsavoury smells in the locality, it was generally known as "stink piquet." The whole Volunteer Brigade stood to arms during the siege at 3.30 a.m., and (whilst food for the horses was plentiful) their horses were exercised round the town in the dark. The shell fire was at times fast and furious. The enemy's gunners seemed rather partial to the locality of the Volunteer Camp, but for some time they did no damage. At first precautions were taken by putting the men and horses in a donga on the other side of the Klip River, but this practice was not carried out for long, and on all sides there soon was a charming disregard of the death-dealing missiles. "Familiarity breeds contempt."

9th November.—No. 5 Squadron took part in a reconnaissance along the Weenen road, and came in touch with the enemy near Hodgson's Hill.

9th November.—The Boers this day made their first attack on Ladysmith, but were repulsed on all sides with, it is said, heavy loss, whilst our casualties were practically nil. The Regiment was slightly engaged below Caesar's Camp, but the Boers were not taking on anything that day.

Nothing of note occurred for some time after, and, by the aid of cricket, football, tennis matches, poker, nap, and the like, the siege dragged on its weary way.

15th November.—Armoured train D.L.I. disaster near Chievely. No. 5 Squadron with the I.L.H. marched out to render assistance.

19th November. No. 5 Squadron left Estcourt for Willow Grange, and on the 20th engaged the enemy near Highlands.

21st November.—Squadron returned to Estcourt.

22nd November.—Re-advanced on Willow Grange. The Squadron materially assisted to mount a naval gun on Beacon Hill. Returned to Estcourt in the evening.

23rd November.—No. 5 Squadron took part in the battle of Willow Grange. This action is now generally regarded as the mark, though no one claims that it was the cause, of the turning point of the Boer invasion of Natal.

27th November.—Squadron left Estcourt and encamped at Frere.

29th November.—On the night of the 29th November, the Regiment was warned to be ready to march out of Ladysmith at 2 a.m. the following morning—object unknown. At the last minute the order was cancelled. It transpired afterwards that it was intended to take and hold Rifleman's Ridge, but it was found out that the Boers had got wind of it, and so the idea was abandoned.

30th November.—No. 5 Squadron patrolled to Weenen with I.L.H.

2nd December.—On Saturday, 2nd December, orders were received at 8 p.m. to saddle up and be ready to go out of Ladysmith. It proved to be a false alarm, but the Volunteer Brigade was first at the rendezvous, and was complimented by the G.O.C. on its smartness.

7th-8th December.—Surprise of Gun Hill by Natal Mounted Volunteers and Imperial Light Horse. About this time, in anticipation of speedy relief, a "Flying Column" was held in readiness to move out at a moment's notice. Another false alarm parade was held on the night of 12th December, the Volunteers again gaining credit for their smartness in turning out.

11th December.—No. 5 Squadron took part in reconnaissance to Colenso under Lord Dundonald.

13th December.—Advanced on Chieveley and pitched camp there.

15th December.—Battle of Colenso. In conjunction with I.L.H., No. 5 Squadron attempted to take Hlangwane Hill, but the enemy, from an impregnable position, poured in a terrific fire at 80 yards range, and our force had to retire. Casualties in this engagement: Troopers Adie, Gray, Jenner and Warren, killed; Lieut. Mackay and five men severely wounded.

On the 15th, hopes of relief ran high in Ladysmith in consequence of the heavy firing heard from Colenso.

16th December.—An armistice at Colenso. Buried our dead near the railway line.

17th December.—Official intimation was received in Ladysmith that General Buller had "failed to make good his attack."

18th December.—While the men of the Regiment were at stables this morning, a shell from the Bulwana Long Tom struck a horse and exploded before reaching the ground, killing Troopers R. M. M. Miller, W. Buxton, T. Elliott, and W. Craighead Smith, and wounding Corporal M. H. Holley, Troopers C. Craik, S. Daly, J. Gillam, J. E. Greig, A. Nicholson, and W. S. Warwick. Eleven horses were also killed, and several severely injured. After this occurrence, precautions were taken against shell fire. Shelter pits were dug, and a trumpeter was always on duty. When he saw the smoke of Long Tom he sounded the regimental call as a warning for all to take shelter. These precautions were of avail, for although afterwards many shells struck in camp, only a few horses were killed by them.

20th December.—One troop of No. 5 Squadron, under Lieut. Silburn, surprised some Boers who had come out to rob a Hussar who had been killed the previous day. Two of the Boers were killed.

24th December.—With Bethune's Horse, No. 5 Squadron formed the escort to General Buller, who made a reconnaissance in the direction of Doorn Kop.

In Ladysmith, sports were held on Christmas Day, and all enjoyed themselves as far as possible in their untoward circumstances.

Rations were now getting short, and the terrible amount of sickness among the Ladysmith garrison was most depressing. The work of defence, however, had still to be done and, consequently, it fell very hard on those who were fortunate enough to be fit for duty. So the siege dragged on. Rumours of all sorts were in the air.

1900.

6th January.—Repulse of Boer attack on Caesar's Camp, Waggon Hill, and Waggon Point.

The volunteer section piquet on the night of the 5th January was composed partly of Natal Carbineers and partly of Natal Mounted Police under Captain Lucas, N.C. It has been stated that the enemy got through this piquet; but the statement is quite untrue. Those of the Regiment who were with the piquet were the only Carbineers in the actual fighting on the 6th, one man, Trooper Haine, being wounded. On the night of the 6th the Regiment furnished the piquet and support, who were under a heavy fire whilst going out in the evening, Trooper Heckler being wounded. Next day a party from the Regiment was employed in the gruesome task of collecting the Boer dead on Caesar's Camp, carrying them down the hill, and handing them over to the enemy. Twenty-two bodies were thus handled by our men.

10th January.—No. 5 Squadron left Chieveley and seized Upper Tugela bridge.

11th January.—No. 5 Squadron encamped on Spearman's farm.

17th January.—No. 5 Squadron crossed Trichardt's Drift with cavalry under Lord Dundonald. Several men who were washed down the river by the strong current were saved by Troopers D. Sclanders and F. F. Wood, the former receiving the Royal Humane Society's silver medal for his action.

18th January.—No. 5 squadron advanced on Acton Homes with I.L.H. and K.R.R. Carbineer Scouts reported that the enemy were advancing to seize Kopjes. Major McKenzie with the N.C. and others galloped for five miles and reached the Kopjes a few minutes before the Boers came up, on whom, at 100 yards, fire was opened and several saddles were emptied. The Boers retired in confusion to a position 200 yards off and, after an hour's continuous firing, they put up the white flag. Upon our men standing up the Boers recommenced firing, wounding Trooper Higgins. The enemy were then shouted to that if firing did not stop instantly no surrender would be allowed, whereupon the firing ceased. 25 prisoners were taken : 14 of the enemy were killed and 40 wounded. The I.L.H. had two men wounded and the K.R.R. two killed.

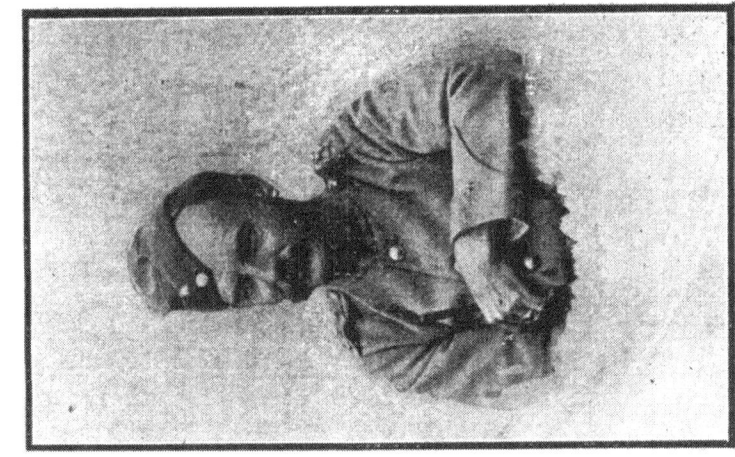

Major G. F. Tatham,

Lt.-Colonel Bede Crompton, D.S.O,

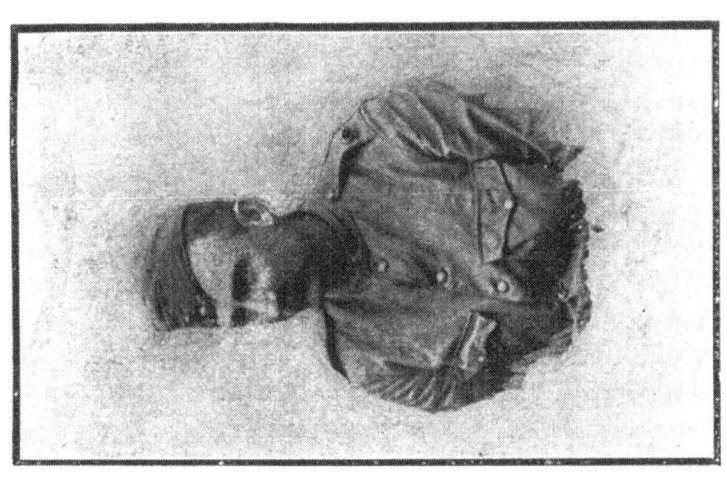

Lt.-Colonel C. B. Addison,

21st January to 14th February.—During the series of military operations which ended in the abandonment by the Relief Column first of Spion Kop and afterwards of Vaal Krantz, commanding heights captured in the face of stout resistance, No. 5 Squadron was employed under Lord Dundonald and was frequently under heavy shell fire.

The failure of the Relief Column to hold Spion Kop and Vaal Krantz was a grave disappointment to the Ladysmith defenders. Sickness and famine were now their deadliest enemies, and by them two-thirds of the Regiment was at this date unfit for duty. The extremity to which the garrison was reduced was humorously described, after the war, by a versifier in a New Zealand newspaper, in what might have been the lament of many a trooper saved from starvation, though metamorphosed it is feared, by a regretful diet on horse flesh:—

"I eat that horse in a week or less,
    And as I a-eatin' be
The last of his chops, why I almost drops,
    For old Buller in sight I see.

"And I never smiles, and I never laughs,
    And I never larks nor play,
But I sit and croak, and a single joke
    I have, which is—to neigh:—

"'Oh! I'm the colt of the roadster too,
    And the lead of the tandem pair,
A war horse bold, and a hunter old,
    And the foal of the Doctor's mare'."

15th February.—With the I.L.H. No. 5 Squadron attacked and took Cingolo Hill. Trooper Goldstein, N.C., killed.

16th February.—Seized the extreme right of Monte Cristo.

17th to 21st February.—Occupied and held Hlangwane. Lieut. Mackay rejoined the squadron.

22nd to 24th February.—Advanced towards Pieters Station.

25th and 26th February.—Returned to Monte Cristo.

27th February.—Returned to hill overlooking Pieters Station.

28th February.—Scouting the whole day on hills to the south of Ladysmith. About 5 p.m., finding that the Boers had fled, entered Ladysmith in conjunction with I.L.H. The Squadron after this joined the Regiment, whichh ad been besieged in Ladysmith.

At midday on the 28th the cheering news was given out in Ladysmith that the Boers were in full retreat. Every available man of the Carbineers saddled up to go out. But they had not gone more than a mile before, to their delight, horsemen were seen galloping towards the town. This delight was greatly enhanced by the fact that amongst the horsemen were their comrades of No. 5 Squadron under Major McKenzie.

1st March.—Patrols of the Regiment scoured the country around Ladysmith, and the remainder assisted in the engagement of Pepworth's Hill, which so materially hurried the enemy's departure. No casualties.

7th March.—On the 7th March the whole Regiment marched for Highlands to recuperate and refit; and here they stayed till the 5th April Many recruits joined, and remounts in place of the chargers lost in Ladysmith were obtained. During the month's stay all felt better for the good diet, the bracing climate of Highlands, and a few days' leave.

5th April.—On the morning of the 5th April the Regiment marched by road to Estcourt and entrained for Ladysmith, the last squadrons not getting to camp there till past midnight. They joined the 3rd cavalry brigade under Lord Dundonald at Star Kopje. Next day tents were pitched and sundry rumours were current as to the ultimate destination of the Regiment. However, there was no long delay, for the following day the brigade marched to Elandslaagte, then the most advanced British position in Natal.

8th April.—The Regiment furnished outposts on the 8th and 9th April. The following day the Boers shelled and, in a faint-hearted way, attacked the camp. Without being actually engaged the Natal Volunteers were under a very heavy shell fire, the enemy's gunners, as usual, showing a marked partiality for their lines. Fortunately no casualties occurred. About midday they moved to the east of the camp and reconnoitred in that direction without seeing any signs of the enemy. A return to the camp was made at dusk, tents struck, and at 9.30 p.m. the brigade moved to the vicinity of Buys's farm.

11th April.—A permanent camp was formed at Buys's farm, where the whole brigade stayed till the 7th May. The Volunteer Brigade furnished the outposts along the hills overlooking the Sunday's River Valley besides other minor posts, and opportunity was taken of this period of comparative inactivity to practice field firing.

21st April.—Firing was heard in the direction of Elandslaagte, and the Brigade marched a few miles towards it, but nothing of note happened.

6th May.—The brigade joined General Buller's force moving toward Helpmakaar road, the Regiment furnishing scouts, and bivouacked at Pieter's farm.

9th May.—The column marched to Sunday's River drift which had been occupied on the previous day by two squadrons of the Regiment under Captain Nourse, N.C. A halt was made there, and the main column under General Buller arrived.

11th May.—A move was made to Waschbank. Here the advanced squadrons came into touch with the enemy and Trooper R. A. Lindsay, No. 3 Squadron, was wounded.

12th May.—The column proceeded to Vermaak's Kraal, the Regiment furnishing flanking squadrons. Some slight skirmishing ensued but there were no casualties.

13th May.—As the column was leaving Vermaak's Kraal the Boers began shelling from the Biggarsberg with one gun which, without having done much damage, was promptly silenced by our 4.7. Part of the Regiment acted as scouts to the column, whilst the remainder stayed the night at Vermaak's Kraal and formed the rearguard. The Boers did not make much of a stand at Helpmakaar and soon retired along the Biggarsberg, setting the grass on fire as they went and followed by our men through dust and blinding smoke. Our scouts occasionally came under heavy shell and rifle fire but there were no casualties.

15th May.—Dundee was re-occupied by our troops who halted there for the next day. Detached troops of the Regiment were sent out all round and succeeded in taking several rebels prisoners.

17th May.—The column arrived at Dannhauser and more rebels were captured.

18th May.—Newcastle was re-occupied.

19th May.—The column marched to within a few miles of Lang's Nek to ascertain the enemy's position, and found them in strong force on the Nek. An attempt was made to draw the enemy's fire but without success and eventually the column retired to the Ingogo River.

21st May.—Owing to the persuasions of Brigadier-General Dartnell the Regiment with the U.M.R. was sent to occupy Mount Prospect and Inkwelo Hill. The wisdom of seizing and fortifying Inkwelo was apparent when it was found that both Lang's Nek and Botha's Pass could be commanded by guns on this position. The work entailed on General Dartnell's small force, weakened by No. 4 Squadron under Captain Lucas having been left at Buys's farm, was exceedingly hard, especially in the cold and windy weather of this time of year. No. 4 Squadron shortly afterwards joined General Lyttleton's column and took part in that General's move into the Transvaal as far as Utrecht.

28th May.—The 4th Brigade with guns arrived and took up a position on the slopes of Inkwelo. It had been a matter of debate whether the enemy had a Long Tom on Pougwana Hill, but doubts were soon set at rest by its opening fire on our guns as they were being placed in position. A reply was soon made and a long range duel ensued but without much damage being done.

30th May.—A party, under a flag of truce, was sent to the Boer Commandant, C. Botha, on Lang's Nek, suggesting that he should surrender. The proposal, referred by him to Pretoria, was refused; hostilities, however, ceased for some days while the subject was pending.

2nd June.—General Buller met the Boer Commandant, Assistant-General C. Botha, on the question of surrender, but the result of their meeting was not satisfactory. During these three days of negotiation there was a good deal of sniping between the outposts.

6th June.—Shelling re-commenced. Several shells fell in the camp during this and next day and two of the Royal Scots were killed.

8th June.—This day General Buller succeeded in forcing Botha's Pass. The guns on the west slopes of Inkwelo afforded valuable assistance in this operation.

11th June.—The immediate consequence of General Buller's victory at Alleman's Nek was the retreat of the Boers from Lang's Nek which was then occupied by our men. The Regiment, first to reach Lang's Nek, moved on to Charlestown where it bivouacked for the night.

14th June.—General Buller stated that, the Boers now having been driven out of the Colony, the Natal Volunteers might return home, but he wished them to garrison Dundee for a short time.

SPECIAL NATAL ARMY ORDER.

Headquarters,
Laing's Nek,
15th June, 1900.

As the Natal Field Force is now leaving Natal, it loses the services of the Natal Volunteers.

The G.O.C. desires to place on record his high appreciation of the services rendered by Brigadier-General Dartnell, C.M.G., and the Natal Volunteers.

In the arduous operations, which have resulted in the expulsion of the enemy from Natal, they have borne their full share, and their efforts throughout the last eight months have largely contributed to this successful issue.

The G.O.C. fully realises the sacrifices they have cheerfully made to remain in the field, and he feels that the time has come, when he ought to release as many as possible from the duties they have so patriotically undertaken. He has therefore asked General Dartnell to undertake the defence of the Dundee Section of the Eastern Frontier, and to allow those Volunteers not required for this duty to return to their avocations.

While with the Field Force, the Natal Volunteers have earned the respect and confidence of everyone in it, and when leaving it they carry with them the best wishes of all their late comrades.

By Order,
(Sgd.), H. S. G. MILES, Col.,
Chief of Staff.

15th June.—In obedience to General Buller's order the Regiment left Charlestown en route for Dundee and arrived there on the 18th, having bivouacked at Ingogo, Newcastle, and Dannhauser on their way down. On their arrival at Dundee the Volunteer Brigade took over the outposts at Glencoe, De Waal's, Gregory's Nek, Maybole farm, and Malungeni.

24th June.—His Excellency the Governor visited the camp.

28th June.—A reconnaissance in force was made as far as Maybole farm, but nothing of interest happened.

8th July.—One troop under Lieutenant Tanner was sent to protect Dannhauser.

28th July.—While a patrol of eight men of the Richmond troop under Captain Foxon were on duty near the Buffalo at the distance of about eight miles from their outpost, a party of between thirty and forty Boers suddenly crossed the river with the evident design of surrounding and capturing them. The patrol retired 500 yards and then opened fire, but the enemy pressed them hard and took three of them prisoners, Troopers Ward, Gordon, and Hewitt. As the rest were endeavouring to make their escape Trooper Saner fell dangerously wounded. Thereupon Captain Foxon returned to him, took and used his rifle and bandolier and, while thus protecting him, was himself wounded in the neck and for a short time lost consciousness. The Boers were standing over him and Saner when he recovered but, seeing that the wounded men were unable to walk or ride and being unwilling to encumber themselves with dead weight, they left them lying on the veld and retreated across the Buffalo with their three prisoners. Captain Foxon behaved very pluckily in this little scrap. At night the two wounded men were brought into Dundee by ambulance. The Boers lost in this brush with the Carbineers two killed and a native wounded. A strong reinforcement was sent out by General Dartnell but did not come into touch with the enemy. The three captured Carbineers were soon afterwards restored to their troop by exchange of prisoners. Trooper Bowman rode back, under a heavy fire, with a dismounted man's horse up to within 150 yards of the enemy and by his plucky action saved his comrade.

For the next few days patrols were sent in the direction of the passes in the Drakensberg. Boers were seen on the Berg from time to time but they did not come in contact with the patrols.

9th August.—The camp, which had been pitched on the farm Craigie Burn, was shifted close to the town on the eastern side.

22nd August.—The brigade stood to arms at 3 a.m. to-day and for many mornings afterwards, and went out to hold Talana and Smith's Hills as an attack was expected. An additional piquet was also furnished on the flats beyond Talana.

24th August.—A column, which included the Natal Carbineers, was sent to try to intercept the enemy who were supposed to be moving on Newcastle. A long and trying day in the saddle was spent but no traces of the enemy were seen. For several weeks the Brigade stood to arms at 3.30 a.m.

5th September.—The Brigade demonstrated as far as Maybole farm in the direction of the Buffalo and our guns shelled the other side of the river without any apparent result. A return to Dundee was made on the 7th.

16th September.—The Brigade moved out towards the Buffalo to advance on Vryheid. Maybole was reached that night, and on the following day the river was crossed at De Jager's drift without opposition. Next day an advance was made in the direction of the Blood River, and there General Hildyard's Brigade, which had come from Utrecht, was met. A halt was made at the Blood River for the night. On moving towards

Scheeper's Nek the column was opposed by a commando of the enemy. Several of the scouts supplied by the Regiment were engaged in this affair. The next morning the Regiment was ordered to patrol to the east of Vryheid. They succeeded in taking several prisoners amongst whom was the notorious Ludovic de Jager. The Volunteers were greatly disappointed on hearing that they were not to go on to Vryheid, that place being regarded by them as belonging by rights to Natal. After a long day in the saddle de Jager's drift was regained that night, and the following day the Regiment returned to Dundee. A large number of stock was captured in the course of this patrol.

30th September.—Orders were received to return home, but on the following day a convoy proceeding to Vryheid was captured by the enemy between the Buffalo and Blood rivers which necessitated the cancellation for a time of the orders to return.

8th October.—The Regiment finally left Dundee and reached Maritzburg next day—the anniversary of the Boer ultimatum to the British Government—after an absence on active service of one year and eight days.

1901.
22nd September.—From this day the Ladysmith squadron was for some time employed in watching the western border.

29th September.—The rest of the Regiment left Maritzburg for Greytown to form part of a mobile column, under Colonel Mills, sent to the eastern border of Natal in consequence of a threatened inroad of the Boers by way of Zululand. One squadron was sent on to Untunjambili.

1st October.—The column moved on the Magistracy at Krantzkop and remained there patrolling the neighbourhood till the 13th.

13th October.—The Regiment returned to Greytown and, after a halt of one day there, proceeded to Maritzburg.

GOVERNMENT CUP TEAM, 1895 (WINNERS.)

Top Row.—Tr. J. L. Armitage, Tr. J. Davies, Tr. English, Tr. P. W. Stride, Tr. F. Ellerker.
Seated.—Sergt. T. M. Owen, Sergt. C. N. H. Rodwell, T.-Sergt.-Major Tranner, Corpl. J. Armitage, Tr. Joughin.

1902.

11th March.—The Ladysmith squadron set out for the Upper Tugela district in consequence of an inroad by the Boers, but fortunately their services were only required for a few days.

CIVIC BANQUET TO SIR REDVERS BULLER AND THE NATAL CARBINEERS, 17TH NOVEMBER, 1900.

The projected visit of General Sir Redvers Buller to Maritzburg on his way Home from the seat of war, a few weeks after the return of the Carbineers from their year's service at the front, was an opportunity not to be missed of giving thanks publicly to him who had routed the invaders of Natal and at the same time to that part of the Ladysmith garrison that had their head quarters in the city. The Mayor and Corporation prepared a public luncheon for them in the Market Hall, on Wednesday, the 17th November, and invited the leading citizens to assist by their presence in doing them honour. A novel feature of the festival, meant and recognised as a special compliment to the entertained, was the voluntary service of a number of young ladies in helping to wait on the guests.

"None but the brave deserves the fair."

The Mayor (Major G. J. Macfarlane, N.C.), in the course of his speech proposing the toast of the Navy, Army, and Volunteers, with which he coupled the name of General Sir Redvers Buller, said:—"As the head and leader of the army, with which we in Natal have been so closely associated, we have only to mention the name of Sir Redvers Buller to evoke universal and heartfelt enthusiasm. As one of those many here to-day who underwent the hardships, trials, and anxieties of that long four months' siege of Ladysmith, we personally owe him deep and lasting thanks as our rescuer and deliverer. The difficulties that had to be overcome can only be fully realised by those who have gone over the ground through which he had to force his way."

In his reply General Buller said:—"Mr. Mayor, ladies," (the waitresses), "and gentlemen, the navy is England's first line of defence and, as usual and always, has done its duty in every way it has been called on, and has done more than was expected of it in this war. As regards the army, I may say I was here with an army 20 years ago. The privilege of all of us Britons, and we are very fond of it, is to abuse ourselves. We do not like other people to do it. We do it ourselves, and we see in English papers continual references to the shortcomings of the army. But I stand here, in the presence of many men who are quite separate from any feeling and desire to be unfair and unfriendly to the army, and I can say without fear of contradiction, that any men who compare the army—the English army as it has shown itself in Natal during the past twelve months—with the English army they knew 20 years ago, will all agree with me in acknowledging the advances both officers and men have made. And when I say that, I believe I give the poor old English army the highest possible credit, and no more than it deserves. I might say very much the same of the Natal volunteers. There were here 20 years ago, as there are now, a very large number of very gallant men, but they were not then, as they have been since, thoroughly organised, well led, and well conducted troops. It is an immense difference, and I congratulate the Colony on the growth of military spirit and military ardour—in short, it is patriotism; and it is nationalism grown during that period. Whether that immense difference is due to the fact that meanwhile it has become a self-governing colony I do not know, but I hope it may be, because before the whole of Natal and the whole of South Africa there is a potentiality arising that will require a nationality to carry it out. This hall is not easy to speak in, and I could wish to make those at the lower end of the room hear the things I would like to say about the volunteers whom I lately had the honour of commanding. I will only say there is nobody who knows anything of the siege of Ladysmith but joins with me in regretting the death of Colonel Royston. There is nobody who knows anything of the operations of the last twelve months who is not aware of the debt the Empire owes to General Dartnell, and the many other volunteer officers. I would especially mention Major McKenzie and Major Leuchars. I am very diffident about mentioning names, as there are many I could mention, but those three men came specially before me, and I only give them as examples of what I could mention."

On behalf of the volunteers Colonel Greene said:—"The toast in years past had been the 'Navy, Army, and Volunteers,' but the General had changed it into 'Her Majesty's Forces,' and they took it as a compliment that no distinction between the regulars and volunteers had been made by him."

Before the next toast on the list was proposed the General got up again and, playfully charging Colonel Greene with having in his reply forgotton those who might be termed "the best volunteers here," said:—"I have the honour to call for three cheers for those kind lady volunteers who came here to wait on us."

BOER WAR.

SUMMARY OF N.C. RECORD.

Strength on being called out, 508 officers, non-coms, and men; strength on return, 412 officers, non-coms, and men; 2 officers, 116 non-coms and men remaining in the field; returning to Maritzburg, 240 officers, non-coms, and men.

Casualties:—1 officer (Major Taunton) and 10 non-coms and men killed in action; 2 died of wounds; 2 officers (Capt. Lucas and Lieut. A. Wylde-Brown) and 21 non-coms and men died of disease; 34 non-coms and men wounded in action. Total 70, equals 13.78 per cent.

Engagements.—Bester's Station, 19th October, 1899; Tinta Inyoni, 24th October, 1899; Lombard's Kop, 30th October, 1899; End Hill, 3rd November, 1899; Siege of Ladysmith, 2nd November, 1899 to 28th February, 1900; Gun Hill, 7th and 8th December, 1899; Colenso, 15th December, 1899; Caesar's Camp, 6th January, 1900; Acton Homes, 17th January, 1900; Monte Cristo, 17th and 18th January, 1900; Helpmakaar, 11th May, 1900.

RECORDS OF THE PART PLAYED BY THE NATAL CARBINEERS DURING THE REBELLION OF 1906, AND THE ZULULAND EXPEDITION OF 1907.

PREFACE.

In acceding to the request of my Commanding Officer to write the following narrative, I did so with feelings of pleasure but without realising the difficult task involved.

From the diary of daily events written in the field by me, and from other sources, I have endeavoured to record the doings of the Regiment during the Natal and Zululand operations as correctly as possible. If I have failed in compiling an interesting narrative, I ask for indulgence from my readers and critics. It has been difficult to decide what to put into the narrative and what to leave out of it, and my object has been, not to write a military record, so much as a plain narrative of the part played by the Regiment in the field. I can state without hesitation that all the events recorded here are, to the best of my belief, absolutely correct.

HUBERT WALTON, Capt.,
Adjutant, Left Wing, N.C.

Ladysmith,
     24th February, 1910.

A narrative of the part played by the Natal Carbineers in suppressing the Native Rebellion in Natal and Zululand, February to August, 1906; and in the expedition to Zululand in December, 1907, which culminated in the arrest and subsequent trial of the Zulu Chief—Dinizulu.

1906 OPERATIONS.

At the commencement of 1906, grave fears were entertained of a rising among the natives in Natal and Zululand, owing to serious disaffection among various tribes. These fears were justified when, during the first week of February, 1906, a section of the tribe of Chief Mveli, in the Richmond District, defied the authority of the Government and refused to pay the Poll Tax to Mr. T. R. Bennett, Magistrate of the Umgeni Division, when he attended to collect it. In consequence of this conduct, a detachment of Natal Police proceeded to arrest the ringleaders, when a skirmish ensued between the Police and natives, resulting in the killing of Sub-Inspector Hunt, the Officer in Command, and Trooper Armstrong. This occurred on February 8th, and immediately Martial Law was proclaimed throughout the Colony, and the Active Militia were called out for service in the field—the Carbineers being the first Corps ordered to mobilise.

COMPOSITION OF THE REGIMENT.

The Regiment mobilized at a few hours' notice on February 9th, and was at that time comprised as follows:—

Numerical strength—all ranks—675.

Officers on service, including the Staff, were:—

Staff:—

    Lt. Col. Duncan McKenzie, C.B., C.M.G., V.D., O.C. Regiment.
    Bt. Lt. Col. Weighton, V.D., O.C. Right Wing.
    Bt. Lt. Col. D. W. Mackay, O.C. Left Wing.
    Major C. N. H. Rodwell, Regimental Adjutant.
    Capt. T. M. Owen, Adjutant Right Wing.
    Capt. A. W. Smallie, Adjutant Left Wing.
    Lt. E. W. Baxter, Quartermaster Right Wing.
    Lt. J. McKenzie, Quartermaster Left Wing.
    Lt. F. H. Stiebel, Base Officer.
    Sergt.-Major W. Burkimsher, Regtl. Sergt.-Major.
    Sergt.-Major Higgins, Sergt.-Major Left Wing.
    Sergt. D. Thompson, Quartermaster Sergt.
    Sergt. R. Watts, Orderly Room Sergt.

Upon formation of the Field Force, the Extra Staff Appointments were as follows:—

Bt. Lt. Col. W. S. Shepstone, Provost Marshal.
Bt. Lt. Col. A. Hair, Asst. Remount Officer.
Bt. Lt. Col. B. Crompton, D.S.O., Special Service.
Major R. A. Cockburn, Transport Officer.
Lt. E. B. Hosking, Intelligence Officer.

Field Officers:—

Major W. T. Gage, H. Squadron.
Major A. C. Townsend, A. Squadron.
Major W. Comrie, D. Squadron.

Squadron and Troop Officers:—

Right Wing—A. Squadron:

Capt. E. W. Barter, O.C. Squadron.
Lt. R. W. Smith, Troop Leader.
Lt. J. H. Smith, Troop Leader. ⎱ Promoted, 6.3.06:
Lt. H. Walton, Troop Leader. ⎰

B. Squadron:

Lt. P. W. Stride, O.C. Squadron.
Lt. C. M. Paterson, Troop Leader.
Lt. A. E. Todd, Troop Leader. Promoted 9.2.06:
Lt. J. O. Smythe, Troop Leader. Promoted 13.2.06:

C. Squadron:

Lt. G. R. Richards, O.C. Squadron.
Lt. R. A. Lindsay, Troop Leader.
Lt. J. W. Johnston, Troop Leader.
Lt. S. R. Merrick, Troop Leader. Promoted 6.3.06.

D. Squadron:

Capt. J. W. V. Montgomery, O.C. Squadron.
Lt. B. W. Martin, Troop Leader.
Lt. W. H. Home, ,,
Lt. W. E. Antel, ,,

J. Squadron:

Capt. T. J. Allison, O.C. Squadron.
Lt. R. M. Tanner, Troop Leader.
Lt. A. S. Langley, ,,
Lt. P. G. Dickinson, ,, Promoted 4.2.06.

Left Wing—E. Squadron:

    Lt. W. Park Gray, O.C. Squadron.
    Lt. W. Black, Troop Leader.
    Lt. C. F. J. Cope, ,,
    Lt. G. E. Blaker, ,,

F. Squadron:

    Lt. R. A. L. Brandon, O.C. Squadron.
    Lt. J. G. Fannin, Troop Leader.
    Lt. H. C. Thornhill, ,,

G. Squadron:

    Lt. H. Ryley, O.C. Squadron.
    Lt. B. A. Hampson, Troop Leader.

H. Squadron:

    Lt. J. E. Briscoe, O.C. Squadron.
    Lt. A. B. Vanderplank, Troop Leader.
    Lt. C. G. Kemp, ,,

Upon mobilisation, Lt. Colonel D. McKenzie took command of the Column, and Lt. Colonel Weighton took command of the Regiment, but owing to an accident to his knee sometime previously, resulting in a severe case of synovitis, he was unable to go into the field. He, however, acted as Commandant at Richmond during the period up till April 1906, and sat as President of the Courts-Martial during many of the trials, mention of which will be made later on.

Major Rodwell acted as Chief Staff Officer to the Column, and Major Townsend commanded the Right Wing, N.C., in the field.

Capt. J. P. S. Woods was in Hospital with Enteric Fever in Harrismith, and did not serve with the Regiment in 1906, but re-joined in December, 1907.

ON SERVICE—FEBRUARY 9th, TO MARCH 31st, 1906.

The Headquarters Squadrons (A., B. and J.), under the command of Lt. Colonel McKenzie, marched out of Maritzburg at 3.30 p.m. on Saturday, February 10th, for "the Front," accompanied by C. Battery, N.F.A. After encountering a drenching thunderstorm, the Force reached Nel's Rust farm at 7 p.m., and bivouacked at the Umlaas Drift for the night. Colonel McKenzie remained with the Intelligence Staff at Thornville Junction to mature his plans. The next day,—Sunday—was spent in Camp. Nothing exciting happened till afternoon, when two native prisoners were taken on suspicion while attempting to evade the troops. They were despatched to the Intelligence Camp under escort, but within a few hundred yards of the bivouac lines they boldly attempted to escape. The escort called on them to stop, but the call was unheeded, and they were promptly fired on. One was shot instantly and the other surrendered. Next day, 12th, Camp was struck early, and the Column marched to Hosking's farm (the scene of the recent attack on the Police), arriving there at 8 a.m. The same day the remaining Squadrons of both Wings arrived, the Left Wing having travelled by rail from up-country through the night. The Natal Police Field Force and the Border Mounted Rifles also arrived, and Brigade Camp was at once formed, the whole force being in command of Lt. Colonel McKenzie, N.C., and known as "McKenzie's Field Force."

That night a Squadron was despatched under Capt. Barter to Nel's Rust, about 13 miles off, to repel an expected attack by Chief Tilonko's impi, which was then supposed to be in rebellion. What a ride it was! The men started at a hard gallop over broken country at about 4 p.m. with stripped saddles. A storm came on and drenched every man to the skin. The Squadron rode through the rain and darkness along a terrible road, and reached Nel's Rust at 9 p.m. The only mishap en route was the loss of a pack pony. Corporal Chater pluckily tracked the animal single handed and returned to the Squadron the following day. He narrowly escaped being shot within a few yards of a farm house during his search for the pony. The farmer hearing him approach challenged him in the darkness and was about to fire at a few yards distance, when Chater saved himself by shouting, "Don't fire, I'm a Carbineer!"

The Squadron, on reaching Nel's Rust, were amused to find all the farm and Creamery Buildings beautifully lit by electric light, and every man and woman, Indian and Native as well, armed for the attack with guns and farming implements, such as hoes, pitch forks, etc., and bravely doing duty at all doorways and windows. It was indeed a comical sight.

The attack by rebels never came off, but strict sentry duty

CAMP, BALGOWAN, 1899.

Standing—Capt. G. F. Tatham, Lieut. Nourse Varty, Lieut. D. W. Mackay, Lieut. W. Comrie, Lieut. B. Crompton, Lieut. E. Lucas, Capt. A. Lyle, Capt. A. Hair, Lieut. D. Sparks, Lieut. C. N. H. Rodwell.

Seated—Capt. C. G. Willson, Major D. McKenzie, Lt.-Col. E. M. Greene, O.C., Capt. & Adj. J. Weighton, Surgeon Major J. Hyslop, Capt. F. E. Foxon Capt. W. S. Shepstone, Lieut. W. J. Gallwey.

was kept up all night. The men off duty slept in the stable close to their horses. The next day at sundown the Squadron returned to Camp and again encountered a heavy storm en route, reaching their lines wet to the backbone, tired and hungry, only to find all tents down and their kit mainly "non est." While at Nel's Rust the greatest kindness was shown the men by the Hon. Jos. Baynes, C.M.G., M.L.A., and Mrs. Baynes.

The next day the whole Brigade, numbering 1,000 men, moved out along with Chief Mveli's levies to capture Majonga, Chief of the rebels, and his gang, who were responsible for the death of Sub-Inspector Hunt and Trooper Armstrong, N.P. These rebels were hiding in the Enon Bush, —a dense forest several miles long. That afternoon, two of Majonga's accomplices, named Uzondweni and Njwezi, were captured in the bush, and after trial by Court Martial, presided over by Col. Mansel, N.P., they were found guilty of the murder of the Police Officer and Trooper and sentenced to death. At about 3 p.m. the whole of the Troops were paraded, making three sides of a square on the plateau overlooking the bush which, with its precipitous slopes and krantzes, made an impenetrable barrier against escape or any trouble at the hands of the native rebels. A thick mist enveloped everything. The doomed men acknowledged their guilt, and, in the presence of the troops and Native levies, were escorted blindfolded to where their graves had been dug. The firing party, consisting of four men each from the Carbineers, Natal Police and Border Mounted Rifles, was paraded thirty yards or so from the prisoners. One half of them had loaded rifles and the other half rifles with blank cartridges, no one of the party knowing which of the rifles were loaded. The grim sentence was interpreted by Lieut.-Col. Royston, B.M.R., to the Native levies, who responded with three royal "Bayetes." The next moment was one never to be forgotten. The order, "Ready, present, fire!" was given just as a cloud of mist rolled past, and in a second all was over for the victims. Before the interment the levies, in Zulu custom, filed past the dead bodies, singing a war song and touching the bodies with their assegai points. The moral effect of this incident prevented any further rising in that district, for the news of the execution travelled with lightning speed among the natives, and by breakfast time next morning it had reached the Magistrate at Ixopo Village, some 40 miles away, by Native intelligence. The news caused many natives to remark "If that is what the

Government does with Commoners, what will be done with the Chiefs when found guilty!"

The order to march was given, and the Column, in half sections proceeded down the slopes of Enon Mountain, through bush and in heavy rain to Richmond, which was reached at about 8 p.m. Camp was pitched close to the road bridge, and the Column remained stationary for four days, during which time supplies were augmented and kits and horses were seen to.

On February 19th the Column, accompanied by C. Battery, N.F.A., left for Chief Mskofeni's district, south of the Umkomaas river. This Chief was already giving considerable trouble to the authorities and required a strong force to overawe him. A halt was made at mid-day at Umkomaas Drift in the broad valley, but owing to the most intense heat there the order to march was soon given. Waterfall Hotel was reached by night and a halt was made. The next day the Column reached Springvale Mission Station and halted. While there Chief Mskofeni was summoned before the O.C. and was seriously warned to keep his tribe under control. The following morning the march was continued to High Flats and the Column bivouacked there for the night, proceeding to Stuartstown next day (22nd). This village was reached about 4 p.m., and for the first time standing camp was formed. The Column remained here for 18 days until March 13th, during which time the O.C. dealt with several troublesome Chiefs, including Mskofeni, who, with others, was tried by Court Martial and fined heavily for disloyalty to the Government. Whilst at Stuartstown Sergt. J. H. Smith and Trooper H. Walton received first Commissions in A. Squadron. Life in camp was dull, but the residents of the village extended the troops every hospitality. The weather was continuously wet for 11 days and very cold. The small patrol tents afforded little shelter but all remained as cheerful as possible. Mounted drills and skirmishing were the main parades, and occasionally a football match and camp concert were indulged in.

The most exciting incident of this camp life was the stampeding of all the horses and mules one night. A memorable night it was! Owing to the cold and rain some 1,100 odd horses were let loose in a large paddock to seek for shelter, when some mules caused them to stampede. Away they went in a wild gallop in column formation. They made a circuitous course several miles in length and every hour or so throughout the night this mad troop of animals galloped past the camp. The noise of their tread was audible a long way off and grew almost deafening as they galloped past camp each time. At early dawn they ceased their stampede through sheer exhaustion, and at daybreak were seen in batches all over the veld. Many of them were terribly cut in many ways through being driven against barbed wire fences in their stampede and some were "cast" as permanently injured. During the stampede the horses galloped through the picket lines, and sentries were obliged to leave their posts and bolt into camp to escape what would have been certain death to many by being trampled on. The course of the stampede was turned into a veritable roadway and the long grass was trampled under foot beyond all vision in places.

The column at last got marching orders and on March 13th moved off to Umzinto. Bivouacs were formed at High Flats and Dumisa en route, and Umzinto was reached on the afternoon of the 15th. The following morning Umtwalumi was reached, and camp was pitched until the 30th. On the 19th Chief Charlie Fynn with his tribe appeared by summons before the O.C. They numbered about 1050 men, and looked very defiant. This tribe had "taken up arms," and would certainly have devastated the district but for the timely arrival of the troops. Chief Fynn personally remained loyal. The whole of the troops paraded before the tribe as a guard, and after certain interviews the Chief's Indunas and several "ringleaders" were arrested. The tribe was fined 1,500 head of cattle and confiscation of all arms. During the following week the troops were engaged in bringing in cattle and assegais and the ringleaders of the disloyal tribe were tried by Court Martial and punished. Chief among them were M'Chesi, the "ringleader" and Batamani. Other Chiefs dealt with were Jack, N'Komeni and Matomeli, ruling over neighbouring tribes. M'Chesi and Batamani were sentenced to death, but the sentences were commuted to long terms of imprisonment. These tribesmen, according to sworn evidence given by witnesses in Court, fully intended to kill the Magistrate (Mr. J. L. Knight, J.P.), and his Staff at Knox' Store and plunder through Umzinto killing everyone, the women and children last of all, and even go so far as to mutilate the women's bodies for war-doctoring purposes. Throughout the evidence reference was repeatedly made to Dinizulu and his influence, and well-founded suspicions arose as to this Chief's implication in the trouble. On the night of March 28th, 300 Carbineers left Camp at 9 o'clock in a heavy rain to patrol the Umzumbi district to within a few miles of Port Shepstone. They returned late the next day after having had a very rough outing. It was while at Umtwalumi Camp that the Troops heard of the resignation of the Natal Ministry owing to Lord Elgin's interference with the death sentence on the Richmond murderers. Great excitement was caused by the news, and at Umtwalumi Station a mad rush was made for the newspapers. The writer remembers a copy of the "Natal Mercury" containing the cable news from England being eagerly purchased for half-a-crown. The Umtwalumi Camp was a pleasant one excepting when rain fell. Being close to the seashore bathing was allowed and each day or so a couple of Squadrons disported themselves and their horses in the briny ocean—quite an enjoyable item for many country members who had never before set eyes on the sea.

On March 30th orders for the de-mobilisation of the Column were received. The Carbineers bivouacked at Umtwalumi Station that night and entrained for "Home" the next day—all feeling fit after their seven weeks' field service, but, nevertheless, entertaining the idea that they would soon be in the field again, as "trouble" was by no means over.

During this period several members of the Corps were detailed for special Militia duty, and Officers in many cases sat on the Courts Martial. Lt.-Col. Weighton, N.C., besides his duties as Commandant of Richmond, was kept busy as President of the Military Court there, which tried 22 rebels, 12 of whom were found guilty of the murder of Sub-Inspector Hunt and Trooper Armstrong, N.P., and were shot after the friction with the English Government was smoothed over. He was also President of the Military Courts at Greytown and Pietermaritzburg. At the Pietermaritzburg Session the Chiefs Tilonko and Skukuku were found guilty of sedition and sentenced to heavy fines and long imprisonment.

The foregoing account indicates somewhat the nature of the operations in the Southern portion of the Colony. The Field Force carried out an important duty in demonstrating to the native tribes the fact that the Government was prepared to immediately subdue any attempt at insurrection, and without the aid of troops other than the Colony's own forces. During the period referred to, Lt.-Col. Leuchars, C.M.G., of the Umvoti Mounted Rifles who was in command of a mobile column in the Umvoti Valley and at Mapumulo, suppressed a rising by Chief Gobizembi, who was eventually captured, tried and punished.

The experience gained by all ranks helped considerably

towards the great success of the subsequent operations in Natal and Zululand, which, in so far as the Natal Carbineers shared therein, will now be recorded. But for the success of the first expedition above recorded the subsequent insurrection of the natives would probably have taken place sooner and have been far more serious.

ON SERVICE.—17th APRIL to 2nd AUGUST, 1906.

Subsequent to the return of McKenzie's Field Force at the end of 1906, fresh trouble arose in Umvoti County. Chief Bambata had been deposed for misconduct, civil debt, and insubordination to the Government. He attacked the Natal Police Field Force at Impanza, near Greytown, and ultimately fled into Zululand, closely pursued by the Natal Police Field Force, under Chief Commissioner Col. Mansel, C.M.G. This flight was sympathised in by certain Zululand Chiefs, and even Dinizulu was under further suspicions of disloyalty. The Natal Militia were once more called out for service, and on April 17th the Natal Carbineers received orders to mobilise. The whole of the Regiment was not required at once. On the 18th April the Left Wing mobilised, along with 150 men of the Headquarters Squadrons in Maritzburg. The 150 men proceeded by rail to Dundee and joined the Left Wing, and this Force was placed under the command of Lt.-Col. D. W. Mackay, O.C. Left Wing. The Headquarters Squadrons were commanded by Capt. E. W. Barter.

The remainder of the Right Wing mobilised on May 1st, with the exception of D. Squadron. They proceeded to Helpmakaar under the command of Lt.-Col. Weighton, who assumed command of the Regiment—Col. McKenzie having been appointed to command the Zululand Field Force. Col. Weighton however, was unfortunately obliged to return to Maritzburg soon after reaching Helpmakaar, owing to his still suffering from a prolonged attack of synovitis in the knee. Major A. C. Townsend took command of the Right Wing, but on May 18th, owing to ill-health, he was invalided home, and was succeeded by Capt. T. M. Owen, who afterwards became Staff Officer to Lt.-Col. Mackay's Column on Major Smallie's return to Dundee at his own request. Lt.-Col. Mackay's column at first comprised the Left Wing, about 400 strong, and the 150 men from Headquarters. Capt. Brandon took command of the Left Wing, and Lt. Kemp acted as Wing Adjutant. Capt. Barter commanded the Right Wing in succession to Capt. Owen when the latter became Staff Officer to the Column. Capt. Barter acted as his own Wing Adjutant. Lt. and Quartermaster Baxter was appointed to a combatant commission in B. Squadron on the appointment of Lt. Richmond as Quartermaster of the Right Wing.

On May 15th the whole of the Carbineers (both Wings) came under the command of Lt.-Col. Mackay and were known as "Mackay's Field Force." Lt. D. Walton and Lt. J. D. Walsh were appointed to Commissioned rank in G. and H. Squadrons respectively.

Early in June, D. Squadron mobilised and proceeded to Mapumulo District with the Border Mounted Rifles, where they were attached to Lt.-Col. Leuchars' column until they joined Lt.-Col. Mackay's column in July. The strength of the Carbineers during this second service in the Field reached 918 of all ranks, including special service men. The Regiment of 918 was the largest Natal Volunteer Corps ever put into the Field.

The doings of the Corps in the Field during this period cannot be properly recorded without dividing this chapter into six parts, as follows, each of which will be taken in consecutive order:—

1. "Mackay's Column's" march to Nkandhla and return to Fort Murray Smith at Helpmakaar.

2. Operations of the Right Wing Squadrons in the Umsinga District.

3. "Mackay's Column's" operations at and after leaving Fort Murray Smith.

4. C. Squadron's operations at Nkandhla as "Body Guard" to Col. McKenzie.

5. D. Squadron's operations at Mapumulo prior to rejoining "Mackay's Column."

6. Lt.-Col. Mackay's Column's later operations in Natal.

PART I.

Lt. Colonel Mackay's Column as already mentioned mobilised at Dundee on April 18th. On that day wagons were loaded with Column supplies and provisions for the Nkandhla garrison of Natal Police and Zululand Mounted Rifles who were reported to be on half rations.

On the 19th, the Column, accompanied by one section of B. Battery, N.F.A., under Lt. F. Acutt, marched from Dundee about noon for Nkandhla with some 40 wagons. That night a halt was made at Moyman's farm in the Malangeni Valley, where the Noodsberg Troop of A. Squadron with Lts. R. W. and J. H. Smith joined their Squadron. At daybreak the Column marched and Vant's Drift was reached by breakfast time. The Buffalo River was full and some trouble was experienced in fording the wagons. Breakfast over, a long day's march brought Nqutu in sight and at 6.30 p.m. camp was pitched close to the Magistracy. The weather was bitterly cold and rations were not too plentiful. The march was continued at 9 a.m. next morning and Nondweni was reached in the afternoon. The column bivouacked for the night and stood to arms at 4 a.m. next morning. Having entered well into Zululand, every precaution against night attack was now taken. Each night laager was formed with the wagons, and a rough barbed wire fence was erected 50 yards from the laager. The whole force stood to arms at 4 o'clock each morning. On the 23rd Fort Lewis, near Babanango, was reached at 5 p.m. and the next day the Column halted at the Umhlatuzi River, near Itala mountain. Here the first decent water for horses and man was obtained since crossing Vant's Drift into Zululand. On the 25th Nkandhla was reached at 1 p.m., after a six days' dreary slow march through barren and hilly country. Wagons were soon parked and off-loaded for the "starving" garrison who appeared to be far better off for food than was the dusty relieving force. The Z.M.R. and Natal Police extended the Column every hospitality. Camp was pitched on the Eshowe side of the Magistracy, and the Officers of the whole Column were invited to lunch in the Z.M.R. Mess. All troops stood fast on the 26th, and usual Camp duties were the order of the day. On the 26th the Z.M.R. and Natal Police left for Ntingine and Fort Yolland respectively. The same day B. and E. Squadrons N.C. accompanied the Staff to the Nomanca Ridge overlooking the great Nkandhla forest in which Bambata and

Chief Sigananda with his tribe were hiding. The enemy's scouts were surprised, and the first shot was fired by the Carbineers at some 28 rebels who hastily retreated into the forest. The reconnaissance party then returned to Camp. That day Carbineer outposts got into touch with the rebels and at sundown Trooper E. S. Mack of A. Squadron brought into camp the first prisoner from the forest. The man was fully armed in Zulu warrior style, and his assegais and shield were handed to Tpr. Mack, his captor, who subsequently handed them to his Troop Officer, Lt. H. Walton, as a souvenir of the occasion. On the 30th a reconnaissance in force was made to try and draw the enemy, but no rebels ventured out of the forest.

The Artillery tested their ranges over absolutely unknown country, with steep hills, valleys and forest, and with the technical assistance of Lt. D. Walton N.C. (a Government Surveyor), fairly accurate distances from peak to peak were measured off for Artillery fire. The next day was spent in Camp, and on May 2nd a combined movement was made by the whole force through the valleys down to the Ufeni Gorge and along the ridges overlooking the forest. Many hundred head of cattle were captured, but only once during the day did the rebels offer determined resistance. Capt. Park Gray with 20 men of E. Squadron were scouting at the extreme end of Nomanci Ridge, when about 100 rebels attacked them at close quarters, having been in hiding behind the numerous large rocks. The engagement was short and sharp, the rebels being so close as to throw their knobkerries in amongst the Carbineers. They, however, soon retreated and Capt. Gray retired after killing four and wounding several rebels. The Artillery, seeing the enemy in flight, opened fire at about 3,000 yards and succeeded in dropping the second shell among them. It came out in evidence in the Courts-Martial trials later on that this shell fire caused many rebels to leap over a krantz, resulting in eight of them being killed, including one of Chief Sigananda's sons. In this encounter Sergt. Craythorne and Tpr. Beattie, N.C., behaved very pluckily. Craythorne shot one rebel at not more than 30 yards distance. By sundown the whole force returned to Camp. On the 3rd a further reconnaissance in force took place and considerable stock was captured. A few shots were fired, but the enemy kept well to the forest. Many huts belonging to important rebels were burnt and valuable information was gathered.

That evening Col. Mansel at Fort Yolland on the Eshowe side of the forest sent word by heliograph that his force was

SERGEANTS, 1898.

Top Row—E. W. Barter, J. Mapstone, P. J. Stevens, T. J. Lyle, T. M. Owen, W. A. Bartholomew, P. W. Stride, F. G. Holmes, R. A. Cockburn, J. W. Armitage.
Second Row—E. Colville, A. Ashdown, T. Mitchell, J. Mackillican, A. C. Tewnsend B. R. Buchmnn Reg.-Sergt.-Major Bowen, Q.-M.-Sergt. Munro, Bandmaster Kielly, C. J. Meares, J. W. Johnston, A. H. Cockburn.
Third Row—R. Carbis, A. E. Todd, P. Lawrence, A. Peel, W. T. Gage.

likely to be attacked, and every precaution was taken at Nkandhla against a surprise attack from the rear-guard of the rebel forces. All ranks were on the alert and double pickets were posted. At 7 p.m., during "Mess" the alarm was raised, as word was sent from the Magistracy to the effect that the rebels were marching on the Camp. The man who was despatched with the message gave the alarm verbally to the men along the line before reaching the Commanding Officer. It was dark and very misty. The men heard the verbal alarm before their Officers who were at "Mess." Instantly and quietly all ranks got down to cover behind their saddles in the open and waited for orders with rifles all ready for action. The Officers, moved by the quietness in Camp, left the Mess to make enquiries, and were astounded to find the men ready to repel an attack. The attack never came off, for the supposed rebels turned out to be a large number of women and children who came to Camp to claim protection, as their huts had that day been burnt down. Many amusing incidents happened during the alarm. The Right Wing Mess Tent was pulled down by Lt. Tanner on the heads of the occupants, and the roast beef was knocked over into the mud and grass. Corporal Chater fired through the mist at a horse not 20 yards off in a wattle plantation—thinking it was a rebel—and missed his object. One or two men pulled off their rifles accidentally, and, most amusing of all, one Artillery gun loaded with shell was discovered to have been trained right on to the Staff Mess wagon, which had that evening been moved into a new position just outside the saddle lines, and round which 18 officers were seated at the time.

On the 4th and 5th further reconnaissances in force were made, the object being to try and estimate the enemy's strength without engaging them, prior to Col. McKenzie's arrival with the newly formed Zululand Field Force. On the 5th just as the Column was retiring from the Nomanci Ridge, a party of rebels opened fire at about 900 yards on the rear-guard, consisting of E. Squadron and one troop from each of A. and J. Squadrons, all under Captain Gray. Orders were given not to engage the enemy as they were only a few scouts, and it was getting late. It was impossible to see the enemy concealed behind the huge granite boulders, but one of them exposed himself full length and challenged the Carbineers to "come on." He was promptly treated to some sharp-shooting by Capt. Gray and Tpr. Samuelson and then disappeared. It was discovered that day that the rebels had constructed a stone wall 3 feet high right across the main road to the forest, and afterwards evidence given in Court by rebels explained that the wall was built that morning in order to check any advance to or retreat from Fort Yolland where Col. Mansel was attacked the same day at Bobe Ridge. On the 6th Canon Roach conducted divine service in Camp. On the 7th more cattle were captured, but the rebels kept well out of sight and range.

On May 8th McKenzie's Zululand Field Force, consisting of the T.M.R., Royston's Horse, D.L.I. and Artillery, arrived at 3 p.m. from Dundee. What a magnificent spectacle it was! The entry to Camp past the Post Office at Nkandhla commenced at 3 p.m. and it was 6 p.m. before the last man and wagon passed. The Carbineers, on the arrival of this new Force had greater hopes of seeing some real fighting, but bitter disappointment followed their hopes, for a short time after, orders came for "Mackay's Field Force" to proceed to Helpmakaar for service in that district as, so it it stated, a rising in Natal was then expected daily.

The Corps did not leave at once. The next day was spent in Camp "cleaning up" and off-loading supply wagons. On the 10th Lt. Colonel McKenzie, who on May 5th had been given command of all the Field Forces with the brevet rank of Colonel, paraded the Brigade, including the Carbineers, at 3 a.m. The Forces marched at 4.30 a.m., the Carbineers forming the flankers, advance and rear-guards, and proceeded to the Nkandhla forest, where operations were carried out all day. Very hard work was put in by all units, and few rebels were fired at.

On the 11th the Carbineers left for Natal with a convoy of 138 empty wagons. Before leaving they were paraded in mass and addressed by Col. McKenzie, who in most feeling terms thanked one and all for the good pioneer work done in Zululand, and expressed his deep regret at not being allowed to utilise the Corps in his forthcoming operations in the forest. He shook hands with each Officer, and bade him a personal "Good-Bye." Col. McKenzie kept with him Troopers Hopkins and Ken Phipson of A. Squadron, N.C. Hopkins afterwards received a commission in Royston's Horse, and Phipson did duty as the Colonel's Orderly throughout the Nkandhla and Umvoti operations. The force was heartily cheered out of Camp and commenced the long march to Helpmakaar. The route as far as Nqutu was the same as already traversed, and nothing exciting occurred. Each Wing took it in turn to lead the Column, and a careful watch was kept daily for any designs on the part of the Natives. Nondweni was reached at 9 a.m. on the 13th, and a halt was made for breakfast. After breakfast Lt.-Col. Mackay with a large party, including the writer, rode off to visit the spot on the bank of the Ijojosi river where, during the Zulu war of 1879, the Prince Imperial was killed. The Memorial Cairn and graveyard were inspected, and the details of the incident were related in graphic style by an old native care-taker named Gayene who was one of the party of Zulus who surprised and killed the Prince. Capt. Jas. Stuart, N.F.A., acted as **Interpreter** and related the sad story in detail. Meanwhile the Column moved off from Nondweni and the Colonel's party overtook the main body near Nqutu which was reached at 5 p.m. That night orders were received to proceed in haste to Helpmakaar. Next day at 7 a.m. the Convoy wagons were sent to Dundee in charge of the Dundee Squadron and the Column proceeded via Rorke's Drift where a midday halt was made. Nearly everyone indulged in a bath in the Buffalo River—the first decent bath obtainable since crossing Vant's Drift, nearly a month previous. Many visited the fine Memorial Church at St. Augustine's Mission Station, and also the Rorke's Drift ruins and Church where the plucky stand was made by the British troops in 1879.

The Column pushed on and reached Helpmakaar at 10 p.m. after a wearisome march up the Biggarsberg heights in a freezing cold wind. Many men were completely "bowled over" by the cold, and owing to fatigue and hunger, a halt was made within two miles of Fort Murray Smith to enable men and horses to get some food. That day's march was the longest up to that date—the column with all transport having covered nearly 30 miles since 7 a.m. The order to "Stand to Arms" at 4 a.m. was that night relaxed for the first time since the first entry into Zululand—a concession which the men fully appreciated. Early next morning a move was made and by 9 a.m. the Column was once again in a Standing Camp at Fort Murray-Smith. Tents were pitched for the first time since leaving Dundee on April 19th, and the Column was welcomed by the remaining Headquarters men and C. Squadron, who had been at that base since May 2nd. The Regiment was now intact with the exception of D. Squadron.

PART II.

Before proceeding to narrate the further movements of "Mackay's Column," it will be interesting to note the doings of the Headquarter's men and C. Squadron who had hitherto been attached to Major Murray Smith's Column at Helpmakaar base.

This detachment arrived in Dundee on May 2nd and were camped there till the 5th when they joined a composite Column consisting of N.F.A., N.R.R., N.M.R., and N.M.C. under command of Major Murray Smith, N.M.R. The Column left Dundee at 2 p.m. on the 5th and bivouacked for the night at Blesboklaagte. Helpmakaar was reached on the 6th and a fort was constructed—afterwards known as Fort Murray Smith. Camp duties followed, and strong sod entrenchments, supported by barbed-wire fencing, were set up—it being necessary to guard against attack from Chief Kula's tribe, which was then on the verge of open rebellion. The Carbineers were under the command of Major Townsend. On May 8th Major Murray Smith, N.M.R., took command of the whole force known as the Helpmakaar Field Force with Captain Hurst as Staff Officer. The First and Second Reserves from Estcourt northwards were also attached to this Field Force. On May 10th Lt. G. R. Richards in command of C. Squadron N.C., moved out with some of his men to Pomeroy, eventually succeeding, in conjunction with a detachment of the D.L.I., in arresting the powerful Chief Kula and six of his Indunas. This was an important measure, for doubtless the Chief, who was suspected of sedition would, as the result of overtures from Chief Mehlokazulu have very quickly joined the latter and gone into open rebellion. Kula was escorted to camp and eventually lodged in Gaol in Dundee and subsequently removed from the district.

On the 12th Major Murray Smith completed a big movement into the Umsinga Valley and along the Sibindi Valley with his force, and attacked the kraal of Mteli, Chief Induna to Kula. It was a heavy day's work and resulted in 29 rebels being killed. Daily patrols followed, and on the 14th the Right Wing, N.C., with the N.M.R. Reserves, and Artillery, worked along the valleys down to the Buffalo and back as far as Rorke's Drift. During the day's operations several rebels were killed and the final blow was given to those men of Kula's tribe who had risked taking up arms. The Carbineers, like all the others, had a very heavy day's work, covering fully 50 miles over terrible country. The force marched back to Camp late that night and en route joined with Mackay's Field Force which, as stated above, was marching to Helpmakaar.

PART III.

We now return to the further operations of Mackay's Field Force comprising the whole of the Carbineers, excepting D. Squadron, a half battery of Artillery and the Reserves.

On May 17th C. Squadron N.C. left Fort Murray Smith with the Band troop for Nkandhla together with the Natal Mounted Rifles. They remained with Col. McKenzie as his body guard until the Nkandhla operations ceased, and their doings during that period will be recorded later.

The remainder of the Corps stood fast at Fort Murray Smith until the 23rd when at 6 a.m. all available men were sent off at a gallop to defend Helpmakaar Village against an expected attack from Mehlokazulu's impi, which was reported to have come into Natal from Zululand. The report turned out to be unfounded. Later in the day the Column moved off to the Nazareth Mission Station near the Buffalo River with light transport and remained in that neighbourhood two days capturing stock, burning huts, and sniping at rebels. The country was very rough, and the horses suffered terribly. The Mission House had been pillaged and looted by the rebels in a shocking manner. The Column returned to camp on the 25th and on the 26th left for Zululand—being accompanied by the Reserves and Native levies. Rorke's Drift was reached at 9 a.m. on the 27th At 4.30 p.m. Isandhlwana was reached and a stay was made there for three days to allow of operations in the Mangeni Valley, below the Malagato and Hlasagasa Mountains. Each morning at dawn a strong reconnoitring force, accompanied by Artillery, left camp and returned at night. On May 28th the Mangeni Valley was thoroughly searched for rebels. Several were shot, and during two days' operations something like 1,500 head of cattle and 1,000 goats were seized. The Chief—Mehlokazulu—was located in hiding under a ledge of some rocks when his horse was shot dead at his side by a Carbineer. This fact was made known afterwards by natives. The Chief intended, according to native intelligence, to attack the Camp the following night, but that morning (29th) he attacked Col. Leuchars' force at Bekinyoni about 15 miles from us and was thoroughly routed. Before leaving Isandhlwana Camp a force of Carbineers proceeded to Mehlokazulu's huts near the Buffalo River and utterly destroyed them—a fine collection, built in semi-European style.

During the operations in the Mangeni Valley one afternoon, Major Owen sent Tpr. "Bob" Culverwell of A Squadron to Col. Mackay with a despatch, and meantime the Carbineers shifted their position. Culverwell returned to the spot where he thought the force was, and was somewhat surprised at being fired at by some rebels who had been watching his movements. They were not more than 40 yards off when first seen by Culverwell and they shouted to him to "hands up." He promptly returned the fire, and thinking discretion the better part of valour put spurs to his horse and eventually reached the Column, narrowly escaping with his life. This Isandhlwana camp was most interesting to one and all. The camp was pitched close to the site on which the ill-fated Carbineers, 1st Batt. 24th Regiment and others, suffered severely by the Zulus in 1879.

From May 20th to June 23rd the Column operated along the Buffalo valley down to the junction of the Tugela near the Umfongosi river. Hundreds of cattle were captured and some rebels were shot. The column was operating to check the retreat of Bambata and Mehlokazulu who had joined forces in the bush at Macala Hill, and eventually received orders to push on and join up with McKenzie's Field Force at Nkandhla. The column bivouacked along the route at Nqobonga Spruit, Mangeni Store (which had been looted by rebels and burnt out completely), Mahlosi Valley (where protection was afforded to Chief Matshana ka Mondisa, who remained loyal), and on the Qudeni Mountain. The weather was bitterly cold and though the Column had patrol tents, many suffered severely. Owing to ox transport, movement was slow, but a move was made each morning at about 4 a.m. and distances were soon covered. On June 5th the Reserves were ordered back to Helpmakaar for demobilisation and received well earned thanks from Col. Mackay for their excellent services whilst in the Field. On June 9th a detachment of the Natal Rangers, under Capt. Forsbrook, an irregular Corps of Infantry which had been attached to us, left the Column and marched to Nkandhla to join the remainder of their unit under Lt.-Col. Dick, D.L.I. The Rangers' place was taken by the Lancashire and Yorkshire Volunteers ("The Rosebuds") from the Transvaal, 150 strong, under Lt.-Col. Peakman, C.M.G., with Captain Helbert as Adjutant. This was the first occasion on which the Officers of the Carbineers had the good fortune to meet Captain Helbert, and the acquaintanceship grew closer every day, resulting, as it did, in the subsequent appointment in 1907 of this gallant Officer as Regimental Adjutant to the Carbineers —a position which at the time of writing he still holds. The Column was from this date assisted by a Field Search Light apparatus in charge of Sergt. Goertz, N.M.R. On June 10th Lt.-Col. Peakman was appointed second in command of "Mackay's Field Force," and his contingent remained with the column until demobilisation in August following. The column was also strengthened by a detachment of the Cape Mounted Rifles, with one Maxim, in command of Capt. Humphries. On June 22nd, at 8 a.m., B. and G. Squadrons, N.C., with the mounted section of the 'L.' and 'Y.' and the Native levies, moved out from Madhlozi Camp, under Lt.-Col. Peakman and patrolled down to the Buffalo River. Lt.-Col. Mackay having received news by helio on June 11th from Col. McKenzie of the defeat of Bambata and Mehlokazulu in the Mome Gorge fight on the 10th, hurried on to join hands with the Zululand Field Force, and on the 20th the Column got in touch with Col. Leuchars in the Umfongosi valley after operating through the Qudeni Forest. Col. McKenzie was found to be halted with his column in the Ndikwa valley a few miles from the Qudeni mountain, and operations having ceased for a day or so on the surrender of Siqananda the Carbineers were allowed to ride across country and meet their comrades of C. Squadron who were with Col. McKenzie.

Whilst camped on the Qudeni mountain, a portion of "Mackay's Column," consisting of A. and J. Squadrons, was left in charge of the supplies whilst the column moved off to Madhlozi valley. At sundown a strong gale sprang up bringing with it a grass fire from the valley below. In camp were the supply wagons, containing about 20,000 rounds of ammunition. The wagons were quickly drawn to the centre of the camp, whilst all available hands turned their attention to checking the fire which was rushing on to the camp like a hurricane. Three fire breaks were burned simultaneously and were, none too many. The fire leapt the first two breaks and was broken in its mad rush at the third break. After strenuous work under the direction of Lt. Riby Smith, N.C., the wagons were saved, but not before the fire had got within a few yards of them.

On June 24th the column, whilst at Madhlosi Camp, received orders from Col. McKenzie to join him at once at Nkandhla and proceed to Natal for service in the Mapumulo district. Lt.-Colonel Mackay prepared at once for the march and left in person at 6 a.m. on the 25th with No. 1 Troop of A. Squadron under Lt. H. Walton as escort. A hard ride it was, covering a distance of nearly thirty miles through the Little Insuzi valley and past the Itala Mission Station. Nkandhla was reached at 10.30 a.m. just as Col. McKenzie and his staff were about to leave for Natal. Mackay's Column, with all transport, marched the same day from Madhlozi Camp, reaching Nkandhla at midday on the 26th after a heavy march through rough country past the Ntingine Bush, the Tshengabantu Store, through the Little Insuzi Valley and via the Itala Mission Station. A halt was made for lunch at the old Nkandhla Magistracy, and then the column pushed on through the Nkandhla forest.

Col. Mackay left Lt. H. Walton at Nkandhla to conduct, in conjunction with Lt. Clarkson, D.L.I., the defence of Chief Sigananda and his seven sons, who were to be tried by Court-martial for sedition. Meanwhile Lt. Walton's troop was handed over to Lt. P. G. Dickenson of J. Squadron. Lt. Walton rejoined the column at Thring's Post on July 5th, after proceeding to Eshowe with the Court-martial staff and then on by rail to Stanger. Lt. Col. Shepstone, and Troopers Oxland and Braatvedt, N.C., also remained at Nkandhla for the trials, Col. Shepstone being a member of the Court-Martial, and the last two named were engaged as Zulu interpreters. They also returned to Field duty at Thring's Post on July 5th.

Mackay's column reached Fort Yolland on June 27th when Capt. Barter assumed command of the Right Wing, N.C. Middledrift on the Tugela was reached on the 28th and the long climb up the Ntunjambili Mountain to Krantzkop in Natal was negotiated. The Krantzkop Magistracy was reached on the 29th, Balcomb's store on the 30th, Otimati Spruit on July 1st, and Thring's Post on the 2nd. Here the column was brigaded with McKenzie's Field Force and fresh operations of a more hostile nature commenced, details of which will be narrated later.

PART IV.

C. Squadron did not rejoin the Regiment until July at Thring's Post, and it is of interest to note the part played by this squadron in the Nkandhla operations.

The Squadron under Lt. G. R. Richards and the Band Troop of B. Squadron under Bandmaster J. Kielly, left Fort Murray Smith on May 17th as part of the convoy escort which accompanied the N.M.R. under Major Murray Smith to Nkandhla. The route taken was via Nondweni and Babanango, and the convoy reached Nkandhla on May 24th. The Carbineers were detailed for special duty as bodyguard to Col.

Colonel J. Weighton, V.D.,
Commanded Regiment 1907 to 1910.

McKenzie, C. Squadron being the Squadron formerly commanded by him when a Squadron Officer in the Regiment.

At sundown on the 25th May, Col. McKenzie moved his force to engage Bambata in the Ensingabantu bush on the side of the Qudeni Mountain. The Column marched along the bridle path across the "Devil's Gorge" at the Insuzi to the Ntingine, then to the Madhlosi Mountain on the Qudeni range. A terrible journey it was! The Insuzi river lay about 1,000 feet beneath and a slip would have been fatal in almost every case. It took three hours to cross the drift in the dark. At 2 a.m. Ntingine was reached, and a halt was made at 4 a.m. at the edge of the Ekombe forest. At 6.15 the column moved on and at 7 a.m. the mist lifted showing the bush completely surrounded. Bambata had fled however, and after being in the saddle for fourteen hours the column rested. The return march was commenced and a halt was made for the night at Calverley's store. Nkandhla was reached at 10 a.m. on the 27th.

On the 28th at 10 a.m. the Carbineers proceeded with the column for the Nkandhla forest, and the force bivouacked at the source of the Itale stream. At 6.30 a.m. next day operations began. On reaching London Kop the Carbineers descended the Gorge and searched the valley down to the stream. Operations by all Corps lasted throughout the day, some rebels being killed and 460 cattle were captured. The column bivouacked for the night to the east of London Kop. Operations were renewed early on the 30th. At noon the Itale Gorge was again attacked. The Carbineers rode in advance and held a position at the west side of the Gorge to cut off any retreat to the Macala Hill. The enemy was tracked by the smell of burnt porridge, and fighting began, lasting nearly all day. Twenty-one rebels were killed. The column returned to camp and plans were prepared for the attack on the Mome stronghold.

On June 1st the big attack commenced, and the forest was entered by a force of nearly 2,000 men. The Carbineers remained at Gun Hill with Col. McKenzie while the advance to the stronghold was made. Very little fighting ensued, and the troops retired after the enemy beat a hasty retreat. It was a hard day's work, however, and tested the endurance of the men greatly. Sigananda's chief kraal was, however, burnt, and the enemy fled from the Mome Gorge.

Col. McKenzie moved his camp along the Nomanci Ridge to the eastern side near the Mome Stream. Early on the third, the force marched out for the Bonvana Ridge and were placed in position. At 2 p.m. firing was heard on the right below the ridge, and the cry of "Usutu" rang through the forest. The Carbineers and Z.M.R. entered the forest and all units engaged in the drive through the bush. Fighting was confined to Royston's Horse, and Capt. Clerk here made his plucky stand against great odds. With his force was Trooper W. H. E. Hopkins, of "A" Squadron, N.C., who was severely wounded in the head. The wound necessitated a serious operation, and injured Hopkins' hearing permanently. That day many rebels were killed in the Manzipambana fight.

On June 4th the forest drive was continued. The Carbineers operated on the right flank towards the Sibudeni Hill. The enemy was not met with all day, and the force returned to camp in the evening footsore and exhausted. On the 6th a further "drive" was made from the Bonvana Ridge to the Bobe Ridge. It was a terrible day's work, and those engaged will never forget the hardships endured. The column bivouacked for the night on the bank of the Nkunzana River, near Cetewayo's grave. That night intelligence arrived that Sigananda and his followers were located, and the whole force was moved early next morning up the Bobe Ridge. The enemy, however, was not found, and all troops returned to Nomanci Camp "done up." Nothing exciting happened until the 10th. On the night of the 9th Sigananda was located near the Mome stronghold, and news came that Mehlokazulu and Bambata were joining him with 1,000 rebels. At 3.30 a.m. on the 10th all mounted men moved off, the Artillery and Infantry having preceded them at 3 a.m. The Carbineers, as bodyguard to the O.C., moved westerly with the other units. A halt was made at Gun Hill, and the forces were disposed for attack—the Z.M.R. being given the place of honour in the advance. The enemy was located and a memorable gallop was made towards the Mome. The fight began and in a short while the enemy was surrounded.

The Carbineers were operating below the Gorge and eventually joined hands with the T.M.R. Lieut. Lindsay was in charge of this Troop. The firing continued all day and the rebels were utterly routed, leaving among their dead the rebel ringleader Bambata, and the Chief Mehlokazulu.

Col. McKenzie, not knowing then that Bambata was dead, formed a strong column, including the Carbineers, for further operations under his personal command. Lieut.-Col. Royston was placed in command of a separate column to work in conjunction with him. McKenzie's Column left on June 12th for the Ekombe Forest by the road to the Qudeni Mountain. The Colonel, with the Carbineers, went across country from the Nomanci Ridge to the Ntingwe. It was reported that Makahlaleke, one of Sigananda's principal sons, was in hiding in the Ofeni Gorge. One troop of Carbineers, with the Z.M.R., commanded the junction of the Ofeni and Insuzi Rivers. The remainder of the Carbineers, with the N.D.M.R., thoroughly searched the chasms, which were from 300 to 400 feet in depth. In one chasm the Carbineers put up a rebel who, in the failing light, threw away his coat and a revolver, and managed to escape, although wounded. This rebel turned out to be the man Makahlaleke, who was being searched for. He afterwards surrendered with his father. An hour's halt in the dusk was made at Insuzi River, and the column eventually arrived at the Ntingine at 9 p.m., bivouacking at Titlestad's store. The column moved at 2.30 a.m. the following morning and marched to the Insuzi Valley and Fort Yolland. A halt was called at the summit of the Macala Hill in order to "drive" the bush. The Carbineers were ordered to make for the centre of the crescent-shaped bush. The drive was completed by 11 a.m. and a halt was made for breakfast. While in the bush a few Carbineers, under Lieut. Lindsay, were standing on rocks, when a rebel beneath them thrust his assegai at a passing friendly native, with the result that the Carbineers put up a hunt and killed two rebels in ambush. It was here that Col. McKenzie shot Malaza, the Basuto witch doctor, who had "doctored" Bambata's impi. The column returned to Titlestad's store at 4.30 p.m., where news came that Sigananda had surrendered. At 5.30 a.m. on June 14th the column marched to the Ekombe Forest again. The Carbineers, with Royston's Horse, then descended to the Mfongosi Stream and took part in "driving" the bush up an altitude of about 3,500 feet. The horses became knocked up with the two days' hard work, for no wagons and rations had been seen for days.

The news that Bambata's dead body had been identified was received the next day, and the good news cheered the men tremendously. The column marched to the Ekotongweni and a most exhausting drive was made towards the Tugela, eventually returning to camp. The column then moved to Ndikwa Valley and rested for a few days. Whilst here the Carbineers got into touch with their comrades of Lieut.-Col. Mackay's column for the first time since May 17th, and right hearty were the mutual greetings between officers and men.

Many of "C" Squadron were in shreds of clothing—some had resorted to skin patches on their breeches, and many were without leggings, and their boots were held together by string.

The appearance of one and all was proof of the arduous work done, but all were cheerful and ready for the next of Col. McKenzie's night marches—commonly dubbed "night-mares"!

C. Squadron returned to Nkandhla, and on June 25th marched with the Staff for Natal, via the Forest, Fort Yolland, Middle Drift, and Krantzkop, eventually reaching Thring's Post, the base of new operations, on July 1st.

On July 2nd they rejoined their regiment, and once more came under the command of Lieut.-Col. Mackay.

Having now narrated the doings of C. Squadron, the writer must proceed to relate the doings of D. Squadron during all this time, and before the Regiment was once again all together. Trooper Ken Phipson, of A. Squadron, remained at his post as Special Orderly and Despatch Rider to Col. McKenzie throughout the subsequent operations.

PART V.

Whilst the Nkandhla surrenders were coming in, fresh trouble broke out in the Mapumulo district in Natal. Two Chiefs, Messeni and Ndhlovu ka Tumeni, with some 5,000 to 7,000 followers, had openly rebelled, and immediately Major Murray Smith with the N.M.R., two Squadrons of the B.M.R., under Lieut.-Col. Arnott, D. Squadron of the Carbineers, under Capt. Montgomery, and other details were despatched to the scene of trouble before the Zululand forces could co-operate. By now the whole of the Carbineers were in the field once more. On June 19th a convoy was attacked by rebels at Otimati Stream, resulting in the death of Tpr. Powell, N.M.R., and the wounding of Sergt. Knox, N.M.R. The rebels were eventually defeated by the N.M.R., under Lieut.-Col. Ritchie. On the same day Thring's store was burnt down. Mr. Sangreid, the storekeeper, was brutally murdered, and Mr. Robins, the Stock Inspector, was nearly killed, being left for dead.

On June 21st operations began in earnest. Col. Leuchars, of the U.M.R., with a strong column consisting of D. Squadron Natal Carbineers, and others details made a reconnaissance from Thring's Post down the Hlonono Ridge to the Mission Station. The rebels were surprised and a hot engagement followed—many close encounters taking place. The Artillery eventually routed the enemy and the column returned, leaving many rebels dead on Hlonono Hill. Camp was pitched for the night at Otimati Spruit.

The Carbineers Squadron was not again engaged until after they rejoined the Regiment, but during the week following the Hlonono fight the men were kept hard at work doing patrols and preparing for the coming Zululand columns. On July 1st they moved Camp to Thring's Post, and on the 3rd joined the Regiment. Thenceforth the Regiment was intact, and for the first time since April 17th it operated as a column under Lieut.-Col. Mackay. All further reference to the Regiment in the next Chapter will refer to the entire Corps unless otherwise stated.

PART VI.

All forces having now got into touch with each other, Col. McKenzie commenced making a cordon of troops round Messeni's location. The Carbineers up till now had accomplished much hard and useful work, but had not had the fortune to get much actual fighting, excepting C. and D. Squadrons, which were more fortunate. The Regiment was well seasoned and the largest unit in the field. On July 2nd the general movement began. The Carbineers, all but D. Squadron, which accompanied Col. Leuchar's column, were to move towards Messeni's Kraal via Hlonono Ridge. D. Squadron was to proceed via Glendale. At 10 o'clock that night a native spy reported the capture and murder of Mr. Geo. Veal, of the Natal Public Works Department. At 4 a.m. on the 3rd the Carbineers, accompanied by Col. McKenzie and General Dartnell, left Thring's Post. They reached Hlonono Mission Station at daybreak and surprised some rebels who fled. A. Squadron gave chase and headed them off. The other column co-operated, and by evening many rebels were killed, the brunt of the fighting falling to the N.D.M.R. That day the mutilated body of Mr. Veal was discovered by the Carbineers, and the horrible condition of the ill-fated man's body caused a feeling of horror to run through every Carbineer. The forces bivouacked at Umvoti Drift and the following morning worked up the Umvoti Valley. After a long day's work bivouac was made on the bank of the Umvoti

River. Early on the 5th the retirement to Thring's Post took place, all valleys and bushes being well searched. On this sad day the Carbineers lost their only man during the whole of the Rebellion. The victim was Lance Corporal Vernon Christopher of J. Squadron Maxim Detachment—a fine soldier and athlete, a staunch "Old Hiltonian" and a promising law student. This young man at the age of 22 lost his life in the service of his native land, and a brass Mural tablet is shortly to be erected to his memory by the Regiment in All Saints Memorial Church, Ladysmith. "Chriss," as he was popularly called, whilst on the march back to Thring's Post, went to a kraal near the Hlonono Mission Station, when on arriving near the kraal he was suddenly stabbed by a rebel who sprang from behind the outer kraal fence. The poor fellow's horse was also stabbed in the chest, and both horse and rider fell almost instantaneously, the horse dying on the spot. Christopher, however, with unbounded pluck, fired two shots from his revolver at the rebel but was unable to hit him. The young soldier died within two minutes of being stabbed. The body was respectfully borne to Camp on an improvised stretcher and eventually interred on July 8th in the Ladysmith Cemetery with Military honours. The deceased's Squadron provided the escort from Thring's Post to Stanger under command of Lt. R. M. Tanner. The native rebel who killed Christopher bolted into the bush and evaded capture. The Column reached Thring's Post at midday on the 5th. The same morning, Lt. H. Watlon and Troopers Oxland and Braatvedt returned to duty from Nkandhla treason trials.

On July 6th, news was received to the effect that Chief Messeni was hiding in the bush overlooking Glendale. At about 2 p.m. Col. McKenzie ordered out three squadrons of Carbineers for instant duty. The order was for the first men available to parade. Horses were out grazing, but in less than half an hour the required number of men were on parade. The little force left camp at a gallop, as Messeni was reported to be on the run. A few miles out native messengers reported that Messeni was a considerable distance away, and the day being far spent Colonel McKenzie ordered a retirement to camp.

The next day the Carbineers had a tough bit of work. At 3.30 a.m. the whole Brigade in three columns moved off to try and capture Messeni and his followers in the Umvoti Gorge some 8 to 10 miles away. The Gorge, near Mr. Nicholson's Mill, was an almost inaccessible place. The Carbineers worked in the centre of the cordon and descended the gorge after breakfast. Above the bush was a precipice nearly 300 feet high. This was descended by a single track. A. Squadron held the right of the line and entered the bush first, the other Squadrons following. By midday the bush was "driven" from end to end, but Messeni had made his escape over night. Six rebels were shot and thirteen taken prisoners. Trooper Reed, of Newcastle Troop, N.C., met with a nasty accident in the bush. He slipped, and to save himself jammed his loaded rifle against a rock. The impact fired off the rifle and Reed was shot through the lungs.

It transpired that Messeni had escaped and joined forces with Chief Ndhlovu ka Tumeni in the Tugela Thorn belt. The Columns retired to camp in the evening after a very heavy day's work. Success, however, was not far off. On the night of the 7th, news was received that the two Chiefs were located in the Isimba Valley, about 8 miles off towards the Buffalo. At 11 p.m. the whole Brigade received "after orders" to parade with stripped saddles at 3 a.m. on the 8th and march at 3.30 a.m.—no talking or smoking to be allowed on the march. The moon was shining brightly and a heavy dew was falling. Within two miles of Chief Matshwili's big kraal the Column halted and dismounted. A. and G. Squadrons, N.C., under Captains Barter, Brandon and Park Gray, with fixed bayonets were ordered to surround the kraal. It was a stirring sight. Within 75 wards of the kraal the order to "Charge" was given. Bayonets glistened in the moonlight and men bent forward stealthily and scrambled over rocks and through long grass. The kraal was surrounded, two men were placed at each hut door, and the search began. The door of the Chief's hut was smashed in, but alas! he had gone. Not a rebel was there, only a few welcome fowls. The troops mounted and pushed forward to the Insimba valley. As dawn broke the valley was surrounded by all three columns. The enemy was located in the valley on the banks of the Insimba Stream. There were krantzes, kloofs and bush to negotiate. The trumpeters sounded the general advance. The Carbineers, who were entrusted with the heaviest work, descended the valley dismounted. No alignment could be maintained and each man had to look after his own safety. Down they went—a descent of nearly 2,000 feet. Rifle fire commenced at the mouth of the valley. The N.M.R. and B.M.R. drove up the valley and the rebels were "pinned" in a trap. For two hours the rattle of the firing continued mingled with cries of "Usutu" from the rebels.

All columns combined. Hand-to-hand engagements ensued. Parties of rebels made final charges at close quarters but were soon placed out of action by magazine fire. It was the warmest piece of work since the Mome Gorge fight. Assegais were thrown at passing troops and many narrow escapes were experienced. Lt. Home, of D. Squadron, N.C., had the back of his wrist watch and one sleeve cut by an assegai thrown at close quarters. The enemy was demoralized and beaten. By afternoon many rebels were left dead in that valley—the grave of the Rebellion in Natal. The Chief Matshwili, his son, his chief Induna, and his Native Minister, were all shot whilst attempting to escape out of a cave. The Minister was armed with a battle-axe, two assegais and a Bible—truly a brave warrior, and, of course, not a rebel! A few rebels escaped.

The back of the Rebellion was completely broken, and the troops marched back to Thring's Post by moonlight. The next day all troops rested. On the 10th the Columns moved off to the Tugela Thorn Belt to hunt for the Chiefs Messeni and Ndhlovu. The Carbineers marched at 3 a.m. The Otimati Stream was crossed and the Isiwazimbuzi Krantz was reached by daylight. This was a huge precipice overlooking the Tugela Valley. The Column descended dismounted in file, and so dangerous was the descent that horses had to be closely held. Col. Shepstone's pack pony fell over the krantz and has never been seen again! The valley was reached and a terrible march through thorn bush lasted all day. No rebels were found and the Chiefs had escaped into Zululand. The men were exhausted by the evening and had no reserve rations. A halt was made at the Imati River and the column bivouacked. On the 11th the search continued in terrible country—no water for man or horse being available for hours. The Column returned in the evening calling at Mapumulo en route. Many men were knocked up and had to be left at Mapumulo. Horses also were left behind to recover from their exhaustion. The bush track was so bad in parts that the men were obliged to lead the horses in file. The Rebellion was practically ended—as the fugitive Chiefs surrendered to Sir Charles Saunders in Eshowe.

On the 12th and 13th all troops rested in camp. On the 14th camp was struck and all units moved to the Mapumulo Magistracy. Here a standing camp was pitched until the 18th. The troops patrolled daily and brought in numbers of surrendered rebels. The Court Martial trials were continued, and a general preparation for home was made.

OFFICERS IN LADYSMITH DURING SIEGE, DECEMBER, 1899.

Back Row—Lieut. Nourse, Capt. Hair, Lieut. Townsend, Lieut. Comrie, Lieut. Sparks, Lieut. Rodwell, Lieut. Smallie.
Second Row—Lieut. Tanner, Surgeon-Capt. Buntine, Capt. Lyle, Surgeon-Capt. O. J. Currie, Lieut. Crompton, Lieut. Lucas, Lieut. Bartholomew.
Third Row—Capt. Shepstone, Surgeon Major Hyslop, P.M.O., Major Macfarlane, Lt.-Colonel Greene, O.C., Major Addison, Capt. & Adj. Weighton, Lieut. Gage.
First Row—Surgeon-Lieut. H. B. Currie Lieut. Vanderplank, Lieut. G. F. Tatham, Capt. Foxon, Vet.-Lieut. J. P. Byrne.

Capt. Brandon, N.C., was one of the Courts-martial Board of Officers, and Lieut. H. Walton, N.C., and Lieut. Smythe, N.C., were engaged as Counsel for the defence in the trials of Chiefs Messeni and Ndhlovu and other rebels. Lieut. Walton was, with Corporal A. Carter, N.C., as Interpreter, also engaged as Prosecutor to work up the cases in connection with the murder of Mr. Veal.

On July 18th the Carbineers' Left Wing moved to Bulwer and patrolled that district near Bond's Drift, and on the 23rd the Right Wing moved to Otimati Spruit. On the 28th the two Wings united at Thring's Post, and on the 29th the Regiment received orders for demobilisation. All preparations being completed, Lieut.-Col. Mackay's column marched to Stanger that day and bivouacked for the night. On the 30th and 31st the various Squadrons entrained for Pietermaritzburg, which was reached on August 1st. On August 2nd the Regiment took part in the Review on the Market Square in Maritzburg, when His Excellency the Governor thanked the forces of the Colony, on behalf of the Government, for their services.

Mention must be made of the magnificent reception given to the Regiment by the members of the Loyal Women's Guild all along the route home.

The foregoing pages contain a narrative of the Regiment's services in 1906, and before proceeding to narrate the 1907 expedition to Zululand it will be of interest to record a few promotions and statistics.

STRENGTH OF REGIMENT ON SERVICE.

Between February and April, 1906 675
Between April and August, 1906 918

OFFICERS PROMOTIONS.

Captain A. C. Townsend ... ... to Major	...	6/2/'06
Lieut. R. A. L. Brandon ... ... to Captain	...	9/2/'06
Lieut. W. Park Gray ... ... to Captain	...	9/2/'06
Lieut. J. E. Briscoe ... ... to Captain	...	17/4/'06
Capt. A. W. Smallie ... ... to Major	...	1/5/'06
Captain T. M. Owen ... ... to Major	...	28/6/'06
Lieut. R. W. Smith ... ... to Captain	...	1/5/'06
Lieut. R. M. Tanner ... ... to Captain	...	1/5/'06
Lieut. G. R. Richards ... ... to Captain	...	1/5/'06

During the 1906 operations only 14 N.C.O.'s and men were discharged as medically unfit.

MERITORIOUS AWARDS.

Sergt. E. I. Dicks ... H. Squadron ⎫ Meritorious Service
Sergt. T. P. Catchpole, C. Squadron ⎭ Medal.

Sergt.-Major P. J. Higgins
S.S.M. A. Swan
Sergt. G. L. Thomson
Sergt. C. L. H. Mulcahy
Sergt. J. Humphries ⎫ Mentioned to His Majesty the
Sergt. B. Wray ⎬ King for good service in the
Trooper H. A. Taylor ⎭ Field.
Trooper H. Brown
Trooper C. P. Francis
Trooper A. O. Zunckel
Trooper G. Leathern

OPERATIONS, 1907.

Notwithstanding the severe blow given to the Natives in 1906, subsequent events proved that embers of sedition were still smouldering and only required a little breeze to fan them into a flame of rebellion. Several loyal Chiefs had been murdered in Zululand, and a crisis was reached towards the end of November, 1907, when Mangati, the fighting General of Bambata's "impi" in 1906, who had made his escape from the Mome fight, surrendered himself to the Government and gave detailed evidence of a conspiracy, hatched in Zululand, to bring about a general rising of tribes throughout the country. This conspiracy was traced to the Chief Dinizulu and some of his councillors, and his Royal Kraal at the Usutu was reported to have become the hot-bed of sedition. How far Dinizulu was personally implicated in the matter was never fully disclosed at his subsequent famous trial at Greytown, but his conviction on some of the charges in the indictment on which he was arraigned, justified the steps taken by the Government as hereinafter narrated.

The Government were faced by a serious danger and acted promptly. It was not a surprise, therefore, when on November 30th, 1907, the whole of the active Militia were again called out for active service in Zululand—primarily for the purpose of preventing further trouble, and also in order to effect the arrest of Dinizulu and Cakijana, the latter having been in hiding ever since his escape from the Mome fight of the previous year.

On Sunday, December 1st, the Carbineers, with commendable alacrity, were completely mobilized. Special Service men were enrolled at Headquarters under the supervision of Capt. C. M. Paterson, the Base Officer. At 5.15 p.m. on the 2nd the Headquarters Squadrons left by rail for Ginginhlovu Station in Zululand, arriving there at 5.35 a.m. on the 3rd. The remaining Squadrons, including the whole of the Left Wing, followed very quickly, and reached Ginginhlovu at about 5 p.m. on the same day. The weather was wet and cold, and, like the rest of the Brigade, the Regiment had to bivouac, no tents being then available. The Regiment was all together and remained intact throughout the operations. The mobilization was carried out in record time considering that officers, men, and horses, had to come from great distances covering an area from Charlestown to Camperdown, and from the Drakensburg to the Buffalo and Tugela Rivers. One of the Natal newspapers referred to the mobilization in the following complimentary terms:—

> "The unrest reported in our issue of a few days ago has become very real, and all the Militia regiments have been ordered out. The Carbineers were the first to get orders last Sunday, and in an incredibly short space of time were on their way to Zululand. The Regiment is to be congratulated on being referred to in a despatch by the Prime Minister to the Governor stating that they had performed 'one of, if not the quickest mobilizations on record.'"

Some of the Imperial Officers in Maritzburg who witnessed the mobilization remarked that they had never seen, nor known, such smart work even amongst the Regular Forces.

The strength of the Regiment during the operations was 610, and in addition some 200 Special Service men were enrolled, but did not all become attached to the column.

The Regiment was commanded by Lieut.-Col. J. Weighton, V.D., who was assisted by the following Officers and Warrant Officers:—

STAFF.

Captain G. Helbert	Regimental Adjutant.
Lieut. A. S. Langley	Adjutant Right Wing.
Lieut. H. Walton	Adjutant Left Wing.
Captain C. M. Paterson	Base Officer at Maritzburg.
Lieut. L. C. Tennent	Paymaster.
Lieut. D. Paton	Quartermaster, Right Wing.
Lieut. D. G. Sclanders	Quartermaster, Left Wing.

Sergt.-Major W. Burkimsher ... Regimental Sergt.-Major.
Staff-Sergt. M. Madsen ... ... Right Wing Sergt.-Major.
Staff-Sergt. A. Swan ... ... Left Wing Sergt.-Major.

WING COMMANDS.

Brevet Lieut.-Col. C. N. H. Rodwell ... ... O.C. Right Wing.
Major E. W. Barter ... ... 2nd in Command.
Brevet Lieut.-Col. D. W. Mackay ... ... O.C. Left Wing.
Major J. P. S. Woods ... ... 2nd in Command.

SQUADRON AND TROOP OFFICERS.

Right Wing.

A. Squadron:

    Capt. R. W. Smith ... ... Commanding.
    Lieut. J. H. Smith ... ... Troop Leader.
    Lieut. A. B. Chater ... ... Troop Leader.

B. Squadron:

    Capt. P. W. Stride ... ... Commanding.
    Lieut. J. O. Smythe ... ... Troop Leader.
    Lieut. E. W. Baxter ... ... Troop Leader.

C. Squadron:

    Capt. G. R. Richards ... ... Commanding.
    Lieut. R. A. Lindsay ... ... Troop Leader.
    Lieut. J. W. Johnston ... ... Troop Leader.
    Lieut. S. R. Merrick... ... ... Troop Leader.

D. Squadron:

    Capt. J. W. V. Montgomery .. Commanding.
    Lieut. B. W. Martin ... ... Troop Leader.
    Lieut. A. Praetorius ... ... Troop Leader.
    Lieut. E. C. Hosking ... ... Troop Leader.

J. Squadron:

    Capt. R. M. Tanner ... ... Commanding.
    Lieut. H. Hathorn ... ... Troop Leader.
    Lieut. G. C. Anderson ... ... Troop Leader.

LEFT WING.

E. SQUADRON:

    Capt. W. Park Gray ... ... Commanding.
    Lieut. C. F. J. Cope ... ... Troop Leader.
    Lieut. G. E. Blaker ... ... Troop Leader.
    Lieut. E. C. Zunckel ... ... Troop Leader.

F. SQUADRON:

    Lieut. H. C. Thornhill ... ... Commanding.
    Lieut. J. G. Fannin ... ... Troop Leader.

G. SQUADRON:

    Lieut. H. Ryley ... ... Commanding.
    Lieut. R. J. R. Hearn ... ... Troop Leader.
    Lieut. J. Mackenzie ... ... Troop Leader.

H. SQUADRON:

    Capt A. B. Vanderplank ... Commanding.
    Lieut. W. Black ... ... Troop Leader.
    Lieut. C. G. Kemp ... ... Troop Leader.
    Lieut. J. D. Walsh ... ... Troop Leader.

Lieut. R. A. Richmond (B. Squadron) was unable to take the field owing to his having met with a revolver accident whilst preparing to mobilize. Lieut. E. W. Baxter was recalled from Ginginhlovu for service at Headquarters.

ON SERVICE: DINIZULU EXPEDITION.

Ginginhlovu Camp was anything but comfortable. Wet weather prevailed, and owing to bad railway service, caused by congestion of traffic and urgency in mobilizing, the Force was very badly off for patrol tents. The Officers' Mess was "rigged up" at one end of a blacksmith's shop, and meals were eaten to the tune of the anvil and the kicking of horses being shod under the same roof. December 4th was occupied in camp duties and the branding of horses. The remainder of the Field Force having arrived, a general move was made on the 5th for Somkele, the northern railway terminus in Zululand. A portion of the Field Force had already proceeded, under Lieut.-Col. Dick, D.L.I., via Eshowe. The Carbineers commenced entraining at 10 a.m. for Somkele. The Left Wing arrived there at 5 p.m. and the Right Wing at daybreak on the 6th. At 2.45 p.m. on the 6th the Column advanced for Nongoma. Lieut. J. Mackenzie, N.C., remained at Somkele as Regimental Depot Officer. Lieut.-Col. Weighton was in command of the Column, which also comprised the Natal Royal Regiment and the Natal Naval Corps. All transport was by mule wagons. A halt was made for the night at Rodwell's Kop, about 6½ miles out, near the Ntseleni Spruit, after a tedious march over hilly country.

At 5 a.m. the Column marched and at about 8.40 a.m. reached the Hluhluwe River, where a halt was made. This was the hottest spot ever created. Men and horses were positively exhausted by the heat, and not a breeze of any kind helped to cool the atmosphere. The valley in which the Column halted was covered with thornbush, which only intensified the heat. At noon Major Barter reported that the Column wagons had stuck along the wet and heavy roads. C. Squadron was sent back to assist, but a heavy storm made matters worse. Anticipating damage to the supplies by the rain, and considering the great distance from Nongoma, the Column was placed on half rations. The Commissariat, however, was augmented by buck, which were shot by order of Col. Weighton—the sport being confined to a few Officers only, of whom Capt. Gray and Lieut. Smythe were the most fortunate, both of them bagging several fine specimens. In the afternoon a thunderstorm came on and drenched every man and beast. The Column wagons arrived by 8 p.m., and an issue of rum was greatly appreciated after the drenching one and all had received. On the 8th the march was continued at 2 p.m., and by evening Hlabisa Magistracy was reached, where a halt was made for the night. At 10 a.m. next day the march continued to Dore's store where, owing to scarcity of water, only a short off-saddle was made, and after another six miles' trek a good drift was reached and a halt made for the night, the Column having marched 18 miles that day. At 5 a.m. on the 10th the Column moved off, and after a twelve miles march reached Nongoma Magistracy at 8 a.m., when we learned that Dinizulu had surrendered the previous day and was safely lodged in the Nongoma Gaol. At 5 p.m. the Right Wing horses were inspected by the P.V.O., and at 8 p.m. all ranks were ordered to be ready to parade at 10 p.m. with stripped saddles and one day's rations, as a night march to

Dinizulu's kraal was contemplated for the purpose of surprising and capturing certain rebels who were supposed to be there. The Regiment was on parade all ready to march at about 10 p.m., when the order was cancelled owing to news of the projected movement having reached the rebels in question, and under the circumstances it would have been futile to carry out the expedition. The 11th was spent in Camp, and during the day the Left Wing horses were inspected by the P.V.O. and the P.M.O. made an inspection of the Camp. On the 12th Horse Insurance parades were held, and Col. McKenzie addressed a large gathering of surrendered Zulus, dealing in detail with the objects of the expedition and of the imprisonment of Dinizulu and his Councillors, among whom was the notorious Mankulumana, who for many years carried out the duties of Prime Minister to Dinizulu. The Colonel gave the Zulus permission to return to their kraals and bring back their assegais and other weapons. He further invited them and the Zulus throughout the country to fight if they were so disposed, and gave them two days in which to commence fighting or surrendering unconditionally.

At 8 p.m. Brigade orders announced that at 11 p.m. all the mounted troops would march with stripped saddles and one day's rations. Very soon the news leaked out that the Usutu kraal was the objective. At 10.30 p.m. the Regiment paraded and formed a Column working in conjunction with other Columns formed of the Natal Mounted Rifles, Border Mounted Rifles and the Natal Police. The plan of operation was to surround the Usutu kraal by daybreak. Men who have served through almost every campaign in South Africa and who took part in the ride to the Usutu kraal styled the undertaking as the most arduous piece of field work they had ever witnessed. The Usutu kraal lay about 18 miles off to the south side, but it could only be reached by circuitous routes along some of the roughest country in Zululand, and large numbers of rebels were still about the hills and bush intervening. It was lucky that the columns were able to concentrate at the rendezvous in the time actually taken.

Shortly after parading, as noiselessly as possible the several columns took their respective routes. The Carbineers' column was accompanied by the Commandant (Col. McKenzie) and his Staff. As the Columns marched off the searchlights were brought into play and enabled all ranks to move off without confusion. The night was intensely dark and misty. The Carbineers took the main road, the Left Wing leading. After about 12 miles, George's Store was reached, and then the Column swung off due west into the bush country. The route from thence was by a bridle path only, and the Column was dependent for direction upon a couple of native guides. The march that followed was memorable! On, on, moved the the Column along the Kafir footpath, and often off it, over boulders, through dense bush, down steep inclines, across dongas, and frequently leading the horses, until one felt absolutely giddy from peering ahead through the darkness to keep touch with the file ahead. About midnight, owing to a couple of the advanced Squadrons having pushed on very fast, the remainder of the Column, having lost touch with the lead, and the guides being in front, finding it impossible to follow the invisible track, decided to halt until dawn. They continued the march at daybreak and arrived at the Usutu kraal soon after the others. The advance portion of the Column, comprising F and H Squadrons, kept well in touch with Col. McKenzie, and had some rough experiences.

The sun beginning to shew itself, and Col. McKenize being anxious to reach the royal kraal before full daylight, in order, if possible, to surprise the inmates, the order to gallop was given. The Usutu kraal was seen five miles ahead and between the Column and the kraal lay the Dallala Flats, the scene of Dinizulu's dances and race meetings. Most of the distance was covered at a hand gallop; men came down in ruts and holes, only to mount again and follow the lead. On reaching the hills overlooking the Royal kraal, F. and H. Squadrons were extended in skirmishing order along the summit, and advanced down the side towards the Kraal, upon reaching which about 80 natives of all ages immediately crawled out of the huts and were considerably surprised at the presence of troops. Cakijana, alas, had escaped from the Royal kraal! This was a great disappointment, as the man's personality was of powerful influence amongst the rebels. He was the son of Gezindaba who, many years ago, held the position of "body-servant" to Cetewayo the last of the Zulu Kings and father of Dinizulu. Cakijana grew up at the Royal kraal as a playmate and companion of Dinizulu. After Dinizulu's repatriation from his exile on Robin Island a few years ago Cakijana renewed his companionship, and at Dinizulu's invitation resided near the Usutu kraal. When the Rebellion broke out in 1906 Cakijana was the man who met the rebel leader, Bambata, at the Tugela and enticed him to cross into Zululand and join forces with Chief Sigananda's impi. Caki-

Lt.-Colonel D. W. MACKAY,
Commanding Officer, 1911-1912.

Lt.-Col. Mackay served in Matabele War, 1896, Medal. Joined Natal Carbineers March, 1899. Commanded No. 5 Squadron with Buller's Relief Column. Severely wounded at Colenso, December 15th, 1899. Subsequently joined Volunteer Composite Regiment, and later the 2nd Imperial Light Horse, in which he was Second in Command. Queen's Medal, five clasps. King's Medal, two clasps. Commanded "Mackay's Column" during the Rebellion in Natal and Zululand, Medal. Took over command of Regiment from Col. Weighton in February, 1911.

jana then organised the rebel forces in the Nkandhla Forest, and actually commanded the impi in the Bobe Ridge fight already referred to. He held the position of Adjutant to Bambata's impi, and was under the immediate command of Mangati, who was the actual fighting general of all the rebel impis. (The above facts were brought to light during the trial of the aged Chief Sigananda, in which the writer took part). Cakijana surrendered to the Government in 1908, and after trial was sentenced to a long term of imprisonment. During the night of the march to the Usutu Kraal, the rebels who had congregated there escaped. Almost simultaneously with the arrival of Col. McKenzie at about 6 a.m. on the 13th, the two other Columns were seen coming over the hills from other directions and the remainder of the Carbineers arrived immediately afterwards.

Bully beef and biscuits over, a thorough search was made of all the huts at the kraal, and many valuable papers were found. By the irony of fate almost, a gramaphone which was found in Dinizulu's office was set going on the record in the instrument at the time, and to the amusement of all present the selection happened to be "Auld Lang Syne"—quite appropriate to the troops in the Field and to Dinizulu confined in his cell in Nongoma Jail! The Usutu Kraal as a "Royal House" was a disappointment to all who saw it. Filth and weeds abounded everywhere. Heaps of empty gin and whisky cases and bottles outside Dinizulu's personal apartment testified to the teetotal habits in the Royal household. At about 8.30 a.m. one of Dinizulu's wives reported to Col. McKenzie that her "Royal" Master's cash box containing about £70 in cash had been stolen. Instantly a careful search was made for the missing box but it could not be found.

Lt. Walton suggested a thorough search of the Chief's bedroom from which the box was reported to have been taken. The wisdom of this course was soon apparent for upon turning over a few mattresses and other things, the box was discovered quite intact.

The incident was a very disagreeable one, and there is little doubt that the Zulu woman devised the scheme with a view to bringing discredit on the troops.

Shortly after the box was found the order to saddle up was given, and the troops commenced the return journey to Nongoma Camp. The Carbineers marched back by a different route to that by which they had come, and through equally rough country. On seeing the previous night's route it seemed almost incredible that mounted troops had, by night, negotiated such terrible country. The Column reached Camp at about 7 p.m. after a ride of about 18 miles, and one and all were glad of a good night's rest. The 14th was spent quietly in Camp. At 2.30 p.m. all ranks lined the main road to witness the departure of Dinizulu and his "suite" for Maritzburg. Not a shout was raised as the prisoner drove past in a Government mule wagon under an escort of the Natal Royal Regiment. His departure was soon followed by the breaking up of the Camp.

On the 15th at 3.30 p.m. the Carbineers left Nongoma under orders for Ngotshe. Owing to wet weather the roads were heavy and the mules were soon exhausted. A halt was made at sundown, and during the night a heavy storm broke over the Camp, thoroughly soaking everybody. At 4 a.m. on the 16th horses were turned out to graze. At 6 a.m. the march was continued. Mr. Grove's farm was reached by midday, and a halt was made for the night. The roads were in very bad condition and progress was very slow. Treble mule teams in addition to men were put on to each wagon in turn, at one hill it took two hours to get the 15 wagons up. The Column bivouacked for the night. While outspanned at midday a runner arrived from the Commandant with a copy of a letter from the Magistrate of Ngotshe stating that he had doubts about Chief Maboko's loyalty. Col. Weighton sent a message to Ngotshe stating that he hoped to be at Ngome at about noon the next day and asked the Magistrate to order the Chief, with his Headmen, to be there to meet him. On the 17th at 4 a.m. the horses and mules were turned out to graze. At 7 a.m. the wagons started to cross the Drift, the whole Regiment having to turn out to help get them across. The wagons were all got over by 8 a.m. The Regiment then paraded and marched, only to find a second drift, almost as bad as the first. The wagons were all got over this drift by 9.30, and owing to the very bad state of the roads it took two hours and a half to go three quarters of a mile. There was then good travelling for about three miles, when, on Robert's farm, a bad hill was encountered. The O.C. decided to outspan as the mules were badly in want of water. Helio communication was tried with Nongoma, but although answered a message could not be got through. Col. Weighton and staff pushed on to Ngome arriving there at 1.30 p.m. and interviewed Messrs. Roberts and Crossley. The O.C. then proceeded to the Police Camp and sent messages to Chiefs Maboko, Mapovela, and Kambi to come in and see him on the following morning. The

Column arrived at Ngome at 5 p.m. the mules being completely done up.

On the 18th Col. Weighton interviewed Mapovela and the Headman of Chief Kambi (who was too ill to appear, but who sent a beast in as a present). Communication was got by helio with Nongoma, and the O.C. suggested to Col. McKenzie that instead of going right into Ngotshe, the same purpose would be served if the Column halted at the junction of the Vryheid-Ngotshe-Ngome roads. This movement Col. McKenzie approved of, and he also gave instructions that Maboko was to be arrested, but not Mapovela, as the latter evidently meant well. The O.C. wrote to the Magistrate at Ngotshe instructing him to have Maboko arrested, and informing him of his own intended movements. During the day, time was spent in Camp repairing kit and laying in fresh provisions from Crossley's store. The men indulged in washing kit and bathing, and many visited the famous Nkombe Forest, distinguished as being the bush in which Cetywayo, the last of the Zulu Kings, and father of Dinizulu, hid for three months after his defeat at the battle of Ulundi, and was there captured by the British Troops. Cold weather set in and a huge bon-fire was made at night, round which a jolly smoking concert was held by all in Camp, duly presided over by the genial O.C., Col. Weighton.

At 8 a.m. on the 19th a despatch was received from the Magistrate, Ngotshe, stating that Chief Kambi was too ill to appear. Another despatch was received from the same source at 2 p.m. stating that Chief Mnyisa of the Abaqulasi tribe was reported to be truculent and would refuse to give up his arms. In reply the O.C. stated that he would summon this Chief to meet him at the cross roads. The Column marched at 2 p.m. to Liversage's farm on the Vryheid Road. The road was good but the drifts were stiff. On the 20th Reveille was sounded at 3.30 a.m., and the Column marched at 5 a.m. till 8.30 a.m. and then outspanned till 1.30 p.m. The march was resumed and the cross roads were reached at 5 p.m. Major Barter went in to Vryheid to arrange about rations for the Column. A despatch was received from Col. McKenzie stating that the Column was to entrain on the Monday (23rd), at Vryheid for Colenso, and a message was sent after Major Barter to let him know of the departure of the Column for Vryheid. During the day Col. Weighton sent a message to Chief Mnyisa and Induna Skobobo to appear before him on the following morning, and the next day Chief Mnyisa appeared with 50 followers. The O.C. addressed him, Tpr. Lugg interpreting. Maboko, who had been arrested by the Magistrate at Ngotshe, arriving in Camp under arrest was sent into Vryheid under escort in command of Lt. Martin. On the 22nd Reveille was sounded at 4 a.m., and the Column marched at 6 for Vryheid, arriving there at 9.30 a.m. Col. McKenzie came in at 11.30 a.m., the order for entraining still holding good. All train arrangements were fixed and the first train was to leave at 6 p.m. on the 23rd. The Commandant and staff left by special train for Maritzburg at 4 p.m. The Column camped outside the Railway Station. On the 23rd the morning was spent in Camp, and at 2 p.m. a wire was received from the Commandant stating that the Regiment was to demobilize at once; a composite Regiment of 200 Volunteers to be formed. This order necessitated a complete change of orders. C. and E. Squadrons left for home at 6.45 p.m., F., G., and H. Squadrons followed at 8.15 p.m., the Camperdown troop, Dalton men, Special Service and remounts leaving at 10.30 p.m. On the 24th Reveille was sounded at 4 a.m., and the remainder of the Regiment entrained at 6 a.m., leaving at 7.15 a.m. for Maritzburg.

Before leaving Vryheid some 70 odd men were enrolled in the Composite Force and remained in Camp in charge of Lt. Thornhill. Later on Major Montgomery joined the Militia Composite Regiment at Vryheid as also did Lieuts. Praetorius, Merrick and Chater. Lt. Thornhill was in command at Vryheid until relieved by Major Colin Wilson, N.F.A., who assumed command of the composite Regiment when fully organized. The Carbineers all managed to reach their homes by Christmas day, and the Dinizulu Expedition was thus concluded so far as the Regiment was concerned.

This expedition to Zululand was not eventful with the exception of the famous night march to the Usutu Kraal, but much hard work was done and the route taken was through very rough country. What with wet weather and hills, the transport had a heavy task and frequently wagons had to be pulled through drifts and up steep hills by mounted Squadrons. The Regiment did its work well and the conduct of all ranks was exemplary. By the arrest and subsequent trial of Dinizulu no further risk of trouble in Zululand was feared, and doubtless the expeditious manner in which the Active Militia of the Colony was poured into Zululand prevented what would probably have been a general rising amongst the disaffected tribes in the country. Peace was once more restored and the subsequent operations of the Composite Force were confined to searching for fire-arms and receiving the surrender of rebels. The Carbineers had done their share of duty, and this narrative can now be concluded. The Commandant of Militia subsequently published in Militia Orders (No. 3, of 1908), his thanks for the ready manner in which all the active militia had mobilized on the further call to duty, and for the excellent services rendered by all.

The writer has now completed his task, but should the Carbineers ever again see service in the Field, doubtless some member, if not the present writer, will carefully note the movements of the Regiment in order to keep the History of the Corps up-to-date.

"PRO PATRIA."

ANNALS.

1855. 15th January is the Foundation Day of the Natal Carbineers (see Cap. I.).

The first drill took place on the 20th February, and was attended by the Lieut.-Colonel, Captain, R.S.-Major, and twenty troopers.

The fifth of the rules for the formation of a mounted volunteer corps for Maritzburg and its neighbourhood reads:—"They shall be called out for exercise twenty days in the course of the year," and the tenth bye-law of the Carbineers divides the prescribed period of exercise into quarterly drills of five days each. The first of these began on the 5th of March, and was attended by a total of fifty-five.

List of members who attended the first quarterly drill from March 5th-9th, 1855:—

MARITZBURG TROOP.

Lieut.-Col. Sir Th. St. George, Bart.

Captain Sargeaunt, W. C.

Lieut. and Adjutant Allison, A. B.
Lieut. Allen, P.

Sergt.-Major Weston, G. K.

Sergt. Wirsing, J. O.
Corporal Player, J.
Trooper Allison, T.
Trooper Anderson, J.
Trooper Ablett, J. P.
Trooper Baker, W. G.
Trooper Bressler, F.
Trooper Caldecott, F. W.
Trooper Clough, E. B.
Trooper Coakes, H.
Trooper Collins, W. M.
Trooper Fannin, T. W.
Trooper Freshwater, G.
Trooper Greaves, F.
Trooper Hall, E.
Trooper Hutchinson, W.
Trooper Jardine, J.
Trooper Maxwell, W.
Trooper Maxwell, T.
Trooper Millan, J.
Trooper Moodie, Donald.
Trooper Macleroy, G.
Trooper McKenzie, W.
Trooper McCabe, H.
Trooper McCabe, J.
Trooper Mayne, W. H.
Trooper Osborn, M.
Trooper Pepworth, H.
Trooper Parish, S.
Trooper Pitcher, J.
Trooper Williams, S.
Trooper Wiggett, J.

RICHMOND TROOP.

Lieutenant Nicholson, J. D.	Trooper Hutton, H. J. C.
Sergeant Weir, J.	Trooper Hambridge, W.
Corporal Dacombe, C.	Trooper McKenzie, W.
Trooper Baseley, J.	Trooper McLeod, W.
Trooper Cooke, W. H.	Trooper Nicholson, W.
Trooper Daine, W.	Trooper Pigg, W.
Trooper Dykes, J.	Trooper Ratsey, E.
Trooper Ely, J.	Trooper Styles, R.
Trooper Godden, J.	Trooper Strapp, S.

The effect of the quarterly drill in March was a marked improvement in the troops at their next turn-out on the 4th of April.

In conjunction with the Royal Artillery, the 45th Regiment, and the Cape Mounted Rifles stationed in Natal as police, the Carbineers paraded on the Queen's Birthday, and gained much credit for their smart appearance. In an account of the day's doings, the "Witness" of 15th June says:— "Another phase of this spirit of union, so characteristic of the present day, is seen in the band of our noble defenders who muster under their Colonel, Sir Theophilus St. George's command, in full uniform and mounted, ready for any laurels of glory with which the fates may deign to adorn them."

At this time the Regiment was armed with a carbine and a light cavalry sabre. But as the carbine when served out was as long as an ordinary musket, it had to be shortened and re-sighted by a civilian gunsmith at the trooper's expense.

On the 5th June sixty sat down to a regimental dinner in the Crown Hotel, Maritzburg. A most enjoyable evening was spent, and the proceedings were kept up till a late hour.

On the following 13th the first Carbineer Ball was held, and proved to be a great success, the leading citizens of Maritzburg, and the representatives of Her Majesty's Regulars, then stationed at Fort Napier, being present.

At a banquet given by the Royal Durban Rangers, Lieutenant Wirsing was present on behalf of the Regiment, and responded to the toast of the Carbineers, which was pledged by their comrades in arms with much enthusiasm.

On the 3rd September the quarterly drill was attended by the Richmond Troop, who came into town thirty-one strong. This parade was the largest of mounted troops which had till then been held in the Colony, and the movements, and parade in general, were highly creditable both to officers and men.

In September, Captain Sargeaunt was promoted to the rank of Major, Lieutenant Allen of Captain, and G. O. Wirsing and W. Nicholson of Lieutenant.

In November, Sir George Grey, Governor of the Cape Colony and Lord High Commissioner, arrived in Natal, and was escorted from Uys Doorns to the City by the Carbineers. His Excellency was so pleased by the creditable turn-out, both of men and horses, that he sent Colonel Sir Theophilus St. George a cheque for £90 for the purchase of great coats,—a gift which, it is hardly necessary to say, was much appreciated.

1856. The following amended bye-laws were adopted:—

PROCLAMATION NO. 32, 1856.

By His Honour Henry Cooper, Esq., Colonel, Acting Lieutenant-Governor, administering the Government of the District of Natal.

Whereas, by a Proclamation dated the 6th day of March, 1855, I did publish certain Rules and Bye-laws made by the "Natal Carbineers," for the regulation of the duties of the members of that Corps, and did proclaim my sanction to the said Rules and Bye-laws:

And whereas the said Corps have submitted to me the following amended Rules and Bye-laws, and have requested that the same may be proclaimed, under the provisions of the Ordinance No. 11, 1855, to be of force in lieu and instead of the Rules and Bye-laws so published, as aforesaid:—

Now, therefore, I do hereby repeal and annul my said Proclamation of the 6th day of March, 1855; and I do further proclaim, that I have, under the provisions of the said Ordinance No. 11, 1855, sanctioned, and do hereby sanction, the aforesaid amended Rules and Bye-laws, and hereby direct their publication for general information.

God save the Queen!

Given under my hand at Pietermaritzburg, in the District of Natal, this 29th day of February, 1856.

(Signed) H. COOPER.

By command of His Honour the Acting Lieutenant Governor,

(Signed) WILLIAM C. SARGEAUNT,
Colonial Secretary.

Lieut. H. B. Currie,
Natal Medical Corps.
Attached to Regiment, Siege of Ladysmith.

Captain R. A. Buntine,
Natal Medical Corps.
Attached to Regiment, Siege of Ladysmith.

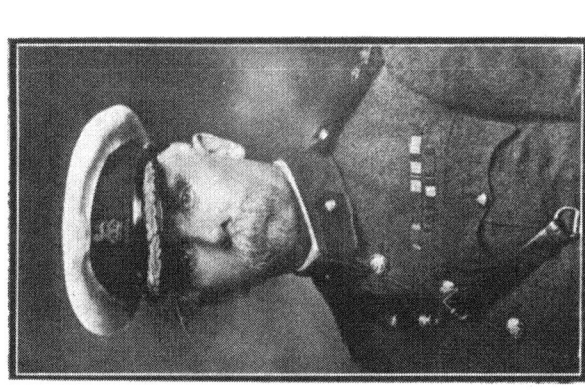

Major O. J. Currie,
Natal Medical Corps.
Regimental Surgeon 1895 to 1899.
Attached to Regiment, Siege of Ladysmith.

Lieut.-Colonel J. Hyslop, D.S.O., V.D.,
Natal Medical Corps.
Regimental Surgeon, 1886 to 1899.

RULES OF THE NATAL CARBINEERS.

1.—The Corps shall consist of two or more troops, each troop to consist of not more than 50 men (including officers), to be called the "Natal Carbineers."
2.—There shall be one Lieutenant-Colonel, one Major, the Adjutant, the Surgeon, and Quartermaster, to be elected by the corps; and one Captain, one Subaltern, and non-commissioned Officers to each troop, to be elected by the troop.
3.—They shall wear a simple and inexpensive uniform.
4.—Their arms shall be a single or double-barrelled gun and a sword.
5.—They shall be called out for exercise 20 days in the course of the year.
6.—They shall be bound to proceed to the appointed place of meeting without delay (within two hours after receiving notice), and to serve in any part of the County of Pietermaritzburg, or in any part of the District, not being more than 30 miles from the general place of rendezvous.
7.—Non-commissioned officers shall call out the troop.
8.—Any part of the Corps, provided not less than twenty men (with discretionary power in the commanding officer to increase the number), may be called out within the limits aforesaid, to support the authority of the civil power, when it appears likely to be resisted.
9.—It shall be in the power of the commanding officer, in cases of great emergency, for the protection of the town, to call out the corps, or part of the corps, without waiting for orders from Government, and also when Governors, or other distinguished persons are arriving at, or leaving the colony.
10.—Rules shall be framed by the Corps, in accordance with the provisions of Ordinance No. 11, 1855, for enforcing discipline. Offenders shall be tried by court martial, chosen by the Corps; punishment shall be by fine; the amount of fines to go to the general fund of the Corps.
11.—The uniform of the Corps shall be blue, with white facings, consisting of a shell jacket, overalls (strapped), helmet of leather, with white cover, and forage cap.

Bye Laws.

1.—Applications, for leave of absence, shall be laid before, and decided upon, by a Board, consisting of the Colonel and four members of the Corps.
2.—If any member be desirous of leaving the Corps, he may do so by giving six months' notice thereof to the commanding officer, or at any time by finding a substitute (to be approved of by the committee named in the 1st Bye-law,) or on payment of £5 to the funds of the Corps.
3.—The commanding officer shall have power at any time to call for volunteers, in case their services be required, without the limits of the county.
4.—It shall be the duty of officers commanding troops, at the request, in writing, of any member thereof, on sufficient cause being shown by the applicant, to call a court martial, to investigate any cause complained of, either against officers or men.
5.—The court martial shall consist of a President and six members, the former to be drawn from the commissioned officers of the Corps, by rotation, the latter by ballot from the whole Corps; the Quarter Master to be Acting Judge Advocate. The proceedings of such court martial shall be forwarded to the commanding officer, for his approval, and it shall be lawful for such commanding officer to authorise and approve of the sentence of every such court martial, or he may order such court to re-assemble once, and reconsider their finding, or sentence, and no sentence of any such court martial shall be carried into execution until confirmed by the commanding officer; and it shall likewise be in the power of such commanding officer to remit the whole, or any part of such sentence, as to him may seem fit.
6.—Any member of the Corps absenting himself from drill or service, unless absent on leave (except in cases of sickness or indisposition, when a certificate from the regimental surgeon, or his assistant, must be produced), shall be fined in a sum not exceeding £10.
7.—Any member guilty of insubordination, disobedience of orders, or drunkenness when on duty, shall be liable to a fine, not exceeding £2 for the first offence.
8.—It shall be lawful for the commanding officer, on any member appearing at muster in a slovenly state, either in person or accoutrements, to inflict a fine, not exceeding 5s.,

on any offender who has been twice warned, and if the irregularities are further persisted in, after the infliction of such fine, to order a court martial on the party so transgressing.

9.—Any member not appearing at muster at the appointed time, shall be liable to a fine not exceeding 6s., according to the order of the commanding officer. The trumpet for saddling up shall sound half-an-hour before the time appointed for muster, and again five minutes before rollcall.

10.—The quarterly musters shall take place on the first Monday, and four following days in March, June, September, and December, in each year, the Corps to muster on the Market Square, at 6 a.m., for three hours, and at 4 p.m., for two hours' drill on each day.

11.—In the event of any officer dying, or retiring from the corps, his successor shall be elected by nomination and ballot; the commanding officer to have power to fill up all vacancies temporarily, whether occasioned by death or otherwise. No new election shall be made without fourteen days' previous notice.

12.—It shall be competent for the commanding officer to call a general meeting of the corps, or upon receiving a requisition signed by not less than ten members thereof, for the purpose of altering the Rules, or amending Bye-laws, etc.

13.—No member of the Corps shall be considered eligible for promotion as commissioned or non-commissioned officer, until he shall have received a certificate of his fitness or capability from the Adjutant, and be approved of by the Lieutenant-Colonel.

14.—An Orderly Book shall be kept, in which the Rules, Bye-laws, etc., as sanctioned by Ordinance, shall be entered; such Orderly Book to be open at all times for inspection by any member of the Corps. The expenses of printing, advertising, etc., shall be paid out of the general fund of the Corps.

Bushman Raids (see Chapter II.).

1857. On the 24th March, at the opening of the first Legislative Council of the Colony, the Carbineers furnished an escort for His Excellency the Lieutenant-Governor, an honour which the Regiment has enjoyed on every subsequent occasion of the kind, except that referred to in the subjoined Notice and Minute:—

GOVERNMENT NOTICE NO. 253, 1874.

His Excellency the Lieutenant-Governor directs the publication of the following Minute to the Commandant of the Volunteer Force.

By His Excellency's command,

B. P. LLOYD,
Acting Colonial Secretary.

Colonial Office, Natal,
July 31st, 1874.

MINUTE.

Lieutenant-Governor to Commandant of Volunteers.

The Lieutenant-Governor regrets that, owing to some unavoidable misapprehension, the "Natal Carbineers" had not sufficient notice to enable them to escort him to the opening of the Legislative Council. His Excellency would have been proud of their escort, as the Carbineers, in common with the Volunteer Forces in general, continue to possess his undiminished confidence.

By Order,
(Signed) W. H. BEAUMONT,
Private Secretary.

Government House,
July 31st, 1874.

It may interest Natalians of to-day to read with what ceremonies the First Session of their Colonial Parliament was opened: "Tuesday, 24th March, 1857. To-day was appointed for the opening of the House by His Excellency. From ten o'clock the town was in commotion. The Rifle Corps (under Captain Leathern), and the Carbineers (under Colonel St. George), turned out as a guard of honour. The Government School was fitted up for the occasion and, the arrangements having been carefully made, secured the accommodation of the largest assemblage ever witnessed in this City. The Bishop of the English Church, and his Clergy in their canonicals; the Recorder, and the members of the bar, in their togae; the Commandant of the forces, and the officers, all in full uniform; Captain Conolly of the Artillery, decorated with his Crimean laurels; Captain MacDonald of the Cape Mounted Rifles; G. C. Cato, Esq., in full dress as Swedish and Norwegian consul; Philip Ferreira, Esq., Mayor; and nearly all the ladies of the city, including Mrs. Scott, were amongst those present. His Excellency, escorted by a guard of honour of the Carbineers and Rifles, arrived, and was received by a guard of honour of the 45th regiment, the band playing the National Anthem. His Excellency, accompanied by Sir Theophilus St. George and Captain Lucas, took his seat on the platform. A Royal Salute of twenty-one guns having been fired by the Artillery in attendance, His Excellency proceeded to read his speech."

Isidoi (see Chapter III.)

On the 23rd July the Carbineers sustained a severe loss by the death of their gallant and popular commanding officer, Lieutenant-Colonel Sir Theophilus St. George, Baronet, who had played such a prominent part in their formation and development. It may not be too much to say that the discipline and esprit-de-corps, which have always been characteristic of the Carbineers, had their origin in his personal influence and example.

Obituary Notice:—"Death of Sir Theophilus St. George. Our small community had a deep gloom cast over it yesterday morning about ten o'clock by the announcement of the sudden death of Sir Theophilus St. George, Baronet, the magistrate of this city. It appears that Sir Theophilus had caught cold during the last rainy season whilst out collecting the taxes from the natives, but was not too indisposed of late to attend to his official duties, until within the last few days. Since Saturday he had been confined to his bed, but on Monday his symptoms took a favourable turn, and hopes of his recovery revived. The disease, however, baffled medical skill and terminated in inflammation. Sir Theophilus has been some five years in the Colony, and was one of those frank, generous, warm-hearted Irish gentlemen towards whom it was impossible not to reciprocate a kindly good-will. The most sincere sympathy is felt for Lady St. George and Sir Theophilus's family. We understand the funeral proceeds from the residence of the lamented deceased at three o'clock to-day, and that several of the principal places of business will be closed from two till four p.m."

It was the gallant Baronet's dying wish that he should be accorded a military funeral and be borne to his last resting-place by members of the Richmond Troop. This was done, the Regiment furnishing a firing party, and he was laid to rest with all the usual military honours.

A monument was erected to his memory, and bears the following inscription :—

"Sir Theophilus St. George, Baronet,
Lieutenant-Colonel,
Natal Carbineers,
died 23rd July, 1857.
aged 47
years.

"A humble Tribute of Respect by the Members of the Corps to their Beloved Officer."

Extracts from Diary of Sir Theophilus St. George, Bart., first Officer Commanding, Natal Carbineers: beginning with the date of his election as Lieut.-Colonel, and continued at intervals till within two months of his death, they are evidence of the interest and pride which Sir Theophilus took in the Regiment.

1855.

7th February.—Elected Lieut.-Colonel Pietermaritzburg Horse.

20th February.—First Drill of Natal Carbineers at 6.30 a.m.
1 Lieut. Colonel.
1 Captain.
2 Subalterns.
1 R.S.-Major and 20 Privates.

23rd February.—First Drill with swords at 5 p.m.

5th March.—First Drill (Pay) of Natal Carbineers.

6th March.—Our first Mess Dinner.

28th April.—Parade of Carbineers at 4.30 p.m., greatly improved.

1856.

6th March.—Left Pietermaritzburg with 1st detachment of Carbineers for Spijoen Kop and outspanned for the night at Prellar's farm.

7th March.—Left Prellar's and B——— at McDonald's Drift on the Little Impafane beyond the Dargle.

8th March.—Arrived at the Military Post at 11 o'clock and pitched our camp. McDonald left us.

9th March.—Left 8 a.m. and after 5 p.m. off-saddled for the night on the Drakensberg.

10th March.—Returned to the camp at 1 p.m.

11th March.—Military Post to Pietermaritzburg. Left at 6 a.m., returned Pietermaritzburg 5 p.m.

1st May.—First day of 3 days' drill for those Carbineers who did not go to Spijoen Kop.
24th May.—Review on the Parade Ground, Pietermaritzburg 45th, C.M.R., Artillery, N.C., and R.R.
25th May.—Capt. McDonald left with 15 men for Umkomaas.
9th September.—Richmond. Quarterly Drill with Hawkins'* Troop, Natal Carbineers.
4th November.—Lieut.-Governor Scott arrived 3 p.m. Carbineers met him.

1857.

3rd March.—First day Quarterly Drill. Received £90 for Carbineers' cloaks.
6th April.—Sargeaunt (Colonial Secretary) left. Natal Carbineers accompanied him out of town.
23rd May.—Marched out and escorted in the Richmond Troop. First day Quarterly Drill.
Held a large meeting of Carbineers at Woodside.
24th May.—Church Parade and 60 Carbineers attended.
25th May.—Attended with Natal Carbineers at the Review.
26th May.—Drill at 8 o'clock.

The Hon. W. C. Sargeaunt succeeded to the command of the Regiment. Captain Allen received his majority, and was succeeded as Captain by Lieutenant A. B. Allison. Quarter Master Wood was promoted to the vacant lieutenantcy, Sergeant Player taking his place as Quarter Master.

1858. Matyana. (See Chapter III.).

The Queen's Birthday this year was celebrated by the most admirable review, says a contemporary report, that has ever been witnessed here. The Royal Durban Rangers, who rode up from the Port to take part in it, were met some miles out, and welcomed to the city, by their comrades of the Carbineers. Just before the review, the Durban Rangers and the Pietermaritzburg Carbineers, accompanied by the band of the 45th Regiment, drew up in front of Government House for the ceremony of the presentation of colours to the first-named corps. His Excellency, in presenting the colours after their consecration by the Bishop of Natal, said:—"Royal Durban Rangers, I am desired on the part of Mrs. Scott to state that she has much pleasure in being made the medium of presenting to your corps this beautiful standard. In accepting a banner em-

---

* A. C. Hawkins, Magistrate, Richmond, late Capt., Royal Scots. His old Regiment was in Pietermaritzburg when he died, and buried him with military honours.

broidered with the arms of the Colony of Natal, you are receiving an important, a sacred trust; you are now associating your corps with the armorial bearings of the Colony. I need scarcely tell you that such a banner, bearing such a device, should not—must not—ever fall into the hands of an enemy." The impressive ceremony which followed, of trooping the colours of the 45th emblazoned with the names of the battles and campaigns of the gallant regiment, was taken advantage of by the Governor to incite, in eloquent words, the two volunteer regiments before him to emulate the heroism and fame of the regular army.

1859. For many years after the expedition against Matyana there is little in the records of the Carbineers except what could only be, even to the members of the corps themselves, of no more than a momentary and rather languid interest. This dearth of exciting incidents may be taken as indirect but sure evidence that in those years the Colony was enjoying the blessing of peace; for since the Carbineers were enrolled, there has never been trouble, within or on its borders, that they have not been called on, and found ready, to assist in allaying. The notes of tame routine that have been preserved, such as parades and escorts, only serve to show that from its beginning the Regiment's performance of duty, whether monotonous or extraordinary, has been unbroken.

During 1859 a number of the Richmond Troop migrated to the coast. But they carried the spirit of volunteering with them, and became foundation members of a new troop of Carbineers, the Umzinto, under the command of Captain Arbuthnot.

At the opening of the Legislative Council the Carbineers supplied the escort of His Excellency, and in the Queen's Birthday parade they took their part under command of Major Allen with Captain Allison and Adjutant J. O. Wirsing.

1860. The opening of the Victoria Suspension Bridge, over the Umsindusi, was an event marked with a degree of ceremony which testified to the pride which the City felt in the successful accomplishment of an undertaking rightly regarded as an enterprise of great credit to the young and poor Colony. After the delivery of the speeches customary on such occasions, His Excellency, attended by a Carbineer escort, crossed and recrossed the bridge, and formally declared it open. It had cost £3,360, of which only £500, it was proudly said by the Mayor, had been spent out of the Colony.

Regimental Sergeant-Major
W. Knott.

Regl.-Sergt.-Major
B. Bowen.

Regl.-Sergt.-Major
W. Burkimsher.

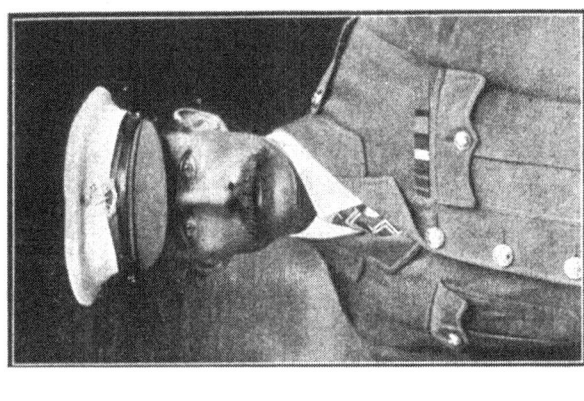

Regl.-Sergt.-Major
W. H. A. Molyneux.

From a paragraph in the "Witness" of the 6th April, it appears that the volunteer movement was at this time checked by some unexplained cause of friction between the Government and the various corps that had been enrolled in the Colony. Of them all, the Carbineers and the Rangers alone were sufficiently sturdy to resist the withering influence, whatever it was. The others, sensitively shrinking from the outside intermeddling, dwindled away. "We wish," says the "Witness" newspaper, "there was a more hearty response in Natal to the national call for volunteer arming which has made such enormous progress in England. The real fact is, the public are jealous of official interference, and the officials say, 'Without us you shall have no encouragement to form yourselves into rifle corps.' We are pleased to be able to report, however, that the Durban Rangers and the Maritzburg Carbineers are exceptions in favour of a volunteer mounted force. Their gallant doings shall always be duly recorded in our columns, and, as far as the pen can co-operate with the sword, they will always command our services and support."

The Queen's Birthday was kept with the usual ceremonial and state by the garrison of Fort Napier. At twelve o'clock all the men of the 85th Regiment, then stationed here, the troop of Cape Mounted Rifles, the Pinetown troop of the Durban Rangers, and the Carbineers of the City, were reviewed by His Excellency, the Commander-in-Chief and Acting Lieutenant-Governor, Major Williamson.

The arrival in Maritzburg of Prince Alfred, on the 3rd September, stirred the hearts and revealed the loyalty of the colonists of Natal. Great preparations were made to do honour to the Sailor Prince, and at the same time advantage was taken of his visit, and a lasting memorial of it was sought, by praying him to grace Maritzburg by laying the foundation stone of its future Town Hall. The arrangements made for the festivities were—1st day, triumphal arches at the bridge and in Church Street; address by the Mayor and Corporation; general illumination in the evening. 2nd Day—Laying the foundation stone of Town Hall, children to sing the National Anthem and be afterwards entertained; public dejeuner in the market shed; games on Market Square; citizens' ball in the evening. 3rd Day—Review of troops, and presentation of colours to the 85th Regiment; Kafir dance; ball at Government House. With the exception of the Klip River Corps, the whole volunteer force of the Colony, comprising the Carbineers of Maritzburg, Richmond, and Umzinto, the Durban Rangers, and the Pinetown Foresters mustered in the City for escort and other duty. His Royal Highness was met at Ladysmith by Colonel Allen and Lieutenant Mesham; couriers were despatched to herald his coming; and on his arrival the streets were lined by the volunteers and regulars. Colonel Allen and Captain Proudfoot were appointed his Aides-de-Camp during his stay, and on his departure were honoured by him with gifts and a letter in acknowledgment of their services. "In addition," says the "Witness," "to the handsome portraits forwarded to our Corporation by the Prince, in recognition of his hearty reception among us, he has sent Colonel Allen and Captain Proudfoot (Carbineers), his Aides-de-Camp during his visit, some tokens of his appreciation of their services. Colonel Allen's is a photograph of His Royal Highness, with an autograph, and a breast-pin, the head-piece of which is a sailor's straw hat, with the name of the ship "Victory" on the band. The presents are accompanied by a complimentary letter, in which reference is made to the Prince's 'happy visit to Natal.'"

The following October the Karkloof Troop of Carbineers was formed, with headquarters at Howick, Captain Proudfoot being in command, with Mr. E. Parkinson as his Lieutenant.

1861. The return of Lieutenant-Governor Scott to Natal in the beginning of this year, after his important mission to England, was hailed with other than the usual feelings that welcome the arrival of a Colonial Governor; for on this occasion the minds of the colonists were filled, not only with the hope of what he might do, but also with gratitude for what he had done, for their Colony. At Durban, in reply to an address, he had said:—"I have completed all arrangements necessary for the immediate commencement of the harbour works, and from my conference with men of science in England, I am more confident than ever that the plans proposed, and now about to be carried out, will effectually remove the difficulties with which commerce has hitherto had to contend in connection with our harbour." On which the newspaper comment was:—"There were many doubts as to the probable result of the mission undertaken by Mr. Scott, and the happy success that has attended his efforts will mark a new era in the history of the settlement. Once let our harbour be known as a safe port, and our future as a Colony is made." When such hopefulness marked the reunion of Governor and governed, we can imagine that it was to discharge no mere perfunctory ceremonial that the Carbineers rode out some miles to meet His Excellency and escort him into the City.

In July the Regiment was called out to guard the border against a threatened invasion by the Zulus under Cetywayo (see Chapter IV.).

A rifle, presented by Prince Alfred, was offered for a shooting competition.

1862. A change in the command of the Regiment took place this year. Lieutenant-Colonel Allen, who had practically been Commanding Officer ever since the death of Sir Theophilus St. George, resigned, and was succeeded by Major Erskine, the Colonial Secretary.

In February, while the Karkloof Troop were assembled for drill at Howick, news was brought to them that Bushmen had driven off some cattle from Mr. Spiers's farm in the neighbourhood. A party was at once formed to go in pursuit, and chased the raiders as far as the Double Mountains in Basutoland. There the minds of the pursuers were diverted from the purpose on which they set out, for no further mention is made of the stolen cattle, and the chase was stopped, by a shooting accident which caused the death of Trooper Hodgson. He was buried where he died.

The comments of the local press at this time bear witness that the Maritzburg Carbineers had reached a high state of efficiency. This it may have been that suggested a proposal to build them stabling for fifty horses. A lease of land for the site from the Maritzburg Corporation was actually applied for and granted. The intention, however, was carried no farther.

At the opening of the Legislative Council on May 15th, His Excellency, Governor Scott, thus referred to the volunteer movement:—"I have advised a small appropriation to provide ammunition and prizes for the volunteer corps. Both at Home and in the Colonies we find our fellow British subjects entering into this voluntary service with energy and perseverance, which gives a stamp of permanency to the movement. Natal has long had its volunteer corps, and in so worthy a race it will not, I am confident, be last; but there is still wanting that earnestness which is all-essential in the organization and maintenance of volunteer corps depending on the voluntary energy and public spirit of individuals. I shall have much pleasure in giving effect to any measures you may devise by which the colonists may be stimulated to organize themselves into armed and disciplined corps, and thus be prepared on any emergency to feel a greater confidence in the self-protective power of the Colony."

At a subsequent opening of the Council, His Excellency,

in the course of his speech, said:—"On the last occasion of the opening of the Council, I alluded to the expediency of some means being adopted for stimulating the formation of volunteer corps. Since that time several corps have been formed, and there has been exhibited a willingness and activity in a portion of the community in support of the movement which merits the highest praise. There remains, however, a large amount of the inhabitants who do not voluntarily come forward, and the question is often mooted whether the necessity does not still exist for the enactment of a militia law, by which the services of those not disposed to enrol themselves amongst the volunteers may be rendered available. By the ordinance enacted in 1855, the Lieutenant-Governor is empowered to cause pay to be issued to every man belonging to a volunteer corps for a period not exceeding twenty days in any one year when called out for muster, and under this enactment pay is yearly issued to volunteer corps. Seeing that the number of the volunteer corps has so largely increased, I cannot but be sensible that so large an amount of pay as is authorized by the ordinance would absorb an amount of revenue possibly not contemplated at the passing of the ordinance, and I have deferred acting with regard to such pay till you shall have considered the matter on a broader basis. Not only do we call upon those persons who voluntarily enrol themselves in the corps, to devote a considerable portion of their time to the acquirement of that skill and discipline so essential to a military body, but an actual monetary outlay on their part is required. It is not possible perhaps to relieve them entirely from their personal expenses, but I think some relief should be afforded them from the public funds. I shall have pleasure in supporting any measure that the Council may devise which may tend to support and stimulate the organization of these corps."

The men who heartily supported the volunteer movement at the cost of their time and money, and with but little assistance from the Government, would have welcomed the enactment of such a measure as was outlined by Governor Scott, provided that those defensive bodies already in existence, which had shown their alacrity to serve the Colony when called on, and had developed a distinct esprit-de-corps, should still be recognised under the proposed Act. A Bill was prepared to make colonial defence a general obligation, but as it was not brought before the Council till too late in the session to receive the consideration due to its importance, it was withdrawn. Natal had to wait quite forty years before its claim on all its able-bodied men for defence was at length asserted by the Militia Law of 1903.

1863. Captain Rolleston was appointed Inspector of Volunteers.

Mr. Saunders, M.L.C., introduced a Bill into the Legislative Council to promote the establishment of a mounted volunteer force. A Select Committee, appointed to report, recommended the offering of prizes for shooting; the providing of arms, equipment, and uniform; a free issue of one hundred rounds per man annually; the payment of a capitation grant of £3 per annum for efficients; and in time of active service the payment of six shillings per diem and compensation for horses lost.

This year cavalry sabres were issued in lieu of the straight sabres hitherto in use. The Enfield rifles were also called in, and replaced by "Terry" carbines.

On the departure of the 85th Regiment from Maritzburg, where they had been quartered for some years, they were escorted out of town by the Carbineers, under the command of Major Erskine.

A party of the Karkloof Troop, under Captain Proudfoot, proceeded to the Berg for the purpose of erecting a stone at the grave of Trooper Hodgson, who had been accidentally killed the year before whilst in pursuit of Bushmen cattle thieves. On their way they fell in with twenty-nine horses which had been stolen by Bushmen, and sent them back under charge of two of their number.

Thursday, the 18th of June, was set apart as a public holiday to celebrate the marriage of the Prince of Wales with the Princess Alexandra of Denmark. At nine o'clock there was divine service. At ten, the colonial officials and the representatives of public bodies and institutions were marshalled on the Market Square for a procession to the ground marked off for a public park across the Umsindusi. There two commemorative oak trees were planted, and the park received its name, "The Alexandra." The part of the Carbineers in the day's arrangements was to escort His Excellency from Government House to the Market Square, and then in his place in the procession to the Park.

1864. The Umzinto Troop, which owed its origin to the zeal in the volunteer cause of some Carbineers who had removed from Richmond to Umzinto, found itself strong enough this year to secede amicably from the parent corps, and formed itself into a new regiment under the name of the Alexandra Rifles.

The Karkloof Troop were threatened with a serious loss by the intended resignation of Captain Proudfoot and Lieutenant Parkinson. Happily, however, these gentlemen were persuaded to remain in office on receiving an address signed by all the other members of the Troop.

A Bill for the disbandment of all volunteer corps then existing and the formation of one force, to be called the Natal Rifles, consisting of twelve troops, was introduced by Government, but did not pass the Legislative Council.

New rules and bye-laws of the volunteer corps of Natal Carbineers were passed on 31st March, and published in the "Government Gazette" of 18th October, 1864.

RULES AND BYE-LAWS OF THE VOLUNTEER CORPS OF "NATAL CARBINEERS."

1. All former Rules and Bye-laws are hereby cancelled.
2. The Regiment shall consist of one or more Troops, and shall be called the "Natal Carbineers."
3. Each Troop shall consist of not less than twenty or not more than fifty members, exclusive of Commissioned Officers.
4. Headquarters of the Regiment shall be the City of Pietermaritzburg.
5. The uniform of the Corps shall consist of a dark blue shell jacket with white cloth facings, viz.—collar and cuffs; overalls to be made of Oxford grey cloth with a side stripe one inch and one-eighth wide, dark blue cloth forage cap with white cloth band and patent leather peak. Members must also provide themselves with a fatigue dress, consisting of a dark blue serge, or Volunteer cloth fatigue jacket, white duck and tan mole skin trousers; all belts to be made of white buff leather.
6. REGIMENTAL OFFICERS.—These shall be one Lieutenant-Colonel, one Major, one Adjutant, Surgeon, Quarter Master, and Sergeant Major as Regimental Officers to be elected from the whole of the Regiment at a general meeting called for that purpose, of which not less than fourteen days' notice shall be given in the "Government Gazette."

7. At any General or Special General Meetings of the Corps, Regimental Questions and Business only shall be brought forward for consideration.

8. The Commanding Officer may call a special general meeting of the Corps on receiving a requisition signed by not less than ten members and stating the object of such meeting.

9. TROOP OFFICERS.—Each Troop shall have attached to it one Captain, one Lieutenant, one Troop Sergeant Major, and one Assistant Surgeon.

10. All Commissioned Officers of Troops shall be elected by nomination and ballot from the members of the Troop in which such election is required.

11. All Commissioned Officers shall, previous to receiving their commissions or appointment, pass an examination of their fitness to the satisfaction of a Board chosen for that purpose by the Commanding Officer, who shall be President.

All Non-commissioned Officers shall be elected by nomination and ballot from the Members of the Troop in which such election is required. The Captain or Officer in charge may appoint provisionally a Lance Sergeant or Corporal as a temporary appointment without proceeding to an election.

12. The Commanding Officer shall have power to suspend from service any Commissioned Officer who shall be charged with conduct unbecoming an officer and a gentleman, provided the charge be immediately investigated—that is to say, within twenty-one days after the charge is made, unless good cause can be shown for further delay.

13. Non-commissioned Officers may be suspended by the Captain of their Troop or by the Officer in charge for the time being, but in every case of suspension the charge shall be proceeded with in twenty-one days after the charge is made, unless good cause be shown for further delay.

14. Each Troop shall have power to make Bye-laws for its own guidance and good discipline, but such Bye-laws must be in conformity with the Rules and Bye-laws of the Regiment and in accordance with Law No. 11, 1856; but no Troop Bye-laws can be carried into effect until they have the sanction of the Commanding Officer.

15. All charges against Commissioned Officers shall be tried by a Court of Inquiry, consisting of four Commissioned Officers, who shall be ballotted for from the whole of the Regiment. The Senior Officer of the Court shall be President, and shall have the casting vote. The Officer in command of the Regiment shall not be a Member or President of the Court.

16. It shall be lawful for any Member of the Corps to forward any charge or charges he may think it his duty to bring against any Commissioned Officer of the Regiment for the consideration of the Commanding Officer, who may order the assembling of a Court of Enquiry, as per preceding Rule, to investigate such charge or charges, the proceedings of such Court to be forwarded to the Commanding Officer for his approval or otherwise, and who shall have power to revise the proceedings of the Court once, and to direct the Court to re-assemble and re-consider their finding. Such Court shall have power to fine, reprimand, or dismiss such Officer from the Corps, and to recommend that his Commission be cancelled by the Lieutenant Governor.

17. Any charge which may be preferred by any Member of the Corps against the Commanding Officer may, at the discretion of the next Senior Officer of the Corps, be forwarded by him to the Lieutenant Governor for his consideration.

18. Any Commissioned Officer who shall become Insolvent, and whose name appears as such in the "Government Gazette," shall thereafter cease to act as an Officer of the Corps until a preliminary Court of Inquiry shall be appointed by the Officer in Command of the Corps for the time being, to inquire into the nature of such Insolvency, and to report whether in their opinion it is necessary to bring charges against such Officer with a view to his being dismissed or otherwise dealt with.

19. All proceedings of Courts of Inquiry will be entered in the Orderly Book of the Troop, kept by the Sergeant-Major.

20. Every Member of the Corps will be required to take and subscribe the Oath of Allegiance to Her Majesty.

21. Any Member absenting himself from drill or parade twice in succession without obtaining leave of absence from his Commanding Officer, shall be struck off the roll of his Troop if satisfactory cause for his absence is not shown to the Troop Committee, or he may be dealt with as the Committee may decide.

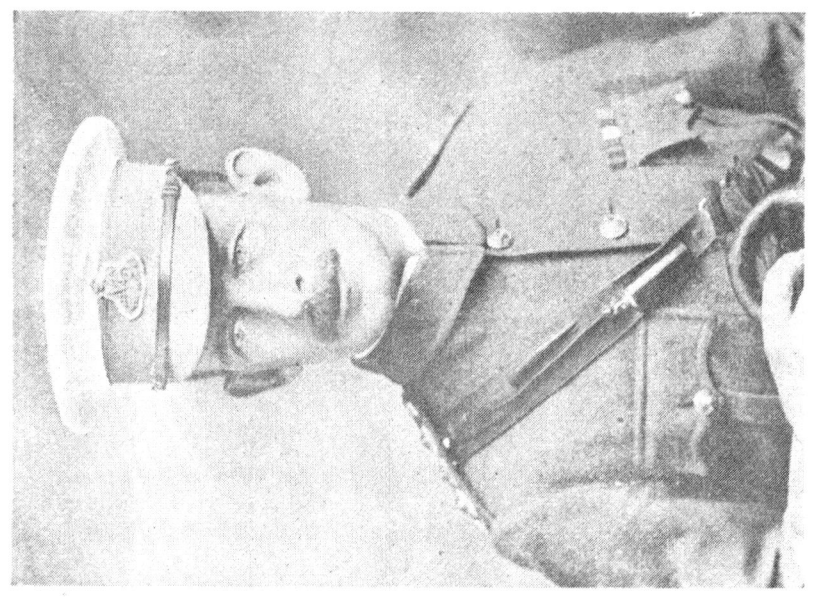

Captain G. H. Helbert,
Regimental Adjutant.

Lt.-Col. W. S. Shepstone, V.D.

BYE-LAWS OF THE NATAL CARBINEERS.

MEMBERS, HOW ELECTED.

1. Any person desirous of joining the Corps must be proposed and seconded by Members of the Troop to which he wishes to be attached, and must deposit with his proposer or seconder the sum of one pound sterling as an entrance fee, which sum shall be returned if he be not elected, but if he should be elected such sum to go to the general fund of the Troop.

2. If any Officer or Member be desirous of leaving the Troop or Regiment he may do so by giving his Captain or Commanding Officer six months' notice in writing, or on payment of five pounds sterling to the fund of his Troop or Regiment by consent of his Troop Committee.

3. The place of rendezvous for Troops shall be decided by each Troop, and the rendezvous of the Regiment by the Officer commanding. Each member shall be bound to proceed to the appointed place of meeting and report himself at the time he is ordered to do so, and to serve in any part of the respective localities or district within a radius of thirty miles of the place of rendezvous; but it shall be lawful for the Commanding Officer to call in Volunteers from the whole of the Regiment in cases of emergency to proceed to any part of the colony.

4. Each Troop will inform the Commanding Officer of their place of rendezvous as soon after their formation as possible.

5. Any part of the Regiment, provided not less than seventy men, with discretionary power in the Commanding Officer to increase the number, may be called out for service under rule 3 to support the power of the civil authority when it appears likely to be resisted.

6. It shall be the duty of Non-commissioned Officers to call out the Troop.

7. Every Member on signing the muster roll shall agree to pay to the general fund of the Regiment the sum of one shilling and sixpence per annum for petty expenses.

8. Honorary Members may be elected in any of the Troops on a payment of ten pounds ten shillings as a life entrance or two pounds ten shillings annually, such sum to go to the general fund of the Troop to which he is elected.

9. Each member shall be individually responsible to the Captain of his Troop for all arms, accoutrements or any other articles which may have been supplied to him by Government as a Member of the Corps, and when called upon to do so by his Commanding or any Subaltern Officer shall deliver them up in good order. No member shall be permitted to shoot for any prize given to or by the Regiment until he has paid all fines and subscription due by him to his Troop, and has been an enrolled member not less than six months.

10. At all meetings of the Regiment or Troops, the Senior Officer shall of right preside, and in the event of an equality of votes he shall have a casting-vote. Members may vote by proxy, duly signed. No member shall be allowed to vote who has not paid all fees and fines due by him to his Troop or Regiment.

11. At all Committee Meetings the members present shall elect their own Chairman, who shall in the event of equality of votes have a casting-vote, and four members shall form a quorum for the dispatch of business.

12. The Commanding Officer, or, if on detachment, the Officer in command, shall, on receiving a requisition in writing of any three members, or at his own discretion, a sufficient cause being shown, call a preliminary Court of Enquiry to investigate any matter or complaint against any member, such Court to consist of a President and six members, the former to be drawn from the Commissioned Officers (the Commanding Officer excepted) in rotation, the latter to be balloted from the Troop in which complaint is made, such Court to have power only to report for the information of the Commanding Officer.

13. The proceedings of all Courts of Enquiry shall be forwarded to the Commanding Officer for his information, such proceedings to be copied in the Regimental Minute-book.

14. Any member absenting himself from parade, drill or service, without first having obtained leave of absence from his Commanding Officer, except in cases of sickness, which must be certified by a duly-qualified Surgeon, shall be fined in any sum not exceeding five pounds sterling, at the discretion of his Commanding Officer.

15. Any member guilty of insubordination, disobedience of orders, or insolence to any superior Officer or Non-commissioned Officer when on duty, shall, in the discretion of the Officer in command for the time being, be fined in any sum not exceeding five pounds sterling for the first offence, or he can be brought before a Court of Enquiry.

16. Any member who shall fail to appear at parade punctually at the hour specified, or who shall appear in a slovenly state either as to his uniform, horse, saddle, arms, or accoutrements, shall for the first offence be subject to a fine not exceeding ten shillings, but if the offence be repeated shall be subject to a fine of two pounds ten shillings sterling, or may be brought before a Court of Enquiry, at the discretion of a Committee to be appointed by the Commanding Officer for the time being.

17. Any member who shall commit any act or deed which shall tend to injuriously affect the peace, honour or prosperity of the Corps, shall, on proof thereof before a Court of Enquiry, be liable to be fined any sum not exceeding ten pounds, or to be expelled.

18. All fines imposed under the Rules and Bye-laws of this Corps, or any of the respective Troops thereof, shall be sued for and recoverable by distress on the goods and chattels of the member fined, in the Court of the Resident Magistrate of the District in which the rendezvous of the Corps or Troop is located for the time being, and shall be sued for in the name of any member of the Regiment appointed by the Commanding Officer for that purpose.

19. There shall be one General Muster of the Regiment during each year, which shall be at the Headquarters of the Corps. Troops will hold Quarterly Drills during the months of February, May, August, and November.

20. An Orderly Book shall be kept by the Adjutant of the Corps, which shall at all times be open for the inspection of any member of the Regiment, and a copy of all Rules and Bye-laws of the Regiment shall be entered and all general and regimental orders.

21. The Rules and Bye-laws of the Regiment may be altered at any time when a General Meeting of the whole of the Regiment is duly called for that purpose upon a requisition to the Commanding Officer signed by not less than Twenty Members duly enrolled. All such meetings to be called by advertisement in the "Government Gazette," giving at least three months' notice with a copy of the proposed alterations.

22. The Commanding Officer of the Corps shall have power to call out the Regiment, or any part thereof, on show or especial occasions.

23. That every present member, and all who may hereafter join the Corps, shall be bound to sign the muster-roll within one month from the time of the passing of these Rules

Passed at a General Meeting held at Pietermaritzburg, the roll unless he can show cause to the contrary.

Passed at a General Meeting held at Pietermaritzburg, the 31st day of March, 1864.

D. ERSKINE, Lieut.-Col. Com.,
Chairman.

On the departure of Governor Scott at the end of the year the Carbineers formed his escort, and presented him with an address as follows:—

"To His Excellency, J. Scott, Esq., Lieutenant-Governor,

"May it please Your Excellency,

"We, the officers, non-commissioned officers, and men of the Natal Carbineers, beg to express to Your Excellency our grateful feeling for the honour conferred upon the corps in being permitted to furnish an escort on your departure from amongst us as Lieutenant-Governor, and to assure you that, individually and collectively, we feel great pleasure in offering you this last mark of our respect. We also beg to thank Your Excellency for the many acts of kindness during the term of your administration, and heartily hope that Your Excellency and Mrs. Scott will have a pleasant voyage and a cordial welcome on your arrival in our dear native land, and that the peaceful condition in which the Colony has remained during Your Excellency's administration, now over eight years, and the flourishing condition in which you leave us, will prove such testimonials as will speedily ensure your appointment to a yet more honourable post. In conclusion, we wish every comfort and happiness both to yourself and Mrs. Scott, and may God bless you is the prayer of your obedient servants."

1865. In March, the Karkloof Troop was inspected by Captain Rolleston, and praised for the efficiency on the parade ground which it had reached under the instruction of Sergeant Currie, late of the Cape Mounted Rifles. The press, in giving a notice of the inspection, added compliments on the Troop's esprit-de-corps and proficiency in shooting.

The Regiment mustered in good force for the Queen's Birthday parade. More than the usual amount of time and attention was given to manoeuvres, in which all ranks acquitted themselves well.

Government offered, as prizes, three Whitworth rifles, to be competed for by teams of fifteen from the Volunteer Corps of the Colony, the rifles to become the property of the best marksmen. The ranges were to be 200, 300, 400, and 500 yards.

3rd July. Inroad of Basutos looting and killing (see chapter V.)

14th July. Expedition sent back by order of Sir P. Wodehouse. Carbineers' revenge (see Chapter V.)

1866. This year was marked by an increased interest in shooting.

The Regiment, as usual, attended the Queen's Birthday parade.

1867. Governor Keate, on coming to take up the duties of his office, was met at Thornville, and escorted into Maritzburg by the Carbineers.

On September 17th, the Regiment enjoyed a useful field day at Howick under command of their popular Adjutant, Captain Sam Williams.

In November, Mr. Charles Barter was appointed to the Captaincy of the Karkloof Troop. The vacancy thus filled was caused by the resignation of Captain Proudfoot who, as commanding officer from the formation of the Troop, had so gained the esteem and respect of his men, that it was considered a pleasure as much as a duty to attend the drills under his command.

The inspection of the Regiment by Colonel Browne, Commandant of Her Majesty's forces, was followed by a gratifying letter from His Excellency:—

"Colonial Office, Natal,

"18th Novemebr, 1867.

"Sir, I am directed by His Excellency, the Lieutenant-Governor, to inform you that His Excellency has received from His Honour, the Commandant, the annual inspection return of the Natal Carbineers, and that His Excellency is happy to perceive that Colonel Browne reports that, in his opinion, the Regiment deserves every encouragement, the Town Troop in particular, and that the Corps is well mounted and equipped, and that the shooting of the men was good. I am to request that you will communicate to the men His Excellency's satisfaction of the favourable report which the Commandant has been enabled to make as to the efficiency of the Regiment, and that you will inform the Town Troop of the special mention made of them.

"I have, etc.,

"D. ERSKINE, Colonial Secretary.

"The Officer Commanding, Natal Carbineers."

1868. In February the Regiment was again inspected by Colonel Browne, and was addressed by him in complimentary terms for its efficiency.

The customary escort attended Lieutenant-Governor Keate, on his departure for Aliwal North.

A newspaper report of the Queen's Birthday parade states:—"The Natal Carbineers turned out in force under Lieutenant-Colonel Erskine and Captain Williams, presenting a front of unusual vigour, especially as regards the improved style in which they were mounted."

Sergeant Clark was appointed drill instructor to the Karkloof Troop on the 27th June.

1869. A commission, appointed to enquire into the state of the colonial forces, recommended the amalgamation of the whole of the volunteer regiments into one, armed and clothed alike; the appointment of some officer of standing and experience to command the whole; the adoption of one set of rules and regulations for the management and discipline of the whole force; the force to be divided into troops, each retaining its respective a   'ation and to elect its own officers and members. These r jmmendations, however, were found to be impracticable.

The Regiment was unfortunate this year in losing the services of Lieutenant Pepworth. When it became known that he had tendered his resignation, the following letter was addressed to him:—"Dear Sir, we, the undersigned members of the Right Troop, Natal Carbineers, have learned with regret of your resignation as Lieutenant of our Troop. The length of time during which you have been attached to the Corps, the unwearying zeal which you have ever displayed in promoting its interests, and above all, your efficiency and qualifications as an officer, deservedly entitle you to the warmest acknowledgments of every member. We cannot, therefore, in taking leave of you, refrain from expressing to you, as we now desire to do, our high appreciation of your services, and our sincere regret that you should have decided to resign the post which you have proved yourself so thoroughly fitted in every respect to occupy. With our best wishes for your future welfare and prosperity, we subscribe ourselves,

"Dear Sir, Yours faithfully,

"S. WILLIAMS, and Twenty-five Others."

On 6th October a dinner was given to Major Williams, who had succeeded Major Allison, resigned, as a complimentary acknowledgment of the esteem in which he was held, and of his services as Captain. Colonel Erskine presided over the festive gathering, which was attended by forty-seven members, the room being decorated with great taste.

1870. In May, Trooper T. Shepstone was elected to succeed Lieutenant Pepworth, resigned.

At the opening of the Legislative Council, the escort to His Excellency, supplied as usual by the Regiment, was thanked for their attendance and complimented on their turn-out.

The discovery of the Diamond Fields, and the rush thither of young men from all parts of South Africa, caused the loss to the Headquarters Troop of no less than twenty of its members.

The Government rifle this year was won by Trooper St. Vincent Erskine.

On 28th September the Headquarters Troop marched out to Captain Barter's farm, "The Start," for a day's drill in conjunction with the Karkloof Troop. An enjoyable day was spent.

1871. After a three days' drill, begun on the 6th February, the Regiment was inspected by the Commandant, Colonel the Hon. B. M. Ward. The men were drawn up in line under command of Captain Williams and Lieutenant T. Shepstone in front of Government House and in the presence of His Excellency, Governor Keate. After inspection, several manoeuvres, and a march past, Colonel Ward, in his address, said that as a soldier he had been long connected with volunteers in England and elsewhere, that the march past which he had just witnessed was highly creditable, and the other movements were fairly well done, and showed that the men had profited by the instructions of their officers. He advised punctuality on parade, and attention to the minutiae of drills. He was pleased at receiving a request to inspect them, and would be glad to have field days in which the volunteers might take part with the regulars.

A sham fight with the Maritzburg Rifles was carried out successfully.

Regulation gloves, spurs, and chains were imported for the Regiment.

At the Queen's Birthday parade the Carbineers were unable to appear in such force as in the year before, so many of the men being away on leave at the Diamond Fields.

Lieutenant Shepstone was appointed to the rank of Captain, which he held till the year 1880.

The Karkloof Troop was inspected by Captain Foll, of the 32nd Regiment, who addressed them and said he was much pleased with the state of the arms and accoutrements and the manner in which the drill had been gone through, the skirmishing being particularly good.

In July a field day was held in conjunction with Her Majesty's forces. A series of military manoeuvres was executed in the direction of New England. Under the command of Captain Shepstone the Carbineers threw out a line of videttes, on the left flank in advance, communicating with the infantry piquets. The enemy was supposed to be driven back in their march on Maritzburg. The officers of the regular army present expressed unqualified praise of the excellent manner in which the Carbineers performed their duties as vidette sentinels, a sure test of the discipline and ability of the Corps.

The Government rifle was won this year by Captain Shepstone.

1872. A Carbineer escort was provided for Governor Keate on his departure from the Colony.

At the conclusion of the quarterly drill in May, the Regiment, under the command of Captain Shepstone, was inspected by Lieutenant Clark, R.A. The movements elicited strong remarks of approbation from the onlookers, especially from the military officers present. The inspecting officer complimented the men on the way they had gone through their drill. He said that he had come on the ground to find fault if he could, but he had nothing to find fault with. The rapidity of the movements, both in the saddle and in the skirmishing on foot, was deserving of great praise. He also praised the thorough discipline evinced throughout the drill, and stated that it would give him much pleasure to make a most favourable report to the Government. Colonel the Honourable D.

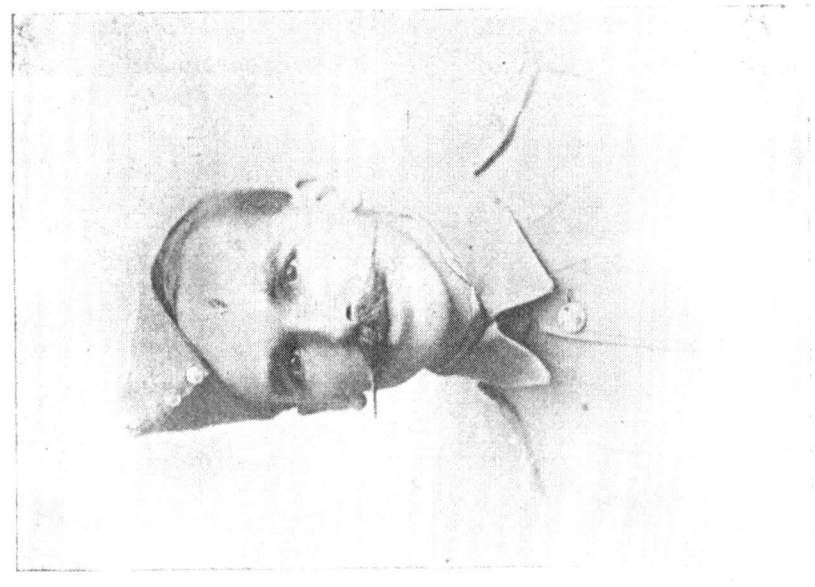

Major J. W. V. Montgomery.

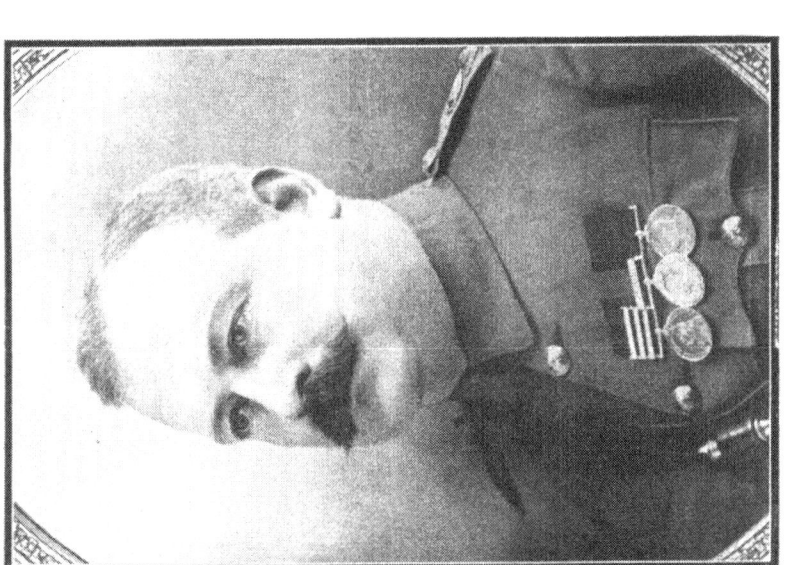

Lieut.-Colonel C. N. H. Rodwell.

Erskine also expressed his satisfaction with the manner in which the drill had been carried out.

The Regiment attended the Queen's Birthday parade under Captain Shepstone, the whole of the mounted volunteers being under the command of Lieutenant-Colonel Erskine.

On the arrival of Lieutenant-Governor Musgrave, the Regiment furnished an escort which met His Excellency at Thornville and accompanied him into the City. An escort was also furnished on occasion of His Excellency being sworn in.

In August of this year a wish was expressed that Mr. H. Pepworth, who had held a commission in the Regiment previously, should be asked to re-accept a commission, and the following correspondence ensued:—

"5th August, 1872.

"Sir,—We, the undersigned members of the Right Troop, Natal Carbineers, beg to address you with a view to inducing you to rejoin our Corps, in which you formerly served so long and efficiently. Should you accede to our request, we feel sure that your return will be heartily welcomed by every member of the Troop, and we promise to use our best endeavours to secure your re-election to the now vacant post of lieutenant.

"We are, Sir, etc.,

"(Signed by fifteen members.)"

"13th August, 1872.

"Gentlemen,—I beg most respectfully to acknowledge receipt of your letter of the 5th instant, requesting me to rejoin the Carbineers and to resume my old position in your Troop. I should have replied sooner, but that I wished to give the matter my most serious consideration; and now, while I thank you most heartily for the honour you intended me, I feel it my duty, after much deliberation, to decline your kind invitation. I am sure that you will feel with me that I do so with much reluctance, when I tell you that I always have had, and I trust, always shall have, the welfare of the Right Troop at heart.

"I have, etc.,

"H. PEPWORTH."

This year the Government rifle was won by Trooper Whitelaw.

A new volunteer law was passed by the Legislative Council which affected the Carbineers immediately after its publication in the "Government Gazette." Section 3 runs:—"The volunteer force of the Colony may consist of, but shall not exceed, one thousand men, in the proportion of six hundred cavalry, three hundred infantry, and one hundred artillery, and the establishment of a cavalry corps shall be one captain, two subalterns, one quartermaster, one surgeon, and sixty rank and file." Section 42 says:—"In the interpretation of this law the word 'Corps' shall include a troop, company, or battery of artillery, a troop of cavalry, or an infantry company, and shall comprehend and include the officers, non-commissioned officers, and privates of the corps." One result of the law, which restricted, in the sections quoted, the rank of the officers and limited the strength of each corps, was the formation of the Karkloof Troop into a separate regiment: it took the name of the Karkloof Carbineers. Another was the resignation of Major Williams, who had been a member of the Regiment from the time of its foundation. As showing the high respect in which he was held, the following resolution was unanimously passed and forwarded to Major Williams:—"That the Troop desires to express its regret that the new volunteer law compels Major Williams to resign his membership, and requests Captain Shepstone to convey the same to Major Williams, heartily thanking him for the great interest he has always taken in the Natal Carbineers."

1873. The Regiment furnished an escort to Sir Benjamin C. C. Pine on his arrival as Lieutenant-Governor for the second time.

The "Witness" of 30th May reports:—"The last day of the holidays—the Queen's Birthday—was to many quite as enjoyable as any of the week. The review was more than usually interesting. It was enlivened by the presence of the Hilton College Cadet Corps, which, with the Maritzburg Troop of the Natal Carbineers, and the Maritzburg Rifles, constituted the muster of volunteers."

In July, the Hon. Theophilus Shepstone, Secretary for Native Affairs, set out, attended by a voluntary escort, for Zululand, to crown Cetywayo (see chapter VI.)

November, Langalibalele Expedition (see Chapter VII.)

1874. This year that gallant officer, Major Dartnell (now Sir John), was appointed Commandant of the Volunteers, a position which he held for more than quarter of a century, admired and trusted in it by the whole volunteer force of the Colony.

The Regiment attended the funeral of the late Chief Justice Harding.

An escort was furnished for Sir Henry Barkly, High Commissioner, on his arrival in Maritzburg.

On the 4th November, the first anniversary of the Bushman's Pass affair, a monument erected to those that fell was unveiled by Mrs. Pepworth, wife of the Mayor of Pietermaritzburg (see chapter VII.)

1875. "Snider" carbines were issued this year in place of the "Terry."

At a meeting held on the 20th February, it was resolved that an effort should be made to re-invigorate the Regiment, which had declined in numbers since the lamentable affair at the Bushman's Pass, and get it up to its full strength.

A four days' drill was held in March.

The Regiment supplied an escort for Sir Garnet Wolseley on his arrival.

In April the Regiment was inspected by Sir Garnet Wolseley, who expressed himself as much pleased with the smart appearance of the men and the capital way in which they drilled.

The Regiment attended the Queen's Birthday parade.

R.S.-Major Taylor and Mr. A. Moodie were appointed Lieutenants.

The Regiment furnished escorts on the arrival of Sir Henry Bulwer, the new Lieutenant-Governor, and the departure of Sir Garnet Wolseley.

It has already been mentioned that, after the disaster at the Bushman's Pass, the numbers of the Regiment dropped very low. But owing to the exertions of a few public-spirited members who, to their credit, stuck to the corps through its time of depression, not only was it kept in existence but its former strength had gradually and regularly been recovered some considerable time before the second anniversary of the disaster came round.

On 30th December, the Regiment marched to Durban to attend the ceremony of the cutting of the first sod of the railway. No pay was drawn, and the men went at their own expense. They met with a cordial and gratifying reception from their Durban comrades.

1876. New revolvers were issued this year.

The Regiment came out in grand style at the Queen's Birthday parade, and called forth the admiration of General Sir A. Conyngham, who said they were well mounted and as active and fine a body of men as he had ever met with.

At the distribution of the Sports' prizes, Captain Shepstone, addressing the men, said, that the remarks made by Sir A. Conyngham on them were highly complimentary. The General had remarked to him in private conversation that their movements on the Queen's Birthday parade were such that he could not praise them too highly. He had said that he had never seen a finer body of men in the field. Captain Shepstone congratulated them on the way in which they had performed their manoeuvres.

1877. Sergt. Royston was appointed Sergt.-Major early in the year.

The Regiment formed an escort to Sir A. Conyngham on his departure for the Transvaal.

On the 13th August the Regiment mustered in good force for a six days' drill at Inchanga in conjunction with the Durban Mounted Rifles. Captain Shepstone and Lieutenant Moodie were the officers present. They returned on the 18th August well pleased with the results of their encampment. Major Dartnell conducted a patrol through the Inanda Location, his men sleeping out without tents and in very rainy weather.

Shortly before this encampment white helmets with plumes were issued.

The following sketch of this outing will be found extremely interesting:—

"On Monday morning, the 13th instant, this corps, Durban Mounted Rifles, in command of Capt. W. E. Shepstone, marched out of town to meet at Camperdown flats—38 miles distant—the Natal Carbineers from Maritzburg, for the usual annual week's drill, in addition to the quarterly drills in town.

"The camping ground was reached early in the day, a spot judiciously selected by Quartermaster Scott, of the Carbineers, combining the advantages of wood, water, grazing and unlimited drill ground. The Carbineers, under Capt. Theo. Shepstone, had arrived on the ground the previous day, and received the wet Durban Mounted Rifles with a warm reception, in the shape of hot coffee—may their shadow never decrease! Major Dartnell, Commandant of Volunteers, was also in camp, and referred smilingly to the hitch in the Commissariat arrangements, which was bombshells and grapeshot to the genial and kindly Quartermaster Sergeant, who, however, retaliated cleverly by pointing out that even in the British Army hitches occurred; for the troops then on the line of march between Durban and Maritzburg had not been supplied with waterproof sheets, although plenty were in store at Durban, and the men were in consequence sleeping on the wet grass!!

"The unfortunate commissariat wagon having now arrived, horses were knee-haltered, and sent out under horse guard to graze. Tents were pitched; sheep cut up, and issued with rations of bread, potatoes, sugar, coffee, dried vegetables, and grog; and the sun now coming out, lifting the clouds and showing the surrounding country clad in the exquisite verdure of early spring, all began to feel comfortable again, although the weather was very cold still.

"The cooks, one for each tent, were told off for the day, and were not long in producing such savoury messes as would have made the mouth of a Soyer water; and, indeed, throughout the week, it was astonishing what a number of toothsome changes were rung upon the very homely ingredients provided.

"The usual drill occupied the rest of the day, and at sunset the retreat was sounded, ensign hauled down, horses driven in and picketed, and rations of maize served out for them, and a blanket strapped over each. Sentries were posted for the night, which came in with a dense fog and raw wind, rendering the post anything but a pleasant one, especially with a lot of fractious and restive horses to keep in order—lest biting and kicking should result in a general stampede.

"Horse guard during the day was another very trying duty; the sentries provided with a horse, without either bridle or saddle, using a folded blanket for the latter, and the end of the halter for former, have to accompany and guard the horses sent out to graze, and if there are a few high spirited ones among them their post is no sinecure, for unless constantly on the *qui vive* their troop is off scampering over the country, leaving them a weary gallop to bring them back. Both these duties were, however, accepted cheerfully as a matter of course, by all in turn.

"The "orders" for the next day brought round by the orderly sergeant, intimated that, leaving the camp standing, and in charge of two men, both troops would move off in the morning, to patrol the wild tract of country known as the kafir location; quartermasters to provide two days' rations. The novelty of the thing made it interesting to all, and the morrow was looked forward to with expectation. A pack saddle was soon improvised, and meal bags cut up for wallets. Rations of sugar, coffee, and bread, were packed therein, and a sheep slaughtered and thrown on top, a few kettles tied on the sides completed the preparations of the Commissariat department. The morning of Wednesday broke gloriously for a change. The "reveille" at sunrise turned out the reluctant sleepers to groom and feed their horses and prepare for the march, and a right pleasant, because so suggestive sight, it was always, to see the young fellows with their shirt sleeves rolled up, in the keen morning air, grooming their own horses, a process never dreamed of at their homes, but insisted upon in camp as a test of self reliance and soldierly bearing.

"Most of your readers will remember that on the road to Maritzburg from Durban, after passing Mrs. Welch's Halfway House, ascending the hill beyond, and passing round the serpentine cutting, a narrow plateau is reached, just before beginning the ascent of the Inchanga; here looking to the left, the country, in the most uncomfortable proximity to the road, falls away suddenly from the traveller's feet into a series of gorges hundreds of feet below, their sides clothed with freshest verdure, sprinkled with flowers, and dotted over with the handsome scarlet flowers of the aloe, giving it a wonderful beauty, but a beauty like that of some of our snakes, which you must admire even while you shudderingly shrink from.

"These gorges are the termination in this direction of the enormous basin or depression known as the Table Mountain and Inanda kafir locations, which extend for a distance of some 30 by 50 miles, and form one of the most astonishingly wild and grand scenes to be met with in South Africa.

"This vast area resembles in the distance a stupendous ocean, petrified while its mighty waves were being angrily tossed upwards and to and fro in some terrific storm, the whole district being one mass of steep hills and deep kloofs running into and across each other in the wildest confusion, and apparently utterly inaccessible.

"Each kloof or valley has its little stream, which, uniting, form, or materially swell, rivers which are of considerable volume. The Umgeni is one of these and the largest.

"The sides of the hills are in some places densely wooded, and perched on many of them are kafir kraals of large size, which look as if they could be reached by baboons and goats only. Roads there are none; kafir and cattle paths, like sheep tracks on the mountains at home, run in every direction, apparently without either beginning or end, and utterly confusing and baffling to the traveller.

"This basin forms one of the happy hunting grounds of thousands of our natives, and, except by the wiry sportsmen, is very rarely visited by the white colonist, the physical conformation of the district raising a serious barrier to any intercourse with its occupants, and here, therefore, barbarism reigns supreme and rampant.

"Down into this location we were marched on the morning of Wednesday, down, down, ever descending, tripping over the stones, slipping and wading through the long yellow grass, until we seemed likely to spend the day in reaching the bottom; and right glad were we when we did reach it, and found ourselves in the dry bed of a large water course, where we were able once more to re-mount, and ease aching knees and ankles. Our march now lay in the bed of the river, following its windings for a considerable distance. The high banks were in many places pierced with numerous nests of the kingfisher, and abundant "spoor" of bucks proved that they were to be found in the thickets of mimosa, which fringed the river and dotted the landscape. Hæmanthus were beginning to peep out of the hard stiff soil, as if their delicate stalks had been tipped with steel, and everywhere the glorious scarlet blossoms of the erythrina lent life to the scene. The advanced guard proceeding noiselessly on the soft sand of the river bed, came suddenly upon some kafir women digging for water in the gravel. The unexpected sight of soldiers made the younger ones leave their calabashes and fly into the bush, but one old lady, trusting probably to her ugliness for immunity, stood her ground, and asked what they wanted there. "Oh," said one of the troopers, "we are going to take this place." "Ah," she replied, with the ready wit of an Irishwoman, "and where are you going to put it?"

"I may here remark that this was the only instance in our patrol where any alarm was exhibited, and here, only, because the women were alone and taken by surprise. Everywhere, we were met with the utmost friendliness, and men, women, and children alike crowded out of their huts as we passed, exchanging the usual "sa-u-bona" with the utmost cordiality. All seemed fat and sleek, and in every kraal were fine strapping young fellows lolling about, the beau ideal of manly beauty and strength, Apollo Belvederes in bronze, and with even less covering than the Grecian one.

"Leaving the bed of the river our course now lay towards

Table Mountain, crossing several fine streams, dismounting frequently and forcing our way through the bush, up hill and down dale. Some of these streams would, later in the season, prove very formidable, as, even now, there was a good volume of water. In one, an unfortunate trooper came to grief; and a gallant officer of Carbineers, superintending the ford, was so tickled and convulsed by the doleful spectacle, that his nether garments, unprepared for such a sudden strain, gave way, and were shattered beyond recovery, leaving him to perform the rest of the day's ride in a costume as airy and cool as that of a Scottish Highlander; borne, however, with all the characteristic nonchalance of that gallant officer. Skirting the base of Table Mountain, which towered in massive grandeur over us on our left, and opening out as we went along some charming little kloofs and dells, suggestive of hidden treasures, in ferns, lycopods, and begonias, we now struck across towards the Inanda location, and early in the afternoon halted on the banks of a large stream. Horses were soon off-saddled, knee-haltered, and allowed to graze; the pack-saddle wallets explored, and the inner man satisfied; and, after a brief roll on the grass, and the invariable post prandial pipe, the march was resumed.

"We here passed through a dense forest of euphorbias, of an entirely different character to the one so familiar to us on the coast. This one has a clean, straight, woody looking trunk, surmounted by a dense mass of dark green *quill*-like foliage, and in numbers has a very fine effect. We observed here also a handsome plumbago, its clusters of pale blue blossoms being shown off to the greatest advantage by its dark surroundings; festoons of a sweet little primrose-coloured thumbergia further graced the path, while a charming little scarlet lily in clusters of three or four flowers on one stem, gracefully pendant like a fuchsia, enlivened the open glades in the bush.

"The kafirs met here assured us there was no road; no horses had ever been here before *nor could they go*, but as the sequel proved they could and did go. The track now descended precipitously to the banks of the Umgeni and skirted it closely, occasionally leaving it and penetrating the bush to avoid serious obstacles necessitating incessant dismounting, many a weary clamber and the use of swords occasionally to clear the way, notwithstanding which more than one trooper found himself an Absalom, and not a few left shreds of blankets and garments on the projecting thorns as guides for the rear guard. The difficulties here were so many and persistent that the writer, who was with the rear guard, more than once saw the

Memorial Brass Erected in St. Saviour's Cathedral, Pietermaritzburg, in Memory of the Members who Fell in Action or Died during the Boer War, 1899 to 1902.

head of the column emerge on a hill quite a mile and a half distant from us, the rest of the column in single file struggling along as well as it could, now in the dense bush, now wading on the river sand, and again clambering over huge masses of granite, which seemed as if they could only have reached such spots, hurled there by the hands of some Titan.

"One of these enormous masses, by some convulsion of nature, had been rent in twain, forming a natural gateway or pass, with, however, a sloping and slippery ascent of smooth granite on either side. This was a ticklish place to pass with horses, and the Major, therefore, with characteristic thoughtfulness, remained by it until he had seen the column safely through, not, however, until many a suspended pannikin had been squeezed flat as a pancake, and more than one warrior laid prone.

"Such a spot, defended by a couple of resolute men armed with rifles, could bar the way against an army; indeed, the impression gathered by the patrol, as a whole, was that—without a swarm of native allies to occupy the bush on the flanks—no European force could possibly penetrate this district, and even then a mountain howitzer attached to each troop would be found of inestimable advantage.

"The scenery here was very fine in many places, the brawling river tumbling over rocky ledges, adding to the charm, deliciously suggestive of much desired, but impossible baths, and equally impossible pic-nics.

"Leaving the river's windings and striking off now to the right, we were confronted by a hill so long and steep, that both horses and men were completely blown on reaching the top; and even the untiring and ever active Quartermaster-Sergeant found himself here knocked out of wind.

"This brought us, towards sunset, on the top of a long, high and narrow ridge, the former site of a kafir kraal, where it was determined to bivouac for the night.

"Horses were accordingly off-saddled, and under charge of a horse-guard allowed to pick up what they could. Rations issued, fires were lit, and soon, over hot coffee, and rudely grilled crops, which needed no Lea and Perrin's, the fatigues of the day were forgotten, and the incidents humorously discussed.

"As night began to close, the horses were driven in, and tethered wherever a stout enough bush permitted. Sentries were posted for the night; and as they had to make a circuit outside the space occupied by the scattered horses, their duty was no sinecure.

"The moon rose calmly, and the stars looked down on us with a merry twinkle, and soon after, wrapped in their blankets, the weary warriors, picking the softest six feet of the sun-baked hill each could find, were off into oblivion: the saddle, the only pillow; mother earth, the downiest of mattresses. Officers might be picked out here and there by the white helmet stuck on the hilt of the sword, which was thrust upright into the ground, and the belts suspended therefrom, gleaming in the moonlight like some ghostly monumental trophy over the grave of a slain knight.

"The gentle rustle of the night wind in the surrounding tree tops, the unceasing murmur of the river, far away down at the foot of the hills, and the occasional roar of a tiger in the kloofs below, formed a lullaby, which was irresistible; and the writer having selected a snug little depression on the hill side, on the softest of ironstone gravel, soon also passed into dreamland, only to be brought back again therefrom an hour or two after, and to have the romance of the situation cruelly dispelled by a heavy downpour of rain, which eventually it became impossible to sleep through, the blankets being soaked, and the nice little hollow converted into a pond.

"Reader—pull on a pair of top boots over your unmentionables, get into a closely buttoned coat, lie on your back in your bath, and get your kafir to pour a couple of buckets of cold water gently down your back inside your coat collar, rise now suddenly to your feet, and you will find a great many pounds weight of water in your breeches and boots. Now throw over you a brown paper Government cloak, and having chosen a wet and cold night for your experiment, go out and promenade your garden until daylight doth appear, and you will understand this phase of the pleasures of volunteering, as experienced by the writer. I commend the attempt to Mr. John Millar, M.L.C.—the always consistent admirer and supporter of Volunteers.

"The rain continued all night, but many of the men, too tired to care, slept soundly all through it; others, raised by hydraulic pressure, made a huge fire and sat or walked round it till the "reveille" once more reminded the sun it was time to rise; and great was the fun and chaffing as one after another the sleepers came on the hill top, all draggled, like fowls on a fence in the rain, although anything but forlorn.

"A cup of hot coffee, the wet blanket wrung out and strapped on the saddles, the shivering horses saddled, the "fall in" sounded, "half sections right" followed by "form files," and we were once more off.

"The rain continued to accompany us as we picked our way carefully along the narrow, and now slippery kafir tracks, often on the steep sides of the hills, now up hill, and again down or winding along the crest. Occasionally the rain lifted for a few moments, revealing wild and grand bits of scenery away below us, and although the thick white fog spread out along the valleys like vast sheets, and hid the depths, yet sufficient was revealed to give us glimpses of landscape which would have delighted the heart of a Turner, or Thos. Baines.

"Our route now lay eastward, through the location, and brought us to several kraals. The hills hereabouts were covered with huge aloes, which standing apart, and having only a few of the upper leaves erect, the rest, dried and black, falling close along the stem, at a distance looked exactly like a swarm of kafirs in war feathers scattered over the hill, and had our mission not been a peaceful one, would probably have led to the word of command being passed along quietly, "with ball cartridge, load."

"Towards afternoon the troop once more emerged on the high road, on the hill above Padley's, and passing the Halfway House again, struck across the country on the left hand side of the road near Inchanga, and reached camp again in the afternoon, entering from the opposite side to that we had emerged from on the previous morning, so that we had completed a circle in our patrol.

"The rain now ceased, and the men, after a good meal, were soon busily engaged burnishing-up their rusty accoutrements, and before parade next morning every trace of the recent journey, except the sunburnt faces, was washed and pipeclayed out.

"Friday proving fine, there was a general turn-out of wet blankets and garments, and the day was fully occupied with squadron drill, foot drill, and skirmishing.

"Major Dartnell, at the close of the latter, addressed the men, expressed himself gratified at the result of the week's work, and hoped that next year he might find even more proficiency, and certainly a better muster.

"Three cheers were called for the Major, and heartily responded to, the Commandant of Volunteers having earned the respect, esteem, and confidence of every man wearing a volunteer's uniform. A horse race, foot races, jumping, and football brought a very pleasant day to a close.

"The following morning early tents were struck, kits packed, and the two troops moved off homewards, exchanging cheers as they passed each other, the utmost harmony and good feeling having existed between them during their stay, both commanding officers, gallant scions of the same good old stock, having done their best to foster this feeling by their unvarying courtesy and affability to all.

"The results of the week's work may be summed up thus:— The mettle of both men and horses was tested, and those who did not join the force for such work, had the opportunity of learning what is expected of them, and can at once resign if it is unpalatable. The officers, and the Commissariat have learnt duties they could never acquire on parade. The Commandant says he has learnt he can depend upon his branch of the service; and the kafirs have learnt that their fastnesses can be reached if necessary by an armed force; and if all this be so, the members of the two troops may conclude that their week from home and their usual occupations have not been lost or mis-spent, and that their capitation grant has been fairly earned."

In November the Carbineers joined in a field day with the regulars. A pleasant day was spent, and they were complimented by the Commandant.

1878. The Regiment, to the number of thirty-two, attended the Queen's Birthday parade.

On the 12th August the Carbineers encamped with the Durban Mounted Rifles at Botha's Hill.

Lieutenants Taylor and Moodie having resigned their commissions their places were worthily filled by Sergt.-Major Royston and Quarter-Master Durrant Scott.

The Regiment formed an escort for Sir Bartle Frere on his arrival, all the officers being presented to His Excellency.

At this time the pending Zulu War was much talked of, and at the distribution of prizes shortly after the annual prize shooting, Captain Shepstone, who presided, intimated that the Regiment would be ready and willing to cross the border if necessary.

29th November. The Carbineers leave Maritzburg for the Zulu War (see chapter VIII.)

1879. 22nd January. Isandhlwana (chapter VIII.)

28th July. Carbineers leave Landtman's Drift for Maritzburg.

In the Drill Shed, at the distribution of the annual shooting prizes of the Regiment, Captain Shepstone announced his intention of resigning, and referred to the gallant conduct of Trooper Barker in the retreat from Isandhlwana.

1880. The Regiment attended the Queen's Birthday parade, which was held on the market square.

Sir George Colley, on his arrival as Lieutenant-Governor, was met by a detachment from the Regiment at Thornville, and by them escorted to town.

The Regiment formed part of the procession in the demonstations at the opening of the railway line from Durban to Maritzburg.

On 3rd December a ten days' drill was held in the city. Sergeant G. J. Macfarlane was elected second lieutenant.

1881. On the 18th July a combined camp with the Durban Mounted Rifles was held at Inchanga. There was not, however, a large attendance.

In August Captain Shepstone's resignation was accepted, he being allowed to retain his rank and wear the uniform of his Regiment "in consideration of his long and arduous services in the corps."

In December Sir Evelyn Wood distributed Zulu War medals (see chapter VIII.)

1882. An encampment was held at Pinetown beginning on the 6th April. Before leaving it, a meeting was held at which Lieutenant Royston was unanimously elected Captain. The camp broke up on the 13th April. Before dismissing, Captain Royston addressed the men, informing them of his pleasure at the manner in which the various duties had been carried out, and mentioned that their late Commanding Officer, Captain Shepstone, had expressed his admiration for the way in which they had turned out, and for their exertions to keep up the credit of the Regiment.

On 28th April there was unveiled in the Maritzburg High School, by His Excellency Sir Henry Bulwer, a tablet (since re-erected in Maritzburg College) in memory of those old boys who had fallen at Bushman's Pass and in the Zulu War. It bears this inscription, penned by Mr. R. D. Clark, M.A., Head Master:—

"Dulce et decorum est pro patriâ mori."
In piam memoriam
hujus scholae alumnorum
qui ut olim pueri inter studia ludosque
aemuli fuerant
sic juvenes contra barbaros pro aris et focis
alius alio fortius
pugnantes
mortem oppetiverunt
hoc monumentum
icti desiderio condiscipuli magistrique
hic erigendum curaverunt.

R. H. Erskine, N.C., apud "Bushman's Pass," prid. non. Nov. MDCCCLXXIII.

J. P. Archbell, N.N.C.
J. A. Blaikie, N.C.
H. W. Davis, N.C.
F. G. Doyle, L.H.   } apud "Isandhlwana,"
E. J. D. Scott, N.C.   } xi. kal. Feb. MDCCCLXXIX.
G. T. Macleroy, N.C.
G. J. P. Shepstone, N.N.C.

C. A. Potter, W.N.C., apud "Hlobane," V. kal. Apr. MDCCCLXXIX.

I. Ferreira, C.D., apud "Kambula," IV. kal. Apr. MDCCCLXXIX.

C. Mears, apud "Secocoeni" fines, IV. kal. Dec. MDCCCLXXIX.

Pietermaritzburgii, mense Januario, MDCCCLXXXII.

In the course of an address Mr. K. H. Hathorn referred feelingly to the manly and honest character of those to whose memory the tablet was erected, some of whom had been his school-fellows.

This year is signalised in the annals of the Regiment by a large increase in its numbers, Captain Royston and his officers giving every encouragement to the right sort of recruits.

1883. There is little to record of the Regiment this year. The numbers on the roll gradually increased, and the reputation for smartness and discipline, which have ever been distinctive features of the Corps, was well maintained.

The annual encampment was held at Pinetown, where, it is stated, the Regiment took the palm for muster and discipline. At the conclusion of camp the following general order was issued:—"The Commandant desires to express to the officers and men of the several corps lately encamped at Pinetown, his appreciation of the highly creditable manner in which they turned out, and of their ready and cheerful performance of duty, and obedience of orders, which so largely contributed to make the encampment a success. He especially congratulates the Natal Carbineers and Maritzburg Rifles on their increased strength, efficiency, and general appearance on parade, and trusts that, before long, the other corps will be enabled to emulate them in every respect.—By order, N. E. Davey, Capt. and Adj. Volunteers."

1884. The prizes won at the annual shooting were presented by Captain Shepstone, C.M.G., who, in the course of his speech, said he trusted that the credit of the Regiment, borne testimony to by many distinguished officers, would be kept up.

The annual camp was held at Pinetown from the 10th April. The Regiment's numbers were still increasing, and His Excellency, the Lieutenant-Governor, complimented it highly after its march past.

At a meeting held on the 25th September, Sergt.-Major E. M. Greene was elected Second Lieutenant.

The monument to those who fell in the Zulu campaign was unveiled on 11th October by Sir Henry Bulwer, the Lieutenant-Governor. The Regiment, it is hardly necessary to say, was present at the ceremony in full force. The following address was presented to His Excellency on the occasion:—

May it please Your Excellency:

We, the members of the Zulu War Memorial Committee, and as representing the subscribers to that memorial, beg to express the pleasure we feel in meeting Your Excellency here to-day.

To the events from which this memorial has sprung, and which it is designed to commemorate, Your Excellency is no stranger, and it is therefore, not now necessary to recall them. It is sufficient to remember that Your Excellency shared with Colonists the risks and perils of a grave crisis, and to assure

Your Excellency of our appreciation of the peculiar fitness of Your Excellency's presence to take part in to-day's ceremony.

Although mainly intended to commemorate the names of those Colonists who so nobly fell in the discharge of their duty to their Queen and country, this memorial, we would remind Your Excellency, is no less intended as a tribute of gratitude on the part of Colonists towards all those, whether Her Majesty's regular troops, or Her Majesty's subjects of all nationalities in this or the adjoining Colony, who took part in defending colonial homes.

We would now respectfully request Your Excellency, by unveiling this monument, to dedicate it publicly to the memory of those Colonists who honourably laid down their lives at the call of duty, in the hope of the establishment of that lasting peace which is worthily purchased by the blood of brave men.

Signed on behalf of the Committee,

H. GRIFFIN,

Mayor.

Pietermaritzburg, Natal,

11th October, 1884.

His Excelleny, in replying said: Mr. Mayor and members of the Zulu War Memorial Committee—I receive your address with satisfaction, and I need not to assure you that I have accepted your request that I should take part in this ceremony with the profoundest personal sympathy in the object for which it is held. This is not the first occasion on which it has been my privilege to speak in this place of those who fell in the Zulu war of 1879, and to bear testimony, in the name of the Colony at large, to the sentiments of grateful affection in which we hold their memory. The events of that war are fast passing, with the passing years, into the back ground of our personal recollections and experiences. By those here amongst us who had a part in those events, whether in active service in the field or in the councils and administrations of the Government, or through the lives of those who fought and fell, it is not likely, indeed, that that stirring time or the incidents of it will ever be forgotten; and therefore, for us of this generation, it might be claimed that no marble monument is needed to remind us of what is written for ever in our own memories and hearts. But it is only right that we, in this our day, should do honour to the

CAMP, TAYLOR'S CAMP, 1905.

Back Row—Lieut. Thornhill, Lieut. Autel, Lieut. Hampson, Lieut. Tatham, Lieut. Ryley, Lieut. James, Z.M.R., Lieut. Fannin, Lieut. Tanner, Lieut. Lindsay, Lieut. Allison, Lieut. Hulley, Z.M.R., Capt. Flindt, Z.M.R.
Second Row—Capt. Lyle, Capt. Gray, Lieut. Black, Lieut. Richards, Lieut. Paterson, Lieut. Smollie, Lieut. Brandon, Capt. Owen, Capt. Townsend, Lieut. Martin, Lieut. Stiebel, Lieut. Smith, Lieut. Hone, Lieut. Briscoe, Capt. Barter.
Third Row—Major Gaze, Major Rodwell, 3t. Lt.-Col. Hair, Bt. Lieut.-Col. Shepstone, Bt. Lieut.-Col. Weighton, Lt.-Col. McKenzie, O.C., Bt. Lt.-Col. Mackay, Bt. Lt.-Col. Foxon, Bt. Lt.-Col. Crompton, Capt. Woods.
Front Row—Lieut. Stride, Lieut. Vanderplank, Major Vanderplank, Z.M.R., Lieut. Walton, Z.M.R., Capt. Montgomery, Major Comrie.

dead, and should seek, in some fitting manner and permanent form, to commemorate their fate and the manner in which they met it, for their death was that which is of all deaths the most honourable to men, dying as they did in the performance of their duty and giving up their lives in the service of their Queen and of their country. It is only right and proper that some such memorial as this should record their worthy fate and the grateful recollection of those for whom they died; and only right also that this should be done for the sake of those who come after, that there may be set always before them, not merely the monumental stone of a memorable event, but a record of brave lives given up in the public service of their country and in the performance of duty that was faithful unto death. In unveiling, then, this memorial, which is raised to the memory of those colonists who fell in the Zulu War of 1879, and to serve at the same time as a tribute of gratitude and respect on the part of the colonists of Natal to all those—the officers and soldiers of Her Majesty's regular forces, and the subjects of Her Majesty of all nationalities and races— who perished in that war, I dedicate it to that memory and to that purpose in order, and in the trust, that it may be held in enduring honour by succeeding generations in this country, and that it may ever be a means of pointing out to the young the path of honour and of duty—a lesson the usefulness and beauty of which will long outlive the service rendered by those who died.

The monument bears the following inscription: —

"In memory of honour and in hope of peace.
This monument, inscribed with the names of Natal Colonists
who fell during the Zulu War
is erected by Public Subscription.
'They being dead yet speak.'"

On one side are inscribed the names of those Carbineers who fell in the war.

1885. An athletic club was formed in connection with the Regiment and regular practices were begun.

The camp was held this year at Emberton when, Quartermaster Slatter having resigned, Mr. J. Weighton was elected to the vacancy. Remarks were made on all sides that the Regiment made a brave show, the physique of men and horses being excellent. There was the usual wet weather on the march to camp, and a most unpleasant ride was the consequence. Before dismissing, Captain Royston addressed the men, and congratulated them on the manner in which they had performed their duties which had been to the utmost satisfaction of the Commandant.

The Queen's Birthday parade was attended as usual, and the following General Order, by the Colonel on the Staff, was issued :—

DISTRICT ORDER, NATAL.

NO. 134.

Pietermaritzburg,

14th June, 1885.

1. The Colonel on the Staff, Commanding Troops, desires to express his satisfaction with the appearance and the working of the Troops on the recent parades and field days.

On the occasion of the Queen's Birthday parade, the Soldierlike appearance of the Troops, their smartness and steadiness under Arms, were all that could be desired. The appearance of the horses of the Cavalry and Mounted Infantry was excellent, their condition reflecting the greatest credit on those branches of the Service. Trooping the Colours was very effectively performed by the 1st Battalion A. and S. Highlanders. The march past was good. The Colonel Commanding desires that his remarks with reference to the Troops should equally apply to the Volunteer forces who were present on the ground—the Natal Carbineers and the Maritzburg Rifles. The appearance of these Corps was most creditable in every respect, and their movements on parade were executed with great steadiness and accuracy.

The Colonel Commanding has much pleasure in notifying that His Excellency the Governor was pleased to express the gratification afforded to him by the soldier-like and efficient appearance of the whole of the troops that were present on the Queen's Birthday parade.

By Order,

J. M. GORDON, Major,

D.A.A. General.

In August a meeting was held at Howick for the purpose of forming a troop in that district. Sixteen members were elected. This meeting may be said to have inaugurated the county troop system which has been such a success in adding to the numbers of the Regiment.

At a meeting held in October, Sergeant-Major D. McKenzie, Corporal C. B. Addison, and Trooper W. W. Barker were elected lieutenants in consequence of the increase in the numbers of the Regiment.

The annual Regimental Ball was resuscitated this year, and Regimental Races were held.

1886. The Regiment was fortunate in obtaining Dr. Hyslop for its surgeon, who was for so many years its popular medico.

To the then large number of 125 the Regiment attended the Pinetown camp from 22nd April, being played out of town by the band of the Maritzburg Rifles. A review was held by His Excellency, the Lieutenant-Governor, who addressed the men as follows:—

"Volunteers of Natal, you have already a history, and a history you have good reason to be proud of. The volunteer movement in Natal, dating as far back as 1855, is, I believe, older than that of the Mother Country. The Volunteers of Natal have probably seen more active service than any other volunteer force in Her Majesty's dominions. In the year 1865 you were called out for the Basuto war; during the rebellion of 1873 your services were again employed; during the Zulu War of 1879 you were in the field—or many of you were —for eight months, serving side by side with Her Majesty's regular troops. You fought and bled at Rorke's Drift, at Isandhlwana, Ugingindhlovu, and to repeat the words of a distinguished soldier, personally known to you, "the melancholy field of Isandhlwana is a record of what colonists did, in silence and death, but none the less a living record now and for ever." You know, and I know, the many difficulties and hindrances that hamper volunteering—the sacrifice of time, the loss of money which are inseparable from it. Many a volunteer corps, unable to withstand all these trials, has in its infancy sickened and died; but you, as a body, have passed through the troubles of childhood, and have arrived at robust manhood. And now, although there are all these difficulties and troubles in the way of volunteering, I must say there is a great deal of compensation. The movement itself is essentially a healthy movement, and when it develops into a camp of exercise, such as this is, it is difficult to exaggerate the benefit and advantage it confers both bodily and mentally. In addition to that I am sure we must all feel that it is a most pleasant thing in itself. The volunteer forces of the Colony now bear over 1,000 names on the roll, of these 834 are present on parade to-day. There are in the Colony twelve different corps. Of these nine are present to-day. To mention them in the order of seniority, that is, with regard to the date at which they were first formed, the Natal Carbineers come first, then, close together, the Victoria Mounted Rifles and the Alexandra Mounted Rifles, and in order of seniority follow the New Germany Rifles, the Maritzburg Rifles, the Durban Volunteer Artillery, the Durban Mounted Rifles, the Royal Durban Rifles, and last, but not least, the Natal Naval Volunteers. The corps that are absent from parade to-day are the Natal Hussars, and nobody regrets more than I do the cause of their absence; it is the prevalence of horse-sickness among them. The Stanger Mounted Rifles are not at this meeting—I am not aware of the precise reason why they are not here. The Umzimkulu Rifles are also absent; the great distance from the site of the camp gives some reason for their absence. Of your tenacity of purpose no better proof could be given than that afforded by the fact of your having been, as I have already mentioned, engaged in the field during the Zulu War of 1879 for eight consecutive months. The severity of such a strain on the volunteer organisation must be felt to be realised. Of your soldierlike qualities, of your discipline, and of your efficiency, abundant proof has been given in times past under most trying circumstances. The perfect order and good conduct that has marked this camp of exercise, and the admirable manner in which you have performed the evolutions and manœuvres I have already witnessed, show that the Natal volunteers are zealous to maintain the high reputation they have already gained. I am glad to observe that the Government and Legislature have, by making a liberal grant, shown that they attach due value and importance to the volunteer force; and Colonel Dartnell, officers and men, I rejoice with you in the warm interest and the pride that the Colony at large has learned to take in its volunteer force. Natal is proud of her volunteer force; and I am proud to be called the commander-in-chief of the force."

Before leaving the camp Captain Royston, addressing the men, complimented them on their excellent discipline, and stated that he understood from the Commandant that he was thoroughly satisfied with their behaviour both off and on parade. He trusted the efficiency of the corps would be zealously maintained.

Meetings were held at Richmond and Camperdown and attended by Major Greene, Captain Macfarlane, and others, and troops were formed in these districts.

In August meetings were held at Richmond Road and Estcourt at which centres troops were formed.

The revolvers were called back to store, and have not again been issued.

Owing to virulence of horse sickness the remount fund was started.

At a meeting held on 10th September the following gentlemen were elected lieutenants.—Quartermaster J. Weighton, Sergeant Henderson, Trooper W. Shepstone and Mr. C. E. Taunton (Headquarters), J. W. Harvey (Camperdown), and P. Flack (Estcourt). Orderly Room Sergeant Hicks was elected Quartermaster.

The Annual ball was held on 26th November, in Simmer and Jenkins' new buildings.

A shooting club was formed this year, Sergeant Whittaker officiating as Honorary Secretary.

The horse allowance was reduced to £7 10s., and capitation grant to £2.

1887. In April a troop was formed at Ladysmith.

In May the Regiment sustained a loss by the resignation of Lieutenant Barker who, as has been elsewhere mentioned, had done such good service in the Zulu War.

The encampment was held on the 14th June, close to Maritzburg, and was well attended, the Regiment outstripping all others in numbers. The new country troops made a good show.

On Jubilee Day a review, held in conjunction with the regulars, was followed by a sham fight on a large scale. The mounted men had a hard day of it, being in the saddle from 10 a.m. to 7 p.m.

The Richmond Troop was formed in August.

The Annual Ball was held in the old Theatre Royal, proving as usual a great success.

A supplementary camp was held at Sterkspruit for those who had been unable to be present at the general camp.

In consequence of the amalgamation, which was effected this year, of the Natal Hussars with the Natal Carbineers, the following promotions were made:—Major Royston to be Lieutenant-Colonel, Captain Greene to be Major, and Lieutenants Taunton, Addison, and Ross to be Captains.

1888. Instead of attending the general camp of volunteers this year, the Carbineers held a regimental camp at Nottingham Road with great success. The Regiment left the city on 29th March, being played out by the band of the Inniskilling Dragoons. As no regimental sergeant-major had been appointed since the resignation of R.S.M. Molyneux, the Regiment was lucky in obtaining the temporary services of Q.M.-Sergeant Steele of the Inniskillings, who proved himself to be the right man in the right place, and evidences of his smartness and tact were soon seen and long remained. The camp passed off without any exciting incidents, and a lot of good practical work was done. In the absence of Lt.-Colonel Royston the command devolved on Major Menne.

On 24th October the Regiment (headquarters) attended the funeral of the late Colonel Stabb, Commandant.

The annual Regimental Ball was held in the Foresters' Hall on the 2nd November, the evening after the annual race meeting, everything passing off most harmoniously, owing to the exertions of the honorary secretary, Trooper A. S. Lister, who, it should be mentioned, officiated in a like capacity at the races .

The Dundee Troop was formed this year.

1889. Captain G. J. Macfarlane, who had been Adjutant for several years, resigned and was succeeded by Captain J. Weighton.

Camp was held this year at the Umlazi from 18th April. Colonel Royston resumed command of the Regiment and issued the following General Order:—"The commanding officer expresses his pleasure at resuming command of the Regiment and feels assured that the conduct of every man will be such as to maintain the high reputation the Regiment has ever borne." The camp was visited by His Excellency the Governor, Sir A. Havelock, and also the O.C. Troops, Natal, Colonel Curtis, C.M.G. At the conclusion of the camp the following General Order was issued:—"Before breaking up camp the Commanding Officer wishes to express his entire satisfaction at the general good behaviour and soldierly conduct of every man under his command. Although the numerical strength of the Regiment now under canvas is less than it ought to be, yet this fact is outweighed by the proved efficiency of the corps generally, for out of a total strength of 225, only six have been found by the inspecting officer to be below the efficiency standard. This is all the more satisfactory when it is borne in mind that at least one third of the whole strength are recruits. It is a pleasure to the Commanding Officer to record that not one case of breach of discipline or misconduct has come under his notice. The Estcourt, Ladysmith, and Dundee Troops are to be congratulated on their efficiency and numerical strength, the Estcourt Troop especially, mustering as it does 28 N.C.O.'s and men. The members of the Corps residing at the remote western confines of the Colony have shown praiseworthy zeal in attending camp from such a distance, and the Commanding Officer expresses his pleasure at having for the first time under his command such a useful and well proved body of men as the Left Wing of the Regiment. The Commanding Officer recognises with pleasure the interest taken in volunteers by the military authorities, practically evinced by the visit paid to the camp by the Officer Commanding Her Majesty's troops in Natal, and also the courtesy of the Officer Commanding the 6th Inniskilling Dragoons in lending the services of such a smart soldier as R.S.M. Steele, to whose hard work and zeal the success of this camp is in a great measure due The Commanding Officer hopes that at the next encampment the same healthy desire, as has been shown at this one, may actuate every member of the Regiment to be good volunteers and of practical use to the Colony in time of need."

On 15th July Trooper C. Brown ("Barley"), of Headquarters Troop, died. The soul of fun and wit, he was the life of every camp fire and sing-song, and a good volunteer. A tombstone, subscribed for by his comrades, was erected to his memory.

On 30th July the volunteer force of the Colony sustained a loss by the death of Captain Davey, Adjutant of Volunteers, who had filled that post of honour and responsibility for many years. He was buried in the military cemetery, the Regiment furnishing the firing party.

Lieutenant-Colonel Royston was appointed to fill the vacancy, and, as a consequence, resigned from the Regiment, in the command of which he was succeeded by Major E. M. Greene, who was promoted to the rank of Lieutenant-Colonel.

Acting Regimental Sergeant Major Steele, of the 6th Inniskilling Dragoons, was the recipient of a testimonial from the non-commissioned officers and men, in the shape of a handsome gold watch bearing the following inscription:—"Presented to Acting R.S.M. Steele by the N.C.O. and men of the Natal Carbineers."

On 5th November a party from the Regiment proceeded

to Ladysmith for the purpose of escorting the Orange Free State delegates to the turning of the first sod of the O.F.S. line. The guests were duly escorted into Ladysmith, and next day were attended by a guard of honour at the ceremony. Captain Addison was in charge of the party, with Lieutenants Cooke and G. F. Tatham.

1890. A general camp was held this year at Pinetown. The whole Regiment paraded on the Market Square on 3rd April and began the march to camp. As on a previous year they were played out by the band of the gallant Inniskilling Dragoons, who were always ready to recognise and encourage the local volunteers. After passing the night at Camperdown the site of the camp was reached next morning, the other regiments coming in during the day. A review was held by His Excellency the Governor, who, at the conclusion addressed the men, complimenting them on the large numbers and the noticeable improvement in shooting. A two days' patrol was taken in the direction of the Umlazi, a sham fight being held on both days. The whole of the mounted men bivouacked on the banks of the Umlazi, the river being much appreciated owing to the lack of water at the camp. Before the breaking up of the camp the opportunity was taken to present Lieutenant-Colonel Royston with an address, and a testimonial consisting of a gold watch suitably inscribed and a piece of plate. Colonel Dartnell, the Commandant, in making the presentation, referred in feeling terms to the loss which the Carbineers had sustained in Colonel Royston's relinquishing command of a Regiment with which he had been so honourably connected for so many years, and at the conclusion of the proceedings three hearty cheers were given for the gallant officer. The address read as follows:--

"Natal Carbineers,

"Pinetown Volunteer Camp,

"April, 1890.

"To Lieutenant-Colonel Royston, Staff Officer of Volunteers.
"Sir,—

"We, the undersigned Officers, Non-Commissioned Officers and Men of the Natal Carbineers, in presenting you with the accompanying piece of plate and watch, beg you to accept them as a slight and affectionate token of our regard and esteem for you on your retirement from the Corps.

Major C. E. Taunton,
Killed in action near Ladysmith, November 3rd, 1899

"During the seventeen years in which you have served in various capacities as a member of the Corps, you have made yourself deservedly popular, and have earned the respect of all of us as a good comrade, an able soldier, and a good and just Commanding Officer, in whom we have always had the fullest confidence, and our regret at your retirement is only tempered by the feeling that you have been appointed to a position in which your advice, based as it is upon long practical experience, will be of the greatest value to the Volunteer Department of this Colony, and that in the discharge of your new duties you will continue to be more or less intimately connected with the Corps, in which you have been so long and favourably known.

"In conclusion, we wish you and Mrs. Royston many years of health, happiness and prosperity.

"We remain, Sir,

"Your obedient servants,

"(Signed) THO. MENNE, Major,

"For 316 Officers, Non-commissioned Officers and Men of the Natal Carbineers."

In August the Newcastle Troop was formed under the command of Lieutenant W. A. Vanderplank.

The annual ball was held on 31st October in the Foresters' Hall.

1891. The Headquarters Troops attended the funeral of the late Lieut.-Colonel Birkett, N.R.R., on 25th February, a mounted party escorting the body of the deceased officer from his residence in the suburbs into town.

On 4th April a detachment of the Regiment proceeded to Charlestown as an escort to His Excellency the Governor, and His Honour the President of the South African Republic, on the opening of the line to Charlestown. The escort consisted of Lieutenants F. S. Tatham, G. F. Tatham, and Vanderplank and 75 men, under the command of Captain Taunton. The headquarters detachment left the City on the evening of the 4th April, not arriving at their destination till late next afternoon. Tents were pitched and the ordinary routine of camp life gone through. The following day was spent in drilling, clearing up, etc., but that night a terrific thunderstorm soaked everything. The following morning the escort marched to a temporary station on this side of Charlestown to meet His

Excellency the Governor, Sir Charles Mitchell, and thence escorted him to Coldstream to meet the President of the South African Republic. The rain the night before had made a quagmire of the roads, which are at any time far from good, and as His Excellency drove very fast in a mule wagon, what was a spick and span Carbineer was soon bespattered and eclipsed with mud from head to foot.

As His Honour crossed over into Natal salutes were fired by Transvaal burghers on the one side of the stream and a detachment of Natal Field Artillery on the other. In the transit by rail from Charlestown to Newcastle, where the Carbineers were to be a dismounted guard of honour, how to get rid of the mud and its stains was a problem that pressed for immediate solution on the mind and energy of the men, rather out of respect for the Governor and his guests than for the sake of their own comfort. Without delay they turned the carriages into dressing rooms and, by spending every moment of the journey in vigorous exertion, when they fell in on the platform to receive the distinguished party with the usual honours, each seemed to have vied with his neighbour in the successful effort to restore himself to his tidy and smart appearance of the morning. Hardly had they detrained when the "special" with its distinguished passengers was signalled as approaching, and the men fell in on the platform without delay and received His Excellency and His Honour the State President with the usual honours. After a hasty meal the horses were re-entrained and the return journey began, the headquarters men not reaching the city till 3 p.m. next day. Some of the detachment remained at Charlestown as an escort for the return journey when Captain McKenzie took the command. The following special order was issued by the officer commanding:—

The Officer Commanding has received with much satisfaction a Report from Captain Taunton with regard to the Escort and Guard of Honour furnished by the Regiment to His Excellency the Governor and His Honour the President of the South African Republic, at Charlestown and Newcastle.

The following is an extract from Capt. Taunton's report:—

"It affords me unbounded pleasure to testify to the creditable and soldier-like manner in which every member performed his duty, both on parade and during the journey to Charlestown and back, more especially as these duties were exceptionally heavy and trying.

"Special praise is due to those men who formed the Guard

of Honour at Newcastle, for their smart appearance when they turned out on the platform, considering that they were covered with mud when they entrained at Charlestown, and had to clean their accoutrements during the journey."

The Officer Commanding has great pleasure in issuing this Special Order, expressing to the Officers, N.C.O., and men of the Escort his appreciation of the highly creditable manner in which they did their duty. He is also greatly pleased to learn that all Commissariat arrangements were most satisfactorily carried out by the Quartermaster and his Staff.

By Order,

J. WEIGHTON, Capt.,

Adjutant.

Headquarters.

The annual training this year took the form of a regimental camp at Balgowan when there was a large muster, over 375 men being in camp. At this encampment the regimental signallers made their first appearance. A feature of this camp, due to Lieutenant-Colonel Royston, Staff Officer of Volunteers, was the introduction of the annual field firing competitions. The Greytown troop of the left wing distinguished itself by coming at the top of the list with a score of 124, Nottingham Road (C troop) taking 2nd place, and Dundee troop third. His Excellency the Governor visited the camp, and a review and march past was held terminating with a sham fight.

On 9th October the Regiment furnished an escort to the High Commissioner, His Excellency Sir Henry Loch, at Richmond, on the occasion of His Excellency's visit to Natal.

The annual Ball was held on 30th October in the old Skating Rink when a large number of guests were present and the proceedings went off with eclat.

1892. A meeting was held at headquarters on 18th February, for the purpose of forming another troop, which was successfully carried out.

A general camp was held this year at Reit Spruit beginning on 10th April. A review was held by His Excellency the Governor on Easter Monday, after which His Excellency complimented the volunteers in general, more especially on the large numbers of mounted men, and concluded by stating that no colony could turn out a better volunteer force. A sham fight brought the encampment to a close.

The annual Ball was again given in the old Skating Rink.

1893. A Regimental camp was held at Balgowan from 2nd June, 21 officers and 322 N.C.O. and men being present. His Excellency the Governor attended the camp, inspected the Regiment, and afterwards witnessed some field movements and outpost duty. The field firing competition was won by the Dundee troop.

The annual Regimental Ball took place this year on 8th September in the Town Hall. A feature of the success of this Ball was the kindness of the wives of the officers in providing the supper.

1894. The most important event of this year was the introduction of the Khaki field uniform and the adoption of white helmets, both of which changes were a great improvement.

Another event was the first appearance of the Regimental Band at the mounted parade on 31st March, when the new uniform was worn for the first time.

In conjunction with the Umvoti Mounted Rifles the annual camp was held at Sterkspruit from 8th June. A novel feature of the encampment was the communication maintained by the Regimental signallers with a telephone station some distance from the camp. The field firing competition was won by B. Troop. The Premier, accompanied by other members of the ministry, attended the camp and a review was held in their honour. The Premier afterwards delivered an address expressing the pleasure he and his colleagues felt in being able to review such a large body of men.

A detachment of the Regiment, consisting of Captain Shepstone, Sergeants Rodwell, Runciman, Townsend, Barter, Corporals Holmes, Button and Lawrance, attended a military tournament arranged by the 3rd Dragoon Guards in Durban, and were most successful, winning the section pegging, and the individual tilting at the ring and tent pegging.

The annual ball was held on 31st August, and again was a great success.

1895. Early in the year the new Martini-Metford carbines were issued, taking the place of the Swinburn-Henrys, which had done good service.

The annual camp was held in bitterly cold weather at Nottingham Road from 14th June. An interesting patrol was made to the Giant's Castle, under the Berg. The Regiment bivouacked in the Game Pass for the two nights of the patrol. The field firing resulted in B Troop again coming to the top of the list, with Dundee Troop second. A polo match was played against a civilian team, the Regimental team, consisting of Captain McKenzie, Corporal Duff, Troopers Taylor and Hodgson, inflicting a defeat on their opponents by seven goals to love.

1896. The camp this year took the form of a flying patrol. Leaving Maritzburg on 20th April, the Regiment marched to Hopewell Drift, Umlaas River, where they remained for three days. The next two days were occupied in sham fighting, all the forces eventually uniting at the Umquahumbi. A parade was held at Hopewell for the purpose of presenting Sergeant T. Mitchell with the Long Service Medal, also to present a gold watch from the members of the Regiment to Sergeant T. M. Owen in recognition of his valuable services in promoting good shooting in the Regiment. Lieutenant-Colonel Greene took the opportunity to address the parade on the crisis in Rhodesia, and stated that if a sufficient number volunteered to serve there he would represent the matter to Government with a view to the granting of the necessary permission. The idea was most enthusiastically taken up by all the men. The result of this offer is shown in the following correspondence. Comment is unnecessary.

From Officer Commanding Natal Carbineers to Commandant of Volunteers.

2nd May, 1896.

Sir,—

I have the honour to inform you that I have been authorised by a large majority of the Natal Carbineers, and others who are willing for this special service to join that regiment, to offer their services in assisting to put down the native rising in Rhodesia, and to request that this offer may be forwarded to His Excellency, the High Commissioner, or other proper officer for his favourable consideration. I may say that I can guarantee at least 300 men, and the only condition that they make is that they go as Natal Carbineers under such of their officers as are willing to accompany them. I would, however, on their behalf, like to be advised of the terms upon which the officers and men should be engaged if their offer is accepted, as also to enquire whether they would be permitted to take the arms they now have as volunteers with them. It is, of course, understood that they offer their services as Mounted Infantry, and, as horses are difficult to obtain, the men would in nearly every instance be willing to sell the horses they now own, as mounted volunteers, to the Chartered Co. at a fair valuation to be made before departure from Natal. It is not only possible but very probable that if 500 men were needed they would easily be obtained on the above terms.

I have the honour to be, Sir,

Your obedient Servant,

EDWARD M. GREENE, Lt.-Col.

From Commandant of Volunteers to Lt.-Col. Greene, Commanding Natal Carbineers.

6th May, 1896.

Sir,—

I have the honour to acknowledge the receipt of your letter of 2nd inst., offering the services of your regiment in assisting to put down the native rising in Rhodesia. Your letter was duly forwarded for the consideration of the Government, and in reply I am directed to inform you that the High Commissioner is already aware of the readiness of the Natal Government to render all possible aid in suppressing the rising in case help from this Colony may be needed.

Yours, etc.,

W. ROYSTON, Lt.-Col.

For Commandant of Volunteers (absent on duty).

From Officer Commanding Natal Carbineers to Commandant Natal Volunteers.

7th May, 1896.

Sir,—

I have the honour to acknowledge receipt of your letter of the 6th inst., conveying a reply from the Government to the offer contained in my letter to you of the 2nd May. The reply which the Government has instructed you to convey to me is offensive in its abruptness. On behalf of, and at the request of my regiment, I made an offer of our services to assist a sister British Colony in her difficulties, and I am at least entitled to a courteous reply from the Government, even if they have reasons for not conveying my offer to the High Commissioner. His Excellency the High Commissioner may possibly be aware of the readiness of the Natal Government to render all possible aid in suppressing the rising in Rhodesia, in case help from this Colony may be needed, but as the Government had not the power to offer the services of the volunteers without their consent, the reply which you have been directed to send me is not an answer to my letter. As it is necessary that I should, without delay, advise the men whether their offer is to be communicated to, and accepted by, the High Commissioner or not, I should be obliged if you would secure me a somewhat more definite, and, at the same time, more courteous, reply from the Government.

I have the honour, etc.,

From Commandant of Volunteers to Lt.-Col. Greene.

12th May, 1896.

Sir,—

In reply to your letter of 7th inst., I am directed to inform you that it is not expected that circumstances will require the raising of a force in Natal to assist in the suppression of the native rising in Matabeleland. If any such need should arise the Government will make all proper arrangements for the raising, command, equipment, horsing, and pay of the force which it may be decided to send, and for compensation in cases of wounds and deaths. It will be open to all volunteers to offer their services as members of such a force.

W. ROYSTON, Lt.-Col.,
For Commandant of Volunteers (absent on duty).

From Officer Commanding Natal Carbineers to Commandant of Volunteers.

13th May, 1896.

Sir,—

I have the honour to acknowledge receipt of your letter of the 12th inst. I regret that the Government seem determined to try and put me off with evasive replies to my letters, but I am sure you will agree with me that as the Carbineers, through me, made an offer of their services to the High Commissioner, they are entitled to expect a direct reply from him, and cannot reasonably be expected to be satisfied with curt and evasive replies from this Government. Would you, therefore, kindly ascertain whether the Government have forwarded my offer to the High Commissioner, as requested, or, if not, whether they intend to do so.

I have the honour, etc.,

From Commandant of Volunteers to Lt.-Col. Greene.

18th May, 1896.

Sir,—

I am directed to inform you, in reply to your letter of 13th inst., that the Government have not communicated to the High Commissioner the tenour of your letter of 2nd May, 1896, and, moreover, that they are unable to comply with your request to to so.

W. ROYSTON, Lt.-Col.,

For Commandant of Volunteers (absent on duty).

The field firing competition was held at Umquahumbi camp, the Regiment doing exceedingly well. Competing against all other mounted regiments they took 1st, 3rd, 4th, 5th, 8th, 10th, 14th, 16th, and 18th places. Richmond troop took premier place, closely followed by Nottingham Road.

Addressing the men before the breaking up of the camp, Lieutenant-Colonel Greene touched on various subjects including the new Volunteer Regulations. He said it was also proposed to adopt a felt hat for the field uniform, concluding by expressing his entire satisfaction with the whole of the Regiment during the patrol. The following General Order from the Commandant was issued:—

From Commandant of Volunteers to Officer Commanding Natal Carbineers.

Upon the completion of the Annual Training of the Mounted Corps, the Commandant wishes to thank Commanding Officers for the ready support which they have given in making this year's manoeuvres a success.

The Commandant also wishes to record his appreciation of the excellent discipline and cheerful disregard of comfort shewn by the Officers and Men, and is pleased to notice a marked improvement in the Saddlery and equipment generally.

The Commandant trusts that now the new Regulations are becoming better understood and appreciated, Officers and Men will unite in raising the efficiency of the Force to the highest possible standard.

By Order,

W. ROYSTON, Lieut.-Colonel,

Staff Officer, Volunteer Dept.

Trooper C. E. J. Miller, D.C.M.

Trooper Dacre Shaw, D.C.M.

Sergeant F. C. Farmer, D.C.M.

The Regimental Ball was held on 25th September, followed next day by sports.

1897. Her Majesty Queen Victoria completed the sixtieth year of her reign on the 20th June, and, in token of her subjects' loyalty to the throne and affection for its occupant, representatives of every part of the British Empire were gathered in London that day to unite in the celebration of what was called the Queen's Diamond Jubilee. The men selected from the Regiment to go Home for the occasion as part of the contingent of Natal Volunteers were T.S.M. Bartholomew, Troopers Smalley, R. Hesom, W. Tanner, J. L. Armitage, and C. A. Carbutt. The officers in charge of the contingent were Captain Shepstone and Lieutenant Crompton, N.C., both of whom had served in the Zulu War. The whole troop consisted of colonials, and all but one were Natal born. The men, picked on account of their smartness and physique, averaged 5 feet 10 inches in height and presented a very creditable appearance. Special uniforms and saddlery made in England, and cavalry horses provided by the War Office, were ready for them on their arrival. In the Bisley team the Carbineers were represented by Sergt. Owen, Corporals Armitage and Stride, and Troopers Sclanders and Colville. The Bisley shooting competitions were held between the 13th and 24th July, after which date the Natal men, grateful for the kindness and hospitality with which they had been treated in the Old Country, returned together to South Africa.

Estcourt Encampment. The city contingent, together with the Camperdown and Richmond troops, in all about eighty strong, mustered on the Market Square on Tuesday the 28th April, and at six o'clock marched up Church Street to the station, where they were subsequently entrained for Estcourt. Having arrived there at seven o'clock next morning the men, under Colonel Greene, marched to the camp on the race-course where they breakfasted. They were accompanied by the Newcastle men who arrived by the kafir mail. The next men to put in an appearance were the Weenen and Estcourt troop, followed closely after by about seventy men of the Umvoti Mounted Rifles who had marched from Greytown via Weenen. These were followed at 10.30 by the Ladysmith men, and at four o'clock the last detachment, the Dundee troop, was expected. The total strength, 13 officers, 32 non-coms, and 178 men including the band, was much under last year's, due undoubtedly to so many men doing duty as rinderpest border guards. The place selected for the camp also was not the most suitable for a larger muster. Church parade was conducted by the Rev. G. Pennington. On Monday at 8.30 a.m. the Carbineers and U.M.R. set out on a four days' patrol to the Upper Tugela. After leaving Estcourt the Carbineers made their first halt at Frere where both man and beast had dinner. After a short rest they moved on again as far as the bridge across the Little Tugela near Springfield and halted there for the night. The next morning the column moved on towards Mr. Fred. Zunckel's, where they slept on Tuesday night, and the following morning it was expected they would meet the enemy—the U.M.R. In this they were not disappointed although the enemy was not in the position expected and as laid down in the plans. Through this error, notwithstanding Captain McKenzie and the men under him made a dashing charge and executed a brilliant manoeuvre, the programme was all wasted, hardly a shot being fired the whole time. That night the Carbineers slept at Gourton, and came on from there to Estcourt on Thursday.

On Thursday a most enjoyable dance was held in the Agricultural Hall, given by the residents of Estcourt in honour of the volunteers, invitations being sent to officers and sergeants of both corps. The band of the Carbineers was in attendance and played a selection of twenty-four dance tunes, which was greatly appreciated by all lovers of good music and dancing.

While the main body N.C. and U.M.R. were on patrol those who for various reasons had been left behind held a shooting match, resulting in N.C. 424, U.M.R. 365. Return match, N.C. 373, U.M.R. 342.

At the Carbineers Annual Meeting, held on Saturday night in the open air, Colonel Greene, who presided, after eulogising the conduct of the men during the encampment, criticised the Government's attitude towards the volunteers as shown by their curt refusal of the offer of the Carbineers to go to Rhodesia. He maintained that the volunteers were always ready to make a sacrifice when duty required it of them, and said that it was not true that the Carbineers were discontented with the small capitation grant, or that they wished for paid instructors. They desired a paid official to do necessary clerical work, but would refuse paid drill instructors: their own officers were qualified. The question of extension, too, should not rest with the ministry—that would be to make volunteers subject to political considerations—it should rest with the Commandant. He did not object to any commanding officer retiring on the Commandant's recommendation, but he would have no ministry telling him that if he behaved himself he would get five years' extension, and that if he did not he must go. In conclusion, he appealed to them to do their utmost for the Regiment and for the volunteer cause generally.

1898. Monday, 4th April. In place of regimental camps held in different parts of the Colony, which was the rule for several years past, the Natal Volunteer Department decided to hold a general camp this year and selected ground at Richmond for the purpose. Lines were laid out for and occupied by the Natal Carbineers, Border Mounted Rifles, Natal Mounted Rifles, and Umvoti Mounted Rifles, and behind these were the infantry quarters containing the Natal Field Artillery, Natal Royal Rifles, and the Durban Light Infantry. From Monday to Thursday the various corps were employed in the parades, regimental drill, and attack and defence exercises which properly take up a large part of the time spent in camp. Two evening lectures by Colonel Hay, R.A., on "Modern Field Artillery Tactics," delivered in the large marquee, were attended by crowded and appreciative audiences. On Friday morning General Cox inspected the troops. After the inspection and march past the General addressed the men in complimentary terms. He had seen the men at their parades, he had gone through their camp and found it in good order and thoroughly well pitched, but it pleased him most that the volunteer encampment was not being looked upon as a picnic; but that good hard work was being done. Immediately after the review the troops engaged in a sham fight, the object being to take the camp. On Saturday the whole of the forces were engaged in active field operations against an imaginary enemy. The general opinion was that the operations were carried out fairly well, though, as might be expected with men having so few opportunities of practice, a few slight hitches occurred.

1899. Easter camp at Balgowan, from 27th March.

The Headquarters, Camperdown and Richmond Road Troops, 155 strong, mustered on the Market Square, and, at 8 a.m., headed by their band, left the City on their march to the camping ground at Balgowan. When all the country troops arrived the Regiment in camp numbered fully 350. The neighbourhood of a force of Regulars, stationed between Balgowan and Fort Nottingham, and their participation in the military manœuvres, lent additional interest to the volunteer brigade enampment this year. The whole of the first two days was given up to troop and regimental drill to get the men into shape for the big field day following. The arrangement for that day was that the infantry and artillery, together with a body of Regulars, should act as a convoy of wagons from Mooi River to Howick along the main road. After the vicissitudes of temporary success and defeat on the one side and the other, which are usual incidents of a real battle, when "cease firing" sounded the attacking party had not succeeded in their attempt to stop and capture the convoy. Next day, in cold and damp weather, His Excellency, Sir Walter Hely-Hutchinson, inspected and reviewed the troops in camp. In his address the Governor congratulated Colonel Royston, the officers and men, on the efficient and soldierly appearance of the forces on parade and the manner in which the various evolutions had been carried out. He was glad to see, as was indicated by the large muster in camp, that a great deal of interest was taken in volunteering in Natal, and promised to do what he could to encourage so useful and beneficial an institution. Saturday was another field day. The idea was that a northern army, making for Fort Nottingham, was to be obstructed and repelled. The northern army, under the command of Colonel Greene, N.C., distinguished itself by the strong positions it took up. Its first, being impregnable, was only left in order to make something of a fight. The second was almost equally good, and was held successfully till the end of the engagement. On an early evening of the encampment, Major Dawkins, R.A., delivered an interesting and instructive lecture on his personal experiences during the late Egyptian campaign, including his account as a combatant of the Khartoum and Omdurman battles.

South African War, 1899-1902. (See Chapter IX.)

1902, May. The undermentioned N.C.O.'s and men were selected to represent the Regiment at the Coronation of H.M. the King:—T.-S.-M. A. B. Vanderplank, Sergeants H. J. Harkness, R. Carbis, J. K. Murray, T. McCathie, R. W. Smith, Corporals W. E. Antel, R. C. Boyd, M. Madsen, J. Watson, Trumpeter H. A. Craig, Troopers G. F. Bennett, E. M. G. Bowes, S. Daly, A. F. Grant, J. W. Horsley, J. Lawrence and H. P. Walsh.

Lieutenant T. M. Owen, Corporal W. P. Gray and Trooper D. G. Sclanders were selected as the regimental team at the English Bisley.

1903. Hermansberg Road Encampment, 9th to 18th April.

The strength of the Carbineers in camp was 380, there

having been a large accession of recruits to them since the war. At 8 o'clock on Sunday morning an inspection of the Natal Carbineers was conducted by Lieut.-Col. Duncan McKenzie, C.B., C.M.G. The Corps turned out in a manner that would satisfy the most fastidious martinet. The whole of the troops in camp next assembled and, after a similar ceremony, a church parade was held. Major Pennington, Church of England Chaplain, conducted the service, which was fully choral, the Natal Carbineer band acting as accompanists. On Wednesday His Excellency Sir Henry McCallum was escorted by a guard of honour of the Carbineers to the parade ground, where there was a march past. After luncheon His Excellency presented a large number of war medals to men of the Border Mounted Rifles and the Umvoti Mounted Rifles. At the conclusion of the presentation the Governor expressed the pleasure he felt at being called on to distribute these marks of well-earned distinction. He would not, in these days of peace and conciliation, refer to the past. He hoped that the volunteer forces would be largely extended. He felt that it was the duty of colonists living in town or country, and surrounded by a large coloured population, to put themselves in a state of efficiency so as to be able to meet any emergency that might arise. He would go even further and say that he would like to see every woman in the country taught to shoot. He urged his hearers to get rid of everything parochial and aim at building up and advancing the British Empire. At 8 o'clock on Thursday morning, Lieut.-Col. Greene formally handed over the command of the Natal Carbineers to Lieut.-Col. McKenzie. Colonel Greene feelingly bade his subordinates good-bye, and remarked that he had been 25 years in the Carbineers, 12 of which were spent in command of the Regiment. He had decided to go on the reserve, but would always take an interest in his old Regiment. Colonel McKenzie referred to the present excellent condition of the Carbineers, which was entirely due to Colonel Greene. Thanks to the late commander, he said, the finances were sound and prosperity should be theirs. Three cheers were given for Colonel Greene, who then took his leave and was accompanied to the train by a large number of the officers.

In connection with Colonel Greene's retirement from the command of the Regiment, the following Order was issued by Colonel Leader, the Commandant:—

"Upon the retirement of Colonel E. M. Greene, V.D., from the command of the Natal Carbineers, the Commandant desires to place on record the valuable and able services rendered to the Volunteer Force and the Colony in general by this officer, which has extended over a quarter of a century, the greater half of which was in command of his Regiment.

"Colonel Greene has rendered most valuable service to the Force and has contributed in no small measure to the success of the Volunteer movement in Natal. The Commandant desires to express his sincere regret in losing the services of so distinguished an officer to the active forces of the Natal Volunteers."

On Sunday, 9th August, in the Alexandra Park, Pietermaritzburg, the Governor, Sir Henry McCallum, distributed medals to the officers, non-commissioned officers, and men of the Natal Carbineers and the Natal Royal Regiment who served during the late war. His Excellency, in addressing the troops, said he felt bound to congratulate all ranks on the admirable way in which they had behaved in the late campaign, and remarked that they had more than upheld the reputation of the Colony. Officers and men alike had borne their privations in a spirit worthy of the traditions of the Empire. When the war-cloud had settled on Natal, and they were called to protect their homes from the invader, they responded right well. The Carbineers, whose contribution to the defence force was about 550 men, had borne the brunt of the fighting. In Ladysmith they had made a name for themselves. The exploit of blowing up the Boer Long Tom on Gun Hill was one that deserved special praise, and any regiment would be proud to have the fact registered in their laurels. The Estcourt Squadron of the Carbineers had fought along with General Buller from Willow Grange till they had joined hands with their beleaguered comrades, and had gained praise of the highest order from General Buller, while the services of the Carbineers in Ladysmith had gained unstinted praise by such soldiers as Lord Roberts and Generals White and Hunter for their behaviour at such trying times as Rietfontein, Lombard's Kop, Waggon Hill, Gun Hill, etc. From Botha's Pass to Volksrust they had operated, when, the invaders being cleared out of Natal, they were sent to Zululand and again saw service at Buffalo River and Vryheid. Colonel Greene had led them from start to finish, and he (His Excellency) had mentioned him in despatches for the excellent work he had done, but up to now nothing further had been heard. In his opinion, Colonel Greene had led them in a thoroughly efficient manner, and no word of praise could be high enough for him.

He was sorry such excellent services as his had not been better recognised. As for Colonel McKenzie, his deeds were too well known. It gave him much pleasure to inform his audience that the distinguished conduct medal had been awarded to three of the Boer contingent, lately our enemies and now our fellow-subjects, just returned from Somaliland; and with the words, "The Temple of Janus is closed," he brought to an end his admirable and, in some parts of it, touching address. The following were the officers of the Natal Carbineers to receive the South African medal:—Lieutenants-Colonel Greene, McKenzie, Macfarlane, Addison, and Weighton; Majors Shepstone and G. F. Tatham; Captains Foxon, Hair, Crompton, Rodwell, Comrie, Mackay, Gage, Townsend, Nourse and Captain and Quarter-Master Lyle; Lieutenants Gallwey, Smallie, Woods, Cockburn, Barter, Montgomery, Vanderplank, Holmes, Lindsay, Martin, Sparks, Bartholomew, Richards and Verney.

1904. On Wednesday, 30th March, the local Carbineers paraded on the Drill Hall ground, under command of Colonel Weighton. In full marching order, and headed by their band, they proceeded by Commercial Road and Church Street to the Central Railway Station and there entrained for their Easter encampment at Colenso. Only a very few of the troopers were absent. The ground selected, owing to its historic associations with some of the most memorable events of the late war, as well as its healthy situation, is well suited for a military camp. The advance parties, under Major Hair, had everything ready when the troops arrived. The number of men in camp, 680, was the strongest muster of any volunteer regiment in Natal, and under their Commanding Officer, Colonel McKenzie, there was from the outset the fairest promise that this encampment would be specially distinguished for hard work with its rewards of instruction and experience. Previous to the contemplated sham fights, long distance marches, etc., the men were kept busy with parades, sentry duty, and attendance to horses and equipment. On Wednesday, 6th April, there was full parade before the Administrator, Sir Henry Bale, and General Broadwood. Sir Henry addressed the men, and referred to the fact that the Carbineers were the senior corps in the Colony and the first called out for active service within the Empire. General Broadwood complimented the men in high terms for their smartness and steadiness. He was extremely pleased with the great thoroughness, energy, and work he had seen on the part of all concerned. He had visited all the camps, and in case of eventualities he was sure Natal volunteers could be thoroughly relied on.

The men had not long returned to camp from parade when the alarm was spread of the drowning of two of their comrades in the river. The whole Regiment searched for the bodies till midnight, but without success. The search was renewed with daylight and again continued fruitlessly till long after dark. On Friday the body of Stoffel Boshoff was recovered, and on Saturday that of his equally unfortunate companion, Harry Rainsford. Both were buried at Colenso with full military honours.

On Saturday, before camp was struck, Colonel McKenzie, in the name and presence of the Regiment, presented Colonel Greene with a service of silver plate, on which was inscribed:— "Presented as a token of esteem and regard by the Officers, Non-commissioned Officers and Men of the Natal Carbineers to Col. E. M. Greene, V.D., on his retirement from the Regiment, which he commanded for 12 years." At the same time Distinguished Conduct medals, awarded to Troopers R. Watts, D. A. Shaw and C. J. Miller for gallantry in the Boer war, were presented by Colonel McKenzie.

The local Carbineers returned to the City early on Sunday morning and marched to the Market Square. Before being dismissed they were addressed by Colonel Weighton. He spoke with pride of the work of the troops in camp, cordially thanked the men for the way in which they had comported themselves during the training, was glad to know that in every respect they had by their behaviour and soldierly qualities maintained the prestige and good name of the Regiment, and closed with the hope that when the time came for their next annual meeting it would be spent under more auspicious circumstances.

Wednesday, 8th June. The Headquarters Squadrons and Band paraded at the corner of Boshoff Street and Prince Alfred Street at 4.30 p.m. to attend the funeral of the late Charles Barter, Esq., formerly an officer in the Regiment. Non-commissioned officers and men were selected to form the firing party at the grave.

Sunday, 4th September. The Headquarters Squadrons and Band attended St. Saviour's Cathedral at the unveiling of the Memorial Tablet which, placed in a prominent part of the building, bears the following inscription:—"Erected by the Natal Carbineers in memory of their comrades who fell in

Lt.-Col. J. P. S. Woods,
Commanding Left Wing, 1911.

Lt.-Col. W. E. Barter.
Commanding Right Wing, 1911.

action, or died, whilst serving in the field during the Boer War 1899-1900, 1901-1902.

"Officers:—Major C. E. Taunton, Captain E. Lucas, Lieutenant A. Wylde-Browne.

"Non-commissioned Officers:—Regimental Sergeant-Major B. M. Bowen, Sergeants A. E. Colville, J. W. Durham, F. G. Mapstone, C. Holmes, Corporals C. W. Abel, P. C. Comrie.

"Troopers:—P. Adie, T. P. Bale, F. W. Bassage, J. L. Birkett, F. H. Brittain, W. Buxton, S. Chapman, W. Cleaver, J. B. Cohen, J. S. H. Colville, W. Craighead Smith, J. E. Davies, F. Duke, T. Elliott, M. Goldstein, D. M. Gray, K. W. Greenall, W. J. Harcourt, H. N. Jenner, G. McKellar, G. G. Mann, A. J. Miller, R. M. Milne-Milner, W. R. Moody, P. A. Murphy, D. Patton, J. Price, S. W. Raw, E. H. Shaw, F. W. Taunton, and B. W. Warren."

Tuesday, 4th October. In the Alexandra Park, Pietermaritzburg, Her Royal Highness Princess Christian presented Colours, the gift of His Majesty the King, to the eight Natal Volunteer Corps that served in the late war. Each corps was represented on the ground by a colour party of 30, selected from its own officers and men. To the Natal Carbineers Her Royal Highness said:—"You are the oldest corps in this Colony. You have served with distinction in the Zulu and other native wars, and in the late war. You have established a record of which you may well be proud. In presenting this standard, which the King entrusts to your care, I feel sure that you will guard it with the same devotion to duty that you have shown in the past."

Saturday, 15th October. One subaltern and 30 N.C.O.'s and men of the Regiment formed an escort to Field Marshal Earl Roberts, K.G., etc., on his visit to Maritzburg.

1905. Camp at Taylor's. For the first time since the Boer War the whole of the Volunteer, or, as it was now termed, "Militia" Force, mounted and foot, assembled at Taylor's for the Easter encampment. Instead of proceeding direct to camp the troops were formed into "northern" and "southern" forces and carried out extensive operations before they reached the rendezvous. The strength of the Natal Carbineers in camp was 40 officers and 576 non-commissioned officers and men. The work during the encampment consisted principally of manœuvres, the ground being well adapted for that purpose, and the practical experience there gained proved of great value in the Native Rebellion that broke out the following year. Wednesday, 26th April, was a gala day in camp. In honour of the visit of His Excellency Sir Henry McCallum, and Admiral Durnford, there was a sham fight, a march past, and a kafir dance. Later in the day an impromptu reception was held by the Governor, Admiral Durnford, and Miss Durnford. Volunteer decoration medals were presented to Lieut.-Colonel Hyslop, Lieut.-Colonel Weighton, and Sergeant Lyle; the King's war medals to Colonel McKenzie, Captains Crompton, Smalley, and Woods; and the Queen's war medal to Lieut.-Colonel Watkins Pitchford. A general inspection was held by Sir H. Hildyard, the General Officer commanding in South Africa. Towards the close of the encampment a sad accident happened to Corporal B. H. K. Orchard, which was the cause of his death six days after. He was a young man to whom character and ability promised a useful and honourable career in the profession of the law.

18th August. The annual ball was held in the Town Hall, Maritzburg.

12th December. Farrier Q.M.S. Meares was presented with a gold watch by the members of the Carbineer Band. He was a foundation bandsman. Having been appointed to a lucrative post in the Natal Mounted Police he had to retire from the Carbineer ranks.

1906. Native Rebellion. (See Chapter X.).

26th February. The Duke and Duchess of Connaught and the Princess Patricia visited Maritzburg. An escort of the Natal Carbineers attended the Royal party from Government House to the Town Hall. On account of the outbreak of rebellion in the Colony and the Regiment being on active service, the arrangement for an inspection by His Royal Highness had to be abandoned.

31st July. Extract from the Journals of the Legislative Council:—"His Excellency the Governor directs it to be notified that General Lord Kitchener of Khartoum, G.C.B., O.M., G.C.M.G., has been pleased to accept the appointment of Honorary Colonel of the Natal Carbineers."

In the Legislative Assembly the Prime Minister moved:— "That the cordial thanks of this Assembly are hereby accorded to the Militia and other forces now or lately engaged in the field, for the promptitude with which they responded to the call to arms for the purpose of quelling the rebellion of portions of the Native population of this Colony; that this Assembly, in congratulating the Officers Commanding upon the success which has attended their arms, places on record the appreciation of the gallantry and endurance displayed by all ranks, and of the public spirit with which private interests have been sacrificed by all alike for the defence of the Colony." The motion was carried unanimously.

Friday, 21st September. The annual ball was held in the Town Hall, Pietermaritzburg.

Extract of a letter received by the Officer Commanding the Natal Carbineers from Lord Kitchener:--

"Simla, 17th October, 1906.

"I am very proud of being again closely associated with such a gallant and efficient corps as the N.C., and I hope you will convey to all ranks my very high appreciation of the honour that has been done me. It has given me the greatest pleasure to hear of the excellent services rendered by the Carbineers during the recent fighting in Natal. The Regiment has well maintained the high reputation for loyal and gallant service to King and Country, which it has gained during 51 years' service in the Colony, and has added another page to its already distinguished records. I shall always remember the time when you and the N.C. were under my command, and helped me so efficiently in bringing about peace in South Africa, and you may be sure I shall always take the greatest interest in the future of the Regiment. I hope I may some day have the pleasure of meeting you all again. I am sending you herewith a picture of myself which the Regiment may care to have.

Yours very truly,

(Signed) KITCHENER."

1907. Native Rebellion (see chapter X.)

16th February. The Colony's Memorial in marble and bronze to those of her sons who lost their lives during the Boer War was unveiled by Lady McCallum. At the conclusion of the unveiling ceremony His Excellency the Governor presented Long Service Medals to Lt.-Col. W. S. Shepstone, Majors T. M. Owen and F. J. Choles, Lieutenants P. Stride and J. W. Johnston, and the King's S.A. Medal to Trooper W. W. King.

19th February. Colonel D. McKenzie, C.B., C.M.G., V.D., having been appointed Commandant of Militia, resigned his command of the Carbineers after a membership of 27 years, of which four years were in command of the Regiment, and permission was given him to wear the uniform of the Corps. Brevet Lt.-Col. J. Weighton V.D., was appointed Lt.-Col. to command the N.C., vice Col. McKenzie.

Lt.-Col. Weighton's record:—Colonel Weighton began soldiering in the Galeka and Gaika campaigns of 1877-8 as corporal with the Prince Alfred Guards, Port Elizabeth. During the Zulu War 1878-9 he acted as Commissariat Officer. During the Boer War he was with his present corps, the N.C., and was among the besieged in Ladysmith. His good services were recognised, and he was mentioned in despatches. His regimental record in the Carbineers is as follows:—Elected Quartermaster, March 1885; Lieutenant, Nov. 1886; Captain and Adjutant, March 1889; Major, Nov. 1899; Hon. Lt.-Colonel, Nov. 1900; Brevet Lt.-Col., April 1905. He held the appointment of Adjutant for eleven years and a half until 30th Nov. 1900.

Lord Kitchener, being Hon. Colonel of the Carbineers, received due notice of the change in command of the Regiment. Through his private secretary, Colonel Birdwood, he sent the following reply to Colonel Weighton:—

"Simla, 24th August, 1907.

My dear Colonel Weighton,

Lord Kitchener asks me to thank you for so kindly having written to him and sent him the Militia orders regarding your appointment as Commandant of the Natal Carbineers, and to say that he is very sorry to hear that Colonel Sir. D. McKenzie has terminated his service with the Corps, but glad to hear that you have succeeded him in the command, and he wishes you every success during your tenure of command, and has every confidence that the Corps will continue to maintain its high reputation for efficiency in the field if again called on for active service during your tenure. On my own behalf I congratulate you very heartily, and will be grateful if you will convey my best wishes to all my old friends of the Carbineers, of whom I have so many happy recollections during the time we served together in Natal in '99 and 1900. I wonder if you still have Burkimsher with you? With kind regards,

Yours very sincerely,

W. R. BIRDWOOD."

2nd September. The Regiment furnished the escort to His Excellency, Sir Matthew Nathan, from Government House to the Town Hall.

25th September. The annual ball was held in the Maritzburg Town Hall.

31st October. Sir Duncan McKenzie, Commandant of Militia, was presented with a large-sized photograph of the Carbineer band.

Meritorious Service Medals were conferred on Sergts. E. I. Dicks and T. P. Catchpole, and the names of the following warrant and non-commissioned officers and men, for good service performed during the same operations, were brought to the notice of His Excellency the Governor:—Sergt.-Major P. J. Higgins, Squadron Sergt.-Major A. Swan, Sergts. G. L. Thompson, C. L. Mulcahy, J. Humphries, B. Wray, Troopers H. A. Taylor, H. Brown, C. P. Francis, A. O. Zunckel, and G. Leathern.

1908. 16th June. The Carbineers furnished Sir Matthew Nathan's escort at the opening of the Natal Parliament.

On Sunday, 16th August, a parade, preceded by divine service, at which there were present representatives of all the militia regiments of the Colony, was held in the Alexandra Park, Maritzburg, for the purpose of presenting Native Rebellion Medals. The parade was under the command of Colonel Weighton, and His Excellency was escorted to the ground by Carbineers. The distribution of Rebellion Medals to the officers and men of the various regiments, to native scouts and loyal chiefs, and of Long Service Medals to Lt.-Colonel Molyneux, Bandmaster Keilly, and R.S.M. Burkimsher, was the final act, said Sir Matthew Nathan, of a drama in which the actors then before the curtain had played well their several parts.

Extract from Natal Militia Orders for October:—"His Excellency the Governor directs it to be notified that His Majesty the King has been graciously pleased to approve the grant of the honorary distinction "Natal, 1906," to the following Natal Militia Regiments who took part in the suppression of the Native Rebellion, 1906:—Natal Carbineers, Natal Mounted Rifles, Umvoti Mounted Rifles, Border Mounted Rifles, Northern District Mounted Rifles, Zululand Mounted Rifles, Natal Royal Regiment, and Durban Light Infantry."

1909. Extract from Natal Militia Orders:—"His Excellency the Governor directs it to be notified that His Majesty the King has been graciously pleased to approve the grant of the honorary distinction "South Africa 1879" to the following Natal Militia Corps:—Natal Carbineers, Natal Mounted Rifles, Umvoti Mounted Rifles, and Border Mounted Rifles."

30th March. A special session of the Natal Parliament, convened to consider the Draft Act of Union, was opened by

His Excellency the Governor. The Carbineers as usual furnished His Excellency's escort.

Regimental Camp at Colenso, 9th to 13th April. The Regiment, encamped under command of Colonel Weighton, mustered 353 of all ranks. On Monday the 12th, His Excellency, accompanied by Sir Duncan McKenzie, arrived in camp. After the presentation of the Militia Forces decoration to Captain Lyle and Rebellion Medals to those who, though entitled to them, had not yet received them, His Excellency complimented the Regiment generally on the evidences of their esprit-de-corps and advised the officers and non-commissioned officers specially to study the profession of war from books as well as on the ground. The rest of the day was devoted to a sham fight with an enemy supposed to be advancing from Estcourt, a general parade and inspection, an alarm, and a lecture by Captain Armstrong on "The Lines of Communication." The first half of Tuesday, the last day in camp, was spent in field-firing at targets half hidden among the rocks and placed in the position occupied by the N.C. Troop at the time of the attempt to take Hlangwane Hill at the battle of Colenso. For the fourth time in succession since the Boer War, namely at the camps at Hermansberg Road, Colenso, Taylor's, and Colenso, this competition was won by the Newcastle squadron. At noon a parade was held at which Colonel Weighton addressed the Regiment. He expressed his great satisfaction that the conduct of the men, without a single exception, was such that he had not had to speak a severe word to any one of them, and regretted that the camp, for financial reasons, had been such a short one. He concluded by thanking Lt.Colonel Mackay and Major Barter, the Wing Commanders, and all the other officers for their valuable assistance.

24th September. The annual ball in the Maritzburg Town Hall was largely attended. Of hosts and guests no fewer than 225 couples took the floor.

Tuesday, 9th November, being the King's Birthday, the Carbineers took part in a grand military review on the Polo Ground, P.M. Burg. His Excellency, escorted to the grounds by the Carbineers, inspected the troops, after which a feu-de-joie was fired, three cheers for the King were given followed by the royal salute, and the ceremonial concluded with the trooping of the colours by the Royal Fusiliers.

1910. General Camp at Taylor's, 19th to 28th March. On Friday the 18th the Carbineers left the city for Howick en route to Taylor's and, after a difficult march across country, arrived in camp on Saturday evening. On Sunday morning His Excellency Lord Methuen was an interested spectator of a sham fight between the "White" and "Khaki" forces, the bone of contention being a train of 50 waggons under convoy. He was much pleased with the manoeuvres, especially with the way the D.L.I. scaled the hills during the fight, and expressed the opinion that the manner in which the Colonial troops linked their horses, making it possible for one man to look after from ten to fifteen of them, might well be imitated by the regular cavalry. Operations between the two opposing forces were continued on Monday. The key of the battle-field was a kopje on the left of the road. It was occupied first by the "Khaki" force, but not to a sufficient extent, with the result that the "White" force, seeing its strategic advantage, captured it and shelled the "Khaki" force on the hill opposite and afterwards rushed the hills in fine style. An alarm, supposed to be caused by an enemy approaching from the south, was the means of proving the readiness and efficiency of the troops in camp. Gallopers were instantly sent off to fetch the horses in from the hills some distance away, and in a surprisingly short time the parade ground was occupied by the troops—artillery, cavalry, and infantry—not all in full dress perhaps, but all armed and ready for action. To test the vigilance of the troops, a party of Carbineers left camp to return and make a sudden attack on it. Their attack was so swift and impulsive that, though they met with a warm reception, they managed to get right through the line of outposts without being captured.

The last night in camp was an uncomfortable and dismal one. A frightful thunderstorm broke over the camp and neighbourhood, and soon there was not a tent but was flooded out. Next morning His Excellency arrived and brought sad news with him. It had been arranged that the Wiltshires should surprise the camp the preceding evening, but on their march to carry out the intention, being overtaken by the storm, they were ordered to return to Fort Napier. In attempting to recross the swollen and raging spruits, which they had passed shortly before, three of their number, Privates John Drew, William Newport, and Leonard Clay, were swept away and drowned. (A memorial tablet, bearing their names and regimental numbers, has since been erected by Lord Methuen in Southbroom Church, Devizes, the garrison Church of the Wiltshire Regiment).

After reviewing the troops in camp, addressing Sir D. McKenzie and those members of the Natal Ministry who happened to be present, Lord Methuen said:—"I do not think you could wish for a finer body of men than have been assembled in this camp, and I say so not in a general way but because I do not suppose that if you were to search the whole world round you would find men who are finer horsemen, who have to a greater degree the instincts of being good shots, or who know so well how to make use of ground."

The gift of a purse to Regimental Sergt.-Major Burkimsher, in view of his approaching trip Home on six months' leave, was followed up later on by the following address:—

"Sergeants' Mess, Natal Carbineers.

W. Burkimsher, Esq., Regimental Sergeant-Major, Natal Carbineers.

Dear Mr. Burkimsher,—

The members of this mess desire to take the opportunity, on the occasion of your contemplated visit to England, to express their high appreciation of your comradeship during the eventful ten years in which they have been associated with you and have had the privilege of your counsel. In wishing you bon voyage and a safe return, we ask your acceptance of the accompanying purse of gold, with our goodwill, and as a token of the high esteem in which you are held.

Signed on behalf of the members of the Sergeants' Mess, Natal Carbineers, this 25th day of March, 1910.

GEO. HARKER, Q.M.S., President.
W. H. F. HARTE, S.Q.M.S., Hon. Secretary."

Friday, 20th May. At midday a solemn and imposing memorial service for the late King Edward VII., to synchronise with the funeral service at Windsor, was held in the Alexandra Park, P.M. Burg. The Natal Carbineers, the Natal Royal Regiment, and the Maritzburg Cadets, numbering in all 700, were on the Oval. Sympathetic crowds occupied the Pavilion stand and stood around the Oval. The service began by the Carbineer band playing Chopin's "Funeral March." Prayers and the lesson were read by the Revd. G. Pennington, Chaplain to the Militia, and the Revd. W. Turnbull, Presbyterian. The troops and spectators, led by the N.C. band, joined feelingly in the hymns, "For ever with the Lord" and "O God, our help in ages past." The band then played the "Dead March in Saul," and the sounding of the "Last Post," by the buglers of the Carbineers, brought this impressive service to an end.

BAND, 1908.

Top Row—J. W. Meares, G. Blair, R. Ash, W. Crane, C. Douglas, F. Lamble, A. Devereaux, J. Brouchley, J. M rton, A. D. Kelly, H. Hendry.
Second Row—J. Runcie, C. Meures, E. W. Fairall, V. Hollington, W. Cullingworth, G. Stevenson, W. Bromfield, J. Johnstone, L. Hollington, E. Hollington, J. Barfield.
Third Row—G. Fairall, Q.-M.-S. Thompson, Bandmaster Kielly, Capt. Helbert, Adj., Lt.-Col. Weighton, O.C., Lt.-Col. Rodwell, Capt. Walton, Sergt. Cragg, Corpl. Rowels, F. Crossley.
Fourth Row—A. Isaacs, G. Isaacs, W. Moor, A. Bush, W. F. Fairall.

Friday 19th August. Extract from the report of the Carbineers ball, published in the "Natal Witness," 20th August, 1910. "There was a dazzling scene and a brilliant company at the Town Hall last night, where the officers and men of the Natal Carbineers held their annual regimental ball. Some 250 couples took the floor, and the uniforms of brave men, the floating draperies of fair women, mingling with the flag-draped walls, and the flower-festooned and fairy-lit stage, created a tout ensemble of glittering enchantment which one might almost liken unto a peep into fairyland, or as near an approach to it as one might hope to see in this work-a-day world."

20th November. In the presence of a large congregation at the morning service in All Saint's Memorial Church, Ladysmith, on Sunday the 20th November, Colonel Weighton unveiled a reredos and a tablet to the memory respectively of George Tatham, who was a major, and of Vernon Christopher, who was a corporal, of the Natal Carbineers. The inscriptions on the memorials are:—"The reredos in this church is erected to the glory of God and in affectionate remembrance of Major George Frederick Tatham, of the Natal Carbineers, who, for 16 years, was a church warden of this parish of Ladysmith. Died, 18th August, 1908." "This tablet is erected by the Natal Carbineers to the glory of God, and in memory of their comrade, Corporal Vernon J. W. Christopher, who was killed near Thring's Post, Victoria County, on the 5th July, whilst on active service in the Native Rebellion of 1906."

1st December. During the course of their tour through South Africa, after the opening of the first Union Parliament at Capetown, Their Royal Highnesses the Duke and Duchess of Connaught and the Princess Patricia spent a long and busy day in Maritzburg. A selection of the Natal Carbineers escorted the royal party from the railway station to Government House, to the civic welcome in the Town Hall, to the ceremony of laying the foundation stone of the Natal University College at Scottsville, and to the open-air reception in Alexandra Park.

13th December. In the committee room of the Town Hall, Maritzburg, the fifty-guinea challenge cup, presented by the "Transvaal Leader" to "The Volunteer Regiment best at arms," was handed over to the Natal Carbineers as the winning regiment at the last Transvaal Volunteer Military Tournament. In making the presentation, Mr. D. Jacobsson, of the editorial staff of the "Transvaal Leader," said:—"The executive of the tournament decided that the cup should be awarded to the regiment best at arms, which meant the regiment scoring the most points. The success of the Carbineers was due to the brilliant achievements of Lieutenant Merrick, who, against big fields, took four firsts, and thus scored 64 points, the winning score."

Alliance of the Natal Carbineers with the 6th Dragoon Guards (The Carabiniers).

It was a matter for congratulation, not only to the Natal Carbineers themselves, but to the Natal Militia generally, that an alliance was formed between that regiment and the 6th Dragoon Guards (The Carabiniers) stationed at Bloemfontein. The announcement of this alliance was made in the Provincial Gazette on September 22nd, 1910.

Some time previously it was proposed to affiliate the Natal Carbineers with the King's Colonials. The matter met with some opposition, and was ultimately allowed to drop.

Subsequently Sir Matthew Nathan, who always took a keen interest in the Natal Carbineers, considered it would be more in keeping with the fitness of things if an affiliation could be brought about between the Natal Carbineers and the 6th Dragoon Guards (The Carabiniers). Colonel Greene, who commanded the Natal Carbineers for many years, and who at the time was a member of the Natal Government, on being consulted, at once took an active interest in the matter; and Lieut.-Colonel Weighton, the officer commanding the Natal Carbineers, viewed the proposition with favour.

Correspondence between the parties concerned led to a complete agreement, and eventually the consent of the War Office and of Lord Kitchener, Honorary Colonel of the Natal Carbineers, and the approval of His Majesty King George V., were given.

When Colonel Smyth, V.C., the O.C. the Carabiniers, was approached, he, speaking on behalf of the members of his regiment, unhesitatingly stated that the regiment would be very much gratified if a closer connection of the nature proposed were formed with the Natal Carbineers; and Lieut.-General Sir John Fryer, the Colonel-in-Chief of the 6th Dragoon Guards, on being consulted, said he had heard a very high report of the standing of the Natal Carbineers favourable to that Corps in every way, and was inclined to give the wishes of so good and distinguished a corps a most thoroughly favourable consideration.

Both General Fryer and Colonel Smyth expressed their appreciation of the fine cavalry spirit of the Carbineers, and recognised that they were essentially cavalry and yet mounted rifles, and that from their foundation they had nobly maintained the traditions associated with the title and honour which was granted to the picked horsemen who, in the reign of Queen Elizabeth, were first equipped with the new firearm in place of the long lance of the days of chivalry.

The Natal Carbineers stand high in the favour of the War Office at Home, whose approval to the proposed affiliation was willingly given.

The alliance will result in training and other facilities being given, when opportunities offer, by the Imperial Government to the members of the Colonial unit. Both are mounted corps and were raised for the same nature of service. The title of the Natal Regiment corresponds with the title of honour of the 6th Dragoon Guards (The Carabiniers), and the uniform and weapons of the two corps closely resemble each other.

It is notable that the alliance between these two fine corps is the first instance of a Colonial mounted regiment being affiliated to a cavalry regiment of His Majesty's Forces. The instances of Colonial infantry corps being allied to Imperial infantry regiments are as follows:—

8th Australian Infantry Regiment to the King's Liverpool Regiment.

9th Australian Infantry Regiment to the Norfolk Regiment.

5th Regiment "Royal Highlanders of Canada" to the Black Watch.

63rd (Halifax) Rifles (Nova Scotia) to the King's Royal Rifle Corps.

48th Highlanders (Canada) to the Gordon Highlanders.

91st Highlanders (Canada) to the Argyll and Sutherland Highlanders.

The Natal Carbineers is the senior mounted corps in the Province, distinguished itself in the Zulu and Boer Wars, and has a high reputation for efficiency. Alliance with it, therefore, is not unacceptable to a regiment even with such fine traditions as "The Carabiniers."

The Natal Carbineers now appear in the Army List as allied to the 6th Dragoon Guards (The Carabiniers).

1911. Lieut.-Colonel Weighton, V.D.

In February, 1911, Lieut.-Colonel Weighton, the Officer Commanding the Regiment, having completed his four years' command, decided to retire from the Active List.

In connection with his retirement from the command of the Regiment, Colonel Weighton issued the following Valedictory Order:—

"On parade at Taylor's Camp last year I intimated that the tenure of my command was nearing completion, and that it was not my intention to recommend an extension in my case. I therefore, in February last, informed the Commandant-General of my desire to retire on completion of my four years' command. My retirement has been approved by the Governor-General, and Lieut.-Colonel Mackay has been appointed my successor.

"Upon giving up the command of the Natal Carbineers I have to express great regret at severing my connection with the Regiment, of which I have been a member for six-and-twenty years, and in which I have held a commission for the whole of that period. The severance, unfortunately, will be a complete one, and this I deeply regret, because I would like to be able to keep in touch with the Regiment in some way or other, but, according to my interpretation of the Militia Regulations which deal with the subject, I shall have no claim whatever to consider myself a member of the Natal Carbineers. Having been appointed to the Supernumerary List my position will be that of a Supernumerary Officer attached to the Natal Carbineers, and my services will be, like those of other officers similarly situated, at the disposal of the Commandant-General for general duty when ordered out for military service. I will, however, always take the liveliest interest in the Regiment, and will ever look back with pride and pleasure on my long and intimate association, both in war and in peace, with the Natal Carbineers. It gives me great pleasure to be able to record that, during the period of my command, the discipline of the Regiment has been all that one could desire. Notwithstanding the very heavy calls on the Regimental funds in sending teams to compete at the various Bisleys and Military Tournaments, the financial position of the Regiment is quite satisfactory.

"I have ever considered it my duty to do all in my power to maintain the high position which the Natal Carbineers have always held, not only in respect to general efficiency, but also in the matter of sport; and I have it on the authority of the Commandant-General that with regard to the former the condition is highly satisfactory; and I am pleased to say that our successes at Military Tournaments and Rifle Competitions have been second to none.

"The recent large reductions in the pay and allowances of the Natal Militia made me apprehensive as to the effect such drastic measures might have on members of the Regiment; but I am glad to say that, with the spirit of patriotism which has always been a characteristic of the Natal Carbineers, the members have accepted the situation, which, however, they hope is only temporary. Not a man has resigned owing to the reductions, and recruits are coming in satisfactorily. This speaks well for the spirit of the young men in our recruiting area, and for the popularity of the Regiment.

"The alliance between the 6th Dragoon Guards (The Carabiniers) and the Natal Carbineers is a matter of which every member of our Regiment is justly proud. In replying to a letter of mine to Lieut.-Colonel Smyth, V.C., Commanding the 6th Dragoon Guards, on the subject of the alliance, that officer said:—'I assure you that the sentiments, so happily expressed by you on behalf of the Natal Carbineers, are reflected by the officers, non-commissioned officers and men of the 6th Dragoon Guards, and that the honour paid to this Regiment, by the decision of His Majesty the King in regard to the alliance, is a matter of gratification to all ranks, in view of the most distinguished character and historic services of the Natal Carbineers.'

"In bidding good-bye to the Regiment, I desire to express my sincere thanks to every officer, non-commissioned officer and man, for their loyalty to me during the four years I have had the honour of being their Commanding Officer. My thanks are specially due to the Adjutant, Captain Helbert, whose services to the Regiment have been invaluable. I am sure the same spirit of loyalty will continue during Lieut.-Colonel Mackay's command. Let every officer, non-commissioned officer and man bear in mind that the reputation of the Regiment is in his keeping, and so will be maintained the proud position the Natal Carbineers hold to-day on the roll of the Forces of the British Empire.

"J. WEIGHTON, Lieut.-Colonel,
"Commanding Natal Carbineers.
"Headquarters, Maritzburg,
"March 7th, 1911."

The following is an Extract from Orders for April, 1911, by Lieut.-Colonel Mackay, who succeeded Colonel Weighton in command:—

"Command.—The Officer Commanding, on assuming command of the Regiment, wishes to place on record the appreciation and regard of all ranks for Colonel Weighton, and the deep regret felt by one and all at his determination to sever his connection with the Regiment. There is no doubt that the proud position the Regiment holds to-day is mainly due to the intense interest displayed, and efforts made, by Colonel Weighton throughout his service.

"G. HELBERT, Captain,
"Adjutant, Natal Carbineers

"Headquarters, 1st April, 1911."

Easter Encampment.—The regimental camp of seven days' duration, beginning on Friday, the 14th of April, was pitched on the same spot near Colenso as two years ago, overlooking the place where Lieut. Roberts, son of the Field-Marshal, was killed. The force on the ground came from all parts of central and northern Natal, and numbered 38 officers and 433 non-commissioned officers and men.

At 11 a.m. on Friday the call sounded for dismounted drill. Each squadron was taken out some distance from the camp, and there put through their facings. In the afternoon similar work was done, the men being mounted. The men were out for a couple of hours, and some good work was done, consisting of drill under the squadron leaders, and then under the leaders, Major Barter and Major Woods, of the Right and Left Wings. Finally Colonel Mackay took charge and, as one of the officers remarked, "made them move."

The orders for Saturday included mounted parade at 6.30 a.m.; foot parade, 11 a.m.; mounted parade, 3 p.m.; and a lecture at 8.30 in the evening on "Musketry," to be delivered by Captain Helbert, the Adjutant.

On Sunday, at 9.30 a.m., all ranks attended church parade. The service was conducted by Canon Pennington, the band supplied the music, and at the close three cheers were given for the King.

On Monday the squadrons competed against each other in field-firing, under the new method laid down by the School of

Musketry for the colonial forces of South Africa, with the following result:—"A" Squadron 1, "H" Squadron 2, and "D" Squadron 3. In the evening the lessons of this competition were set forth in a lecture by Adjutant Helbert, in which he dealt with the control and direction of firing, indication of targets, fire discipline, and change of direction of fire.

After the field-firing competition the regimental sports were held on the open ground below the railway line, and the following were the results:—

1. Individual tent-pegging championship: Lieut. Johnston 1, R.S.M. Mitchell 2, Corporal H. E. Dicks 3, Trooper C. D. Gray 4.

2. Section tent-pegging championship: "C" Squadron team, consisting of Lieut. Johnston, Corporal W. J. Hill, Corporal H. Hill, and Trooper Ratsey, 1; "E" Squadron, 2; "B" Squadron, 3.

3. Individual Jumping: Sergt. Culverwell, 1; Sergt. Pottow, 2; Lieut. Zunckel, 3; Trooper Malcolm, 4.

4. Section Jumping: Lieut. Johnston, Corporal Otto, Corporal W. J. Hill, and Trooper Ratsey, 1; S.Q.M.S. McLean's Section, 2; Capt. Cole's Section, 3; Trooper McCullough's Section, 4.

5. Tilting Ring and Peg: Lieut. Johnston, 1; S.Q.M.S. Kean, 2; Trooper Ratsey, 3; Sergt. Malcolm, 4.

6. Fugitive Race: Trooper James and Trooper Steel, 1; Corporal H. E. Dicks and Trooper Bowen, 2; Trooper G. B. Evans and Trooper Schwegmann, 3; Corporal Ryley and G. S. Dicks, 4.

7. Led Horse Race: Sergt. Todd, Sergt. Holcomb, Corporal Cooper, and Trooper Adie, 1; Trooper Schwikkard's Section, 2.

8. Lemon cutting: Lieut. Winter, 1; Corporal H. Hill, 2; Lieut. Zunckel, 3; S.S.M. Harding, 4.

At 7 a.m. on Tuesday the men turned out mounted, 370 strong, under the Commanding Officer, for the purpose of being inspected by the Commandant-General. Various exercises were performed, including the advance at a gallop, and dismounting and linking of horses. The Commandant expressed himself as being highly gratified with the work of the Regiment. There was a foot parade at 11 o'clock, while the officers underwent a written examination on tactical questions. In the afternoon a mounted parade was held under the wing officers, after which Colonel McKenzie took the officers out and put them through a severe test of horsemanship. They had to cross stirrups and mount and dismount at the walk, trot, and canter. He again expressed himself as being exceedingly gratified. Sir Duncan then lectured the officers on the answers given at the examination.

Wednesday was a hard day for both men and horses, the cause being a particularly interesting sham fight. The general idea was that a Khaki Force was lying at Weenen, and the Blue Force was a small independent force out from a large army at Ladysmith, and was lying in camp in order to protect the Colenso Bridge. At midnight on Wednesday the Officer Commanding the Blue Force heard that the Khaki Force would make an attempt to cut him off, so he assumed the offensive, and moved out at 9 a.m. in the direction of Monte Cristo. The Blue Force occupied Hlangwane, and it was almost impossible for the Khaki Force to do anything except try to turn the enemy's right flank to the south, which necessitated crossing a flat, which, in the opinion of the umpire (Colonel Mackay) he would have done had time permitted. The second phase of the operations was that, the Blue Force being defeated, the Khaki Force made an attack on the camp. The O.C. Blue Force, fearing a crossfire from the Khaki Army and the Khaki mounted men, made an effort to regain camp, so he proceeded to attack from Hussar Hill. The O.C. Khaki Force defended camp with a strong line of outposts, and made his disposition so well that it was a hopeless task for the Blue Force to attack camp, owing to his having to cross a large open flat under heavy fire. An attempt was made to rush into camp, but a large number of men were "killed." Major Woods was in command of the Khaki Force, and Major Barter of the Blue. The men were out till 4 o'clock and came into camp very tired.

The competition for the Methuen Cup was held on Thursday, the last day in camp. Major Tanner superintended the firing.

Presentations.—In the interval between the regimental sports and Adjutant Helbert's lecture on Monday, the 17th April, Colonel Weighton was presented with an address and a service of plate as tokens of the esteem of his regiment for him as Officer in Command, and Mrs. Weighton at the same ceremony was presented with a diamond pendant in recognition of the interest she has always shown in the welfare and good name of the Natal Carbineers. The address, artistically executed by Mr. Friggins, of the Tramway Department, was read by Captain and Adjutant Helbert:—"It is with the deepest regret that we, the officers, warrant officers, non-commis-

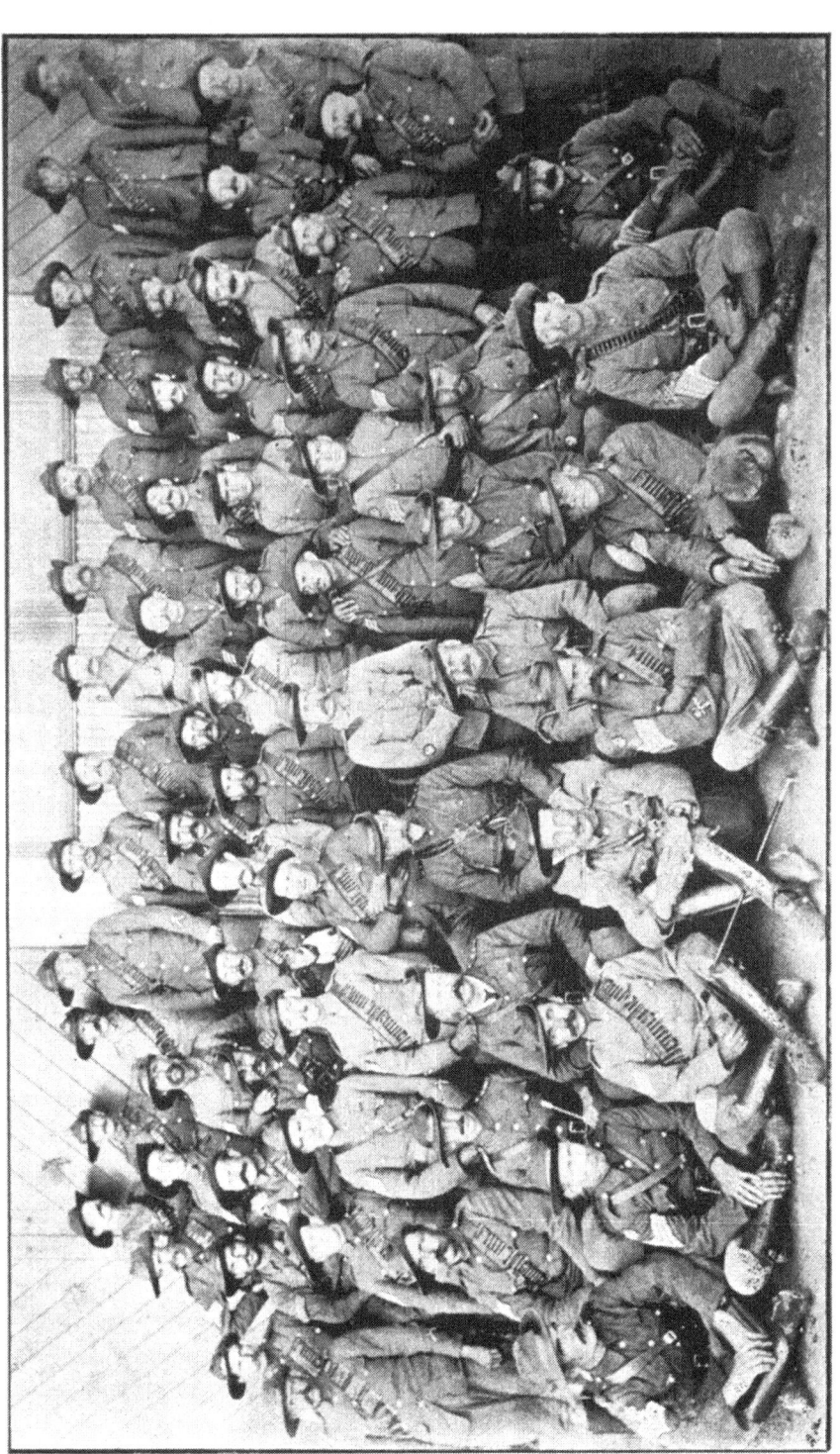

On Service, Vryheid, 1907.

Sergt. Robinson, Sergt. Hayes, Sergt. Dickinson, Sergt. Dicks, Q.-M.-Sergt. Kenn, Q.-M.-Sergt. Dunn, Sergt. Dicks, Sergt. Shaw, Sergt. Thompson, Sergt. Mulcahy, Sergt. King. Sergt. Newlands, Sergt. Bissett, Sergt. Talbot, Sergt. Lyell, Sergt. Teasdale, Sergt. Yirrell, S.-S.-Major Topham, O.-R.-Sergt. Anderson, S.-S.-Major Meyer. Sergt. Pottow, Sergt. Francis, S.-S.-Major Wright, Sergt. Household, Sergt. Jackson, Sergt. Harding, S.-Q.-M.-Sergt. McLean, Sergt. Bunting, Sergt. Swan, Sergt. Anderson, Sergt. Savage, Sergt. Bennett, Sergt. Carter, Sergt. Madsen. Sergt. Moreland Sergt. Peters, S.-Q.-M.-Sergt. Newton, Sergt. Campbell, Sergt. Mitchell, R.-S.-Major Burkim-her, Sergt. Conrie, S.-Q.-M.-S. Buchanan, Sergt. Hardink, S.-S.-Major Mitchell, Sergt. Urquhart. S.-S.-Major McCathie, Capt. Walton, Lt.-Col. Mackay, Lt.-Col. Weighton, O.C., Lt.-Col. Rodwell, Capt. Langley, S.-Sergt. Madsen. S.-Q.-M.-Sergt. Forsyth, S.-Q.-M.-Sergt. Bennett, S.-Q.-M.-Sergt. Bristo, Capt. G. Helbert, S.-S.-Major Warwick, S.-S.-Major Langley, Sergt.-Trumpr. Fairall Q.M.Sergt. Harker,

sioned officers, and men of the Natal Carbineers, learnt that you had made up your mind to sever your active membership with the Regiment with which you have been so closely connected for the last twenty-six years. We owe you a debt of gratitude, which can never be repaid, for all the labour and time spent in the service of the Regiment; for although this Regiment has been extremely fortunate in its commanding officers, still your career—first as Quartermaster, then as Adjutant for eleven years, followed by being Officer Commanding Headquarters Squadrons, and Officer Commanding Right Wing, and lastly as Commanding Officer of the Regiment—has been unique; no one in the history of our Regiment has had the opportunity of serving it as you have had, and certainly no one has made more of his opportunities than you have. You have also done much to encourage the volunteering spirit in the Province of Natal. To refer individually to all the benefits which this Regiment has obtained through your efforts would take up far too many pages for a simple address as this, and, moreover, these are written in large letters in the regimental records, so there is no need to do so here; but there is one event we feel it our duty and pleasure to mention, and that is the completion of the affiliation between our Regiment and the 6th Dragoon Guards, which completion has been brought about by your efforts on our side and those of Lieut.-Colonel Smyth, V.C., on the part of the fine regiment we are now affiliated to. To emphasise this achievement, the honour of which we all appreciate, we have ventured to place the photos of yourself and Colonel Smyth on this address as a lasting reminder to whom we owe this honour. We wish you and Mrs. Weighton, whose interest in the Regiment has always been so keen and sincere, many years of prosperity and happiness, and feel sure that, although not actively connected with the Regiment, it will always be first in your thoughts, and that we shall always be able to benefit by your advice and counsel. To conclude, we feel that the good work done by you, not only for the Regiment, but for the Province, has been actuated by our cherished motto: 'Pro Patria.'

"Signed on behalf of the Regiment,

"D. W. MACKAY, Lieut.-Colonel,
"Commanding Natal Carbineers."

In making the presentations Colonel Mackay said:— "Colonel Weighton,—As you have now decided to take a well-earned rest after your long and successful career in this regiment, we feel we cannot allow you to part from us without taking a formal farewell of you. We have invited you here to-day, Sir, to convey to you the esteem in which you have always been held in the regiment, our appreciation of the work you have done, and the respect you have always commanded from all ranks. You have served this regiment faithfully for the last 26 years, and that has been a time of progress and advance for its welfare. You joined the regiment when it was little more than a Squadron,—I think you have told me four officers and about 70 men. To day you leave it, Sir, as it now stands before you, one of the most efficient and one of the finest volunteer regiments in the British Empire. During your term in the regiment much has been done in the way of history-making, but one event has happened during your tenure of command, and one I know you will always be proud of, that is the affiliation of this regiment with that fine cavalry regiment of His Majesty's Army, the 6th Dragoon Guards, "The Carabiniers," the regiment from which we take our name, and which I am pleased to say is represented here by some of its officers. In all social functions you have been ably assisted by Mrs. Weighton, whose interest in this regiment has always been so keen and so sincere, and to her as well as to yourself we owe a deep debt of gratitude for all that has been done in the interests of the regiment. In saying farewell to you to-day, Sir, we feel that we are not only losing a commanding officer, but one who has been a friend of every member of the regiment, and one who has always had the interests of the regiment deeply at heart. Sir, in presenting you with this address as an expression of our feelings, I have also to present to you this presentation of plate as a token of good-fellowship. You will be pleased to know that this presentation has been subscribed to by every member of the regiment, showing their great regard for you. And I know that in its daily use it will always bring back to you the memory of the happy days you have spent in the Carbineers. On behalf of the regiment I now make this presentation to you. Mrs. Weighton, I have also to present to you a small present from the regiment. We know that you have always taken the keenest interest in the Carbineers, and that you have at all times done all you could to further the interests of the regiment. In the name of the regiment I ask you to accept of this small present as a memento. On behalf of the Carbineers I now wish you both long life, prosperity, and happiness."

Sir Duncan McKenzie also bore testimony to the recipient's ability and worth.

Colonel Weighton in reply, after thanking his brother officers for their eulogies of him, and the donors for their handsome and valuable present, prolonged his speech to considerable length with reminiscences of comrades worthy of mention, and of striking incidents that had happened, in the course of his service of over a quarter of a century in the Natal Carbineers. In conclusion, he read a letter, written by his wife, the daughter of a foundation member of the corps, by which she conveyed her thanks to the regiment for their gift to her of a beautiful necklace.

APPENDIX 1. RACES.

1855. One of the events on the programme of the Maritzburg races held on the 14th and 15th June was strictly reserved for the Carbineers. Horses that were the bona fide property of members of the Regiment were alone eligible to run in it, and they were to be ridden by their owners. Other conditions of the race were:—Entrance £1 1s., half forfeit, with about £10 added; mile heats, and second horse to save his stakes. The finish was:—

    Lieut. Allison's "Robert the Devil" 1
    Lieut. Allen's "Erin" 2
    Tpr. Clough's "Cossack" 3

1858. Maritzburg races came off on the 3rd and 4th June. The weather was very fine and the company numerous. The racing on the first day was hardly so good as on former occasions. The second day the Volunteer Corps Race, a mile and a half, was run.

    Lieut. Wood's "Invicta" 1
    Capt. Allison's "Robert the Devil" 2

This was the most exciting and best contested race of the season.

The band of the 45th Regiment was present the second day.

1863. At the annual Maritzburg race meeting, the Military and Volunteer Corps Stakes, two miles, was won by Mr. T. Shepstone's (N.C.) "Chieftain," owner up.

1864. The Volunteer Race in the Karkloof Races was won by Tpr. Brandon's "Fugleman."

1872. At the May race meeting the Military and Volunteer Race was won by Capt. T. Shepstone's "Solemn Swell."

1877. At the May race meeting the Military and Volunteer Race was won by Tpr. Francis' "Peeping Tom."

1878. The annual races were held on 25th May, the following being the events:—

    Heavy Marching Order Race—Trooper Whitelaw's "King Coffee."
    Carbineer Plate—Tpr. Merryweather's "Tommy Dodd."
    Maritzburg Stakes—Tpr. Wallace's "Pet."
    Hurdle Race—Tpr. Merryweather's "Tommy Dodd."
    Half-mile Scratch—Tpr. Whitelaw's "Lass o' Gowrie"

1880. Races were held in May at which Trooper Duncan McKenzie proved most successful. The following were the events:—

    Trial Stakes—Tpr. McKenzie's "Nancy Lee."
    Carbineer Plate—Tpr. McKenzie's "Whisky."
    Maritzburg Stakes—Tpr. McKenzie's "Whisky."
    Hurdle Race—Tpr. McKenzie's "Rex."
    Troop Race—Tpr. Ross's "Dabulamanzi."

1885. This year the annual Regimental Races were instituted, the first meeting being held on 31st October, with results as follows:—

    Aged Stakes—Tpr. Risley's "Masher."
    Carbineer Plate—Corpl. Foxon's "Remorse."
    Hurry-skurry—Tpr. Windham's "Rebel."
    Hurdle Race—Tpr. Armitage's "Surprise."
    Fugitive Race—Corpl. Foxon's "Remorse."

1886. The annual race meeting was held on 30th November. Results:—

    Maiden Stakes—Corpl. Holmes' "Tormentor."
    Carbineer Plate—Sergt. Ross's "Rex."
    Encampment Stakes—Sergt. Ross's "Rex."
    Hurdle Race—Tpr. Barry's "Little Wonder."
    Fugitive Race—Sergt.-Major Windham & Tpr. Craw.

1887. The races were held on 1st November. Results:—
    Maiden Stakes—Capt. Macfarlane's "Blue Peter."
    Officers' Plate—Tpr. McArthur's "Cohort."
    Carbineer Plate—O.R.S. Tilney's "Vidette."
    Hurdle Race—Lieut. McKenzie's "Goldfinder."

1888. The annual races were held on 1st November. Results:—
Maiden Stakes—Tpr. Holgate's "Comet."
Carbineer Plate—Capt. Taunton's "Petrel."
Officers' Plate—Tpr. Holgate's "Comet."
Forced Handicap—Sergt. Tilney's "Vidette."

1889. Races were held on 1st November. Results:—
Maiden Stakes—Tpr. Townsend's "Harlequin."
Officers' Plate—Tpr. Davis's "Comet."
Carbineer Plate—Capt. Macfarlane's "Blue Peter."
Forced Handicap—Capt. Macfarlane's "Blue Peter."

1890. The annual race meeting was held on 1st November.
Maiden Stakes—Tpr. Risley's "Midnight."
Officers' Stakes—Tpr. Erskine's "Victor."
Tally Ho Handicap—T.S.M. Wood's "Colworth."
Carbineers' Plate—Capt. Macfarlane's "Blue Peter" and Capt. Taunton's "Petrel," dead heat.

1891.—The annual races were held on 31st October.
Maiden Stakes—Tpr. Solomon's "Norman."
Officers' Plate—Tpr. Peters' "Capsome."
Tally Ho Handicap—Tpr. Cochrane's "The Innocent."
Carbineer Plate—Tpr. Peters' "Capsome."
Flying Stakes—Tpr. Risley's "Pony."

1892. The annual races were held on the 26th November.
Maiden Stakes—Tpr. Dick's "Bob."
Carbineer Plate—Capt. Taunton's "Sweep."
Officers' Plate—Corpl. Peters' "Capsome."
Fugitive Race—Tprs. Joughin and Wood.
Tally Ho Handicap—Corpl. Peters' "Capsome."

1893. The annual races this year were held during the regimental encampment at Balgowan. That this alteration of time and place was popular was shown by the splendid fields.

Maiden Stakes—Tpr. Robinson's "Trumpeter."
Balgowan Stakes—O.R.S. Dick's "Greywing."
Heavy Marching Order Competition—Sgt. Townsend.
Hurdle Race—Trooper Madsen's "Briton."
Tent-pegging (Section)—A Troop (Sergts. Rodwell and Townsend, Corpl. Peters and Tpr. Sibthorpe).
Officers' Plate—Tpr. Madsen's "Briton."
H.M.O. Race (foot)—Tpr. Griffin.
Fugitive Race—Corpl. Holmes' "Perhaps."

A race meeting was held in November, with the following results:—
Maiden Stakes—Q.M. Lyle's "Sandy."
Galloway Race—Tpr. Madsen's "Briton."
N.C. Gymkhana Handicap—Sgt. Townsend's "Greywing."
Tent-pegging—3rd Dragoon Guards Team.

1894. Races were held at the Sterkspruit Camp in June.
Maiden Stakes—Tpr. Bullock's "Pilot."
Sterkspruit Stakes—Tpr. Madsen's "Briton."
Hurdle Race—Major Taunton's "Sweep."
Officers' Stakes—Tpr. Bullock's "Pilot."
H.M.O. Competition—Drummer Smith.

A race meeting was held on 1st November.
Maiden Stakes—Tpr. Wylde-Browne's "Clementine."
Carbineer Plate—Tpr. Vanderplank's "Bluebeard."
N.C.O. Stakes—Lieut. Langley's "Freedom."
Hurdle Race—Lieut. Langley's "Freedom."

1895. In June, races were held at the Nottingham Road Camp.
Maiden Stakes—Tpr. Taylor's "Shylock."
Nottingham Road Handicap—Sergt. Townsend's "Montrose."
Hurdle Race—Tpr. Carbutt's "Glencoe."
Officers' Plate—Sergt. Townsend's "Montrose."
H.M.O. Race—Tpr. McLean's "Ginger Nap."
Fugitive Race—Lieut. Gallwey and T.S.M. Dodd.
Band Race—Tptr. Lawrance's "Wallace."
Tent Pegging—Lieut.-Col. Greene's Section (Lieut.-Col. Greene, Capts. McKenzie and Shepstone, and Q.M. Lyle).

A race meeting was held on 9th November.
Maiden Stakes—Tpr. Fisher's "Count."
Open Galloway—Sergt. Townsend's "Montrose."
Band Race—Bandsman Kitchen's "Toby."
N.C. Gym. Handicap—Capt. Taunton's "Diogenes."
Flying Stakes—Tpr. Madsen's "Briton."
Tent Pegging, open—N.C. Section (R.S.M. Bowen, Sergts. Rodwell and Townsend, and Corpl. Button).

1896. A race meeting was held on 31st October.
Maiden Stakes—Sergt. Owen's "Robin Gray."
Carbineer Plate—Corpl. Searle's "Starlight."
Band Race—Tpr. Burn's "Boy."
Officers' Plate—Sergt. Owen's "Robin Gray."
Consolation—Tpr. Syme's "Metford."

1897. Saturday, 13th November. N.C. Race meeting. The feature of the meeting was the riding of Sergt. A. C. Townsend, who rode four winners during the day; an achievement due to good judgment and clever jockeying as much as to the horses he had charge of.

1. Maiden Stakes:—
Corpl. Hesom's "Prince" (Sergt. Townsend) 1
Corpl. Joughin's "Fly" (Tpr. W. J. Armitage) 2
Tpr. Money's "Baby" (R.S.M. Bowen) 3

2. Carbineer Plate:—
Sergt. Townsend's "Montrose" (Owner) 1
Sergt. Owen's "Robin Gray" (Tpr. Craik) 2

3. Open Galloway and Pony Handicap:—
Mr. C. W. Meade's "Naughty Girl" (B. Buchanan) ... 1
Mr. G. P. White's "Briton" (Forsyth) 2
Mr. F. G. Burchell's "Aileen" (J. Posnott) 3

4. Band Race:—
Corpl. Hesom's "Prince" (Sergt. Townsend) 1
Tpr. Daly's "Nansen" (Corpl. Lawrence) 2
Tpr. Meares' "Inspector" (Owner) 3

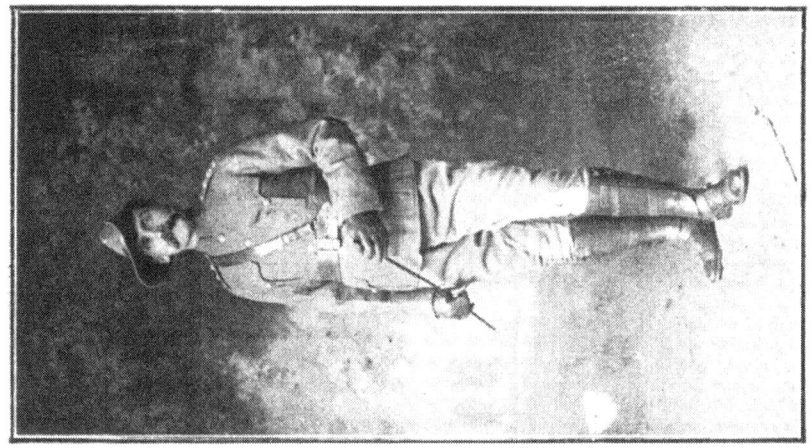

Captain A. Lyle,
Quartermaster, 1889 to 1905.

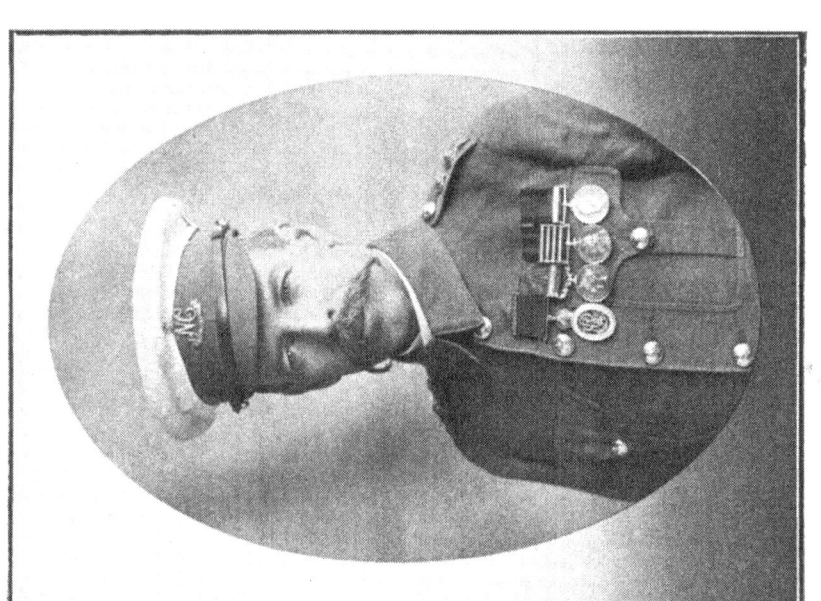

Lieut.-Colonel F. E. Foxon, V.D.

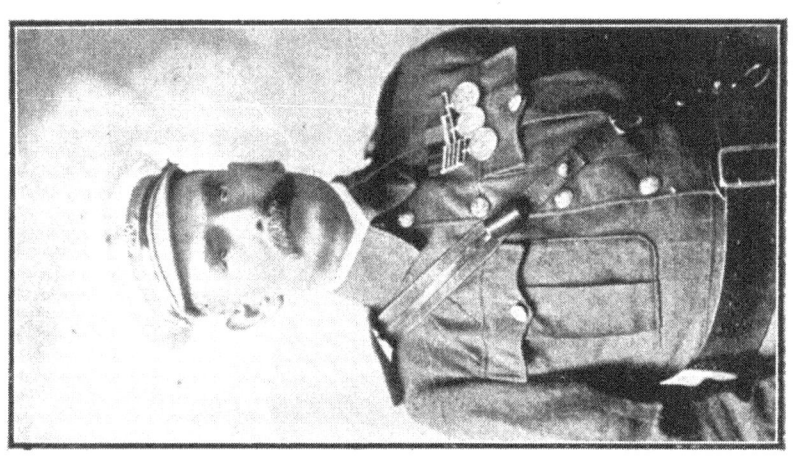

Major W. T. Gage.

5. Military and Volunteer Handicap:—
   Mr. F. G. Burchell's "Induna" (J. Posnott) 1
   Mr. C. W. Meade's "Naughty Girl" (B. Buchanan) ... 2
   R.S.M. Bowen's "Charles Dickens" (Tpr. Craik) 3
   The best race of the day.

6. Officers' Plate Handicap:—
   Sergt. Townsend's "Montrose" (Owner) 1
   Sergt. Owen's "Robin Gray" (Tpr. Craik) 2
   Corpl. Joughin's "Fly" (Tpr. Armitage) 3

1898. Saturday, 5th November. Both the established popularity of the Natal Carbineer races and the delightful weather attracted a large attendance on Saturday. His Excellency the Governor visited the course during the afternoon. The officers of the Regiment were "At Home" and entertained their guests right royally. The band of the Regiment, under the direction of Bandmaster Keilly, played selections during the afternoon and added to the enjoyment of the proceedings.

1. Maiden Stakes, value £7 7s.:—
   Sergt. Barter's "Insimbi" (Townsend) 1
   Tpr. R. M. Tanner's "Bonnie Doon" (Madsen) 2
   Mr. Kelly's "Superbus" (Owner) 3

2. Carbineer Plate Handicap, value £15 15s.:—
   T.S.M. Townsend's "Montrose" (Murray) 1
   Tpr. O. S. McKenzie's "Champagne" (Owner) 2

3. Open Pony Handicap, value £15 15s.:—
   Dr. Platt's "Lone Star" (E. Taylor) 1
   Mr. P. Lawrence's "Sunny Boy" (Palmer) 2
   Mr. B. C. Dent's "Stowmarket" (Owner) 3

4. Band Race Handicap, value £7 7s.:—
   Bandsman Harkness's "Blazes" (Madsen) 1
   Bandsman De Haas's "French Maid" (Townsend) 2
   Bandsman Meares' "Inspector" (Owner) 3

5. Officers' Plate Handicap, value £19 19s.:—
   R.S.M. Bowen's "Charles Dickens" (Townsend) 1
   T.S.M. Townsend's "Montrose" (Murray) 2

6. Military and Volunteer Handicap, value £15 15s. :—
Dr. Platt's "Convener" (C. Taylor) 1
Mr. Scott's "Oleander" (Owner) 2
Mr. F. G. Burchell's "Wolff" (Murray) 3

7. Hurdle Race Handicap, value £15 15s. :—
Tpr. R. M. Tanner's "Bonnie Doon" (Murray) 1
Tpr. O. S. McKenzie's "Champagne" (Crouch) 2
Sergt. Owen's "Robin Gray" (J. Craiks) 3

1903. 10th February. Regimental Races.

1. Long Tom Stakes, of £10 (of which £3 goes to the second horse), for bona fide registered troop horses. Distance, five furlongs :—
Tpr. H. Madsen's "Nabob" (Madsen) 1
Tpr. R. M. Tanner's "Katerfelto" (De Haas) 2
R.S.M. Burkimsher's "Yorkshire Lass" (Burkimsher) ... 3

2. Relief Handicap, of £19 19s., open to all members of His Majesty's forces. Distance, one mile :—
Capt. Landsberg's (U.M.R.) "Berthier" (Player) 1
Mr. J. B. Collyer's (N.P.) "Weary Willie" (Townsend) 2
M. R. Money's (King's Own) "Maori Girl" 3

3. Open Pony Handicap, of £19 19s. Distance five furlongs :—
Mr. W. E. Earle's "Banjo" (Little John) 1
Capt. Landsberg's "Move On" (Landsberg) 2
Mr. F. B. Brown's "Marsa Ba" (Fyrth) 3

4. Gun Hill Handicap, of £19 19s., for bona fide troop horses. Distance 1½ miles :—
Capt. Rodwell's "Bob" (Townsend) 1
Tpr. M. Madsen's "Yabber" (Madsen) 2
Lieut. Townsend's "Montrose" (Pannewitz) 3

5. Led-Horse Scurry, of £7 (of which £2 goes to the second horse), for bona fide troop horses. Distance, 3 furlongs :—
Capt. Rodwell's "Bob" and Lieut. Townsend's "Montrose" 1
Tpr. N. J. Grant's "Dingaan" and Tpr. A. F. Grant's "Lizmoth" 2

6. Tent Pegging Competition :—
Lieut. Owen 1
R.S.M. Burkimsher 2

APPENDIX 2. SHOOTING COMPETITIONS.

1864. The first notice of a shooting match in which the Carbineers took part is the record of a friendly competition between the Weenen County Yeomanry and the Karkloof troop. The latter were successful, winning by forty-seven points. The members of the winning team were:—Lieut.-Col. Erskine (top score), Capt. Proudfoot, Lieut. Parkinson, Tprs. C. Spiers, T. B. Varty, J. Kirby, J. Shires, T. Shires, F. Lean, and G. Fannin. Capt. Proudfoot, who carried off a prize cup presented by Mr. Elliot, generously offered it for a future competition.

1865. At the first meeting of the Natal Rifle Association, the Volunteer Prize was won by Major Erskine, N.C., and the Bankers' Prize was won by Tpr. H. Pepworth, N.C.

1866. At a quarterly shooting by the Karkloof troop, held at Howick on the 20th and 21st February, two rifles were won by Lieut. Parkinson and Tpr. W. T. Shaw, and a revolver by Tpr. R. W. Shaw.

The Regiment was well represented at the meeting of the Natal Rifle Association. The list for the 1st Volunteer Prize was headed by Lieut.-Col. Erskine, Lieut. Pepworth coming second. Lieut.-Col. Erskine came first also in the Competition for the 2nd Volunteer Prize.

In a prize shooting competition at Howick on 21st August, Colonel Erskine again maintained his reputation by taking first place, Tpr. F. Bucknall being second.

A shooting match on the 23rd August was won by the officers of the Carbineers against the officers of the 99th Regiment by 18 points. The winning team consisted of:—

Lieut.-Col. Erskine, Capt. Williams, Lieut. Pepworth, Capt. Proudfoot, and Lieut. Parkinson.

The Headquarters Troop won a match against the Richmond Mounted Rifles. Lieut. Williams had the honour of making the highest score.

In a match between the Cape Mounted Rifles, the Richmond Mounted Rifles, and the Carbineers, the results were:—

    C.M.R. 381
    Carbineers 352
    Richmond Mounted Rifles 329

The following composed the Carbineer team:—Lieut.-Col. Erskine, Capt. Williams, Lieut. Pepworth, Sergts. Corlett and Maxwell, Corpl. Taylor, and Tprs. De Kock, Bowness, Egner, and I. Finnemore.

1867. At Richmond in the early part of this year, the Richmond Mounted Rifles by a large majority beat the following Carbineer team:—Capt. Williams, Lieut. Pepworth, Q.M. Sergt. Corlett, Corpl. Taylor, Tprs. Egner (top score), Finnemore, Bowness, Zeederberg, Wolhuter, and Gilligan. On the way out, Lieut.-Col. Erskine was thrown from his horse, several of his bones being broken, and so prevented from shooting with the city team.

On the 6th June, the Carbineer team, composed of Lieut.-Col. Erskine, Capt. Williams, Lieut. Pepworth, Tprs. Js. Egner, Ferreira, and Jno. Egner, was unsuccessful by 14 points in a match against the Durban Volunteers.

In October an inter-troop competition, for a revolver presented by Government, was held, the headquarters troop being the winner. Their team was:—Tprs. Zeederberg (revolver), J. Niekerk (£1), Js. Egner (cigar case), Jno. Egner, Lieut. Pepworth.

1868. Capt. Williams, Tprs. J. Egner, P. Zeederberg, G. Bowness, J. Freeman, J. Gilligan, F. M. Wolhuter, T. Smith, I. J. Ferreira, and H. Buchanan marched to Durban for a match against a team of the Royal Durban Rangers, and were hospitably entertained by their comrades of the Port. The conditions of the match were five shots at 150, 200, 300, and 400 yards. The Carbineers won by 13 points.

At the Volunteer Prize Shooting this year, Tpr. Egner won a prize of a handsome silver-mounted ram's horn presented by Mr. Padley. Capt. Williams and Tpr. T. Smith were also prize winners at the meeting.

1869. A match against the Maritzburg Rifles was held in a storm of wind and dust. Capt. Williams, Tprs. L. Zeederberg, J. Egner, I. Niekerk, T. Smith, H. Buchanan, H. Adler, and J. Freeman represented the Carbineers, and lost the match by a few points.

At the annual shooting of the Natal Rifle Association the Volunteer Cavalry Prize was won by Tpr. L. Zeederberg.

On 16th October the return match with the Maritzburg Rifles was won by the Carbineers with the narrow majority of two points. The ranges were 200, 300, and 400 yards. The members and scoring of the winning team were:—
Col. Erskine 32, Capt. Williams 18, Q.M. Player 27, Tprs. L. Zeederberg 37, Jno. Egner 13, Niekerk 20, Ferreira 15, Wolhuter 17, Jas. Egner 31, and St. V. Erskine 40.

In a shooting competition by the Karkloof Troop on 13th November, a cup, presented by Capt. Barter, was won by Lieut. Parkinson. The same gentleman was the winner also of one of the three Whitworth rifles presented by the Government.

In another match with the Maritzburg Rifles on the 27th November, Col. Erskine, Capt. Williams, Tprs. Niekerk, L. Zeederberg, Jas. Egner, F. Wolhuter, P. Zeederberg, Clark, J. Allison, and Jno. Egner, representing the Carbineers, were defeated. The Government rifle was won by Tpr. P. Zeederberg.

1870. The Richmond Mounted Rifles were victors in a match against the following members of the Karkloof Troop:—
Lieut. Parkinson 61, Sergt. Methley 48, Corpl. Varty 60, Tprs. C. Shaw 34, J. O. Jackson 39, J. Shires 45, J. Ball 33, A. Spiers 37, H. Kirby 26, and J. Hodson 25.

A match was arranged between the recruits of the Headquarters Troop and Karkloof, with the following result:—

Headquarters.		Karkloof.	
Tpr. J. Martens	16	Tpr. C. Turvin	14
Tpr. H. Martens	17	Tpr. H. Straddy	16
Tpr. J. Zeederberg	26	Tpr. J. Turvin	18
Tpr. G. Martens	12	Tpr. J. King	18
Tpr. H. J. Martens	25	Tpr. Rolandson	6
Tpr. E. Bond	25	Tpr. Stansfield	23
	121		95

1871. A match between the Karkloof Troop and the Richmond Mounted Rifles was won by the latter. For Karkloof Lieut. Parkinson made the highest score.

1872. Natal Carbineers v. Maritzburg Rifles. N.C. team:— Capt. Shepstone, Sergt. Wood, Corpl. Button, Tprs. Murphy, Pistorius, James, Bond, Whitelaw. The Maritzburg Rifles won this match by forty-one points.

1873. At the annual shooting this year, the Government rifle was won by Sergt. Whitelaw, and Capt. Shepstone's cup by Trooper Holliday.

A shooting match was held with the Karkloof Carbineers, resulting in a win for the Maritzburg team.

At the shooting of the Natal Rifle Association, the champion volunteer prize, a silver medal, was won by Tpr. Egner, and the Farmers' prize by Tpr. Royston.

In a match against the 75th regiment, the Carbineer team comprised Sergt. James, Tprs. Egner, Royston, Moodie, Ford and Spettigue. The result was a tie, which being shot off, the Carbineers proved the winners by twelve points.

An intercolonial match was arranged between Cape Colony, Kaffraria, and Natal. In the preliminary shooting by the various volunteer corps in Natal, the Carbineers averaged the highest score, consequently three members of the Regiment were elected to represent the Colony in the match proper, viz. :—Tprs. Royston, Egner, and Spettigue. The final was:—

  Kaffraria 897
  Natal 830
  Cape Colony 638

1874. At the meeting of the Natal Rifle Association, the Regiment was ably represented by Tpr. Royston, who was successful in no less than four of the competitions.

1875. In the annual prize shooting both the Government Prize and the Captain's Cup were won by Tpr. Royston. The conditions were 150, 200, 300, and 400 yards, three shots at each. The Snider carbine was used and gave general satisfaction.

In a match with the Maritzburg Rifles, the Regimental team, consisting of Sergt. Whitelaw, Corpls. Royston and London, Tprs. G. Ford, — Ford, Vanderplank, Pannewitz, Egner, Button, and James, was the winning side by 65 points. A return match, in which the weapons were changed, turned the tables, the Rifles winning by 50 points. Corpl. Royston made the highest score for the Regiment.

At a prize shooting on the 25th June, the events were won as follows:—
Government Prize—Corpl. Royston.
Officers' Prize—Corpl. London.
N.C.O.s' Prize—Sergt. Whitelaw.

At the meeting of the Natal Rifle Association, the representatives of the Regiment were well to the fore, being successful in the following:—
 Fass Cup—Corpl. Royston.
 Champion Volunteer Prize—1. Tpr. Holliday; 2. Corpl. Royston.

Corporation Cup—Corpl. Royston.
Ladies' Prize—Corpl. Royston.
Innkeepers' Prize—Corpl. Royston.

In September the Maritzburg Rifles proved the victors in a match by the narrow majority of one point. The conditions were, 200, 300, and 400 yards, five shots at each distance. For the Carbineers:—

Lieut. Moodie	29	Corpl. London	35
S.-M. James	43	Tpr. G. Ford	40
Sergt. Button	40	Tpr. Pannewitz	33
Sergt. Whitelaw	41	Tpr. MacDonald	40
Corpl Royston	40	Tptr. Holliday	38

On 16th October, in a match against the 13th Regiment, the Carbineers won by 20 points. They also won the return match, by 32 points. For the Carbineers:—

Tpr. Ford	43	Sergt. Button	30
Corpl. Royston	39	Sergt. Whitelaw	14
Tpr. Merryweather	37	Tpr. Thompson	13
Tptr. Holliday	34	Corpl. London	11
Tpr. MacDonald	32		

1876. In a match at Howick between the Maritzburg and Karkloof Carbineers, the latter were the winners by 16 points. The visiting team was most hospitably entertained by their Karkloof comrades.

A return match was shortly afterwards fired, the Regiment, represented by Lieut. Taylor, Q.M. James, Sergts. Button and Royston, Corpl. London, Tprs. MacDonald, Vanderplank, Merryweather, Pannewitz, and Tptr. Holliday being this time successful.

At the Natal Rifle Association meeting the following events were won by members of the Regiment:—
Corporation Cup—Sergt. Royston.
Champion Volunteer Prize—Sergt. Button.
Patron's Prize—Sergt. Royston.
Ladies' Prize—Sergt. Royston.
Aggregate Prize—Sergt. Royston.

Capt. P. W. Stride.

Lt.-Colonel A. Hair, V.D.

The annual prize shooting was held on the 4th October with the following results:—

Government Competition—Sergt. Royston (for the third time in succession. In consequence, he was debarred from shooting in the other competitions).

Merchants' Prize—Tpr. Merryweather.

Consolation Prize—Tpr. W. Francis.

1877. At the meeting of the Natal Rifle Association, Sergt.-Major Royston upheld the honour of the Regiment by winning the Corporation Cup, Ladies' Prize, and the Grand Aggregate.

1878. At the annual prize shooting the following were the winners:—

Government Competition—Sergt.-Major Royston (for 4th time).

Officers' Prize—Capt. Shepstone.

At this meeting the Swinburn-Henri carbines were used for the first time.

In the annual shooting competitions of the Natal Rifle Association Sergt.-Major Royston again distinguished himself by winning the Corporation Cup, Association Prize, and the Ladies' Competition.

At the prize shooting in November the following were the winners:—

Recruits' Prize—Tpr. Moodie.
Government Prize—Lieut. Royston.
Carbineer Prize—Tpr. Moodie.
Merchants' Prize—Corpl. Mileman.
Consolation Prize—Corpl. Methley.
Skirmishing Cup—Corpl. Mileman.

1880. The prize winners at the annual shooting of the Regiment were:—

Government Competition—1. Sergt.-Major Methley; 2. Tpr. Barker; 3. Lieut. Royston.

Consolation—Tpr. Slatter.

1881. The Government Cup for excellence in shooting was instituted this year, and the following represented the Regiment in the Competition for it:—Lieuts. Royston and Macfarlane, Sergt.-Major Methley, Sergt. Merryweather, Tprs. McKenzie, Colville, Ross, Edwards, and W. Hutton.

The annual prize shooting was held in January in very wet weather. Prize winners:—
Government Cup—Lieut. Royston.
No. 2 Competition—Tpr. Edwards.
No. 3 Competition—Tpr. Ross.
Consolation—Tpr. Fowle.

1882. The results of the annual prize shooting were:—
Government Cup—Tpr. G. C. Edwards.
Carbineer Cup—Lieut. Macfarlane.
Third Competition—Tpr. Addison.
Consolation—Sergt.-Major Methley.

At the annual meeting of the Natal Rifle Association, the Regiment was ably represented by its popular Captain, who won the aggregate, and by Tpr. Addison, who won in the Military and Volunteer Competition.

1883 The prize winners at the annual shooting, held in very bad weather, were:—
Government Competition—1. Tpr. J. W. Armitage; 2. Tpr. Edwards.
Carbineer Cup—Tpr. J. W. Armitage.
Consolation—Tpr. Whittaker.

For the Government Cup Competition, the team selected consisted of Capt. Royston, Lieut. Macfarlane, Corpl. Ross, Tprs. Edwards, Addison, C. Colville, E. Colville, Greene, Hutton, and Tptr. Tatham.

Capt. Royston and Tpr. C. B. Addison were again conspicuous at the annual meeting of the Natal Rifle Association, the former winning the Volunteer Competition and the latter the Central.

1884. The following were the winners of the several competitions at the annual prize shooting:—

    Government Prize—Tpr. J. W. Armitage.
    Merchants' Prize—Tpr. J. W. Armitage.
    Carbineer Cup—Tpr. E. Colville.
    Consolation—Tpr. Whittaker.
    Judging distance—Tpr. J. W. Armitage.

The Regiment this year was within an ace of winning the much coveted Government Cup, but just missed it owing to the breakdown of two of the team at the last range. The team and scores were:—

Capt. Royston	67	Tpr. W. Comrie	59
Lieut. Macfarlane,	56	Tpr. E. Colville	62
Corpl. Edwards	62	Tpr. W. Simpson	55
Corpl. Addison	64	Tpr. Whittaker	56
Tpr. Armitage	62	Tpr. Worman	58

At the annual shooting of the Natal Rifle Association Capt. Royston won the 2nd central, and Tpr. Addison the 1st central and aggregate.

1885. The following were the winners at the annual prize shooting, which, for a change, was held in favourable weather:—

    Government Cup—Corpl. Addison.
    Merchants' Prize—Tpr. Ellerker.
    Carbineer Cup—Tpr. Foxon.
    Consolation—Tpr. Hughes.
    Judging distance—Corpl. Addison.
    Aggregate—Tpr. J. W. Armitage.

The team and scores for the Government Cup were:—

Capt. Royston	68	Tpr. Whittaker	63
Tpr. Armitage	67	Tpr. Ellerker	62
Corpl. Addison	65	Tpr. Hughes	59
Tpr. W. Comrie	65	Lieut. Macfarlane	58
Tptr. Worman	64	Tpr. Simpson	58

At the meeting of the Natal Rifle Association, the aggregate was won by Tpr. Armitage.

1886. At the annual shooting in January the winners were:—
Government Competition—Tpr. W. Comrie.
Merchants' Prize—Capt. Royston.
Carbineer Cup—Tpr. E. Colville.
Aggregate—Tpr. Armitage.
Consolation—Tpr. Runciman.

For the Government Cup the team and scores were:—

Lieut. Addison	68	Tpr. Whittaker	59
Tpr. Armitage	65	Tpr. Hughes	59
Tpr. Ellerker	64	Capt. Royston	57
Corpl. Foxon	63	Lieut. Macfarlane	55
Tpr. Comrie	62	Tpr. Tranmer	54

Total score 606

At the annual meeting of the Natal Rifle Association, Lieut. Addison made a record score:—600 yards, 35; 500 yards, 32; 200 yards, 35; total, 102.

The Regiment was successful in winning the Team Competition:—

Tpr. Armitage	64	Tpr. Marwick	58
Lieut. Addison	63	Tpr. Tranmer	58
Capt. Royston	60	Tpr. Colville	56
Tpr. McCullough	58	Sergt. Whittaker	55

Tpr. Armitage distinguished himself by winning the Speakers' Cup, and Lieut. Addison won the aggregate.

1887. The annual prize shooting was held on 22nd January. Results:—

Government Prize—Corpl. Armitage.
Carbineer Cup—Tpr. Colville.
Officers' Prize—Tpr. Hutton.
Aggregate—Corpl. Armitage.
Consolation—Tpr. Lister.

At the annual shooting of the Natal Rifle Association, Major Royston won the aggregate. Other members of the Regiment also distinguished themselves.

A match between A. and B. Troops resulted in a win for the former:—

A. Troop.		B. Troop.	
Lieut. Addison	59	Sergt. Whittaker	51
Tpr. Tranmer	54	Lieut. Taunton	49
Tpr. Runciman	50	Tpr. MacKillican	48
Tpr. Holgate	45	Tpr. C. Brown	48
Corpl. Thring	37	Tpr. W. Brown	27
Tpr. Lister	34	Tpr. Kenny	21
	279		244

In a match between B. Troop and Richmond Troop, the Maritzburg team was beat:—

Richmond Troop.		B. Troop.	
Corpl. Comrie	44	Sergt. Whittaker	48
Tpr. J. A. McCullough	43	Tpr. C. Brown	30
Tpr. J. W. Marwick	42	Lieut. Taunton	27
Tpr. S. P. Ashley	33	Tpr. MacKillican	24
Tpr. A. E. McKenzie	31	Corpl. Hayes	24
Tpr. R. A. Marwick	28	Tpr. Kenny	14
	221		167

1888. The annual prize shooting was held on 21st January. Results:—

    Government Prize—Capt. Addison.
    Carbineer Cup—Tpr. Tranmer.
    Officers' Prize—Sergt. Tilney.
    Aggregate—Tpr. Tranmer.
    Consolation—Tpr. H. Brown.

In a match, on 25th February, between teams composed of officers, and non-commissioned officers and men, the result was:—

N.C.O.'s and men.		Officers.	
Corpl. Tranmer	69	Capt. Addison	65
Tpr. Lister	59	Capt. Macfarlane	60
Corpl. Hutton	58	Major Greene	58
Sergt. Vanderplank	58	Lieut. Weighton	58
Sergt. Tilney	53	Lieut. Shepstone	46
Tpr. Williams	49	Capt. Taunton	39
Corpl. Hayes	40	Q.M. Hicks	25
	386		351

On the 2nd June, in a match against the Inniskilling Dragoons, the Regiment won by 34 points. Scores:—

Capt. Addison	80	Lieut. Weighton	73
Corpl. Tranmer	80	Major Greene	65
Capt. Macfarlane	78	Sergt. Tilney	62
Tpr. Lister	76	Lieut. Shepstone	52

Natal Carbineers 566
Inniskilling Dragoons ... 532

1889. The annual shooting was held on the 21st January:—
Government Prize—Corpl. Comrie.
Carbineer Cup—Tpr. J. W. Marwick.
Officers' Prize—Tpr. Hughes.
Aggregate—Corpl. Williams.
Consolation—Tpr. C. Colville.

In a match against the Natal Royal Rifles on 6th April, the team and score were:—

Tptr. Stride	63	Lieut. Whittaker	60
Tpr. C. Brown	63	Tpr. Lister	58
O.R.S. Blofeld	62	Tpr. C. Rodwell	57
Capt. Weighton	61	Corpl. Tranmer	56
Capt. Macfarlane	60	Tpr. Holgate	54

Carbineer ... ... total 594
N.R.R. ... ... total 581

1890. The annual shooting competitions were held on 25th January:—
Government Competition—O.R.S. Blofeld.
Carbineer Cup—Corpl. Tranmer.
Officers' Prize—Tptr. Stride.
Aggregate—Corpl. Tranmer.
Consolation—Surgeon Hyslop.

The Government Cup for 1889 was shot for on 29th January, the following comprising the team:—

Lieut. Whittaker	69	Tptr. Stride	60
Corpl. Tranmer	65	Sergt. Comrie	60
Capt. Addison	64	Corpl. Hutton	59
Tpr. C. Rodwell	63	O.R.S. Blofeld	57
Capt. Weighton	61	Add	3
Capt. Macfarlane	60		
			621

The cup was won by the left wing of the Regiment.

The Government cup for this year was shot for on a range specially erected at Pinetown camp, the competition being open to all colonial teams, and all shooting together. The Regiment was unlucky in coming behind the winning team by three points—the last man of the Regimental team being so unfortunate as to make a miss with his last shot:—

Lieut. Whittaker	63	O.R.S. Rodwell	58
Corpl. Tranmer	60	Tptr. Holliday	58
Sergt. Comrie	59	Tptr. Stride	57
Capt. Weighton	59	Capt. Macfarlane	53
Tpr. Blofeld	59	Tpr. Owen	44
Total			570

In April a return match between teams of officers, and N.C.O.'s and men, had the following result:—

N.C.O.'s and men.		Officers.	
Corpl. Tranmer	66	Capt. Weighton	68
Tptr. Holliday	65	Major Menne	59
Tptr. Stride	64	Capt. Macfarlane	59
Tpr. Blofeld	61	Lieut. Whittaker	56
Tpr. Gordon	55	Major Greene	50
O.R.S. Rodwell	52	Q.M. Lyle	36
R.S.M. Knott	44	Average 7th man	55
	407		383

On 17th May the Regiment met the N.R.R. in a match:—

Tpr. Blofeld	60	Tptr. Holliday	53
Tpr. Stride	59	Capt. Weighton	51
Capt. Macfarlane	58	Capt. Addison	47
Major Menne	54	Lieut. Whittaker	45
Corpl. Tranmer	53	O.R.S. Rodwell	40
Carbineers			520
N.R.R.			514

1891. The annual prize shooting was held on the 7th February:—

    Government Cup—Tpr. Blofeld.
    Carbineer Cup—Lieut. Foxon.
    Officers' Prize—Tpr. Tomlinson.
    Aggregate—Lieut. Foxon.
    Consolation—Lieut. Willson.

1892. The annual prize shooting was held on 6th February:—
  Government Competition—Corpl. Owen.
  Carbineer Cup—Tpr. Wright.
  Officers' Prize—Tpr. Peddie.
  Aggregate—Tpr. Mileman.
  Consolation—Tpr. Paxton.

The Government Cup (a prize long coveted) for **1891** was won by a Regimental team:—

Tptr Holliday	76	O.R.S. Rodwell	63
Tpr. McCathie	73	Tpr. W. Brown	57
Tpr. H. B. Owen	69	Major Macfarlane	55
Tpr. Taynton	68	Add	4
Sergt. Tranmer	67		
Corpl. Owen	67		665
Capt. Weighton	66		

In the field-firing at the Reit Spruit Camp, B. (headquarters) Troop had the honour of being placed first on the list, D. (Nottingham Road) coming second.

The first Bisley shooting was held on 6th June, thanks to the energetic Staff Officer of Volunteers. The Government Cup Competition was held there, and was won by the N.M.R. (Durban). The following were the Regimental team:—Capts. Addison and Weighton, Lieut. Foxon, O.R.S. Rodwell, Sergts. Owen and Tranmer, Corpl. Marwick, Tprs. Mileman, Armitage, and Stride.

1893. On 21st January a match between A. and B. Troops was held:—

B. Troop.		A. Troop.	
Sergt. Owen	59	Tpr. Stride	54
Tpr. Jackson	54	Sergt. Rodwell	47
Tpr. McDowell	50	Corpl. Peters	46
Tpr. G. C. Armitage	48	Tpt.-Major Gutridge	46
Tpr. R. Owen	47	Tpr. Harte	42
Tpr. J. Armitage	45	Q.M.S. Munro	42
Tpr. Joughin	44	Q.M. Lyle	39
Corpl. Todd	41	Tpr. Leslie	39
Tpr. Baxter	38	Tpr. Butler	35
Tpr. Selvey	27	Corpl. Ashdown	18
	453		408

OFFICERS, COLENSO CAMP, 1909.

Top Row—Lt. W. Black, Capt. G. Cumming, N.M.C., Lt. R. J. Hearn, Lt. S. R. Merrick, Lt. G. C. Anderson, Lt. E. C. Hosking, Lt. B. W. Martin, Lt. C. G. Kemp.
Second Row—Capt. Goole, N.V.C., Lt. J. McKenzie, Lt. C. F. J. Cope, Lt. R. A. Lindsay, Lt. A. Praetorius, Lt. J. H. Smith, Lt. E. C. Zunekel, Lt. J. W. Johnston, Lt. J. G. Fannin, Lt. R. W. Smith, Lt. H. Ryley, Lt. J. D. Walsh, Lt. H. C. Thornhill, Lt. A. R. Chater.
Seated—Lt. D. Paton, Capt. A. S. Langley, Capt. R. M. Tanner, Major J. W. Montgomery, Lt.-Col. D. W. Mackay, Lt.-Col. Weighton, O.C., Major J. P. S. Woods, Capt. A. B. Vanderplank, Capt. G. H. Helbert, Capt. H. Walton.

And on 4th February a match between A. and C. Troops:—

A. Troop.		C. Troop.	
Tpr. Stride	53	Corpl. Armitage	54
Tpr. Harte	52	T.S.M. Tranmer	53
Sergt. Rodwell	49	Tpr. Smith	39
Tpt.-Major Gutridge	43	Tpr. Peel	37
Tpr. Butler	41	Corpl. Hanna	36
Q.M. Lyle	41	Sergt. Knott	34
Tpr. Leslie	33	Tpr. Whitelock	31
Corpl. Peters	29	Tpr. Berriman	25
Q.M.S. Munro	28	Tpr. Gallwey	19
Corpl. Barter	12	Tpr. Dick	10
	381		338

The Regiment lost a match with the 3rd Dragoon Guards on 25th March:—

Tpr. R. Comrie	83	Tpr. Stride	79
Corpl. Armitage	83	T.S.M. Tranmer	78
Sergt. Owen	83	Q.M.S. Munro	70
Sergt. Rodwell	79	T.S. Bowman	57

Carbineers ... 612
3rd Dragoon Guards 649

On 15th April the Regimental team sustained another defeat by the Natal Royal Rifles:—

T.S.M. Tranmer	75	Tpr. Stride	62
Sergt. Rodwell	72	Corpl. Armitage	61
Tpr. Ellerker	70	Tpr. Goodwin	59
Sergt. Owen	67	Tpr. Joughin	57
Capt. Weighton	66	Tpr. Comins	52

Carbineers ... 641
N.R.R. ... 668

In a return match the 3rd Dragoon Guards were again the victors:—

Tpr. F. Ellerker	83	Sergt. Owen	74
Capt. Weighton	83	Tpr. Joughin	71
Tpr. J. L. Armitage	80	Sergt. Rodwell	71
Corpl. Armitage	79	Tpr. T. Ellerker	59
Tpr. Comins	76	Tpr. Kean	54

Carbineers ... 730
3rd Dragoon Guards 825

The annual prize shooting was held on 6th May : —

Government Competition—T.S.M. Comrie.
Carbineer Cup—Corpl. Armitage.
Officers' Prize—Tpr. Kean.
Aggregate—Corpl. Armitage.
Consolation—Tpr. G. C. Armitage.

The Regiment did well at the Bisley shooting, the Recruits' competition being won by Tpr. Goodwin, Queen's by Corpl. Mileman, and the Running Buck by Tpr. McDowell. Major Addison, Corpl. Marwick, and others were also prize winners. The Regimental team selected to shoot for the Government Cup was unsuccessful.

1394. The annual shooting was held on 5th May : —

Government Cup—T.S.M. Tranmer.
Carbineer Cup—Sergt. Owen.
Officers' Prize—Tpr. F. Ellerker.
Aggregate—Sergt. Owen.
Consolation—Tpr. H. Colville.

At the Bisley meeting the representatives of the Regiment had the following successes : —

Field firing—Q.M. Lyle's team.
Running man—Tpr. McDowell.
Recruits—Tpr. Goodwin.
Veterans' Carbine—Tpr. Jackson.
Veterans' rifle—Tpr. Stride.
Queen's Carbine—Corpl. Armitage.

The Government Cup was also won, the following being the team and scores : —

Tpr. Goodwin	70	Sergt. Owen	59
Sergt. Rodwell	70	Tpr. Hackland	59
Tpr. Stride	68	T.S.M. Tranmer	57
Tpr. F. Ellerker	64	Tpr. G. Jackson	51
Corpl. Armitage	62	Tpr. T. Ellerker	42

Total 602

The Regimental team succeeded in winning the Team Competition at the annual meeting of the Natal Rifle Association:—

Tpr. Stride	64	Tpr. Davis	61
Tpr. T. Ellerker	63	Sergt. Owen	60
Tpr. Hackland	62	Tpr. Goodwin	50
Corpl. Armitage	62	Sergt. Rodwell	47

Total 469

1895. The "Brown Cup" was presented for competition by teams from the different troops, B. Troop having the honour of being first winners:—

B. Troop.

Sergt. Owen	91	Tpr. F. Ellerker	80
Tpr. Davies	84	Tpr. English	78
Tpr. Comins	83	Tpr. Pannewitz	76
Tpr. Smallie	82	Tpr. G. C. Armitage	75
Tpr. Joughin	82	Tpr. Francis	73
Tpr. J. E. Armitage	81	Corpl. Todd	70

Total, 955.

A. Troop.

Sergt. Rodwell	86	Tpr. Peel	74
Corpl. Armitage	82	Tpr. T. Ellerker	72
T.S.M. Tranmer	81	Q.M.S. Munro	69
Tpr. Wolhuter	78	Tpr. Harte	62
Tpr. Stride	76	Tpr. Tanner	46
Tpr. Wilkinson	75		

801

The annual shooting was held on 18th May:—

Government Cup—Corpl. Armitage.
Carbineer Cup—T.S.M. Tranmer.
Officers' Prize—T.S.M. Buchanan.
Aggregate—Corpl. Armitage.
Consolation—Sergt. Rodwell.

At the Bisley held on 4th June, the following events fell to members of the Regiment:—

Veterans' rifle—Corpl. Marwick.
Queen's rifle—Tpr. Goodwin.
Queen's carbine—Tpr. J. L. Armitage.
Running man—Tpr. Harte.

Government Cup:—

Corpl. Armitage	...	82	Tpr. Stride	... ...	67
T.S.M. Tranmer	...	81	Tpr. Davies	... ...	66
Tpr. Joughin	... ...	79	Sergt. Owen	... ...	65
Tpr. F. Ellerker	...	74	Sergt. Rodwell	... ...	63
Tpr. J. L. Armitage		69	Tpr. English	... ...	59

Total 705

In the 1st Centrals Sergt. Owen had the honour of taking first place.

On 7th September the headquarters troop was defeated in a match with the 3rd Dragoons:—

Sergt. Owen	... ...	89	Tpr. Davies	... ...	76
Tpr. Stride	... ...	81	T.S.M. Tranmer	...	76
Corpl. Armitage	...	81	Tpr. F. Ellerker	...	74
Tpr. T. Ellerker	...	81	Capt. Weighton	... ...	70
Sergt. Rodwell	... ...	79	Tpr. English	... ...	67

Carbineers 774
3rd Dragoons 840

A triangular match was arranged between A. Troop, B. Troop, and Band and Staff:—

B. Troop.		A. Troop.	
Tpr. J. Armitage ...	86	Corpl. Armitage	83
Tpr. G. C. Armitage	84	Sergt. Rodwell	77
Tpr. Davies	81	Tpr. Stride	73
Tpr. F. Ellerker ...	81	Tpr. Harte	70
Tpr. English	80	Tpr. Peel	65
Sergt. Owen	79	Tpr. Adie	64
Tpr. Joughin	74	Tpr. Kean	58
Tpr. Francis	74	Tpr. Wilkinson	49
Tpr. Pannewitz	72	Sergt. Barter	47
Tpr. Comins	67	Corpl. Pain	35
778		621	

Band and Staff.

Capt. Weighton	77	Tpr. Rowles	58
Sergt. Keilly	76	Capt. Tatham	57
Q.M.S. Munro	71	O.R.S. Dick	56
Q.M. Lyle	66	Surgeon Hyslop	46
Tpr. Hesom	59	Capt. Taunton	45

611

On 16th November the N.C.O.'s of headquarters defeated a team of N.R. Rifles:—

Sergt. Owen	77	Corpl. Armitage	64
R.S.M. Bowen	72	Sergt. Barter	62
T.S.M. Tranmer	69	Corpl. Todd	52
Sergt. Rodwell	65	Q.M.S. Munro	51
Corpl. Taynton	65		
			577

N.R.R. ... 498

1896. The "Brown Cup" was shot for on 11th April, A. Troop having the honour of winning it with a grand score:—

Corpl. Armitage	97	Tpr. Raymond	82
R.S.M. Bowen	96	Tpr. Harte	82
Corpl. Stride	95	Sergt. Barter	81
Lieut. Rodwell	94	Corpl. Peel	81
T.S.M. Tranmer	93	Q.M.S. Munro	79
Tpr. Ellerker	88		
Tpr. R. Smith	83		1051

The annual shooting was held on 16th May:—

Government Cup—Corpl. Stride.
Carbineer Cup—Tpr. J. L. Armitage.
Officers' Prize—Tpr. Hesom.
Aggregate—R.S.M. Bowen.
Consolation—Capt. Weighton.

The marksmen of the Regiment did well at the Bisley shooting on 25th May. Corpl. Armitage won the Fixed Sight, Sergt. Bell the Standing, and Corpl. Stride the Queen's rifle. The Government Cup was also won, the following being the Regimental team:—

Sergt. Owen	90	Tpr. J. L. Armitage	71
Tpr. Ellerker	83	Corpl. Stride	69
Corpl. Armitage	80	Corpl. Joughin	62
T.S.M. Tranmer	79	Lieut. Rodwell	59
R.S.M. Bowen	74		
Tpr. N. Hesom	73		740

1897. Natal Bisley, 7th and 8th June. Carbineer Successes:—

1. Recruits' Competition, restricted to volunteers enrolled since 1st July, 1896:—

   Tpr. W. C. Smith, £5 51
   Tpr. A. Paine £3 49
   Tpr. R. Holliday, 10s. 38

2. Veterans' Competition, restricted to volunteers of six years' efficiency, including reservists:—

   Carbines—
   R.S.M. Bowen, £2 42
   Tpr. J. Davis, £1 5s. 41

   Rifles—
   R.S.M. Bowen, £6 48
   Tpr. N. F. Hesom, £3 46
   Tpr. A. T. Hackland, £2 46
   Tpr. W. D. Raymond, £1 10s. 46
   Tpr. T. Ellerker, £1 46
   Capt. J. Weighton, 15s. 45
   T.S.M. Comrie, 10s. 45

3. Rapid Competition, open to all enrolled volunteers, including recruits:—

   Tpr. J. Davis, £6 42
   Bandmaster J. Keilly, 10s. 34

4. Queen's Competition, open to all volunteers, including reservists; in two stages, carbines or rifles: 1st stage, seven shots at 200, 500, and 600 yards. Any position at 200; kneeling, sitting or prone at the other two distances. First twenty in first stage entitled to fire in second stage; the next twenty receiving prizes. Second stage; ten shots at 800 and 900 yards, sitting or prone:—

   1st Stage—
   Sergt. Colville, £2 81
   Tpr. J. H. Smith, £1 10s. 80
   Tpr. W. D. Raymond, £1 79
   Tpr. A. Comrie, 15s. 78
   Tpr. E. J. Kean, 10s. 76

Entitled to shoot in 2nd stage—
Tpr. J. Davis 92
Bandmaster J. Keilly 89
R.S.M. Bowen 89
Tpr. T. Ellerker 86
T.S.M. Comrie 85
Tpr. N. F. Hesom 84
Tpr. W. Buxton 83
T.S.M. Tranmer 83
Tpr. R. Holliday 82

5. Standing Competition, open to all enrolled volunteers, including reservists:—
Tpr. T. Ellerker, £2 10s. 35
Tpr. A. Comrie, 15s. 29

6. Fixed Sight Competition, open to all enrolled volunteers, including reservists: rifles or carbines. Sights must remain fixed at 200 yards. Distance 400 and 500 yards. Seven shots at each range:—
Tpr. J. Hackland, £3 59
Tpr. T. Ellerker, £2 10s. 59
Tpr. E. A. Stieger, 10s. 54

7. Volley-Firing Competition, by sections of four. No section to contain more than one N.C.O. above the rank of corporal. Officers not to compete. Five shots at 400 yards. Position prone:—
N.C. Section, commanded by R.S.M. Bowen, £3 87
N.C. Section, commanded by T.S.M. Comrie, £2 83

8. Field-Firing Competition, distance from 600 to about 250 yards:—
1st, Carbineers' No. 1 team (Lieut. Rodwell, R.S.M. Bowen, T.S.M. Tranmer, Tprs. Smith, Davis, and Ellerker), £8 142

9. Government Cavalry Cup Competition:—
N.C. No. 1 team (Lt. Rodwell, R.S.M. Bowen, T.S.M. Tranmer, Tprs. Davis, Raymond, Hesom, J. H. Smith, Paterson, Ellerker, and Hackland) 694

The prize for the highest aggregate score in all competitions—the blue ribbon for individual marksmanship—was awarded to Tpr. Davis of the Natal Carbineers.

Queen's Competition, 2nd stage:—

Tpr. W. P. Ellerker, £10	152
T.S.M. Tranmer, £6	145
R.S.M. Bowen, £4	141
Tpr. J. Davis, £3	133
Tpr. F. Hesom, £3	126
Bandmaster Keilly, £2 10s	119
Tpr. W. Buxton, £2 10s.	103
T.S.M. Comrie, £2 10s.	102
Tpr. R. Holliday, £2 10s.	95

10. Unlimited Entry Competitions. A competitor may enter as many times as he wishes, but can only take one prize in the competition, i.e. with his highest score: —

Tpr. Raymond, £4	44
Tpr. Ellerker, £1 10s.	43
Tpr. J. H. Smith, £1	42

11. Running Buck Competition, six shots:—

Tpr. Paine, £2	14
Tpr. Paterson, £1 5s.	14
Lieut. Rodwell, 15s.	12

1898. Natal Bisley. 30th May to 1st June.

1. Recruits' Competition:—

Tpr. T. Hackland, 10s.	42
Tpr. J. B. Nicholson, 10s.	37
Tpr. R. McKenzie, 10s.	35

2. Veterans' Rifle Competition:—

Tpr. J. S. H. Colville, £6	48
Corpl. Paterson, £4	48
Sergt. E. Colville, £3	47
Sergt. M. Armitage, £1 10s.	46
Tpr. T. Ellerker	45

WARRANT OFFICERS AND SERGEANTS, COLENSO CAMP, 1909.

Top Row—Arm.-Sgt. Holloghan, S.-I.-M. L. Clarence, O.-R.-S. D. Anderson, O.R.S. R. Watts, Sgt. E. A. C. Harding, Sgt. E. E. Housholt, Sgt. J. Peters, Sgt. C. E. Hayes, Sgt. W. W. King, Sgt.-Farr. J. Derrick, Sgt. E. H. Hayes, Sgt.-Cook A. J. E. Campbell, Q.-M.-S. D. Thompson, S.-Q.-M.-S. Bennett, Sgt. H. Teasdale, Sgt.-Farr. E. M. Nelson.

2nd Row—Q.M.S. D. J. Dunn, S.-Q.-M.-S. Lyall, S.-Q.-M.-S. A. D. Buchanan, O.-R.-S. C. F. Layman, S.-Q.-M.-S. H. W. Payn, Sergt. F. E. King, Sergt. B. C. T. Pottow, Sgt. A. B. Dickinson, Sgt. F. Davis, Sgt. A. F. Grant, Sgt. C. E. Lugg, Sgt. A. Madsen, Sgt. A. Carter, Sgt.-Farr. J. Nicolson, Sgt. G. Newlands, Sgt. Beattie, N.D.M.R.

Sitting—S.-S.-M. W. P. Stevens, S.-Q.-M.-S. W. H. Forsyth, S.-S.-M. T. E. Warwick, S.-Sgt. M. Madsen, R.-S.-M. W. Burkmister, Lt.-Col. Weighton, Capt. G. Helbert, Q.-M.-S. G. Harker, S.-S.-M. W. E. Wright, S.-Q.-M.-S. E. J. Kean, S.-S.-M. T. McCathie, S.-Q.-M.-S. H. McLean.

Front Row—S.Q.M.S. W. H. F. Harte, Sgt. C. L. H. Mulcahy, Sgt. J. J. Harding, Sgt. H. T. Mitchell, Sgt. Emmerton, N.M.C., Sgt.-Tptr. Fairall, Sgt. Tptr. H. A. Craig, S.-Q.-M.-S. J. Bristo, S.-S.-M. W. H. Mitchell, Sgt. J. Dicks, Sgt. G. Anderson, Sgt. J. M. Comrie, Sgt. J. A. Dicks.

3. Veterans' Carbine Competition:—
    Sergt. Owen, £6 46
    Tpr. T. Ellerker, £4 45
    O.R.S. Stride, £3 44
    Corpl. Paterson, £1 15s. 42
    Tpr. McCullough, £1 5s. 42
    Sergt. J. W. Armitage, £1 42
4. Rapid Firing Competition:—
    Tpr. McCullough, £6 41
    Tpr. Raymond, £3 38
5. 200 yards:—
    R.S.M. Bowen, £3 33
    Tpr. T. Ellerker, 10s. 33
6. Revolver Competition:—
    R.S.M. Bowen, £2 6
    Tpr. Paine, 10s. 6
7. Running Man:—
    Lieut. Comrie, 10s. 9
8. Running Buck:—
    Tpr. R. McKenzie, £1 14
9. Queen's Prize; 1st stage:—
    Tpr. Raymond, £2 88
    Tpr. C. Colville, £2 86
    Tpr. Sclanders, £1 10s. 86
    Lieut. Comrie, £1 84
    Tpr. Holliday, £1 84
    Sergt. Colville, 15s. 83
    Lieut. C. Rodwell, 10s. 81

    Queen's Prize; 2nd stage:—
    Sergt. Armitage 93
    Tpr. J. Hackland 92
    R.S.M. Bowen 92
    Corpl. Paterson 91
    Tpr. Colville 90
    Sergt. Owen 90
    Tpr. A. T. Hackland 90
    Corpl. Marwick 89
    O.R.S. Stride 89
    Tpr. Davis 88
    Tpr. Raymond 88

10. Standing. 200 yards:—
   Tpr. T. Ellerker, £2 10s. 41
   R.S.M. Bowen, £2 39
   Tpr. J. S. H. Colville, £1 36
   Tpr. Davis, 15s. 36

11. Volley Firing:—
   3rd Team, N.C. (R.S.M. Bowen's) 87

12. Fixed Sight:—
   Tpr. A. T. Hackland, £4 64
   Tpr. T. Ellerker, £2 61
   R.S.M. Bowen, 15s. 58
   Sergt. J. W. Armitage, 15s. 57
   Tpr. Davis, 10s. 57

13. Queen's Prize; Final stage:—
   Corpl. J. W. Armitage, £10 168
   Tpr. A. T. Hackland, £6 168
   Sergt. J. W. Armitage, £3 162
   O.R.S. Stride, £3 162
   R.S.M. Bowen, £3 162
   Tpr. Raymond, £3 160
   Tpr. Davis, £2 10s. 157
   Corpl. Paterson, £2 10s. 151
   Tpr. A. J. Hackland, £2 10s. 144
   Tpr. J. S. H. Colville, £2 10s. 143

14. Aggregate:—
   R.S.M. Bowen 219

15. Volley Firing:—
   Natal Carbineers (R.S.M. Bowen), £3 ... 87

16. Field Firing:—
   Natal Carbineers (R.S.M. Bowen), £8 ... 102

17. 200 yards:—
   Tpr. Sclanders, 10s. 33

18. Running Man:—
   Lieut. Comrie, £2 13

   Government Cup (mounted):—
   1st Team Natal Carbineers 781
   2nd Team Natal Carbineers 742

1899. Natal Bisley. Monday, 22nd May.

1. Veterans' Carbine Competition:—

   Sergt. Paterson, £6 47
   Tpr. McCullough, £4 44
   Tpr. J. H. Smith, £3 43
   Tpr. J. S. H. Colville, £2 42
   Lieut. Rodwell 40

2. Recruits' Competition:—

   Tpr. Gray, £5 56
   Tpr. Sclanders, 10s. 46
   Tpr. Rupert Holliday, 10s. 42

3. Queen's Prize; 1st stage:—

   Tpr. Colville, £2 88
   Tpr. Gray, £1 10s. 86
   Tpr. R. W. Smith, £1 10s. 86
   Tpr. J. H. Smith, £1 85
   Tpr. A. T. Hackland, 15s. 84
   Lieut. Rodwell, 15s. 84
   Corpl. F. J. Duke, 15s. 83
   Corpl. McCullough, 15s. 83
   Sergt. E. Colville, 10s. 82
   Sergt. Owen 82

4. Running Buck:—

   Tpr. Sclanders, £2 17
   Sergt. Colville, £1 10s. 16
   Tpr. Gray, £1 14
   Lieut. Rodwell, 10s. 14

5. Running Man:—

   Corpl. Richmond, £2 14

6. Revolver:—

   Lieut. Rodwell, £3 12
   R.S.M. Bowen, £1 8
   Lieut. Comrie, 10s. 6

7. Unlimited Entries. 200 yards:—

   Tpr. Gray, £3 34
   Tpr. Davis, 10s. 32

8. Queen's Prize; 2nd stage:—

    Tpr. Davis.   Tpr. Raymond.
    Tpr. Joyner.   Lieut. Comrie.
    Tpr. Ellerker.   O.R.S. Stride.
    Sergt. Paterson.   Tpr. Sclanders.

9. Troop and Company Competition:—

    Natal Carbineers, £5 407

10. Volley Firing:—

    N.C. (O.R.S. Stride's team), £8 105
    N.C. (Sergt. Owen's team), £3 90

11. Field Firing:—

    N.C. (Lieut. Rodwell's team), £4 75

12. Fixed Sight:—

    Tpr. T. Ellerker, £6 64
    Sergt. McCullough, 15s. 59

13. Queen's Prize; 2nd stage:—

    Tpr. Davis, £6 173
    Lieut. Comrie, £4 168
    Tpr. Joyner, £3 167
    Sergt. Paterson, £3 167
    Tpr. Raymond, £3 166
    Tpr. T. Ellerker, £3 166
    Tpr. Sclanders, £3 163
    O.R.S. Stride, £2 10s. 158

14. Running Man:—

    Sergt. Colville, £1 10
    Corporal Richmond, 10s.   9
    Tpr. Joyner   9

15. Running Buck:—

    Corpl. McCathie, £1 10s. 15
    Lieut. Comrie, £1 15

16. Revolver:—

    Tpr. A. T. Hackland, £3   8
    Lieut. Rodwell, £2   4

17. Unlimited Entries. 200 yards:—
    Tpr. Davis, £2 ... 33
    Sergt. McCullough, £1 ... 33
    Sergt. Paterson, 10s. ... 33
18. Aggregate:—
    Tpr. T. Ellerker, £5 ... 156
19. In the Government Cup Competition the Natal Carbineers, who had a total of 740, were disqualified on the ground of one man having paper under the back sight at 400 yards. The Border Mounted Rifles, with a score of 667, were declared the winners.
20. Maxim:—
    N.C. B. Troop (Sergt. Paterson's team) £5 ... 51
    N.C. B. Troop (Corpl. Richmond's team) 38
21. Running Man:—
    Tpr. A. T. Hackland, £1 10s. ... 11
22. Revolver:—
    Tpr. Hackland, £2 ... 4
23. Unlimited Entries:—
    Tpr. Davis, £2 ... 34
    Tpr. T. Ellerker, £1 ... 33

1904. 25th April. Transvaal Bisley. The Natal Carbineers came first, with a total of 754, in the competition for the inter-regimental cup. The individual scores of the N.C. team were:—Sclanders 98, Zunckel 96, Armitage 96, Gray 95, Paterson 95, Smythe 94, Johnstone 91, Baxter 89. The scores of the other teams were:—B.M.R. 731, N.M.R. 730, 7th Dragoon Guards 723, U.M.R. 721. For the inter-regimental revolver-shooting cup, as also for the inter-colonial challenge cup, the N.C. came second.

20th July. Natal Bisley. The "Royston Memorial" competition, open to squadrons, batteries, and companies of the Natal Militia, was won by B. Squadron team of the N.C., Lieut. C. M. Paterson 95, Corpl. H. A. Campbell 95, Tpr. T. P. Catchpole 90, Corpl. A. J. E. Campbell 89, Capt. T. M. Owen 88, Tpr. J. O. Smythe 81. Total 538.

Of twelve competitors in revolver shooting
Capt. T. M. Owen was 1st with a total of 59
Corpl. D. G. Sclanders 2nd with a total of 55

334

1905. 17th March. Transvaal Bisley. The inter-regimental challenge cup was won by the Regiment for the second year in succession with the following scores:—

	200 yds.	500 yds.	600 yds.	Tl.
Lieut. W. P. Gray	33	34	34	101
Tpr. A. E. Johnstone	35	33	33	101
Tpr. E. C. Zunckel	33	32	33	98
Lance-Sergt. D. J. Sclanders	31	34	31	96
Tpr. J. O. Smythe	30	34	27	91
O.R.S., R. A. Richmond	28	31	31	90
Corpl. H. A. Campbell	30	33	27	90
Lieut. C. M. Paterson	33	31	26	90
Totals	253	262	242	757

Captain of team, R.S.M. Burkimsher.

The Running Man Competition was also won by the Regiment; the following comprising the team:—Lieuts. Gray and Paterson, O.R.S. Richmond and Tpr. Smythe.

17th May. Natal Bisley. The following were the scores made in the competition for the "Emma Thresh" trophy which was won by the Regiment:—

	200 yds.	500 yds.	600 yds.	Tl.
Lieut. W. P. Gray	33	35	31	99
Capt. T. M. Owen	34	33	30	97
Sergt. D. G. Sclanders	33	33	29	95
Corpl. A. J. E. Campbell	33	32	29	94
Tpr. E. C. Zunckel	30	32	30	92
R.S.M., W. Burkimsher	31	31	30	92
O.R.S., R. A. Richmond	31	34	26	91
Lieut. C. M. Paterson	33	31	25	89
Tpr. J. O. Smythe	27	34	27	88
Tpr. C. S. D. Otto	32	27	26	85
Total	317	322	283	922

Captain of team, Lieut. P. W. Stride.

The inter-regimental cup—mounted competitors—was also won by the Regiment, the following comprising the team:—Capt. Owen, Corpls. H. A. Campbell, A. J. E.

Campbell, A. B. Dickinson, and Stirton, and Tprs. J. M. Anderson, W. V. Mason, T. P. Catchpole, and C. S. D. Otto.

1906. 8th October. Cape Colony Bisley. The Western Province Shield, won last year by the Capetown Highlanders with a score of 602, was won this year by the Natal Carbineers with a score of 513:—

Capt. Gray	74	Corpl. H. A. Campbell	63
Lieut. Paterson	70	Sergt. Sclanders	63
Tpr. Johnstone	65	Lieut. Richmond	63
Corpl. A. J. E. Campbell	64	S.I.M. Zunckel	51

1907. 12th April. Transvaal Bisley. In the Booysen's sweepstake, Capt. W. P. Gray, the winner, scored 34. The East Rand sweepstake was won by Lieut. C. M. Paterson with a possible. Tpr. A. C. Adie won the Pretoria cup, 7 shots at 500 and 600 yards. The Brakpan cup, Running Man competition, open to teams of four, was won by the N.C. with 10 hits. Capt. Gray, Lieuts. Paterson, Smythe, and Richmond were the team.

May. Natal Bisley. In the following team competitions the Natal Carbineers gained 1st place:—

Government cup	with 776	points.
Royston Memorial	with 646	points.
Emma Thresh	with 929	points.
Lloyd Lindsay	with $32\frac{1}{2}$	points.
Revolver match	with 284	points.

Members of the Regiment were also conspicuous amongst the successful competitors in the long list of individual events.

1908. May. Natal Bisley. The "Emma Thresh" trophy, open to teams of ten, was won by the N.C. with the following score:—

	200 yds.	500 yds.	600 yds.	Tl.
Lieut. E. C. Zunckel	32	34	32	98
Capt. C. M. Paterson	33	34	30	97
Capt. W. P. Gray	32	33	31	96
Lieut. D. G. Sclanders	34	32	30	96
Sergt. J. J. Harding	31	31	32	94
Tpr. W. S. Anstey	31	30	32	93
Lieut. J. O. Smythe	30	30	32	92
Corpl. C. S. D. Otto	31	31	28	90
O.R.S., R. Watts	32	29	28	89
Corpl. A. J. E. Campbell	31	31	24	86
Totals	317	315	299	931

Revolver match, open to teams of four from any regiment, corps, or rifle association in South Africa. 20 yards, 6 shots right, and 6 left hand. Won by the N.C. team:—

	20R.	20L.	Tl.
Capt. C. M. Paterson	39	38	77
Lieut. J. O. Smythe	38	32	70
S.I.M., L. R. Clarence	33	32	65
Capt. W. P. Gray	28	27	55
Totals	138	129	267

1909. March. Transvaal Bisley. The following scores were made in the competition for the inter-regimental challenge cup won again by the Regiment:—

	200 yds.	500 yds.	600 yds.	Tl.
Capt. C. M. Paterson	31	34	34	99
Major W. P. Gray	32	34	33	99
Tpr. A. E. Johnstone	34	33	31	98
S.I.M., L. R. Clarence	34	31	32	97
Tpr. W. S. Anstey	31	29	32	92
Sergt. A. J. E. Campbell	31	32	29	92
Lieut. E. C. Zunckel	31	32	29	92
Tpr. E. E. Johnson	31	31	27	89
Totals	255	256	247	758

WINNING SECTION—OFFICERS' TENT-PEGGING, MILITARY TOURNAMENT, DURBAN, 1909.
Major T. M. Owen, Major J. P. S. Woods, Lieut. J. W. Johnston, Lieut. S. R. Merrick

The scores made in the "Hollins" cup, an inter-regimental revolver competition, which was also won by the Regiment, were as under:—

	20	50	Tl.
S.I.M., L. R. Clarence	35	31	66
Major W. P. Gray	35	26	61
Tpr. N. O. Berry	31	28	59
Capt. C. M. Paterson	30	27	57
Totals	131	112	243

May. Natal Bisley. The field firing competition, open to teams of eight men from any regiment, corps, or rifle association in South Africa, was won by the N.C. with 22 points, their team being Major W. P. Gray, Capt. C. M. Paterson, O.R.S., R. Watts, S.I.M., L. R. Clarence, Sergt. J. J. Harding, Tprs. W. S. Anstey, N. O. Berry, and A. E. Johnstone

The Royston Memorial competition, open to one team of eight from any of the active militia regiments, was also won by the Natal Carbineers:—

	100 yds.	200 yds.	Tl.
Tpr. Russom	19	21	40
Capt. Paterson	14	23	37
Tpr. Johnstone	12	22	34
Major Gray	12	20	32
S.Q.M.S. Harte	11	20	31
Tpr. Berry	8	17	25
R.S.M. Burkimsher	7	17	24
O.R.S. Watts	7	17	24
Totals	90	157	247

The N.C. missed the Emma Thresh competition by one point only:—

Durban Light Infantry	934
Natal Carbineers	933

In the revolver competition the N.C. team came first. Major Gray 72, Capt. Paterson 66, S.I.M. Clarence 57, Tpr. Berry 54, Total 246.

Maritzburg Rifle Association	242
Natal Police	181

May. The following members of the Regiment were selected to form part of the team to represent the Colony at the forthcoming English Bisley:—

Major W. P. Gray.	Sergt. A. J. E. Campbell.
Capt. C. M. Paterson.	Tpr. W. S. Anstey.
Lieut. E. C. Zunckel.	Tpr. A. E. Johnstone.

May. The Regiment in the "Daily Mail" Empire Day competition obtained the 6th place in the whole Empire and the 1st in South Africa. The following are the scores:—

O.R.S. Watts	100	Tpr. E. E. Johnson	98
Corpl. C. S. D. Otto	99	Tpr. A. B. Coulson	98
Tpr. R. P. Campbell	99	Tpr. J. M. Moreland	97
Boy Franklin	98	Tpr. A. E. Johnstone	97

Total ... 786

1910. 24th May. In the "Daily Mail" Empire Day shooting the following gives the team and scores of the Natal Carbineers:—

	200 yds.	500 yds.	600 yds.	Tl.
Capt. C. M. Paterson	35	33	32	100
Tpr. N. O. Berry	32	34	33	99
R.S.M. Burkimsher	33	34	32	99
Corpl. S. V. Samuelson	33	35	31	99
Tpr. V. K. Russom	33	35	31	99
Tpr. A. V. Edmondson	34	34	31	99
Sergt. W. G. Holcomb	30	34	33	97
Sergt. J. M. Anderson	33	34	30	97
Totals	263	273	253	789

APPENDIX 3.—ATHLETIC SPORTS.

1865. The games arranged this year by the officers of the garrison, stationed at Fort Napier, took place on Monday, 29th May, on the hillside in front of Government House. In the contests open to Volunteers, several of the Carbineers carried off prizes:—

    Volunteer Cup, 600 yards—Tpr. T. Shepstone.
    High Jump—Tpr. Erskine.
    Officers' Hunt Stakes—Tpr. T. Shepstone.
    Champion Belt—Tpr. T. Shepstone.

1866. At the military sports the Officers' Hunt Stakes was won by Tpr. T. Shepstone, N.C.

1875. On the 24th April, Regimental Sports were held on the old Race Course in presence of Sir Garnet Wolseley and a large gathering of spectators. Capt. Shepstone, Sergt. Whitelaw, Corpl. London, and Tpr. Doig formed the committee. The following were the events:—

HORSE RACES.

    Heavy Marching Order Race, value £5, presented by His Excellency, Sir Garnet Wolseley—Tpr. Doig's "Young Natal."
    Carbineer Plate—Sergt. Whitelaw's "Gowrie."
    Hurdle Race—Tpr. Doig's "Sir Garnet."
    Maritzburg Race—Sergt. Whitelaw's "Gowrie."
    Troop Race—Tpr. Doig's "Young Natal."

FOOT RACES.

    100 yards—Tpr. Moodie.
    200 yards Hurdle—Tpr. Player.
    400 yards Hurdle—Corpl. London.

1876. On 6th May, before a large number of spectators, sports were again held on the old Race Course. The band of the 13th Regiment added to the afternoon's enjoyment. The committee was composed of Capt. Shepstone, Sergt. Royston, Corpl. London, and Tpr. D. B Scott. The events and the winners were :—

 Commandant's Race, value £5, presented by Major Dartnell—Tpr. D. B. Scott's "Blesbok."
 Troop Race—Sergt. Royston's "Lancer."
 Carbineer Plate—Sergt. Royston's "Lancer."
 Hurdle Race—Tpr. D. B. Scott's "Blesbok."
 Maritzburg Race—Captain Shepstone's "Metropolitan."
 Consolation Stakes—Tpr. Bower's "Doubtful."
 100 yards (foot)—Tpr. Francis.
 300 yards (foot)—Tpr. Francis.
 400 yards (hurdle)—Corpl. London.

1877. Sports were held on the Race Course on 28th April and were attended by a large number of spectators, the band of the 3rd Buffs adding to the enjoyment :—
 100 yards race—Tpr. Francis.
 Heavy marching order race—Tpr. Whitelaw's "Gowrie."
 Troop Race—Capt. Shepstone's "Buzzard."
 Hurdle Race—Tpr. W. S. Shepstone.
 Carbineer Plate—Sergt.-Major Royston's "Lancer."
 Hurdle Race—Tpr. W. S. Shepstone's "Boojum."
 Consolation Stakes—Tpr. Merryweather's "Tommy Dodd."

1879. On the 27th July at Landtman's Drift, the last camp of the Carbineers in the Zulu war, they arranged a day's sports, the first relaxation that, as a regiment, they had indulged in since they left Maritzburg for the front on the 29th of the preceding November. Judge, Lieut. Royston; Committee, Sergt. Macfarlane, Q.-M.-Sergt. Mileman, Corpl. Merryweather, Tprs. Greene, Hair, Lavender and Cooke; Starter, Tpr. Brewer; clerk of the course, Tpr. Grainger :—

Trial Stakes :—
 Tpr. Greene's "Gatling" 1
 Tpr. Lloyd's "Paddy" 2

100 yards foot race:—
    Sergt. Macfarlane ... 1
    Tpr. Greene ... 2

Throwing cricket ball:—
    Sergt. Macfarlane ... 1

Carbineer Plate:—
    Tpr. Ross's "Dabulamanzi" ... 1
    Tpr. Crawford's "Charlie" ... 2

Bareback Race:—
    Tpr. Brewer's "Social" ... 1
    Tpr. Ross's "Dabulamanzi" ... 2

Sack Race:—
    Tpr. Brown ... 1
    Sergt. Macfarlane ... 2

Hurdle Race:—
    Tpr. Crawford's "Charlie" ... 1
    Tpr. Sibthorpe's "Ulundi" ... 2

Galloway Stakes:—
    Tpr. Lloyd's "Paddy" ... 1
    Tpr. Hair's "Cockalorum" ... 2

Long Jump (Open):—
    Tpr. Sibthorpe ... 1
    Sergt. Macfarlane ... 2

Consolation Stakes:—
    Lieut. Royston's "Rob Roy" ... 1
    Corpl. Merryweather's "Failure" ... 2

1883. Sports were held at the Encampment in Pinetown, the following events being won by members of the Regiment:
    Trial Stakes—Tpr. Armitage.
    100 Yards—Tpr. Simpson.
    Military and Volunteer Race—Tpr. Peters' "Cowper."
    High Jump—Tpr. Simpson.
    Steeplechase—Corpl. Ross's "Death or Glory."
    Officers' Race—Lieut. Macfarlane.
    Heavy Marching Order Race—Corpl. McKenzie.
    Tug of War—Natal Carbineers.

1884. In the sports at the Pinetown Encampment, the principal prize winner was Trooper Ross.

1885. The following events were won by members of the Regiment in the sports at the Emberton Camp:—
    100 Yards—Tpr. Hughes.
    Mile Race—Tpr. Simpson.
    Tent-pegging—Lieut. Greene.
    Hurdle Race—Sergt. Ross's "Death or Glory."
    Fugitive Race—Sergt. Ross's "Death or Glory."
    Tilting the Ring—Tpr. Armitage.

In May a Gymkhana was held, the following being the events:—
    Tilting the Ring—Sergt. Addison.
    Tent-pegging—Tpr. Armitage.
    Flat Race—Corpl. Foxon's "Remorse."
    200 Yards—Tpr. Vanderplank.
    Hurdle Race—Lieut. Greene's "Solano."
    Flat Race, One Mile—Tpr. Simpson's "Jupiter."
    Fugitive Race—Corpl. Foxon and Tpr. Lys.

Shortly afterwards another Gymkhana was held with the following results:—
    Half-mile Race—Tpr. Peters' "Timekeeper."
    Tent-pegging—Corpl. Addison.
    Mile Race—Tpr. Peters' "Volunteer."
    Hurdle Race—Tpr. Peters' "Timekeeper."
    Tent-pegging (Open)—Lieut. Greene.

Sports were held on the 10th October, the following being the winners:—
    Half-mile Flat Race—Tpr. Risley's "Masher."
    200 Yards—Tpr. Runciman.
    Tent-pegging—Tpr. MacKillican.
    Mile Race—Tpr. Risley's "Masher."
    Hurdle Race—Tpr. Peters' "Carbineer."
    Tent-pegging (Open)—Tpr. Armitage.
    Tilting the Ring—Tpr. Whittaker.
    Fugitive Race—Corpl. Foxon.
    Consolation—Tpr. Buchanan's "Cutlet."

1886. At sports held on 3rd April the results were:—
Three-quarter Mile Race—Tpr. Risley's "Masher."
Tent-pegging—Tpr. Runciman.
Leading Race—Tpr. Risley's "Masher" & "Swindle."
Tilting the Ring—Tpr. Hughes.
Hurdle Race—Tpr. Venning's "Crocon."
Bareback Race—Tpr. Risley's "Masher."

At sports in the Pinetown Camp on 5th June:—
Three-quarter Mile Race was won by Tpr. Jackson's "St. George."
Leading Race—Tpr. Jackson's "St. George."
Tilting the Ring—Tpr. Armitage.
Tent-pegging—Tpr. Runciman.

1888. On the 18th February a Gymkhana was held, the following being the events and winners:—
Maiden Stakes—Tpr. Jackson's "Toby."
Foot Race—Corpl. Runciman.
Tent-pegging—Corpl. Runciman.
Fugitive Race—Tprs. Risley and Parry.
Tilting the Ring—Tpr. Williams.
Fugitive Race, Mounted—Tprs. Mackillican and Risley.

A Gymkhana was held on the 5th May. Results:—
Maiden Stakes—Tpr. Stride's "Dingaan."
Tent-pegging—Corpl. Runciman.
Lemon Cutting—Corpl. Runciman.
Tent-pegging (Sections), Officers v. N.C.O. & Men—The Officers' team, consisting of Major Greene, Captains Macfarlane and Addison, and Lieut. Shepstone, beat the team of N.C.O.'s and Men, consisting of Sergt. Tilney, Corpl. Runciman, Tprs. MacKillican and Rodwell.
Fugitive Race—Tpr. Risley.

1891. At a sports meeting held on 15th August in Maritzburg, the Regimental Section (consisting of Sergt.

Rodwell, O.R.S. Rodwell, Corpls. Runciman and Townsend), were successful in winning the Section Tent-pegging, competing against teams from the 11th Hussars and others.

1892. On 17th September sports were held in conjunction with the N.R.R.
    100 Yards—Tpr. Leslie.
    Sack Race—Corpl. Townsend.
    Walk, Run, and Ride—Tpr. Player.
    Three-legged Race—Tprs. Cotter and Cook.
    Potato Picking—Corpl. Townsend.
    Tug of War—Natal Carbineers.
    Trotting Race—Tpr. Tanner's "Brandy."

1893. At the military sports held on 15th June, the Regimental Section (Sergts. Rodwell and Townsend, Corpl. Peters and Tpr. Sibthorpe) beat the representatives of the Garrison in tent-pegging, a success which they repeated at a military tournament on 10th September.

1894. Sports were held on 1st September.
    Tent-pegging—Capt. Shepstone.
    100 Yards—Tpr. H. Joughin.
    Putting Shot—Tpr. Smith.
    150 Yards Boot Race—Sergt. Townsend.

1895. On 22nd July a Detachment of the Regiment, consisting of Sergts. Rodwell, Townsend and Barter, Corpls. Button, Lawrence and McDowell, Tprs. Joughin and F. Ellerker, competed at the military tournament held by the 3rd Dragoons in Durban, and won in section tent-pegging, tug-of-war, and wrestling on horseback.

1896. On 13th January, at the Royal Artillery Sports, in the Section Tent-pegging the Regimental Section, consisting of Lieut. Gallwey, R.S.M. Bowen, Sergts. Rodwell and Townsend, were successful, beating no less than **nine teams.**

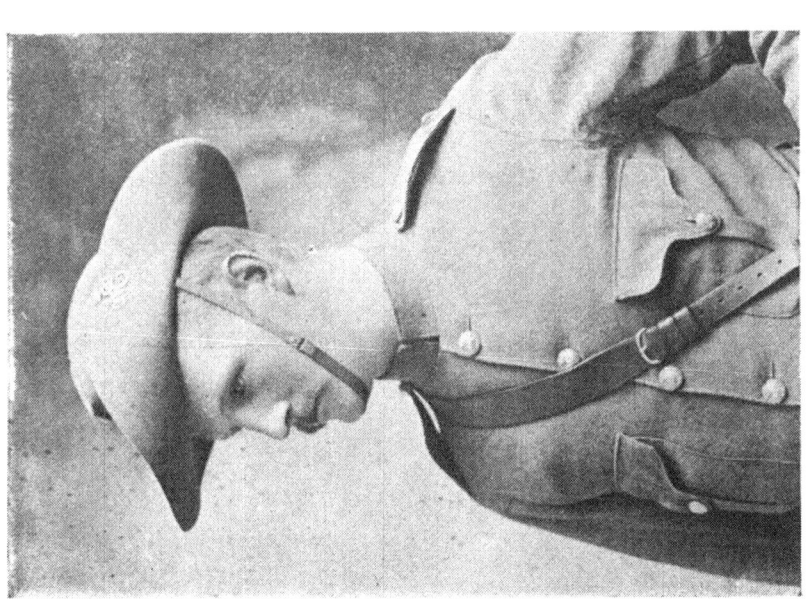

Major A. C. Townsend.

Major T. M. Owen.

Sports were held on 26th September.
  H.M.O. Competition—Bandsman Hesom.
  Tent-pegging—R.S.M. Bowen.
  100 Yards Race—Corpl. Joughin.
  Mounted Melee—B. Troop.
  Variety Race—Lieut. Rodwell.

1897. At the Estcourt encampment sports were held on the afternoon of May 6th. The weather was delightful, and the attendance larger than has ever been seen on the Estcourt Race Course before. While the sports were in progress General Cox arrived and witnessed several of the competitions:—

1. Heavy marching order competition. 1st prize £2, 2nd prize £1. Points for best turned-out man and horse:—
    Tpr. Fisher, A Troop (Headquarters) 1
    Tpr. W. J. Armitage, B. Troop (Headquarters) ... 2
        Five competitors.

2. Maiden Stakes. Value £10 10s., for horses that have never won a race (sports included). Catchweights over 11st. 7lb. Distance four furlongs:—
    Lieut. Nourse-Varty's "Prosper" 1
    Tpr. Smith's "Secret" 2
    Bandsman Ridgway's "Comrade" 3
    Fifteen entries. "Prosper," Mr. Varty's newly imported Australian horse, had it all his own way from start to finish, winning easily.

3. Mounted tug-of-war. 1st prize £2 2s. In teams of four (bareback):—
    K. Troop (Dundee) 1
    D. Troop (Nottingham Road) 2
        Seven troops competed.

4. Encampment Stakes (handicap). Value £15 15s. Distance $1\frac{1}{2}$ mile:—
    Tpr. Mattison's "Briton" (12st.) 1
    Sergt. Townsend's "Montrose" (11st. 11lb.) 2
    Lieut. Varty's "Prosper" (12st. 3lb.) 3
    Eight ran. By some error this race was made two miles instead of $1\frac{1}{2}$, and Mr. Varty lodged an objection, which was not upheld.

5. Lloyd-Lindsay Race. Value £4. In teams of four:—
 D. Troop (Nottingham Road) 1
 K. Troop (Dundee) 2
  Four entries.

6. Hurdle Race (handicap). Value £10. Distance two miles, over eight 3ft. 6in. hurdles:—
 Q.M.S. Munro's "Robin Gray" (Craig), 11st. 2lb. 1
 Tpr. Mattison's "Briton" (Owner) 12st. 2
 Lieut. Varty's "Prosper" (Raw), 12st. 3
 Five ran. Both "Robin Gray" and "Briton" swerved at the last hurdle, and Mr. Varty lodged an objection against the winner, which was over-ruled.

7. Band Race. Value £5 5s. Half a mile. Catch-weights:—
 Ridgway's "Comrade" 1
 Daly's "Nansen" 2
 Sergt. Carbis's "Masher" 3
  Five ran. A good race.

8. Tent-pegging (in sections). 1st prize £4, 2nd £2. Three runs:—
 B. Troop, 12 points 1
 A. Troop, 9 points 2
  Five teams competed.

9. Fugitive Race. £2 2s. Distance, half a mile, straight:—
 Tpr. McLean 1
 Tpr. Ladds 2
  Won by a neck.

1899. Balgowan Encampment, Monday, 3rd April, was given over to the annual camp sports. The following successes were scored by Natal Carbineers:—

1. Heavy marching order competition:—
 Corpl. Garbutt 1
 Tprs. A. T. Hackland, Teasdale, and Maritz, N.C., divided 2nd and 3rd prizes with Tprs. Johnson and Hurst, N.M.R.

2. 100 yards regimental championship:—
 Tpr. Jackson 2

3. Maiden Stakes: —
 Tpr. Tanner's "Bonnie Doon" 1
 Tpr. Rickett's "Friendship" 2

4. High Jump: —
 Tpr. H. de Barry 1
 Tpr. R. de Barry 2

5. Long Jump: —
 Tpr. M. Madsen 3

6. Camp Plate Handicap: —
 Tpr. W. Taylor's "Shylock" 2
 Tpr. Tanner's "Bonnie Doon" 3

7. Fugitive Race: —
 Tprs. Chadwick and Smyth 1

8. Lemon Cutting: —
 Lieut. Rodwell 1
 Sergt. Perrin 3

9. Flying Stakes Handicap: —
 Tpr. L. O. Fyvie's "Orphan" 2
 R.S.M. Bowen's "Charles Dickens" 3

10. Tent-pegging: —
 2nd Team Natal Carbineers 1
 1st Team Natal Carbineers 3

11. Tug-of-war: —
 Carbineers started by pulling B.M.R. over the line by a tussle, and defeated the N.M.R. in the final with comparative ease.

1903. Hermansberg Road Encampment. Sports at Greytown.

1. Maiden Race: —
 R.S.M. Burkimsher's "Yorkshire Lass" 3

2. 100 Yards Flat Race, Handicap: —
 1st Heat—Tpr. Madsen 1
 3rd Heat—Sergt. Madsen 1
 4th Heat—Corpl. De Barry 1
 Final—Sergt. Madsen 1

3. 120 Yards Flat Race, Hurdles:—
   1st Heat—Corpl. De Barry ... 1
   Tpr. McWilliam ... 2
   3rd Heat—Tpr. Nicholson ... 1
   Tpr. Madsen ... 2
   Final—Tpr. Madsen ... 1
   Tpr. Nicholson ... 2
   Tpr. De Barry ... 3

4. Tug-of-war:—
   Natal Carbineers ... 1

5. Galloway Race:—
   Tpr. J. Sime's "Joe" ... 3

6. 220 Yards Flat Race, Handicap:—
   Tpr. Madsen ... 1

7. 440 Yards Flat Race:—
   Tpr. De Barry ... 2

8. Tent-pegging in Half Sections:—
   Natal Carbineers ... 3

1903. 10th October, Natal Carbineer Gymkhana.

1. 100 Yards Boys' (under 14) Race:—
   C. Hair ... 1
   H. Kenmuir ... 2

2. 100 Yards Handicap, open to Volunteers and Police:—
   Tpr. A. W. Salter, N.C. ... 1
   Tpr. H. N. Shaw, N.C. ... 2
   Tpr. G. H. Phillips, N.P. ... 3

3. 100 Yards Championship, open to Volunteers & Police:—
   Tpr. J. A. Hathorn, N.C. ... 1
   Tpr. L. J. King, N.C. ... 2

4. 220 Yards Handicap (open):—
   Tpr. A. W. Salter, N.C. ... 1
   J. Flanders ... 2

5. 440 Yards Handicap:—
   J. Flanders ... 1
   Tpr. W. Johnstone, N.P. ... 2

6. Tilting the Ring, open to Volunteers and Police:—
   Sergt. Stevens, N.P. (32 points) ... 1
   Tpr. H. N. Shaw, N.C. (25 points) ... 2
   Capt. Townsend, N.C. (24 points) ... 3

7. Tent-pegging in Sections:—
   Natal Carbineers 1st Team (77 points) ... 1
   Natal Carbineers 2nd Team (66 points) ... 2
   Natal Police Team (42 points) ... 3

8. Victoria Cross Race: —
   Tpr. Catchpole, N.C. ... 1
   Sergt. Stevens, N.P. ... 2

9. Market Race:—
   R.S.M. Burkimsher (lady partner, Miss Burkimsher) ... 1
   Sergt. Todd (lady partner, Miss Clark) ... 2

10. Costume Race:—
    Inspector Dimmick, N.P. ... 1
    R.S.M. Burkimsher ... 2
    For best costumes:—Capt. Townsend, N.C. ... 1
    T. J. Kenmuir ... 2

11. Surprise Competition:—
    B. Troop, Natal Carbineers (2 min. 45 sec.) ... 1
    A. Troop, Natal Carbineers (3 min. 37 sec.) ... 2

12. Bandsman's Race:—
    Sergt. Carbis ... 1
    Bandsman Fairall ... 2

1904. 20th August, Natal Carbineer Gymkhana. At the Agricultural Showground, on Saturday afternoon, the Natal Carbineers held their annual gymkhana sports. An interesting "bill of fare" had been arranged, and the only thing lacking was the support of the public. Considering the absence of counter attractions there was a very small attendance, and the sports were of a character that certainly deserved better patronage. The arrangements were carried out by a good committee, with Capt. A. C. Townsend and S.Q.M.S. Kean as secretary and assistant secretary respectively. The other officials were as follows:—Judges, Col. Leader, Commandant of Militia, Lieut.-Col. McKenzie, C.B., C.M.G., V.D., Lieut.-Col. Weighton, V.D.; Starter, Major Shepstone; Handicappers, three members of the Committee; Committee, Lieut.-Col. Weighton, V.D., Major Hair, V.D., Capt. Owen, Lieut. Barter, Lieut. Allison, Lieut. Langley, Lieut. Stride, R.S.M. Burkimsher, Bandmaster Keilly, Q.M.S. Munro, S.S.M. Todd, Sergts. Pannewitz, Shaw, Tomlinson, and Symes, Tprs. Todd and Symes.

The programme consisted of twelve items, and a large number of competitors figured in each. Considerable variety was introduced into the sports, and competition generally was keen. Both the important foot events, 100 yards and 220 yards handicaps were won by Mr. A. C. Marsh, who received a liberal start. The mounted events attracted considerable interest. In the tilting the ring competition some very keen sport was witnessed, and again in the tent-pegging and jumping events some excellent sport was provided. At intervals during the events mounted men engaged in what was described as the Balaclava Melee. Throughout the afternoon the band of the Regiment played a very pleasant programme in excellent style.

RESULTS.

100 Yards Boys' Race (handicap):—
    F. Burns (7 yards) ... 1
    C. Haslewood (5½ yards) ... 2
    A. E. Kean (5½ yards) ... 3
    Another competitor, R. Johnson, was the second past the tape, but he admitted being over the age limit (12), and was therefore disqualified.

100 Yards Handicap.

  First Heat:—
    Sgt. W. J. Johnstone, N.P. (6 yards) ... 1
    Tpr. L. J. King, N.C. (scratch) ... 2
    Tpr. A. W. Cullingworth, N.C. (6 yards) ... 3

  Second Heat:—
    A. C. Marsh (7 yards) ... 1
    Gunner Spiceley, R.F.A. (4 yards) ... 2
    R. A. King (scratch) ... 3

Final:—
    A. C. Marsh 1
    Sergt. W. J. Johnstone 2
    L. J. King 3

All the heats were well contested, and the final heat was very close, only a couple of inches separating first and second. There was about a yard between second and third.

Tilting the Ring:—
    Capt. Townsend, N.C. 1
    Sergt. Stevens, N.P. 2
    Inspector Dimmick, N.P. 3

There were twenty-six competitors, and there was not much to choose between the prize-winners.

Tent Pegging, in Sections:—
    Natal Carbineers Regimental Team (33 points) 1
    Natal Police Team (22 points) 2

Seven teams competed, including three squadron teams from the Carbineers.

220 Yards (handicap):—
    A. C. Marsh (12 yards) 1
    R. A. King (scratch) 2
    Gunner H. F. Dowling, R.F.A. (7 yards) 3

A large field turned out for this event, and Marsh passed the tape a yard ahead of King, who was two yards in advance of Dowling.

Jumping Competition:—
    Lieut.-Col. Leuchars's (U.M.R.) "Yorkshire Lass" 1
    Sergt. Stevens's (N.P.) "Nongai" 2
    Corpl. Otto's (N.C.) "Bricks" 3

Inspector Dimmick rode the winning horse, which took the hurdles very easily. Sergt. Stevens's horse "Nongai" showed plenty of spirit and jumped prettily.

Spearing the Wily Burman:—
    Sergt. Stevens, N.P. 1
    Corpl. Otto, N.C. 2

Another event which attracted a good many entries. The competitors, mounted, with sword in hand, had to jump over a hurdle and spear a dummy placed against the hurdle on the other side.

Victoria Cross Race:—
  Sergt. Stevens, N.P. ... 1
  Tpr. Leighton, N.P. ... 2

Market Race:—
  Corpl. Stirton, N.C. ... 1
  S.Q.M.S. Kean, N.C. ... 2

  This was an amusing event. Each of the competitors was supplied with a ricksha. They had to stop half-way to pick up a lady passenger, who had first to collect vegetables from a heap on the ground according to a list supplied to her by her "puller." The "boy" first home with his passenger and the vegetables was the winner.

Band Race, 100 yards:—
  Bandsman Bush ... 1
  Bandsman Fairall ... 2

1908. 25th April. N.C. Gymkhana. The N.C. right wing held their annual Gymkhana on the Agricultural Show Ground, P.M. Burg. The officers were "At Home" under a huge marquee, where tea and other refreshments were served. In "Robbery under Arms" the coach was captured, the booty removed, and subsequently the principal bushranger was duly hung and cut down.

1. Spearing the Wily Burman:—
    R.S.M. Burkimsher ... 1
    Lieut. Merrick ... 2
    Major Owen ... 3

2. Donkey Race, bare back (open):—
    Tpr. L. L. Phipson ... 1
    S.Q.M.S. Kean ... 2

3. Jumping Competition, over 2 hurdles, open only to Active Militia and Natal Police:—
    Lieut. Merrick, N.C. ... 1
    Sergt. Stevens, N.P. ... 2
    R.S.M. Burkimsher, N.C. ... 3

4. Bun and Gingerbeer Race, open to boys 14 years of age and under, post entries:—
    Master P. Petersen ... 1
    Master A. G. Bell ... 2

OFFICERS, COLENSO CAMP, 1911.

Top Row—Lt. W. Black, Capt. Cope, Qr.-Master Schuders, Lt. Conrie, Qr.-Master Paton.
Second Row—Lt. Johnson, Lt. Richmond, Lt. Winter, Lt. Paunin, Lt. Zunckel, Capt. Thornhill, Capt. Tanner, Lt. Anderson, Lt. Hosking, Lt. Otto, Capt. Tyler, N.V.D.
Third Row—Capt. Helbert, Lt. Tomlinson, Lt. Johnston, Capt. Walton, Capt. Cumming, N.M.C., Capt. Vanderplank, Lt. Harte, Lt. Smith, Capt. Langley, Capt. Ryley, Lt. Chater.
Sitting—Major Park Gray, Major Blew, C.S.O., Capt. Cole, 7th D.G's., Lt.-Col. Woods, Col. Sir D. McKenzie, Lt.-Col. Mackay, O.C., Major Home, 7th D.G's., Lt.-Col. Burter, Major Montgomery, Major Smith, Capt. Lindsay, Lt. Kemp, Lt. Walsh.

5. Tilting the ring, 2 rings and a peg, 3 runs, open :—
     R.S.M. Burkimsher ... 1
     Major Owen ... 2
     Lieut. Merrick ... 3

6. Tent pegging (sections), 3 runs, open :—
     A. E. Todd's team (Todd, Wiles, Clark, and Armitage) ... 1
     "B" team, N.C. (Kean, Shaw, Ladds, and Robinson) ... 2

7. Band Race. Competitors to walk blind-folded and all to play the same tune :—
     Bandsman Crane ... 1
     Bandsman Stevenson ... 2

8. Victoria Cross Race (open) :—
     Lieut. Merrick ... 1
     Tpr. D. Malcolm ... 2

1909. 27th February. N.C. Gymkhana on the Race Course, P.M. Burg.

1. Trial Stakes, for horses that have never won a race. Distance, 5 furlongs :—
     Corpl. Jackson's "Dodger" (Wynne) ... 1
     Capt. Tanner's "Phyllis Dare" (H. H. Henwood) ... 2
     Tpr. Gresham's "Rainbow" (G. J. Henwood) ... 3

2. Balaclava Melee :—
     A. Squadron No. 1 beat B. Squadron No. 1.
     A. Squadron No. 2 beat B. Squadron No. 2.

3. 1st Scurry Race. Distance, 3 furlongs :—
     Tpr. E. C. Wynne's "Mischief" ... 1
     Major Capstick's (N.R.R.) "Wreck" ... 2
     Corpl. Harman's "Fusilier" ... 3

4. Collar and Tie Race. 50 yards :—
     E. W. Dodds ... 1

5. Militia Hurdle Handicap. Distance $1\frac{1}{2}$ miles :—
     Corpl. Phipson's "Nabob" (Owner) ... 1
     Corpl. Culverwell's "Rewi" (Owner) ... 2
     Sergt. Pottow's "Cymru" (H. A. Smith) ... 3

6. Balaclava Melee:—
   A. Squadron No. 1 beat Natal Police.
   A. Squadron No. 2 beat City Reserves.

7. Section tent pegging. 2 runs:—
   N.C. A. team (44 points) 1
   N.C. B. team (28 points) 2

8. 2nd Scurry Race. Distance, 3 furlongs:—
   Corpl. Phipson's "Nabob" (Owner) 1
   Corpl. Jackson's "Dodger" (Wynne) 2
   Corpl. Culverwell's "Rewi" (Owner) 3

9. Wacht-en-beetje Race. No whips or spurs allowed. Riders to draw lots for horses. Distance, 3 furlongs:—
   Corpl. Ladd's "Fairy" (Kavanagh) 1
   R.S.M. Burkimsher's "Redvers" (Merrick) 2
   Major Owen's "Little Mary" (Armitage) 3
   Last horse, Major Townsend's "Nobby."

July. Military Tournament, held at Lord's Ground, Durban.

> Section Tent Pegging Championship (35 entries)—1st Natal Carbineers. The winning team consisted of Major Owen, Lieut. Merrick, R.S.M. Burkimsher, and S.S.M. Mitchell.
> Victoria Cross Race (79 entries)—2nd, Lieut. Merrick.
> Open Tent Pegging (individual) (128 entries)—4th, R.S.M. Burkimsher.
> Officers' Tent Pegging (individual) (44 entries)—2nd, Major Owen; 4th, Lieut. Merrick.
> Officers' Tent Pegging (section) (7 entries)—1st, Natal Carbineers. The winning team consisted of Majors Owen and Woods, and Lieuts. Johnston and Merrick.
> Officers' Riding and Jumping (32 entries)—5th, Lieut. Merrick.
> Officers' Lemon Cutting (28 entries)—1st, Lieut. Merrick.
> Volunteer Tent Pegging (individual) (77 entries)—5th, Major Owen.

Transvaal Military Tournament held in Johannesburg.
  Officers' Tent Pegging (individual) (58 entries)—1st, Lieut. Merrick.
  Officers' Riding and Jumping (37 entries)—3rd, Lieut. Merrick.
  Officers' Lemon Cutting (35 entries)—4th, Lieut. J. W. Johnston.
  Volunteer Tent Pegging (individual) (50 entries)—1st, Lieut. Merrick; 3rd, S.S.M. Mitchell.
  Volunteer Tent Pegging (sections) (14 entries)—3rd, Natal Carbineers.
  Volunteer Lemon Cutting (36 entries)—1st, S.S.M. Mitchell; 4th, Lieut. Merrick.

1910. 26th February. N.C. Gymkhana on Racecourse, P.M. Burg. "The sports were run off," writes the Times of Natal reporter, "without a hitch, and great credit is due to Captain Helbert and his capable assistants for the manner in which they discharged their duties."

1. Individual Tent-pegging:—
    Lieut. Merrick (30 points) ... 1
    R.S.M. Burkimsher (22 points) ... 2
    Corpl. C. D. Jackson (16 points) ... 3
    Lieut. Johnston (12 points) ... 4

2. Tilting the ring and taking the peg:—
    R.S.M. Burkimsher (19 points) ... 1
    Major Owen (18 points) ... 2
    Corpl. Hosken, N.F.A. (18 points) ... 3
    Lieut. Merrick (15 points) ... 4

3. Trial Stakes, for horses that have never won a race. Distance, 5 furlongs:—
    Tpr. W. R. Grant's "Sefton" ... 1
    R.S.M. Burkimsher's "Dandy" ... 2
    Tpr. W. E. Ford's "Stirabout" ... 3

4. 1st Scurry Race. Distance, 3 furlongs:—
    Bandmaster Keilly's "Prince Arthur" (Hendry) ... 1
    Corpl. Holcomb's "Happy" (Owner) ... 2
    Tpr. Stafford's "Sjambok" (Owner) ... 3

5. Spearing the Wily Burman:—
    Lieut. Merrick (16 points) ... 1
    Lieut. Johnstone (15 points) ... 2
    Tpr. Gibbons (12 points) ... 3
    R.S.M. Burkimsher (12 points) ... 4

6. Carbineer Plate (handicap):—
    Tpr. W. R. Grant's "Sefton" (Bennett) ... 1
    Corpl. L. H. Phipson's "Nabob" (Owner) ... 2
    Sergt. Pottow's "Cymro" (Strafford) ... 3

7. Combined Competition:—
    Tpr. W. G. Gibson (40 points) ... 1
    Leader A. E. Todd, C.R. (32 points) ... 2
    Lieut. Merrick (20 points) ... 3

8. 2nd Tent-pegging:—
    N.C. Headquarters A. team (44 points) ... 1
    N.C. Headquarters B. team (42 points) ... 2

9. 2nd Scurry Race:—
    R.S.M. Burkimsher's "Dandy" (Bennett) ... 1
    Corpl. Culverwell's "Rewi" (Owner) ... 2
    Tpr. W. E. Ford's "Stirabout" (Owner) ... 3

10. Siege Hurdle Handicap. Distance, about $1\frac{1}{2}$ miles:—
    Corpl. Culverwell's "Rewi" (Owner) ... 1
    Sergt. Pottow's "Cymro" (Gibson) ... 2
    Corpl. Phipson's "Nabob" (Owner) ... 3

11. Wacht-en-beetje Race. 3 furlongs:—
    Corpl. Ladd's "Demon" ... 1
    Corpl. Holcomb's "Happy" ... 2
    Tpr. Berry's "Breeches" was last.

APPENDIX 4.—CRICKET.

1865. The first appearance of the regimental eleven in the cricket field was in a match against the Maritzburg Rifles. The Carbineer score was:—

	1st Ings.	2nd Ings.
W. W. Wood (not out, 2nd ings.)	6	54
S. Williams	1	3
A. McLean	6	11
A. Gilson	2	8
H. Hansmeyer	1	13
T. Maxwell	22	0
C. Dacomb	0	1
J. Van Niekerk	1	2
F. Wolhuter	1	0
C. Erskine	3	4
L. Zeederberg	1	0
Extras	7	4
	51	100
Rifles' score	60	63

The return match played shortly afterwards, was also a win for the Carbineers:—

	1st Ings.	2nd Ings.
W. W. Wood	14	4
H. D. Gilson	11	6
J. Van Niekerk	6	0
H. Hansmeyer	2	6
T. Maxwell	0	10
S. Erskine	1	0
C. Erskine	5	6
S. Williams	5	4
H. B. Wallis	5	4
H. F. Buchanan	2	0
F. Wolhuter	0	1
Extras	15	7
	66	48
Rifles	40	66

1872. Carbineers v. The Union Club. N.C. score:—

	1st Ings.	2nd Ings.
Tpr. Gilson	9	0
Tpr. Taylor	14	1
Tpr. Button	2	1
Sergt. Clark	2	12
Corpl. Wood	4	1
Sergt. Finnemore	1	0
Tpr. Berning	8	5
Corpl. Niekerk	2	0
Major Williams	0	6
Tpr. Bond	1	2
Tpr. Bamber	0	2

The Union Club won the match by two wickets.

The return match was also won by the Union Club. N.C. score:—

	1st Ings.	2nd Ings.
Corpl. Wood	1	4
Tpr. Freeman	1	0
Tpr. Button	13	4
Tpr. Bond	0	0
Tpr. Berning	0	1
Capt. Shepstone	3	10
Major Williams	1	0
Tpr. James	0	0
Sergt. Clark	0	6
Tpr. Holliday	0	4
Sergt. Finnemore	0	3

1881. In June a pleasant day was spent at Howick by the members of the regimental cricket eleven in a friendly match against the village team. The following were the scores:—

Sergt. Lunn	18
Tpr. Hawkins	14
Tpr. W. Shepstone	6
Tpr. Tandy	41
Corpl. Edwards	13
Tpr. Napier	2

Lieut. Macfarlane	5
Sergt.-Major Methley	5
Tpr. Greene	5
Byes	21
Total	130
Howick, 1st innings	37
Howick, 2nd innings	47

1882. In a match played against the Civil Service the following scores were made by the Carbineer eleven:—

S.-M. Methley	1
Tpr. Greene	1
Tpr. W. Napier	38
Lieut. Macfarlane	5
Corpl. Edwards	61
Tpr. T. E. Edwards	1
Tpr. D. C. Napier	12
Tpr. Hawkins	9
Tpr. Simpson (did not bat).	
Tmptr. C. Tatham (did not bat).	
Tpr. F. Tatham (did not bat).	
Extras	22
	150
Civil Service	91

The return match ended in a draw.

From about this date the Carbineers ceased to have their own football and cricket teams owing to their recruits, in so many cases, being already members of local athletic clubs.

LIST OF OFFICERS OF THE NATAL CARBINEERS FROM THE INCEPTION OF THE REGIMENT TO 31st DECEMBER, 1911.

1855. TOTAL STRENGTH 77.

Lieut.-Col.: Sir T. St. George, Bart.
Major: W. C. Sargeaunt.
Captains: A. C. Hawkins, P. Allen.
Lieut. and Adjt.: A. B. Allison.
Lieutenants: J. D. Nicholson, O. Wirsing.
Quarter-Master: W. Wood.
Surgeon: P. C. Sutherland, M.D.

1856. TOTAL STRENGTH 75.

Lieut.-Col.: Sir T. St. George, Bart.
Major: W. C. Sargeaunt.
Captains: A. C. Hawkins, P. Allen.
Lieut. and Adjt.: A. B. Allison.
Lieutenants: J. D. Nicholson, O. Wirsing.
Quarter-Master: W. Wood.
Surgeon: P. C. Sutherland, M.D.

1857. TOTAL STRENGTH 73.

Lieut.-Col.: W. C. Sargeaunt.
Major: P. Allen.
Captains: A. C. Hawkins and A. B. Allison.
Lieut. and Adjt.: O. Wirsing.
Lieutenants: J. D. Nicholson and W. Wood.
Qt.-Master: J. Player.
Surgeon: P. C. Sutherland, M.D.

1858. TOTAL STRENGTH 74.

Lieut.-Col.: P. Allen.
Major: A. C. Hawkins.
Captains: A. B. Allison and J. D. Nicholson.

Sergt. W. Barker, *Recommended for Victoria Cross, Zulu War.*

Major Park Gray.

Trooper R. Watts, D.C.M.

Lieut. and Adjt.: O. Wirsing.
Lieutenants: W. Wood and J. M. Cockburn.
Qt.-Master: J. Player.
Surgeon: P. C. Sutherland, M.D.

1859. TOTAL STRENGTH 117.

Lieut.-Col.: P. Allen.
Major: A. C. Hawkins.
Captains: A. B. Allison, J. D. Nicholson, J. Arbuthnot, and W. Proudfoot.
Lieut. and Adjt.: O. Wirsing.
Lieutenants: W. Wood, J. M. Cockburn, R. B. Struthers, and E. Parkinson.
Qt.-Master: J. Player.
Surgeon: P. C. Sutherland, M.D.

1860. TOTAL STRENGTH 117.

Lieut.-Col.: P. Allen.
Major: A. C. Hawkins.
Captains: A. B. Allison, J. D. Nicholson, J. Arbuthnot, and W. Proudfoot.
Lieutenants: W. Wood, J. M. Cockburn, R. B. Struthers, and E. Parkinson.
Lieut. and Adjt.: O. Wirsing.
Qt.-Master: J. Player.
Surgeon: P. C. Sutherland, M.D.

1861. TOTAL STRENGTH 116.

Lieut.-Col.: P. Allen.
Major: A. C. Hawkins.
Captains: A. B. Allison, J. D. Nicholson, W. Proudfoot, and R. B. Struthers.
Lieut. and Adjt.: O. Wirsing.
Lieutenants: W. Wood, E. Parkinson, and C. Dacomb.
Qt.-Master: J. Player.
Surgeon: P. C. Sutherland, M.D.
Asst. Surgeon: J. Armstrong.

1862. TOTAL STRENGTH 115.

Lieut.-Col.: The Hon. D. Erskine.
Major: A. B. Allison.
Captains: J. D. Nicholson, W. Proudfoot, R. B. Struthers, and W. Wood.
Lieut. and Adjt.: S. Williams.
Lieutenants: E. Parkinson, C. Dacomb and H. Pepworth.
Qt.-Master: J. Player.
Surgeon: P. C. Sutherland, M.D.
Chaplain: The Very Revd. J. Green, M.A., Dean.

1863. TOTAL STRENGTH 115.

Lieut.-Col.: The Hon. D. Erskine.
Major: A. B. Allison.
Captains: J. D. Nicholson, W. Proudfoot, R. B. Struthers, and W. Wood.
Lieut. and Adjt.: S. Williams.
Lieutenants: E. Parkinson, C. Dacomb and H. Pepworth.
Qt.-Master: J. Player.
Surgeon: P. C. Sutherland, M.D.
Chaplain: The Very Revd. J. Green, M.A., Dean.

1864. TOTAL STRENGTH 82.

Lieut.-Col.: The Hon. D. Erskine.
Major: A. B. Allison.
Capt. and Adjt.: S. Williams.
Captains: J. D. Nicholson and W. Proudfoot.
Lieutenants: E. Parkinson and H. Pepworth.
Qt.-Master: J. Player.
Surgeon: P. C. Sutherland, M.D.
Chaplain: The Very Revd. J. Green, M.A., Dean.

1865. TOTAL STRENGTH 72.

Lieut.-Col.: The Hon. D. Erskine.
Major: A. B. Allison.
Capt. and Adjt.: S. Williams.
Captain: W. Proudfoot.

Lieutenants: E. Parkinson and H. Pepworth.
Qt.-Master: J. Player.
Chaplain: The Very Revd. J. Green, M.A., Dean.
Surgeon: P. C. Sutherland, M.D.

1866. TOTAL STRENGTH 72.

Lieut.-Col.: The Hon. D. Erskine.
Major: A. B. Allison.
Capt. and Adjt.: S. Williams.
Lieutenants: E. Parkinson and H. Pepworth.
Qt.-Master: J. Player.
Chaplain: The Very Revd. J. Green, M.A., Dean.
Surgeon: P. C. Sutherland, M.D.

1867. TOTAL STRENGTH 75.

Lieut.-Col.: The Hon. D. Erskine.
Major: A. B. Allison.
Capt. and Adjt.: S. Williams.
Captain: C. Barter.
Lieutenants: E. Parkinson, H. Pepworth and R. Lawton.
Qt.-Master: J. Player.
Surgeon: P. C. Sutherland, M.D.
Asst. Surgeon: W. Armstrong.

1868. TOTAL STRENGTH 72.

Lieut.-Col.: The Hon. D. Erskine.
Major: A. B. Allison.
Capt. and Adjt.: S. Williams.
Captain: C. Barter.
Lieutenants: E. Parkinson, H. Pepworth and R. Lawton.
Qt.-Master: J. Player.
Surgeon: P. C. Sutherland, M.D.
Asst. Surgeon: W. Armstrong.

1869. TOTAL STRENGTH 80.

Lieut.-Col.: The Hon. D. Erskine.
Major: A. B. Allison.

Capt. and Adjt.: S. Williams.
Captain: C. Barter.
Lieutenants: E. Parkinson and R. Lawton.
Qt.-Master: J. Player.
Surgeon: P. C. Sutherland, M.D.
Asst. Surgeon: W. Armstrong.

1870. TOTAL STRENGTH 89.

Lieut.-Col.: The Hon. D. Erskine.
Major: S. Williams.
Captain: C. Barter.
Lieut. and Adjt.: R. Lawton.
Lieutenants: E. Parkinson and T. Shepstone, Jr.
Qt.-Master: J. Player.
Surgeon: P. C. Sutherland, M.D.
Asst. Surgeon: W. Armstrong.

1871. TOTAL STRENGTH 77.

Lieut.-Col.: The Hon. D. Erskine.
Major: S. Williams.
Captains: C. Barter and T. Shepstone, Jr.
Lieutenant: E. Parkinson.
Qt.-Master: J. Player.
Surgeon: P. C. Sutherland, M.D.
Asst. Surgeon: W. Armstrong.

1872. TOTAL STRENGTH 51.

Captain: T. Shepstone, Jr.
Qr.-Master: L. A. van Niekerk.
Surgeon: P. C. Sutherland, M.D.

1873. TOTAL STRENGTH 49.

Captain: T. Shepstone, Jr.
Lieutenant: C. A. Woodroffe.
Qr.-Master: L. A. van Niekerk.
Surgeon: P. C. Sutherland, M.D.

1874. TOTAL STRENGTH 23.

Captain: T. Shepstone, Jr.
Qr.-Master: L. A. van Niekerk.
Surgeon: P. C. Sutherland, M.D.

1875. TOTAL STRENGTH 36.

Captain: T. Shepstone, Jr.
Lieutenants: J. W. Taylor and A. Moodie.
Surgeon: P. C. Sutherland, M.D.

1876. TOTAL STRENGTH 28.

Captain: T. Shepstone, Jr.
Lieutenants: J. W. Taylor and A. Moodie.
Qr.-Master: George James.
Surgeon: P. C. Sutherland, M.D.

1877. TOTAL STRENGTH 32.

Captain: T. Shepstone, Jr.
Lieutenant: A. Moodie.
Qr.-Master: F. J. D. Scott.
Surgeon: P. C. Sutherland, M.D.

1878. TOTAL STRENGTH 59.

Captain: T. Shepstone, Jr.
Lieutenants: W. Royston and F. J. D. Scott.
Qr.-Master: W. London.

1879. TOTAL STRENGTH 30.

Captain: T. Shepstone, Jr.
Lieutenant: W. Royston.

1880. TOTAL STRENGTH 43.

Captain: T. Shepstone, Jr., C.M.G.
Lieutenants: W. Royston and G. J. Macfarlane.

1881. TOTAL STRENGTH 46.

Lieutenant: W. Royston.
Lieut. and Adjt.: G. J. Macfarlane.

1882. TOTAL STRENGTH 63.

Captain: W. Royston.
Lieut. and Adjt.: G. J. Macfarlane.

1883. TOTAL STRENGTH 77.

Captain: W. Royston.
Lieut. and Adjt.: G. J. Macfarlane.
Lieutenant: E. M. Greene.
Qr.-Master: D. C. Slatter.

1884. TOTAL STRENGTH 93.

Captain: W. Royston.
Lieut. and Adjt.: G. J. Macfarlane.
Lieutenant: E. M. Greene.
Qr.-Master: D. C. Slatter.

1885. TOTAL STRENGTH 116.

Captains: W. Royston and E. M. Greene.
Lieut. and Adjt.: G. J. Macfarlane.
Lieutenants: W. W. Barker, C. B. Addison and D. McKenzie.
Qr.-Master: J. Weighton.

1886. TOTAL STRENGTH 218.

Major: W. Royston.
Captain: E. M. Greene.
Capt. and Adjt.: G. J. Macfarlane.
Lieutenants: W. W. Barker, C. B. Addison, D. McKenzie, G. Ross, J. Weighton, W. M. Henderson, W. S. Shepstone, C. E. Taunton, P. S. Flack, and J. W. Harvey.
Qr.-Master: W. S. Hicks.
Surgeon: J. Hyslop.

1887. TOTAL STRENGTH 283.

Major: W. Royston.
Captain: E. M. Greene.
Capt. and Adjt.: G. J. Macfarlane.
Lieutenants: C. B. Addison, D. McKenzie, G. Ross, J. Weighton, W. S. Shepstone, C. E. Taunton, P. S. Flack, J. W. Harvey, and F. S. Tatham.
Qr.-Master: W. S. Hicks.
Surgeon: J. Hyslop.

1888. TOTAL STRENGTH 393.

Lieut.-Col.: W. Royston.
Majors: T. Menne, E. M. Greene.
Captains: G. J. Macfarlane (Adjt.), C. B. Addison, H. Von Bulow, G. Ross, C. E. Taunton, D. McKenzie.
Lieutenants: J. Weighton, W. S. Shepstone, F. S. Tatham, J. J. Tissimann, W. G. M. Sinclair, J. Ross, C. B. Cooke, C. G. Willson.
Surgeons: D. Birtwell, J. Hyslop.
Quartermasters: T. Smith, W. S. Hicks.
This year the Natal Hussars joined the Natal Carbineers, forming the Left Wing.

1889. TOTAL STRENGTH 376.

Majors: T. Menne, E. M. Greene.
Captains: G. J. Macfarlane, C. B. Addison, H. Von Bulow, G. Ross, C. E. Taunton, D. McKenzie, J. Weighton (Adjt.), W. S. Shepstone.

Lieutenants: F. S. Tatham, J. J. Tissimann, C. B. Cooke, C. G. Willson, A. Hair, W. L. Whittaker, F. E. Foxon, W. A. Tilney, C. Holmes, H. Ehlers, C. Tatham, G. F. Tatham, W. G. M. Sinclair.
Surgeons: D. Birtwell, J. Hyslop.
Quartermaster: A. Lyle.

1890. TOTAL STRENGTH 371.

Majors: T. Menne, E. M. Greene.
Captains: G. J. Macfarlane, C. B. Addison, H. Von Bulow, G. Ross, C. E. Taunton, D. McKenzie, J. Weighton (Adjt.), W. S. Shepstone.
Lieutenants: F. S. Tatham, J. J. Tissimann, C. B. Cooke, C. G. Willson, A. Hair, W. L. Whittaker, F. E. Foxon, W. A. Tilney, C. Holmes, H. Ehlers, C. Tatham, G. F. Tatham, W. G. M. Sinclair, W. A. Vanderplank.
Surgeon: J. Hyslop.
Quartermaster: A. Lyle.

1891. TOTAL STRENGTH 519.

Lieut.-Col.: E. M. Greene.
Majors: T. Menne, G. J. Macfarlane.
Captains: C. B. Addison, H. Von Bulow, G. Ross, C. E. Taunton, D. McKenzie, J. Weighton (Adjt.), W. S. Shepstone, F. S. Tatham, J. J. Tissimann.
Lieutenants: C. B. Cooke, C. G. Willson, A. Hair, F. E. Foxon, W. A. Tilney, H. Ehlers, C. Tatham, G. F. Tatham, W. G. M. Sinclair, W. A. Vanderplank, J. A. Nel, J. McKenzie, D. Timm, C. A. Martin.
Surgeon: J. Hyslop.
Quartermaster: A. Lyle.

1892. TOTAL STRENGTH 429.

Lieut.-Col.: E. M. Greene.
Major: G. J. Macfarlane.

COLENSO CAMP, 1911.

Back Row—Sergt. Farmer, Sergt. Ross, Sergt. Jackson, Sergt. Davis, S.-S.-M. Wright, Sergt. Todd, Sergt. Mitchell, Sergt. Dicks, Sergt. King.
Second Row—Sergt. Grant, Sergt. Robinson, Sergt. Buxton, Sergt. Peters, Sergt. Nicolson, Sergt. Wright, Sergt. Dicks, Sergt. Nelson, Sergt. Gage, Sergt. Holcomb, Sergt. Campbell.
Third Row—Sergt. Phipson, Sergt. Culverwell, O.-R.-Sergt. Watts, S.-Q.-M.-S. McLean, S.-Q.-M.-S. Garbutt, S.-Q.-M.-S. Bristo, S.-Q.-M.-S. Bennett, Sergt. Campbell Sergt. Hayes, Sergt. Walters, Sergt. Mulcahy, Sergt. Wysall, S.-Q.-M.-S. Forsyth.
Fourth Row—O.-R.-S. Anderson, S.-S.-M. Harding, S.-S.-M. McCathie, S.-S.-M. Madsen, R.-S.-M. Stratton (The Carabiniers), Lt.-Col. Mackay, O.C., R.-S.-M. Burkimsher, Capt. Heilbert, Sergt. Mitchell, S.-S.-M. Warwick, S.-Q.-M.-S. Kean, S.-S.-M. Wray.
Front Row—Sergt. Stead, Q.-M.-S. Dunn S.-S.-M. Anderson Sergt. Teasdale Sergt. Malcolm Sergt. Pottow Sergt. Gilbert Sergt. Houshold.

Captains: C. B. Addison, G. Ross, C. E. Taunton, D. McKenzie, J. Weighton (Adjt.), W. S. Shepstone, F. S. Tatham.
Lieutenants: C. G. Willson, A. Hair, F. E. Foxon, W. A. Tilney, G. F. Tatham, W. G. M. Sinclair, W. A. Vanderplank, J. McKenzie, C. A. Martin.
Surgeons: J. Hyslop, G. C. Henderson.
Quartermaster: A. Lyle.

1893. TOTAL STRENGTH 421.

Lieut.-Col.: E. M. Greene.
Majors: G. J. Macfarlane, C. B. Addison.
Captains: G. Ross, C. E. Taunton, D. McKenzie, J. Weighton (Adjt.), W. S. Shepstone, F. S. Tatham.
Lieutenants: C. G. Willson, A. Hair, F. E. Foxon, G. F. Tatham, W. G. M. Sinclair, W. A. Vanderplank, J. McKenzie, C. A. Martin, P. D. Simmons, A. B. Wylde-Browne, W. J. Gallwey, H. C. Langley, B. Crompton.
Surgeons: J. Hyslop, G. C. Henderson.
Quartermaster: A. Lyle.

1894. TOTAL STRENGTH 434.

Lieut.-Col.: E. M. Greene.
Majors: G. J. Macfarlane, C. B. Addison.
Captains: G. Ross, C. E. Taunton, D. McKenzie, J. Weighton (Adjt.), W. S. Shepstone, F. S. Tatham.
Lieutenants: C. G. Willson, A. Hair, F. E. Foxon, G. F. Tatham, W. A. Vanderplank, C. A. Martin, P. D. Simmons, A. B. Wylde-Browne, W. J. Gallwey, H. C. Langley, B. Crompton.
Surgeon: J. Hyslop.
Quartermaster: A. Lyle.

1895. TOTAL STRENGTH 364.

Lieut.-Col.: E. M. Greene.
Major: G. J. Macfarlane.
Captains: G. Ross, C. E. Taunton, D. McKenzie, J. Weighton (Adjt.), W. S. Shepstone, C. G. Willson.

Lieutenants: A. Hair, F. E. Foxon, G. F. Tatham, W. A. Vanderplank, A. B. Wylde-Browne, W. J. Gallwey, B. Crompton, E. Lucas, W. L. Methley, R. H. Ralfe.
Surgeons: J. Hyslop, O. J. Currie.
Quartermaster: A. Lyle.

1896. TOTAL STRENGTH 342.

Lieut.-Col.: E. M. Greene.
Majors: G. Ross, C. E. Taunton.
Captains: D. McKenize, J. Weighton (Adjt.), W. S. Shepstone, C. G. Willson.
Lieutenants: A. Hair, F. E. Foxon, G. F. Tatham, W. A. Vanderplank, W. J. Gallwey, B. Crompton, E. Lucas, W. L. Methley, R. H. Ralfe, G. W. Nourse-Varty, C. N. H. Rodwell, T. R. Bennett.
Surgeons: J. Hyslop, O. J. Currie.
Quartermaster: A Lyle (Hon. Captain).

1897. TOTAL STRENGTH 329.

Lieut.-Col.: E. M. Greene.
Majors: C. E. Taunton, D. McKenzie.
Captains: J. Weighton (Adjt.), W. S. Shepstone, C. G. Willson, A. Hair, F. E. Foxon.
Lieutenants: G. F. Tatham, W. J. Gallwey, B. Crompton, E. Lucas, G. W. Nourse-Varty, C. N. H. Rodwell.
Surgeons: Capt. J. Hyslop, Lieuts. O. J. Currie, G. K. Moberley.
Quartermaster: A. Lyle (Hon. Captain).

1898. TOTAL STRENGTH 390.

Lieut.-Col.: E. M. Greene.
Majors: C. E. Taunton, D. McKenzie.
Captains: J. Weighton (Adjt.), W. S. Shepstone, C. G. Willson, A. Hair, F. E. Foxon.
Lieutenants: G. F. Tatham, W. J. Gallwey, B. Crompton, E. Lucas, G. W. Nourse-Varty, C. N. H. Rodwell, W. Comrie.
Surgeons: Captain J. Hyslop, Lieutenants O. J. Currie, G. K. Moberley.
Quartermaster: A. Lyle (Hon. Capt.'

1899. TOTAL STRENGTH 517.

Lieut.-Col.: E. M. Greene.
Majors: D. McKenzie, *G. J. Macfarlane, *C. B. Addison, J. Weighton (Adjt.).
Captains: W. S. Shepstone, F. S. Tatham, A. Hair, F. E. Foxon.
Lieutenants: G. F. Tatham, W. J. Gallwey, B. Crompton, G. W. Nourse-Varty, C. N. H. Rodwell, W. Comrie, D. Sparks, D. W. Mackay, W. A. Bartholomew, W. T. Gage, A. C. Townsend, W. E. C. Tanner, W. A. Vanderplank, A. B. Wylde-Browne, A. W. Smallie, T. M. Owen, R. Ashburnham.
Surgeons: Major J. Hyslop, Captain O. J. Currie.
Quartermaster: A. Lyle (Hon. Capt.).
*Rejoined Active List on mobilization for Boer War.

1900. TOTAL STRENGTH 428.

Lieut.-Col.: E. M. Greene (Hon. Colonel in Army).
Majors: D. McKenzie, C.M.G. (Hon. Lieut.-Col.), G. J. Macfarlane (Hon. Lieut.-Col.), C. B. Addison (Hon. Lieut.-Col.), J. Weighton (Hon. Lieut.-Col.).
Captains: W. S. Shepstone (Hon. Major), F. S. Tatham (Hon. Major), A. Hair, F. E. Foxon, G. F. Tatham (Hon. Major), B. Crompton, G. W. Nourse, C. N. H. Rodwell (Adjt.).
Lieutenants: W. J. Gallwey, W. Comrie, D. Sparks, D. W. Mackay, W. A. Bartholomew, W. T. Gage, A. C. Townsend, W. E. C. Tanner, W. A. Vanderplank, A. W. Smallie, T. M. Owen, J. P. S. Woods, T. Duff, R. A. Cockburn, E. W. Barter, J. W. V. Montgomery.
Quartermaster: A. Lyle (Hon. Capt.).

1901. TOTAL STRENGTH 418.

Lieut.-Col.: E. M. Greene (Hon. Col. in Army).
Majors: D. McKenzie, C.M.G. (Hon. Lieut.-Col.), J. Weighton (Hon. Lieut.-Col.).
Captains: W. S. Shepstone (Hon. Major), A. Hair, F. E. Foxon, G. F. Tatham (Hon. Major), B. Crompton, G. W. Nourse, C. N. H. Rodwell (Adjt.).

Lieutenants: W. J. Gallwey, W. Comrie, D. Sparks, D. W. Mackay, W. A. Bartholomew, W. T. Gage, A. C. Townsend, W. E. C. Tanner, W. A. Vanderplank, A. W. Smallie, T. M. Owen, J. P. S. Woods, T. Duff, R. A. Cockburn, E. W. Barter, J. W. V. Montgomery.

Quartermaster: A. Lyle (Hon. Capt.).

1902. TOTAL STRENGTH 426.

Lieut.-Col.: E. M. Greene (Hon. Col. in Army).

Majors: D. McKenzie, C. B., C.M.G. (Hon. Lieut.-Col.), J. Weighton (Hon. Lieut.-Col.), G. J. Macfarlane, C.M.G. (Hon. Lieut.-Col.).

Captains: W. S. Shepstone (Hon. Major), A. Hair, F. E. Foxon, G. F. Tatham (Hon. Major), B. Crompton, D.S.O., G. W. Nourse, C. N. H. Rodwell (Adjt.).

Lieutenants: W. J. Gallwey, W. Comrie, D. W. Mackay, W. A. Bartholomew, W. T. Gage, A. C. Townsend, W. E. C. Tanner, W. A. Vanderplank, A. W. Smallie, T. M. Owen, J. P. S. Woods, R. A. Cockburn, E. W. Barter, J. W. V. Montgomery.

Quartermaster: A. Lyle (Hon. Capt.).

1903. TOTAL STRENGTH 727.

Lieut.-Col.: D. McKenzie, C.B., C.M.G., V.D.

Majors: J. Weighton (Hon. Lieut.-Col.)., W. S. Shepstone.

Captains: A. Hair, F. E. Foxon, G. F. Tatham (Hon. Major), B. Crompton, D.S.O., C. N. H. Rodwell (Adjt.), W. Comrie, D. W. Mackay, W. T. Gage, A. C. Townsend, W. A. Vanderplank.

Lieutenants: W. J. Gallwey, A. W. Smallie, T. M. Owen, J. P. S. Woods, R. A. Cockburn, E. W. Barter, J. W. V. Montgomery, J. E. Briscoe, R. A. L. Brandon, W. H. Tatham, G. L. Fraser, A. B. Vanderplank, F. G. Holmes, R. W. Smith, R. A. Lindsay, T. J. Allison, W. P. Gray, B. W. Martin, W. H. Home, R. M. Tanner.

Quartermaster: A. Lyle (Hon. Capt.).

1904. TOTAL STRENGTH 719.

Lieut.-Col.: D. McKenzie, C.B., C.M.G., V.D.

Majors: J. Weighton, V.D. (Hon. Lieut.-Col.), W. S. Shepstone, A. Hair, F. E. Foxon, G. F. Tatham.

Captains: B. Crompton, D.S.O., C. N. H. Rodwell (Adjt.), W. Comrie, D. W. Mackay, W. T. Gage, A. C. Townsend, A. W. Smallie, T. M. Owen, J. P. S. Woods, R. A. Cockburn, E. W. Barter, J. W. V. Montgomery.

Lieutenants: J. E. Briscoe, R. A. L. Brandon, W. H. Tatham, A. B. Vanderplank, F. G. Holmes, R. W. Smith, R. A. Lindsay, T. J. Allison, W. P. Gray, B. W. Martin, W. H. Home, R. M. Tanner, W. Black, E. G. Clerk, W. E. Antel, P. W. Stride, C. M. Paterson, A. S. Langley, G. R. Richards, F. H. Stiebel, H. Ryley.

Quartermaster: A. Lyle (Hon. Capt.).

1905. TOTAL STRENGTH 686.

Lieut.-Col.: D. McKenzie, C.B., C.M.G., V.D.

Majors: J. Weighton, V.D. (Brev. Lt.-Col.), W. S. Shepstone (Brev. Lt.-Col.), A. Hair (Brev. Lt.-Col.), F. E. Foxon, V.D., G. F. Tatham (Hon. Lieut.-Col.), B. Crompton, D.S.O. (Brevet Lieut.-Col.), C. N. H. Rodwell (Adjt.), D. W. Mackay (Brevet Lieut.-Col.).

Captains: W. T. Gage (Brevet Major), A. C. Townsend, A. W. Smallie, T. M. Owen, J. P. S. Woods, E. W. Barter, J. W. V. Montgomery, T. J. Allison.

Lieutenants: J. E. Briscoe, R. A. L. Brandon, A. B. Vanderplank, R. W. Smith, R. A. Lindsay, W. P. Gray, B. W. Martin, W. H. Home, R. M. Tanner, W. Black, W. E. Antel, P. W. Stride, C. M. Paterson, A. S. Langley, G. R. Richards, F. H. Stiebel, H. Ryley, H. C. Thornhill, J. G. Fannin, C. F. J. Cope, B. A. Hampson, G. E. Blaker, C. G. Kemp, J. W. Johnston.

Quartermaster: A. Lyle (Hon. Capt.).

1906. TOTAL STRENGTH 664.

Honorary Colonel: General Viscount Kitchener of Khartoum, G.C.B., O.M., G.C.M.G.
Lieut.-Col.: D. McKenzie, C.B., C.M.G., V.D.
Majors: J. Weighton, V.D. (Brevet Lieut.-Col.), C. N. H. Rodwell (Adjt.), D. W. Mackay (Brevet Lieut.-Col.), A. C. Townsend, A. W. Smallie, T. M. Owen.
Captains: J. P. S. Woods, E. W. Barter, J. W. V. Montgomery, R. A. L. Brandon, W. P. Gray, J. E. Briscoe, R. W. Smith, R. M. Tanner, G. R. Richards, A. B. Vanderplank.
Lieutenants: R. A. Lindsay, B. W. Martin, W. H. Home, W. Black, P. W. Stride, C. M. Paterson, A. S. Langley, H Ryley, H. C. Thornhill, J. G. Fannin, C. F. J. Cope, B. A. Hampson, G. E. Blaker, C. G. Kemp, J. W. Johnston, P. G. Dickinson, E. J. B. Hosking, J. O. Smythe, E. W. Baxter, J. H. Smith, H. Walton, S. R. Merrick, J. D. Walsh.
Quartermasters: J. McKenzie (Hon. Lieut.), R. A Richmond (Hon. Lieut.).

1907. TOTAL STRENGTH 475.

Honorary Colonel: General Viscount Kitchener of Khartoum, G.C.B., O.M., G.C.M.G.
Lieut.-Col.: J. Weighton, V.D.
Majors: C. N. H. Rodwell (Brevet Lieut.-Col.), D. W. Mackay (Brevet Lieut.-Col.), A. C. Townsend, T. M. Owen (seconded), J. P. S. Woods, E. W. Barter.
Captains: J. W. V. Montgomery, W. P. Gray, R. W. Smith, R. M. Tanner, G. R. Richards, A. B. Vanderplank, P. W. Stride.
Lieutenants: R. A. Lindsay, B. W. Martin, W. Black, C. M. Paterson (seconded), A. S. Langley (Local Capt.), H. Ryley, H. C. Thornhill, J. G. Fannin, C. F. J. Cope, G. E. Blaker, C. G. Kemp, J. W. Johnston, P. G. Dickinson, J. O. Smythe, E. W. Baxter, J. H. Smith, H. Walton, S. R. Merrick, J. D. Walsh, G. H. Helbert (Adjt., Local Capt.), A. Praetorious, R. A. Richmond, E. C. Hosking, H. Hathorn, G. C. Anderson, A. B. Chater, E. C. Zunckel, J. McKenzie, R. J. R. Hearn.
Quartermasters: D. Paton (Hon. Lieut.), D. G. Sclanders (Hon. Lieut.).

1908. TOTAL STRENGTH 422.

Honorary Colonel: General Viscount Kitchener of Khartoum, G.C.B., O.M., G.C.M.G.

Lieut.-Col.: J. Weighton, V.D.

Majors: C. N. H. Rodwell (Brevet Lieut.-Col.), D. W. Mackay (Brevet Lieut.-Col.), T. M. Owen (seconded), J. P. S. Woods, E. W. Barter, J. W. V. Montgomery, W. P. Gray.

Captains: R. W. Smith, R. M. Tanner, G. R. Richards, A. B. Vanderplank, G. H. Helbert (Adjt.).

Lieutenants: R. A. Lindsay, B. W. Martin, W. Black, C. M. Paterson (seconded), A. S. Langley (Local Capt.), H. Ryley, H. C. Thornhill, J. G. Fannin, C. F. J. Cope, G. E. Blaker, C. G. Kemp, J. W. Johnston, E. W. Baxter, J. H. Smith, H. Walton (Local Capt.), S. R. Merrick, J. D. Walsh, A. Praetorious, E. C. Hosking, H. Hathorn, G. C. Anderson, A. B. Chater, E. C. Zunckel, J. McKenzie, R. J. R. Hearn, A. P. Craw.

Quartermasters: D. Paton (Hon. Lieut.), D. G. Sclanders (Hon. Lieut.).

1909. TOTAL STRENGTH 440.

Honorary Colonel: Field Marshal Viscount Kitchener of Khartoum, G.C.B., O.M., G.C.M.G., G.C.I.E.

Lieut.-Col.: J. Weighton, V.D.

Majors: D. W. Mackay (Brevet Lieut.-Col.), T. M. Owen (seconded), J. P. S. Woods, E. W. Barter, J. W. V. Montgomery, W. P. Gray.

Captains: R. W. Smith, R. M. Tanner, G. R. Richards, A. B. Vanderplank, G. H. Helbert (Adjt.), R. A. Lindsay, B. W. Martin, H. Ryley.

Lieutenants: W. Black, C. M. Paterson (seconded), A. S. Langley (Local Capt.), H. C. Thornhill, J. G. Fannin, C. F. J. Cope, G. E. Blaker, C. G. Kemp, J. W. Johnston, J. H. Smith, H. Walton (Local Capt.), S. R. Merrick, J. D. Walsh, A. Praetorious, E. C. Hosking, H. Hathorn, G. C. Anderson, A. B. Chater, E. C. Zunckel, J. McKenzie, R. J. R. Hearn, A. P. Craw, R. A. Richmond.

Quartermasters: D. Paton (Hon. Lieut.), D. G. Sclanders (Hon. Lieut.), L. C. Tennent (Hon. Lieut.).

1910. TOTAL STRENGTH 506.

Honorary Colonel: Field Marshal Viscount Kitchener of Khartoum, G.C.B., O.M., G.C.M.G., G.C.I.E.

Lieut.-Col.: J. Weighton, V.D.

Majors: D. W. Mackay (Brevet Lieut.-Col.), T. M. Owen (seconded), J. P. S. Woods, E. W. Barter, J. W. V. Montgomery, W. P. Gray, R. W. Smith.

Captains: R. M. Tanner, G. R. Richards, A. B. Vanderplank, G. H. Helbert (Adjt), R. A. Lindsay, B. W. Martin, H. Ryley, A. S. Langley, H. C. Thornhill, C. F. J. Cope, C. M. Paterson.

Lieutenants: W. Black, J. G. Fannin, G. E. Blaker, C. G. Kemp, J. W. Johnston, J. H. Smith, H. Walton (Local Capt.), S. R. Merrick, J. D. Walsh, E. C. Hosking, G. C. Anderson, A. B. Chater, E. C. Zunckel, J. McKenzie, R. J. R. Hearn, A. P. Craw, R. A. Richmond, C. S. D. Otto, A. H. Winter, W. H. F. Harte, R. Tomlinson, J. M. Comrie.

Quartermasters: D. Paton (Hon. Lieut.), D. G. Sclanders (Hon. Lieut.), L. C. Tennent (Hon. Lieut.).

1911. TOTAL STRENGTH 531.

Honorary Colonel: Field Marshal Viscount Kitchener of Khartoum, G.C.B., O.M., G.C.M.G., G.C.I.E.

Lieut.-Col.: D. W. Mackay.

Majors: J. P. S. Woods (Brevet Lieut.-Col.), E. W. Barter (Brevet Lieut.-Col.), T. M. Owen, W. P. Gray, R. M. Tanner, G. R. Richards, A. B. Vanderplank, G. H. Helbert (Regimental Adjutant).

Captains: A. S. Langley (Adjt., Right Wing), H. Walton (Adjt., Left Wing), R. A. Lindsay, B. W. Martin, H. Ryley, C. F. J. Cope, H. C. Thornhill, C. M. Paterson.

Lieutenants: W. Black, J. G. Fannin, J. W. Johnston, C. G. Kemp, J. H. Smith, S. R. Merrick, J. D. Walsh, E. C. Hosking, G. C. Anderson, A. B. Chater, E. C. Zunckel, R. J. R. Hearn, J. McKenzie, A. P. Craw, R. A. Richmond, C. S. D. Otto, A. H. Winter, W. H. F. Harte, J. M. Comrie, R. Tomlinson, A. L. Johnson, H. P. Walker, F. T. H. Fell, P. I. Davis.

Quartermasters: D. Paton (Hon. Lieut.), D. G. Sclanders (Hon. Lieut.), L. C. Tennent (Hon. Lieut.).

Lieut. PETE OTTO.
Karkloof Troop, 1873.

MUSTER ROLL OF THE NATAL CARBINEERS.
BOER WAR 1899-1902.

Strength of Regiment on mobilization, 508, and on being released from Active Service, 530.

OFFICERS.

Lieut.-Col. E. M. Greene, L
Major D. McKenzie, R
Major C. E. Taunton, L, K
Major & Adjt. J. Weighton, L
Major G. J. Macfarlane, L
Major C. B. Addison, L
Capt. W. S. Shepstone, L
Capt. C. G. Willson, L
Capt. and Q.-M. A. Lyle, L
Capt. F. E. Foxon, L, W
Capt. A. Hair, L
Capt. B. Crompton, L
Capt. E. Lucas, L, D
Capt. G. W. Nourse-Varty, L
Capt. C. N. H. Rodwell, L
Capt. G. F. Tatham, L
Lieut. W. A. Vanderplank, L
Lieut. W. J. Gallwey, P
Lieut. W. Comrie, L
Lieut. D. Sparks, L
Lieut. D. W. Mackay, R, W
Lieut. W. A. Bartholomew, L
Lieut. W. T. Gage, L
Lieut. A. C. Townsend, L
Lieut. W. E. C. Tanner, L
Lieut. A. W. Smallie, L
Lieut. T. M. Owen, Depot.
Lieut. R. Ashburnham, R
Lieut. J. P. S. Woods, R
Lieut. T. Duff, L
Lieut. A. Wylde Browne, SS, D
Lieut. R. A. C. Cockburn, L
Vet.-Lieut. F. A. Verney, SS, R

NON-COMMISSIONED OFFICERS.

R.S.M. W. Burkimsher, R
R.S.M. B. M. Bowen, L, D
Bandmaster J. Keilly, L
Q.-M.-Sergt. W. Munro, L
O.-R.-S. P. W. Stride, L
S.-M.-Tailor W. Walters, Depot
Saddler-Sergt. T. W. Lyle, L
Far.-Sergt. J. Matraves, L
Far.-Sergt. F. Pain, L
Sergt.-Tptr. E. J. Lawrance, R
Sergt.-Cook A. Ashdown, L
S.-S.-Mjr. E. W. Barter, L
S.-S.-Mjr. B. Buchanan, L
S.-S.-Mjr. P. J. C. Deglon, L
S.-S.-Mjr J. W. Johnston, L
S.-S.-Mjr. J. Mapstone, L
S.-S.-Mjr. T. Mitchell, L
T.-S.-Mjr. A. Sclanders, R
S.-S.-Mjr. A. B. Vanderplank, L
S.-S.-Mjr. J. W. Tranmer, R
T.-S.-Mjr. H. C. Fitzgerald, R
S.-S.-Mjr. J. W. V. Montgomery, L
S.-Q.-M.-S. T. Castle, L
S.-Q.-M.-S. T. W. C. Evans, R
S.-Q.-M.-S. J. Hackland, L
S.-Q.-M.-S. R. F. Harte, L
S.-Q.-M.-S. G. Jackson, L
Sergt. J. W. Armitage, L
Sergt. R. Carbis, L
Sergt. A. E. Colville, L, K
Sergt. R. Comins, L

Sergt. J. W. Durham, L
Sergt. H. J. Harkness, L
Sergt. F. G. Holmes, L
Sergt. J. A. McCullough, L
Sergt. F. G. Mapstone, L, W, D
Sergt. W. J. Osborne, L
Sergt. C. McD Paterson, L
Sergt. H. Schwegmann, L
Sergt. S. M. Shaw, L
Sergt. R. W. Smith, L
Sergt. P. J. Stevens, R, W
Sergt. W. P. Stevens, R
Sergt. A. Swan, L
Sergt. A. E. Todd, L
Sergt. F. J. C. Topham, L
Sergt. H. Wilkinson, L
Corpl. J. L. Armitage, L
Corpl. R. C. Boyd, L
Corpl. C. A. Carbutt, L
Corpl. D. M. Craig, L
Corpl. J. Dicks, L
Corpl. T. Ellerker, L
Corpl. J. R. Fayers, L

Corpl. W. P. Gray, R
Corpl. A. T. Hackland, L
Corpl. R. W. Hall, R
Corpl. R. Hesom, L
Corpl. J. H. Holley, L, W
Corpl. C. Holmes, SS, R
Corpl. W. H. Home, L
Corpl. W. A. Lang, L
Corpl. T. McCathie, L
Corpl. J. McCullough, L
Corpl. W. McCullough, L, W
Corpl. H. K. McDowell, L
Corpl. J. McKenzie, L
Corpl. H. McLean, L
Corpl. J. A. Mason, L
Corpl. E. Reed, R
Corpl. R. A. Richmond, R, W
Corpl. H. Smith, L
Corpl. W. H. Sanders, L
Corpl. A. Tanner, L
Corpl. J. Watson, L
Corpl.-Tptr. O. E. Dick, L

MEN.

Tmptr. A. Denness, L
Tmptr. T. P. Egner, L
Tmptr. W. E. Fyfe, SS
Tmptr. J. A. Keith, L
Tmptr. J. H. Mellis, L
Tpr. A. H. Abel, SS, L
Tpr. C. W. Abel, L
Tpr. E. P. Adams, SS
Tpr. H. A. Adams, SS
Tpr. W. T. Adams, SS, R
Tpr. P. Adie, SS, R, K
Tpr. J. Agnew, SS, R, W
Tpr. H. F. Albers, L
Tpr. F. Allerston, L
Tpr. A. F. Anders, L
Tpr. J. M. Anderson, SS
Tpr. W. Anderson, SS, L, W
Tpr. W. N. Angus, SS, R

Tpr. R. J. M. Antel, L
Tpr. W. E. Antel, L
Tpr. E. S. Archer, L
Tpr. A. W. Arnold, L
Tpr. E. J. W. Ashe, L
Tpr. J. W. Aston, SS
Tpr. W. Bailey, SS, L
Tpr. W. J. Baillie, SS
Tpr. R. Baines, SS, L
Tpr. T. P. Bale, SS, D
Tpr. P. Ballantyne, R, W
Tpr. H. M. Ballenden, L
Tpr. C. Banfield, SS
Tpr. A. H. Banwell, SS
Tpr. C. Barnett, L
Tpr. T. Barnett, L
Tpr. T. Barron, R
Tpr. J. Bassage, L

Tpr. J. J. Bassage, L
Tpr. W. F. Bassage, L, D
Tpr. T. Baum, ss
Tpr. G. F. Bennett, L
Tpr. H. Benson, L
Tpr. W. S. Bigby, ss, L
Tpr. J. L. Birkett, L, D
Tpr. H. G. Bizley, ss
Tpr. H. Blaikie, R, P
Tpr. G. R. Blaine, ss
Tpr. G. E. Blaker, L
Tpr. J. W. Bonifant, L
Tpr. E. M. G. Bowes, L
Tpr. A. Bowman, L
Tpr. W. S. Boyce, ss
Tpr. T. H. Brandon, ss, R
Tpr. C. Brazier, L
Tpr. C. Brennen, ss, R
Tpr. F. H. Brittain, ss, L, D
Tpr. F. L. Brown, ss
Tpr. J. H. Brown, L
Tpr. B. B. Buntting, L
Tpr. J. H. Buntting, L
Tpr. F. Burton, L
Tpr. W. M. Busch, L
Tpr. G. W. Butcher, ss, R
Tpr. J. C. Butter, L
Tpr. H. L. Button, ss
Tpr. W. Buxton, L, K
Tpr. A. Cairns, L
Tpr. W. Calder, ss, L
Tpr. D. P. Campbell, L
Tpr. H. C. C. Campbell, ss
Tpr. T. Campbell, ss
Tpr. A. F. Carter, L
Tpr. C. R. Carter, L
Tpr. F. Carter, ss, L
Tpr. H. B. Carter, L
Tpr. H. J. Catchpole, L
Tpr. J. G. Chalklen.
Tpr. W. M. Chalmers, ss, L
Tpr. P. G. Chambers, L
Tpr. E. Chandley, L
Tpr. S. Chapman, ss, L, D

Tpr. R. Charlton, ss, L
Tpr. B. Cheney, R
Tpr. E. Chisholm, L
Tpr. J. P. Christie, ss
Tpr. F. Clark, ss
Tpr. J. F. Clark, ss
Tpr. W. Cleaver, ss, L, W, D
Tpr. A. S. Clouston, L
Tpr. A. E. Cockburn, L
Tpr. J. B. Cohen, ss, L, D
Tpr. J. G. Collins, L
Tpr. R. Collins, L
Tpr. C. Colville, L
Tpr. J. S. H. Colville, L, D
Tpr. A. Comrie, L
Tpr. J. M. Comrie, L
Tpr. P. C. Comrie, L
Tpr. A. O. Cooke, R
Tpr. J. J. B. Cooke, R
Tpr. G. H. Coombes, ss, R
Tpr. C. F. J. Cope, R
Tpr. E. P. Corbet, R
Tpr. W. J. Corrigall, L
Tpr. H. A. Craig, L
Tpr. C. Craik, L, W
Tpr. B. Crathorne, R
Tpr. F. Crathorne, ss, R
Tpr. A. P. Craw, L
Tpr. A. Crickmore, ss
Tpr. G. Crompton, ss
Tpr. A. J. Crosby, ss, L
Tpr. H. W. Cross, ss
Tpr. J. Cross, ss, R
Tpr. H. F. B. Crosse.
Tpr. A. E. Crouch, L
Tpr. B. Crouch, L
Tpr. W. J. Crouch, L
Tpr. J. T. Crowsen, L
Tpr. E. E. Croysdale, ss, L
Tpr. J. Cumming, ss, L
Tpr. W. W. Cummins, ss, R
Tpr. G. T. Cundill, L
Tpr. T. Cunningham, ss
Tpr. T. Curran, L

Tpr. W. H. Currie, L
Tpr. P. B. Curry, ss, L
Tpr. S. Daly, L, W
Tpr. C. F. Davies, L
Tpr. J. E. Davies, L, D
Tpr. F. P. H. De Bary.
Tpr. J. H. M. de Bary, L
Tpr. R. A. H. de Bary, L
Tpr. W. E. Deerans, ss
Tpr. E. J. Dicks, L
Tpr. G. W. Dicks, L
Tpr. H. C. Dicks, L
Tpr. H. E. H. Dicks.
Tpr. J. A. Dicks.
Tpr. C. J. Diot, L
Tpr. W. S. Dobson, ss, L
Tpr. C. Douglas.
Tpr. D. Dowsett, NGR
Tpr. J. Duff, ss, L
Tpr. F. Duke, ss, L, D
Tpr. D. J. Dunn, ss, L
Tpr. D. Dunwoodie, ss, L
Tpr. F. W. Durant, L
Tpr. W. G. Eccles, R
Tpr. W. P. Edwards, ss, R
Tpr. W. T. Edwards, L
Tpr. J. Elliott, ss
Tpr. T. Elliott, L, K
Tpr. J. L. Ennis, ss
Tpr. J. F. Fargerson, ss
Tpr. F. C. Farmer, R
Tpr. R. N. Faulder, ss, L
Tpr. J. G. Ferrand, ss
Tpr. C. J. Fewings, ss, R
Tpr. A. H. Firmstone, ss, L
Tpr. G. A. Firmstone, ss, L
Tpr. J. W. Flett, L
Tpr. F. Ford, ss
Tpr. A. G. M. Forder, ss, L
Tpr. F. Fowler, ss
Tpr. A. P. Francis, L
Tpr. G. L. Fraser, L
Tpr. J. A. Fraser, ss, R
Tpr. W. J. Freeman, ss, L, W
Tpr. L. O. Fyvie, L

Tpr. C. S. M. Gabriel, ss, L
Tpr. M. H. Garson, ss
Tpr. W. Gerhardt, ss, R
Tpr. P. T. Gibson, ss
Tpr. J. Gillam, ss, L, W
Tpr. T. Gill, ss, R
Tpr. M. Goldstein, ss, R, K
Tpr. G. M. Gordon, ss
Tpr. J. K. Gordon, ss, P
Tpr. R. E. Gordon, ss
Tpr. A. F. Grant, R
Tpr. G. J. Grant, R
Tpr. N. J. Grant, R
Tpr. R. Grant, L
Tpr. W. H. Grant, R
Tpr. D. M. Gray, R, K
Tpr. G. D. Gray, L
Tpr. K. M. Greenall, L, D
Tpr. A. H. Greene, L
Tpr. S. Gregory, ss
Tpr. J. E. Greig, L, W
Tpr. C. Groom, ss, L
Tpr. H. C. Groom, ss, L
Tpr. T. Hackland, L
Tpr. H. E. Haddon, ss, L
Tpr. C. C. Haine, L
Tpr. L. P. Haine, ss, L, W
Tpr. H. W. Hale, ss
Tpr. W. A. Hall, L
Tpr. E. A. Hamblin, NGR
Tpr. G. A. Hammond, ss, L
Tpr. J. W. Hammond, L
Tpr. W. J. Harcourt, D
Tpr. E. A. C. Harding.
Tpr. H. Harding, ss
Tpr. F. C. Hardman, L
Tpr. F. O. Harris, L
Tpr. A. E. Harte, L
Tpr. W. H. F. Harte, L
Tpr. C. Hatley, L
Tpr. F. W. T. Hatley, L
Tpr. H. Hatley, L
Tpr. E. H. Hayes, L
Tpr. H. J. Hayes, L
Tpr. A. G. Hazell, L

Chief Langalibalele (in centre), 1873.

Gwaisa (Chum-Chum).
Col. Weighton's Servant.

Tpr. G. C. H. Heckler, L, W
Tpr. O. Hesom, L
Tpr. S. W. Hewitt, ss, P
Tpr. S. R. Higgins, L
Tpr. F. C. Hill, L
Tpr. A. G. Hinde, ss, R
Tpr. C. F. Hodgson, L
Tpr. H. A. Hodgson.
Tpr. T. L. Hodgson, ss, L
Tpr. R. G. Hodson.
Tpr. J. B. Holgate, ss
Tpr. Ralph Holliday, L
Tpr. Rupert Holliday, L
Tpr. F. W. Holmes, L
Tpr. T. Holmes, L
Tpr. W. Hood, ss
Tpr. R. Hope, ss
Tpr. L. Hordern, ss
Tpr. F. S. Hornby, L
Tpr. J. W. Horsley, L
Tpr. H. N. Houghton.
Tpr. A. S. Houshold, ss, L
Tpr. E. E. Houshold, L
Tpr. T. H. Houshold, L
Tpr. F. J. Howden, ss
Tpr. A. Hutcheson, L
Tpr. F. T. Hyde, L
Tpr. T. J. Irving, ss, R
Tpr. G. Izatt, ss
Tpr. R. H. Jackson, L
Tpr. W. Jackson, L
Tpr. J. F. Jacques, L
Tpr. H. N. Jenner, ss, R, K
Tpr. A. C. Johnson, ss
Tpr. W. J. Johnstone, ss, R
Tpr. J. Jones, L
Tpr. W. W. Jordan, ss
Tpr. J. Joughin, ss, R
Tpr. A. S. Joyner, L
Tpr. A. Keachie, L
Tpr. E. J. Kean, L
Tpr. C. G. Kemp, L
Tpr. L. E. Kenmuir, ss, R
Tpr. C. Kennedy, L
Tpr. F. E. King, R, W

Tpr. G. F. King, L, R
Tpr. W. W. King.
Tpr. G. B. Kitchen, ss
Tpr. H. J. Kitchen, L
Tpr. W. T. Kitchen, ss, L
Tpr. C. D. Knapp, L
Tpr. G. F. Kremer, L
Tpr. A. H. O. Kruger, L
Tpr. C. R. Ladbrooke, ss
Tpr. W. H. Ladds, L
Tpr. J. Laing, ss, L
Tpr. G. F. Lane, L
Tpr. P. P. Lang, L
Tpr. R. A. Lang, L
Tpr. A. Larsen, ss
Tpr. J. O. Larsen, ss, L
Tpr. G. Lawrence, L, ss
Tpr. J. Lawrence, L
Tpr. S. W. Lawrence, ss
Tpr. F. W. Lean, ss, L
Tpr. W. Leathern, L
Tpr. J. Leddra, ss
Tpr. H. P. Lefebre, ss
Tpr. J. T. Legge, ss, R
Tpr. P. Lewis, ss, L
Tpr. T. Lewis, ss, L
Tpr. G. Liggett, ss
Tpr. R. E. Lightfoot, L
Tpr. D. P. Lindsay, ss, L
Tpr. R. A. Lindsay, L, W
Tpr. T. J. Locke, ss, R
Tpr. W. Long, ss, R
Tpr. A. H. Loram, ss, R
Tpr. C. H. Luja, ss, L
Tpr. W. E. Lupton, ss, L
Tpr. G. Macfarlane, ss
Tpr. J. McBlain, ss
Tpr. J. R. McCullough, L
Tpr. W. A. McCullough, L
Tpr. A. S. McDonald, L
Tpr. G. McKellar, L
Tpr. N. McKellar, L
Tpr. C. K. McKenzie, L
Tpr. L. R. McKenzie, L
Tpr. O. S. McKenzie, L

Tpr. R. McKenzie, L
Tpr. W. McLean, L
Tpr. F. G. H. McLeod, ss
Tpr. W. S. McLeod, ss
Tpr. A. Madsen, L
Tpr. M. Madsen, L
Tpr. G. G. Mann, ss, D
Tpr. R. J. Marshall, L
Tpr. T. W. Martin, ss, L
Tpr. A. J. Mason, L
Tpr. R. J. Mason, ss, R, w
Tpr. W. F. Mason, L
Tpr. H. Meares, L
Tpr. G. H. Mellis, L
Tpr. E. W. Meyer, L
Tpr. F. Meyer, L
Tpr. H. F. Meyer, L
Tpr. J. Meyer, L
Tpr. A. Miles, L
Tpr. A. J. Miller, L
Tpr. C. E. J. Miller, ss, L, w
Tpr. H. E. Miller, L
Tpr. J. H. Miller, ss
Tpr. R. M. M. Miller, ss, L, K
Tpr. W. J. Milliken, L
Tpr. H. T. Mitchell, L
Tpr. W. J. Mitchell, ss, L
Tpr. W. H. Mitchell, L
Tpr. C. Molyneux, ss, L
Tpr. W. E. C. Molyneux, ss
Tpr. S. G. Monckton, ss, R
Tpr. R. Money, L
Tpr. Q. H. Montgomery, L
Tpr. W. R. Moody, L, D
Tpr. E. B. Moreland, L
Tpr. H. D. Munro, ss, R
Tpr. J. H. Murray, L
Tpr. P. A. Murray, L, D
Tpr. T. R. Murray, ss
Tpr. G. Newlands, L
Tpr. W. C. F. Napier, ss, L
Tpr. D. D. Newton, L
Tpr. T. Newton, L
Tpr. A. Nicholson, L, w
Tpr. B. Nicholson, ss, R

Tpr. J. B. Nicholson, L
Tpr. W. G. Nunn, ss, R
Tpr. D. O'Brien, ss
Tpr. A. H. O. Osborn, ss
Tpr. R. Owen, ss, L
Tpr. A. Paine, L, w
Tpr. F. Palfrey, ss
Tpr. E. C. Palmer, ss, R
Tpr. W. A. Paterson, ss
Tpr. G. S. Paton, ss, L
Tpr. D. Patton, L, D
Tpr. J. Paxton, ss, R
Tpr. H. J. Peake, ss, R
Tpr. J. Pepworth, L
Tpr. H. W. Peters, L
Tpr. G. J. Player, ss
Tpr. B. C. T. Pottow, L
Tpr. J. N. A. Pottow, L
Tpr. J. Price, L, D
Tpr. S. H. Prince, L
Tpr. W. E. Quested, L
Tpr. F. R. Ralfe, R
Tpr. G. Rattray, ss, R
Tpr. R. J. Raw, R, w
Tpr. S. W. Raw, L, D
Tpr. W. G. Raw, L
Tpr. W. H. Rawlings, L
Tpr. R. Read, ss
Tpr. W. L. Read.
Tpr. W. C. Reeves, ss
Tpr. A. B. Richardson, ss
Tpr. J. B. Richardson, L
Tpr. G. H. Richardson, ss, L
Tpr. W. N. Ridgway, L
Tpr. J. Risley, ss
Tpr. S. Robinson, ss, R
Tpr. T. Robinson.
Tpr. T. J. Robinson, L
Tpr. J. Robertson.
Tpr. W. D. Roche, ss, L
Tpr. W. T. Rochester, ss, L
Tpr. E. H. Rose, ss
Tpr. L. Ross, L
Tpr. E. O. Rowles, L
Tpr. B. L. Royal, ss

Tpr. F. S. Rundle, ss, p
Tpr. E. Russell, r, w
Tpr. R. C. Samuelson, l
Tpr. H. E. Saner, ss, w
Tpr. S. Savage, l
Tpr. R. Schofield, ss
Tpr. H. W. Seale, r
Tpr. S. Schofield, ss
Tpr. D. G. Sclanders, r
Tpr. W. J. Sclater, l
Tpr. D. A. Shaw, l
Tpr. A. G. Shaw, ss, l
Tpr. E. H. Shaw, ss, l, d
Tpr. J. G. Shaw, ss, l
Tpr. W. H. Shaw, ss, r
Tpr. W. L. Shaw, r
Tpr. G. H. Shepstone, ss, l
Tpr. M. A. Shepstone, ss, l
Tpr. F. H. Sherman, ss, r
Tpr. G. G. Shores, l
Tpr. G. F. Simon, ss, l
Tpr. W. B. Skottowe, ss
Tpr. C. R. Skottowe, ss
Tpr. P. H. Smallridge, l
Tpr. E. E. Smith, ss, l, w
Tpr. H. Smith, l
Tpr. Jas. Smith, ss
Tpr. J. H. Smith, l
Tpr. R. Smith, l
Tpr. W. C. Smith, l, k
Tpr. E. P. Smithwick, ss
Tpr. P. F. Smithwick.
Tpr. D. W. Smythe, l
Tpr. H. G. Snodgrass, ss
Tpr. J. G. Speirs, l, ss
Tpr. J. Spence, l
Tpr. F. Spencer, l, w
Tpr. G. W. Spencer, ss
Tpr. R. Spencer, l
Tpr. D. J. Spillman, ss
Tpr. C. E. Stainbank, ss, l
Tpr. F. Stanbury, ss, r
Tpr. B. L. Stead, l
Tpr. H. P. Stead, l
Tpr. A. C. Street, ss

Tpr. B. J. Stevens, r
Tpr. F. Stevens, r
Tpr. F. N. Stevens, r
Tpr. A. Stutters, ss, l
Tpr. J. Sullivan, l
Tpr. J. Surgeson, l
Tpr. H. G. Swindon, l
Tpr. O. Swindon, l
Tpr. W. Sutherland, l
Tpr. W. F. B. Sutherland, ss, l
Tpr. J. Symes, ss
Tpr. T. Symes.
Tpr. W. Symes, l
Tpr. G. Symons, ss, r
Tpr. H. E. Symons, r
Tpr. J. Talanda, ss
Tpr. W. A. Talbot, l
Tpr. R. M. Tanner, l
Tpr. H. Tarboton, ss
Tpr. F. W. Taunton, ss, d
Tpr. A. E. Taylor, ss, l
Tpr. B. Taylor, l
Tpr. C. P. K. Taylor, l
Tpr. E. Taylor, r, w
Tpr. E. R. Taylor, ss, r
Tpr. M. Taylor, l
Tpr. R. P. Taylor, ss, l
Tpr. W. F. Taylor, l
Tpr. W. J. Taylor, l
Tpr. J. Taylor, ss, r
Tpr. A. E. Taynton, ss, l
Tpr. G. W. Teasdale, r, w
Tpr. J. Tennant, ss, r
Tpr. A. L. Thompson, l
Tpr. H. W. Thompson, l
Tpr. A. G. Thomson, ss, l
Tpr. G. L. Thomson, l
Tpr. F. C. Thomalla, ss
Tpr. W. A. P. Thorne, ss, r
Tpr. H. Tillett, ss
Tpr. R. Timm.
Tpr. P. Tomlinson, ss, r
Tpr. R. Tomlinson, ss, l
Tpr. R. Trodd, r

Tpr. A. H. Trow, ss, L
Tpr. A. R. Tucker, ss, L
Tpr. H. Turner, ss, L
Tpr. C. J. Tytherleigh, L
Tpr. W. J. Ulyate, ss
Tpr. P. J. Upton, ss, L
Tpr. H. J. Urquhart, L
Tpr. J. P. Urquhart, L
Tpr. W. Urquhart, L
Tpr. F. B. Wade, L, D
Tpr. H. C. Waite, ss, L
Tpr. A. Walker, L
Tpr. A. M. Walker, ss, R
Tpr. H. Walker, ss, L
Tpr. H. P. Walker, ss, R
Tpr. F. W. Walker, ss, R
Tpr. H. P. Walsh.
Tpr. J. D. Walsh, ss
Tpr. L. D. Walsh, R
Tpr. F. A. Ward, ss, W, P
Tpr. H. C. Ward, L
Tpr. B. W. Warren, ss, R, K
Tpr. W. S. Warwick, L, W
Tpr. T. E. Warwick, L
Tpr. R. Watts, ss, L, W
Tpr. S. E. Waugh, L, W
Tpr. C. W. Webber, L, W
Tpr. A. F. Weedon, L
Tpr. F. Westermeyer, L

Tpr. J. Westray, L
Tpr. H. D. Wheeler, ss
Tpr. L. Wheeler, ss, L
Tpr. S. M. Wheeler.
Tpr. G. C. White, ss
Tpr. W. R. A. White, ss
Tpr. C. C. Whitelaw, ss, R
Tpr. W. Whitridge, ss, R
Tpr. S. J. C. Wilkinson, ss
Tpr. J. Williamson, R
Tpr. T. B. Willoughby, R
Tpr. W. J. H. Wilmot, L
Tpr. J. L. D. Wilson, ss
Tpr. R. S. Wilson, ss
Tpr. A. L. Wingfield, L
Tpr. E. A. Woods, R
Tpr. F. T. G. Woods, R
Tpr. M. M. Woods, R
Tpr. W. H. Woodward, ss
Tpr. J. E. Woolley, ss, L
Tpr. B. Wray, L
Tpr. D. C. Wright, L
Tpr. W. E. Wright, L
Tpr. A. J. Yeaman, ss, R
Tpr. G. Yirrell, L
Tpr. E. W. Young, ss
Tpr. E. C. Zunckel, R
Tpr. O. M. Zunckel, R

REFERENCES.

The letters at the end of names signify:—
L—In Siege of Ladysmith.
R—On Relief Column.
ss—Special Service Members.
K—Killed.
W—Wounded.
D—Died.
P—Prisoner.
NGR—On Railway Work.